Black Book

Illustration

THE BLACK BOOK
10 Astor Place. Sixth Floor
New York, New York 10003
Phone: 212 539.9800
Facsimile: 212 539.9801

SALES OFFICES
DALLAS *214 320.3434*
CHICAGO *312 944.5115*
SAN FRANCISCO *415 543.4100*

BLACK BOOK ILLUSTRATION

CHAIRMAN | *William F. Achtmeyer*
PRESIDENT & PUBLISHER | *Marcia E. Miller*
VICE PRESIDENT/ASSOCIATE PUBLISHER | *Donna L. LeVan*
VICE PRESIDENT OF FINANCE | *Laura Branchini*

NEW YORK
NATIONAL ILLUSTRATION DIRECTOR | *Alison Davis Curry*
NATIONAL PHOTOGRAPHY DIRECTOR | *Erica Sturdevant*
PRODUCTION DIRECTOR | *Jason Taback*
DIRECTOR OF SALES & MARKETING AR100 / PRODUCTION MANAGER | *Dana Grossman*
ELECTRONIC MEDIA DIRECTOR | *Paul Cheevers*
MARKETING CONSULTANT - ILLUSTRATION | *David Hoffman*
ILLUSTRATION COORDINATORS | *Alan Carr, Onome Ekeh*
MARKETING CONSULTANT - PHOTOGRAPHY | *Victoria Magno*
PHOTOGRAPHY COORDINATOR | *Brodi Zimmer*
PRODUCTION COORDINATOR | *Cathy Citarella*
TRAFFIC COORDINATOR & JUNIOR DESIGNER | *William F. Dolan*
ASSISTANT LISTINGS MANAGER | *Robert Sefcik*
DISTRIBUTION COORDINATORS | *Lisa Gotlib, Robert Cunningham*
ELECTRONIC MEDIA COORDINATOR | *Jeff McHugh*
ACCOUNTING MANAGER | *Stanley Gong*
SENIOR ACCOUNTANT | *Gayle Walker*
ACCOUNTS RECEIVABLE MANAGER | *Steven Schmidt*
STAFF ACCOUNTANT | *Farida Dhanji*
EXECUTIVE ASSISTANTS TO THE PUBLISHER | *Cynthia V. Riley, Roseanne Mangan*
SPOTCHECK RESEARCHERS | *Timothy Cummings, Joe Roseto, Lori Williamson*
RECEPTIONIST | *Mary Cremin*

CHICAGO
MARKETING CONSULTANT - ILLUSTRATION | *Adrian Johnson*
MARKETING CONSULTANT – PHOTOGRAPHY | *Sandy Rabin*

DALLAS
MARKETING CONSULTANT - PHOTOGRAPHY | *Mary Preussel*

SAN FRANCISCO
MARKETING CONSULTANT - ILLUSTRATION | *Lenore Cymes*
MARKETING CONSULTANT - PHOTOGRAPHY | *Andrea Le Coq*
SALES COORDINATOR | *Maggie Kenny*

BOOK DESIGNER | *Martin Solomon*
TYPOGRAPHIC COORDINATOR | *Alexa Nosal*
Martin Solomon, Co.
28 West 23 Street, 11th Floor
New York, NY 10010
Phone: 212 929.4111
Facsimile: 212 929.2787

Black Book Illustration® was printed in Hong Kong by Everbest Printing Co., Ltd., through Four-Colour Imports, Ltd. Color Separations provided through Four-Colour Imports, Ltd.

Black Book Illustration® is distributed in the U.S. and Canada by Black Book Marketing Group Inc., New York.

Black Book Illustration® is distributed outside of the U.S. and Canada by Hearst Books International, 1350 Avenue of the Americas, New York, New York, 10019. Phone 212-261-6770, Facsimile 212-261-6795.

"The Black Book" and "Black Book Illustration"® are trademarks of Black Book Marketing Group, Inc.

ISBN 0-916098-94-X | ISSN 1045-9855

Welcome to the 1996 Edition of Black Book Illustration.

With this edition, we have strengthened our commitment to you, the illustrator, designer, art director, and the entire creative community. We have taken several bold steps to enhance your visibility and ours, and have completed a modicum of internal restructuring to ensure that you receive the kind of service you've grown to expect over the years. We have also gone to great lengths to make this company more user-friendly and responsive. What's more, we are moving with the times. Since our inception, we have continued to draw the top talent in the field. We now expect to become a driving force in illustration well into the next century.

The first thing you will have noticed is that we've changed the name and cover design. The new name reflects our evolving corporate identity. All of our product titles will begin with the name Black Book, which is a trademark recognizable to the entire visual community as a hallmark of excellence in creative talent and design. Consequently, the Creative Illustration Book has evolved into Black Book Illustration. The cover design, a product of the fertile mind of Martin Solomon, will catch an art director's eye whether it is lying flat on a desk or crowded by other tomes on a bookshelf.

Perhaps of greater importance to some is our revitalized commitment to service with a support team that has evolved as well. I am pleased to have joined the Black Book organization as its President and Publisher, while Alison Davis Curry continues to serve you in her role as National Illustration Director.

Last, and in no way least, a growing awareness of on-line computer services must be met head on. This is, after all, the wave of the future. We are literally riding that wave with our entrance onto the World Wide Web. This will open up whole new frontiers and a new line of communications among creatives around the world. The Web will connect illustrators with designers, art directors, and others seeking their talents. And equally important, this will engender the talents of illustrators to a global design community. Simply stated, that translates into more business, new challenges, and our growing commitment to creatives worldwide.

The growth of the Creative Illustration Book into Black Book Illustration promises to be one that will benefit us all. Whether you take pen, brush, or mouse in hand, you and your clients know that illustration will be a part of our lives always. And we will be there to support your efforts with the best sourcebook available to the industry. More importantly, thank you for your continued support and for brightening all our lives with your talents.

Cordially,

Marcia E. Miller
President & Publisher

Martin Solomon: a sketchbook.

Tel: 212 929.4111   Fax: 212 929.2787

Martin Solomon, Co.

28 West 23 Street, New York, NY 10010

Designer of Black Book

March
*AR100 Deadline for Entries,
Black Book Marketing Group,
New York*

*Deadline for American
Illustration 15th Annual
Competition*

*Showing and Awards,
The Belding Awards, The Art
Director's Club of Los Angeles*

March 16th
*Deadline for entries, Illustration
Annual, Communication Arts
Magazine*

March - April
*Exhibition of the 38th Annual
Showing of American Illustrators,
(Advertising & Institutional), The
Society of Illustrators, New York*

*Communication Graphic Show,
AIGA*

April
*Deadline for entries, Book Show,
AIGA*

*Deadline for entries, ADDY
Awards, American Advertising
Federation*

May
*Show Presentation
The One Show, New York*

May -June
Book Show, AIGA

June
*Deadline for Entries, Applied Arts
Award Annual, Applied Arts
Magazine, Ontario, Canada*

*Deadline for entries, Design &
Advertising Annual,
Communication Arts Magazine*

*The Art Director's Club 74th
Annual Awards and Exhibition,
The Art Director's Club of
New York*

August
*Call to entries, 75th Art Director's
Exhibition, The Art Director's
Club of New York*

October
*Deadline for entries, 38th Annual
Showing of American Illustrators,
The Society of Illustrators,
New York*

December
*Deadline for entries,
76th Annual Exhibition, The Art
Director's Club of New York.*

January 1
New Year's Day

January 15
Martin Luther King, Jr. Day

February 14
Valentine's Day

February 19
President's Day

February 21
Ash Wednesday

March 17
St. Patrick's Day

March 31
Palm Sunday

April 4
Passover

April 5
Good Friday

April 7
Easter Sunday

May 12
Mother's Day

May 27
Memorial Day(Obsvd)

July 4
Independence Day

August 16
Elvis Day

September 2
Labor Day

September 14
Rosh Hashanah

September 23
Yom Kippur

October 14
Columbus Day (Obsvd)

October 31
Halloween

November 5
Election Day

November 11
Veteran's Day

November 28
Thanksgiving Day

December 6
Hannukah Begins

December 25
Christmas Day

January
*Call for Entries, American
Illustration 15th Annual
Competition*

*Local call to entries for the
ADDY Awards*

*Deadline for Entries, Belding
Awards, The Art Directors
Club of Los Angeles*

January 31
*Deadline for entries, The One
Show, New York*

February - March
*Exhibition of the 38th Annual
Showing of American Illustrators,
(Editorial & Book Categories),
The Society of Illustrators,
New York*

January
M 1
T 2
W 3
T 4
F 5
S 6
S 7
M 8
T 9
W 10
T 11
F 12
S 13
S 14
M 15
T 16
W 17
T 18
F 19
S 20
S 21
M 22
T 23
W 24
T 25
F 26
S 27
S 28
M 29
T 30
W 31

February
T 1
F 2
S 3
S 4
M 5
T 6
W 7
T 8
F 9
S 10
S 11
M 12
T 13
W 14
T 15
F 16
S 17
S 18
M 19
T 20
W 21
T 22
F 23
S 24
S 25
M 26
T 27
W 28
T 29

March
F 1
S 2
S 3
M 4
T 5
W 6
T 7
F 8
S 9
S 10
M 11
T 12
W 13
T 14
F 15
S 16
S 17
M 18
T 19
W 20
T 21
F 22
S 23
S 24
M 25
T 26
W 27
T 28
F 29
S 30
S 31

April
M 1
T 2
W 3
T 4
F 5
S 6
S 7
M 8
T 9
W 10
T 11
F 12
S 13
S 14
M 15
T 16
W 17
T 18
F 19
S 20
S 21
M 22
T 23
W 24
T 25
F 26
S 27
S 28
M 29
T 30

May
W 1
T 2
F 3
S 4
S 5
M 6
T 7
W 8
T 9
F 10
S 11
S 12
M 13
T 14
W 15
T 16
F 17
S 18
S 19
M 20
T 21
W 22
T 23
F 24
S 25
S 26
M 27
T 28
W 29
T 30
F 31

June
S 1
S 2
M 3
T 4
W 5
T 6
F 7
S 8
S 9
M 10
T 11
W 12
T 13
F 14
S 15
S 16
M 17
T 18
W 19
T 20
F 21
S 22
S 23
M 24
T 25
W 26
T 27
F 28
S 29
S 30

July
M 1
T 2
W 3
T 4
F 5
S 6
S 7
M 8
T 9
W 10
T 11
F 12
S 13
S 14
M 15
T 16
W 17
T 18
F 19
S 20
S 21
M 22
T 23
W 24
T 25
F 26
S 27
S 28
M 29
T 30
W 31

August
T 1
F 2
S 3
S 4
M 5
T 6
W 7
T 8
F 9
S 10
S 11
M 12
T 13
W 14
T 15
F 16
S 17
S 18
M 19
T 20
W 21
T 22
F 23
S 24
S 25
M 26
T 27
W 28
T 29
F 30
S 31

September
S 1
M 2
T 3
W 4
T 5
F 6
S 7
S 8
M 9
T 10
W 11
T 12
F 13
S 14
S 15
M 16
T 17
W 18
T 19
F 20
S 21
S 22
M 23
T 24
W 25
T 26
F 27
S 28
S 29
M 30

October
T 1
W 2
T 3
F 4
S 5
S 6
M 7
T 8
W 9
T 10
F 11
S 12
S 13
M 14
T 15
W 16
T 17
F 18
S 19
S 20
M 21
T 22
W 23
T 24
F 25
S 26
S 27
M 28
T 29
W 30
T 31

November
F 1
S 2
S 3
M 4
T 5
W 6
T 7
F 8
S 9
S 10
M 11
T 12
W 13
T 14
F 15
S 16
S 17
M 18
T 19
W 20
T 21
F 22
S 23
S 24
M 25
T 26
W 27
T 28
F 29
S 30

December
S 1
M 2
T 3
W 4
T 5
F 6
S 7
S 8
M 9
T 10
W 11
T 12
F 13
S 14
S 15
M 16
T 17
W 18
T 19
F 20
S 21
S 22
M 23
T 24
W 25
T 26
F 27
S 28
S 29
M 30
T 31

Illustrators

2H Studio
54 Old Post Rd, Southport, CT 06490
203 256.9192

A&A
PO Box 330008, Ft Worth, TX 76163
817 292.1855

A.R.T.S. Resource
73 Water St, S.F., CA 94133
415 775.0709

Aagaard, Gary
159 Warren St, Brooklyn, NY 11201
718 694.0458

**Abe, George
2814 NW 72nd St,
Seattle, WA 98117
206 784.1136
fax 206 784.1171
page 354**

Abrams, Ed
PO Box 925, Julian, CA 92036
619 765.2615

Abrams, Jodell
PO Box 925, Julian, CA 92036
619 765.2615

Acuna, Ed
232 Madison Ave, NYC, NY 10016
212 889.8777

Adair, Gary
5711 Sugar Hill, Houston, TX 77057
713 975.9424

Adam, Winky
370 Central Park W, NYC, NY 10025
212 423.0746

Adams, Beth
3700 20th St, S.F., CA 94110
415 648.0355

Adams, Gil
1440 Terrace Dr, Tulsa, OK 74104
918 749.2424

Adams, Jeanette
PO Box 130, Acworth, NH 03601
603 835.2984

Adams, Jenny
724 N Robinson St, L.A., CA 90026
213 665.6155

Adams, Lisa
40 Harrison St, NYC, NY 10013
212 385.8189

Adams, Norman
211 E 51st St, NYC, NY 10022
212 755.1365

Ade & Associates
35 River St, Chagrin Falls, OH 44022
216 241.4990

Adigard, Erik/M.A.D.
237 San Carlos Ave, Sausalito, CA 94965
415 331.1022

Advertising Art Studios
710 N Plankinton Ave, Milwaukee, WI 53203
414 276.6306

Advertising Arts
2402 W Jefferson St, Boise, ID 83702
208 388.0411

Advertising Graphics
27 S Forge St, Akron, OH 44304
216 535.2525

Agrell, Lewis
PO Box 12024, Prescott, AZ 86304
602 445.7038

Aiello, Susan
120 W Illinois St Five E, Chicago, IL 60610
312 527.3533

Air Arts Inc
3323 W Berteau Ave, Chicago, IL 60618
312 583.7627

Air Hero's Studio
30 Duke St, St Catherines, ONT, Canada L2S 6Z4
905 984.6140

Airbrush Ink Studio
58 Forest Ave, Ronkonkoma, NY 11779
516 471.2728

Aitken, Doug
49 Ann St, NYC, NY 10038
212 608.1965

Aizawa, Kaz
6140 Monterey Rd, L.A., CA 90042
213 254.3362

Ajhar, Brian
PO Box 521, Canadensis, PA 18325
717 595.3782

Akgulian, Nishan
42-29 64th St, Woodside, NY 11377
718 565.6936

Akimoto, George
6389 Embarcadero Dr, Stockton, CA 95219
209 476.0483

Akopyan, Loudvik
311 Ave H, #D, Redondo Beach, CA 90277
310 540.5958

Alaimo, Terry M Studio
2233 Martin St, Irvine, CA 92715
714 724.8899

Alanen, Erkki
161 Country Rd, El Paso, TX 79932
915 581.2272

Alavezos, Gus
19050 Merrymen Cir, Monument, CO 80132
719 488.9078

Albano, Trisha Charlotte
Nine Hopes Ave, Holtsville, NY 11742
516 289.5312

Alberg, Kari
68 E Franklin St, Dayton, OH 45459
513 433.8383

Albers, Dave
6549 11th Ave NW, Seattle, WA 98117
206 781.7933

Albrecht, Anne & Associates
68 E Wacker Pl, Chicago, IL 60601
312 853.4830

Alcorn, Stephen
112 W Main St, Cambridge, NY 12816
518 677.5798

Alder, Kelly
1703 Maples Shade Ln, Richmond, VA 23227
804 353.3113

Alder, Kelynn
Five Captain's Walk, Setauket, NY 11733
516 246.5874

Aldridge Reps
758 Brookridge Dr, Atlanta, GA 30306
404 872.7980

Alexander & Turner
232 Madison Ave, NYC, NY 10016
212 889.8777

Alexander, Pat
19 E 83rd St, NYC, NY 10028
212 288.3345

Alexander/Pollard
1841 Lake Cypress Dr,
Tampa Bay, FL 34695
813 725.4438 / 800 347.0734
pages 338-345, 349

Alexander/Pollard
848 Greenwood Ave NE,
Atlanta, GA 30306
404 875.1363 / 800 347.0734
fax 404 875.9733
pages 338-345, 349

Aline, France
1076 S Ogden Dr, L.A., CA 90019
213 933.2500

Alkire, Betty Jo
Historic Taneywood, Rockaway Beach, MO 65740
417 561.8106

Alleman, Keith
2539 Gardenia Dr, Columbus, OH 43235
614 459.8764

Allen, Dave
18108 Martin Ave, Homewood, IL 60430
708 798.3283

Allen, Julian
250 W 57th St, NYC, NY 10107
212 397.7330

Allen, Kelly
2811 McKinney Ave, Dallas, TX 75204
214 922.9080

Allen, Mark Design & Associates
129 20th St, Manhattan Beach, CA 90266
310 796.1443

Allen, Pat
4510 Alpine Rd, Portola Valley, CA 94028
415 851.3116

Allen, Rick
2222 E Third St, Duluth, MN 55812
218 724.4861

Allen, Terry
164 Daniel Low Ter, Staten Island, NY 10301
718 727.0723

Allen, Victoria
31 Walker St, NYC, NY 10013
212 334.0120

Allison, John
7645 Jarboe, Kansas City, MO 64114
816 444.7782

Almquist, Don
353 W 53rd St, NYC, NY 10019
212 682.2462

Alper, AJ
224 Elizabeth St, NYC, NY 10012
212 935.0039

Alpert, Olive
9511 Shore Rd, Brooklyn, NY 11209
718 833.3092

Altamore, Vincent
152-48 Melbourne Ave, Flushing, NY 11367
718 263.2264

Amatrula, Michele
259 W Tenth St, NYC, NY 10014
212 255.7413

Ambre, Matthew Illustration
743 W Brompton, Chicago, IL 60657
312 935.5170

Ambroson, Rodd
141 N State St, Lake Oswego, OR 97034
503 635.6238

Ameijide, Ray
108 E 35th St, NYC, NY 10016
212 889.3337

American Art Studio
124 W 24th St, NYC, NY 10011
212 633.1466

American Artists
353 W 53rd St, NYC, NY 10019
212 582.0023 / 212 682.2462
fax 212 582.0090
pages 177-186, 402
I: **Don Almquist, Nick Backes, Renzo Barto, Keith Batcheller, Roger Bergendorff, Barbara Higgins Bond, Robert Burger, Lynn Butler, Gary Ciccarelli, Will Davis, Jim Deigan, Jacques Devaud, Bob Depew, Brian Dugan, Nicky Dupays, Lane DuPont, Jim Effler, Malcolm Farley, Russ Farrell, George Gaadt, Rob Gage, Bill Garland, Ken Gamble, Jackie Geyer, Garth Glazier, John Hamagami, Pamela Hamilton, Brian Harrold, Karol Havlicek, Doug Henry, Michael Hill, John Holm, Sandy Huffaker, Chris Hopkins, John Hull, Kelly Hume, Mitch Hyatt, Michael Jaroszko, Loris Kalafat, Richard Krieger, Michael Kozmiuk, Alan Leiner, Maurice Lewis, Jerry Lofaro, Shawn McKelvey, Ron Mahoney, Andrzej Malinowski, Roger Mark, Jean-Claude Michel, David Noyes, Chuck Passarelli, Richard Pembroke, Colin Poole, Art Proulx, Tony Randazzo, Nan Rossiter, John Rowe, Michael Schumacher, Joe Scrofani, Barclay Shaw, Dan Smith, Jim Starr, Michael Steirnagle, Wayne Anthony Still, Ethan Summers, Chris Szetela, Cathleen Thole, Linda Thomas, Thomas Tonkins, Sandy Turchyn, Rod Vass, Stan Watts, Jonathan Wright, Gary Yealdhall, Eddie Young, Andy Zito.**

American Graphiti
101 Tremont St, Boston, MA 02108
617 426.6668

Amit, Emmanuel
4322 Sunset Ave, Montrose, CA 91020
818 249.1739

Amorosi, Thomas
20 Sherman St, Brooklyn, NY 11215
718 832.2873

Amos, Jack & Son
18 E Main St, Richmond, VA 23219
804 780.0993

Anatoly
716 Montgomery St, S.F., CA 94111
415 433.1222
fax 415 433.9560
page 400

AnatomyWorks Inc
232 Madison Ave, NYC, NY 10016
212 679.8480

Anderson, A Richard
927 Franklin Ave, River Forest, IL 60305
708 366.5661

Anderson, Charles S Design Co
30 N First St, Mpls, MN 55401
612 339.5181
fax 612 339.3283
pages 428-429

Anderson, Mark
407 N Elizabeth St, Chicago, IL 60622
312 226.4222

Anderson, Paul
182 Christie Ave, Clifton, NJ 07011
201 340.4914

Anderson, Paula
405 N Wabash Ave, Chicago, IL 60611
312 321.0848

Anderson, Phillip
HC 35 Box 1022, St George, ME 04857
207 372.6242

Anderson, Richard
490 Bleeker Ave, Mamaroneck, NY 10543
914 381.2682

Anderson, Sara
3131 Western Ave, Seattle, WA 92121
206 285.1520

Andresen, Mark
6417 Gladys St, New Orleans, LA 70003
504 888.1644

Andrews, Bob
2100 W Big Beaver Rd, Troy, MI 48084
313 643.6000

Andrews, Joanne
40 Waterford Way, Fairport, NY 14450
716 223.9023

Andrews, John
1500 Calico Ln, Sun Prairie, WI 53590
608 837.4235

Angelagraphics/Angela Kamstra
529 S Seventh St, Mpls, MN 55415
612 332.1832

Angelini, George
Four Churchill St, Ossining, NY 10562
914 923.4029

Angelo
1449 Longfellow Ave, Bronx, NY 10459
718 617.2907

Angle, Scott
21051 Barbados Cir, Huntington Beach, CA 92646
714 960.8485

Another Girl Rep/Barb Hauser
PO Box 421443, S.F., CA 94142
415 647.5660
fax 415 285.1102
pages 113-117
Nick Backes, Tracy Britt, Mary Carter,
Lawrence W. Duke, Fred Hilliard,
Paul Kratter, Ed Lindlof, Ben Perini,
Miro Salazar, Marty Smith,
Wilfred Spoon, Judy Unger.

Ansley, Frank
414 Jackson St, S.F., CA 94111
415 989.9614

Anthony, Mitchell
960 Maddox Dr, Palo Alto, CA 94303
415 494.3240

Anton, Jerry
119 W 23rd St, NYC, NY 10011
212 633.9880

Antonio Illustration
Six Humberline Dr, Etobicoke,
ONT, Canada M9W 6X8
416 674.8136

Antonios, Tony
60 E 42nd St, NYC, NY 10165
212 682.1490

Anzalone, Lori
35-02 Berdan Ave, Fair Lawn, NJ 07410
201 796.5588

Apel, Eric
490 Rockside Rd, Cleveland, OH 44131
216 661.4222

Apice, Michael
PO Box 397, Oceanside, NY 11572
516 678.3735

apJones, Todd
817 Westwood Dr S, Mpls, MN 55416
612 374.3169

Applebee, Angie
6628 Floyd St, Overland Park, KS 66202
913 236.8332

Appleoff, Sandy
PO Box 254, Aspen, CO 81612
970 920.9444

Appleton, Doug
360 S Los Robles Ave, Pasadena, CA 91101
818 304.1054

Aquilino, John
158 W 29th St, NYC, NY 10001
212 268.9400

Arbogast, Shane
177 Seventh Ave, Brooklyn, NY 11215
718 832.0149

Arbour, Dennis
PO Box 512, Belfast, ME 04915
207 338.5245

Arce, Alejandro
652 Hudson St, NYC, NY 10014
212 645.8180

Archer, Doug
Box 307, Garnett, KS 66032
913 448.3692

Archey, Rebecca
63 Madrone Ave, Larkspur, CA 94939
415 924.4900

Arday Illustration
616 Arbor Creek Dr, DeSoto, TX 75115
214 223.6235

Arena
144 Royal College St, London,
England NW1 0TA
fax 0171 284.0486
0171 267.9661
pages 420-423

Ariail, Alan
1279 Evergreen, Palatine, IL 60067
708 991.7471

Arisman, Marshall
314 W 100th St, NYC, NY 10025
212 967.4983

Arkle, Dave
1010 S Robertson Blvd, L.A., CA 90035
310 652.7322

Armes, Steve
1509 Glenbrook Dr, Irving, TX 75061
214 721.0614

Armson, Mick
11 Kings Ridge Rd,
Long Valley, NJ 07853
908 813.8718
fax 908 813.0076
page 423

Armstrong, Kathy
7440 La Vista, Dallas, TX 75214
214 320.8232

Armstrong, Robert
200 E B St, Dixon, CA 95620
916 678.2955
fax 916 678.2955
page 337

Arnet, Angela
400 Central Park W, NYC, NY 10025
212 865.0966

Aronson, Ben
33 Wayside Inn Rd, Framingham, MA 01701
508 788.1455

Arrco Medical Art & Design
909 Beacon St, Boston, MA 02215
617 266.2680

Arroyo, Andrea
509 Cathedral Pky, NYC, NY 10025
212 864.6648

Arroyo, Fian
7123 SW 115th Pl, Miami, FL 33173
305 274.3812

The Art Agency
2405 NW Thurman St,
Portland, OR 97210
503 225.9687
fax 503 228.6030
pages 138-141
Represents: **Robin Ator, Dale Champlin,**
Dennis Cunningham, Stephen F. Hayes,
Laurie Heinz-Jenkins, Jim Lommasson,
Sheila Lucas, Joanne Radmilovich,
Ben Killen Rosenberg, Kate Schmitt,
Luis Sola, Gary Whitley, Matt Wuerker,
Jane Zwinger.

Art Attack/Larry Grossman
5309 Coldwater Canyon Ave,
Sherman Oaks, CA 91401
818 907.8626

The Art Director's Studio
419 Park Ave S, NYC, NY 10016
212 689.9888

Art Express
236 W 27th St, NYC, NY 10001
212 206.7125

Art Guy Studios/James Kraus
195 W Canton St, Boston, MA 02116
617 437.1945
pages 24-25

Art Rep Inc
3525 Mockingbird Ln, Dallas, TX 75205
214 521.5156

The Art Source
PO Box 2193, Grapevine, TX 76099
817 481.2212
fax 817 481.2908
pages 74-75
Each of 4 illustrators brings his own
style & experience to your needs.
Further, by combining talents, they can
create almost anything imagined.
Digital pioneers; conventional masters.

Art Source/Diane Barkley
Box 257, Pleasantville, NY 10570
914 747.2220

Art Staff
1000 John Rd, Troy, MI 48083
810 583.6070

Art Works
130 N Marengo Ave, Pasadena, CA 91101
818 449.3840

Art Works Inc
605 Main St, E Rochester, NY 14445
716 377.3126

Artco
232 Madison Ave, NYC, NY 10016
212 889.8777

Artemis
721 Emerson St, Palo Alto, CA 94301
415 325.6596

Artistix
66 Sentinel, Aliso Viejo, CA 92656
714 362.5242

Artists Associates
211 E 51st St, NYC, NY 10022
212 755.1365

Artists Inc
3850 Granger Rd, Akron, OH 44333
216 666.5754

Artists International
320 Bee Brook Rd, Washington, CT 06777
203 868.1011

Artists Representatives of Texas
3352 Walnut Bend Ln, Houston, TX 77042
713 530.5480

Arts Counsel Inc
32 Union Sq E, NYC, NY 10003
212 777.6777

The Artsmith
PO Box 391, Athens, GA 30603
706 543.5555

Artworks Illustration
89 Fifth Ave, NYC, NY 10003
212 627.1554

Aru, Agnes
498 Manning Ave, Toronto, ONT Canada M6G 2V7
416 532.9861

Arvidson, Glenn
333 N Michigan Ave, Chicago, IL 60601
312 629.3525

Arvis, Tom
11228 Troy Rd, Rockville, MD 20852
301 468.0828
fax 301 881.5735
page 384

Asbaghi, Zita
104-40 Queens Blvd,
Forest Hills, NY 11375
718 275.1995
page 237

Asher, Neal & Audette
601 N Park Blvd, Grapevine, TX 76051
817 481.3961

Asher, Terri
21800 Schoenborn St, Canoga Park, CA 91304
818 348.4278

Asmussen, Don
3975 Hortensia St, San Diego, CA 92110
619 298.0414

Aspinall, Neal
1255 Martha Washington Dr,
Milwaukee, WI 53213
414 774.3808

Assel, Steven
29-54 143rd St, Flushing, NY 11354
718 539.5776

Astro Graphics
124 N Park Ave, Westmont, IL 60559
708 969.5854

Atelier Kimberley Boege
PO Box 7544, Phoenix, AZ 85011
602 265.4389

Atkinson, Janet
359 Ovington Ave, Brooklyn, NY 11209
718 836.9335

Atkinson, Steve
3408 Meridian Dr, Mpls, MN 55422
612 522.7756

Ator, Robin
2405 NW Thurman St, Portland, OR 97210
503 225.9687

Atteberry, Kevan
13000 Bel-Red Rd, Bellevue, WA 98005
206 453.6010

Attebery, Craig
1812 Wollam St, L.A., CA 90065
213 227.4120

Auckland, Jim
30166 Chapala Ct, Laguna Niguel, CA 92677
714 495.3664

Auerbach Italic Calligraphy
611 Frederick St, S.F., CA 94117
415 661.8060

Auger, Jacques Design Associates
1130 Washington Ave, Miami Beach, FL 33139
305 534.3200

Austin, Cary
25 W 45th St, NYC, NY 10036
212 398.9540

Austin, Steve
2500 E Menlo, Fresno, CA 93710
209 323.6939

Azar, Joe
1220 N Pierce St, Arlington, VA 22209
703 527.1443

Azzinaro, Lew
11872 St Trinians Ct, Reston, VA 22091
703 620.5155

Babb, Phil
6705 Kemman, Hebron, IL 60034
815 648.4375

Bachem, Paul
89 Fifth Ave, NYC, NY 10003
212 627.1554

Bacher, Nancy
2654 Rodeo Dr NE, Blaine, MN 55449
612 786.1200

Backderf, John
3296 Ormond Rd, Cleveland Hts, OH 44118
216 932.2489

Backes, Nick
PO Box 421443, S.F., CA 94142
415 647.5660

Backus, Michael
1945 Tigertail Rd, Eugene, OR 97409
503 687.0284

Bad Katz Graphics
801 Alakea St, Honolulu, HI 96813
800 636.9669

Badin, Andy & Ella Leffler
50 W 72nd St, NYC, NY 10023
212 877.2390

Baechli, George
6550 Hillcroft, Houston, TX 77081
713 771.7836

Baher, Edward
216 Moorpark Ave, Moorpark, CA 93021
805 529.6228

Bailey, Pat
60 E 42nd St, NYC, NY 10165
212 682.1490

Baker, Don
2814 NW 72nd St, Seattle, WA 98117
206 784.1136
fax 206 784.1171
page 355

Baker, Gary 3D
4101 Linkwood Dr, Euless, TX 76040
817 268.4608

Baker, Joe
35 Wooster St, NYC, NY 10013
212 925.6555
page 266

Baker, Julie
4345 Green Arbors Ln, Cincinnati, OH 45249
513 583.5883

Baker, Kolea
2814 NW 72nd St, Seattle, WA 98117
206 784.1136
fax 206 784.1171
pages 354-357

Baker, Louise
3436 N Racine Ave, Chicago, IL 60657
312 327.7286

Baker, Richard
4230 W Porter Ave, Fullerton, CA 92633
714 994.0459

Baker, Skip
731 N 24th St, Phila, PA 19130
215 232.6666

Balbes, Sydney
9740 Sepulveda Blvd, North Hills, CA 91343
818 891.1370

Balboni, Timothy
165 Ave B, NYC, NY 10009
212 877.0591

Baldwin, Christopher
601 Valley St, Seattle, WA 98109
206 284.8553

Baldwin, Scott
125 Red Schoolhouse Rd,
Chestnut Ridge, NY 10977
914 620.0983

Ball, H/Smile Face Creator
340 Main St, Worcester, MA 01608
508 752.9154

Ballsun, John
18555 Collins St, Tarzana, CA 91356
818 343.1542

Balnaye, Jack
67 Upper Mountain Ave, Montclair, NJ 07042
201 744.4465

Bamundo, David
146 Chandler Ave,
Staten Island, NY 10314
718 370.7726
page 451
**David creates humorous illustrations
with digital media. His art has been
commissioned by over fifty major
publishing, advertising, corporate and
institutional clients, including AT&T,
Comedy Central, Cornell University,
Entertainment Weekly, Forbes, and
The Washington Post.**

Banner, Shawn
53 Duncan Ave, Jersey City, NJ 07304
212 398.9540

Banta, Susan
17 Magazine St, Cambridge, MA 02139
617 876.8568

Banthien, Barbara
250 W 57th St, NYC, NY 10107
212 397.7330

Banyai, Istvan
666 Greenwich St, NYC, NY 10014
212 627.2953

Bapp, Kevin
853 Broadway, NYC, NY 10003
212 677.9100

Baquero, George
Four Westley Ln, New Milford, NJ 07646
201 261.6011

Baradat, Sergio
250 W 57th St, NYC, NY 10107
212 397.7330

Barath, Judith
Six Monterey Ter, Orinda, CA 94563
510 253.9451

Barbaria, Steve
1990 Third St, Sacramento, CA 95814
916 442.3200

Barber, Rob
1963 Esperanza Dr, Concord, CA 94519
510 674.9069

Barbier, Suzette
124 Winchester St, Newton, MA 02161
617 527.8388

Barbour, Karen
PO Box 1210, Point Reyes Sta, CA 94956
415 663.1100

Barboza, Ken
853 Broadway, NYC, NY 10003
212 505.8635

Barcelow, Rick
2299 Pearl St, Boulder, CO 80302
303 447.9164

Barnard, Bryn
PO Box 285, Woodbury, NJ 08096
609 853.4252

Barnes, Barry
3825 Valley Blvd, Walnut, CA 91789
909 594.5979

Barnes, Ken
101 Yesler Way, Seattle, WA 98104
206 447.1600

Barnes, Kim
735 Cypress Rd, Severna Park, MD 21146
410 544.4644

Barnes, Michelle
165 Perry St, NYC, NY 10014
212 219.9269

Barnet, Nancy
8928 Shady Vista Ct, Elk Grove, CA 95624
916 685.4147

Barr, Ken
420 Lexington Ave, NYC, NY 10170
212 697.8525

Barr, Loel
22301 Flintridge Dr, Brookeville, MD 20833
301 774.4634

Barrall, Tim
372 Bleecker St, NYC, NY 10014
212 243.9003

Barrett, Annie / Donna Jorgensen
PO Box 19412, Seattle, WA 98109
206 634.1880
fax 206 632.2024
pages 445-447

Barrett, Robert
Pine Rd HCR, Neversink, NY 12765
914 985.2936

Barrett, Ron
2112 Broadway, NYC, NY 10023
212 874.1370

Barry, Ron
21005 Tamarack Cir, Southfield, MI 48075
810 356.8946

Bartalos, Michael
30 Ramona Ave, S.F., CA 94103
415 863.4569

Bartczak, Peter
PO Box 7709, Santa Cruz, CA 95061
408 426.4247

Bartek, Shelly
8522 Izard, Omaha, NE 68114
402 399.5251
page 331

Bartels, Ceci Associates
3286 Ivanhoe, St Louis, MO 63139
314 781.7377

Bartholomew, Caty
198 Seventh Ave, Brooklyn, NY 11215
718 965.0790

Bartholomew, Sandra Steen
136 Bennington Rd, Charlottesville, VA 22901
804 979.8252

Barton, Kent
5378 Pinecrest Ln, Youngharris, GA 30582
305 431.4652

Baruffi, Andrea
341 Hudson Ter, Piermont, NY 10968
914 359.9542

Baseman, Gary
443 12th St, Brooklyn, NY 11215
718 499.9358

Basso, Bill
38 Ogden Ln, Englishtown, NJ 07726
908 431.5497

Bastiansen, Pete
1503 Briarknoll Dr, Arden Hills, MN 55112
612 631.8480

Batcheller, Keith
1438 Calle Cecilia, San Dimas, CA 91773
818 331.0439

Batchelor, Michelle
34 Meghan Ct, Glassboro, NJ 08028
609 589.0615

Bates, Byron R
328 W Main, Rexbury, ID 83440
208 356.3306

Bates, Harry
853 Broadway, NYC, NY 10003
212 677.9100

Batik Illustration
278 Hwy 105, Lake Mills, IA 50450
515 592.5900

Battles, Brian
6316 Dissinger Ave,
San Diego, CA 92139
619 267.3182
fax 619 267.6649
page 100

Bauer, Ann
2100 W Big Beaver Rd, Troy, MI 48084
313 643.6000

Bauer, Stephen
5811 Kipling Ct, Baltimore, MD 21212
410 323.2393

Baugher, Liz & Associates
333 N Michigan Ave, Chicago, IL 60601
312 553.9888

Baughman, Christi
467 Clearfield, Garland, TX 75043
214 270.5925

Bautista, Vincent
1302 Lyndon St, S Pasadena, CA 91030
818 403.9124

Baviera, Rocco
41 King William St, Hamilton,
ONT, Canada L8R 1AZ
905 570.0004

Baxter, Daniel
RR 3 Box 159 Feller Newmark Rd,
Red Hook, NY 12571
914 758.0909

Beach, Lou
1114 S Citrus Ave, L.A., CA 90019
213 934.7335

Beach, Pearl
4939 Sycamore Ter, L.A., CA 90042
213 256.2170

Beards, Richard
58 W 15th St, NYC, NY 10011
212 741.2539

Beaudoin, Mario
22 E 36th St, NYC, NY 10016
212 685.4580

Beavers, Sean
60 E 42nd St, NYC, NY 10165
212 953.7088

Beck, David
4042 Appletree Ct, Cincinnati, OH 45247
513 741.1228

Becker, Ann Dunphy
9131 Westview, Houston, TX 77055
713 465.3037

Becker, Erika
150 W 55th St, NYC, NY 10019
212 757.8987

Becker, Pamela
PO Box 756, Marshall, CA 94940
415 663.1788

Becker, Paula
6017 Ebonwood, Corpus Christi, TX 78412
512 993.0164

Beckley, Scott
2100 Leeds Dr, Plano, TX 75025
214 919.0069

Bedrick, Jeffrey K
2852 California St, S.F., CA 94115
415 923.1122

Bee, Johnee
30166 Chapala Ct, Laguna Niguel, CA 92677
714 495.3664

Beerworth, Roger
1723 S Crescent Hts Blvd, L.A., CA 90035
213 933.9692

Begin, Maryjane
Three Hidden St, Providence, RI 02906
401 421.2344

Beha, Philippe
NYC, NY
212 581.8338
page 464

Beha, Philippe
18 McKinley St, Rowayton, CT 06853
203 866.3734
fax 203 857.0842
page 464

Behum, Cliff
26384 Aaron Ave, Euclid, OH 44132
216 261.9266

Beilfuss, Kevin
1154 W Barry, Chicago, IL 60657
312 871.8618

Bell, Ron
7118 Upper River Rd, Prospect, KY 40059
502 228.9427

Bellantuono, Jeffrey
292 Britannia St, Meriden, CT 06450
203 639.0665

Bemus, Bart
353 W 53rd St, NYC, NY 10019
212 682.2462

Ben-Ami, Doron
#3 Roxbury Rd, Danbury, CT 06811
203 797.8847

Bendell, Norm
420 Route 206, N Bedminster, NJ 07921
908 221.9030

Bender Illustration
1749 Perrysville Ave, Pittsburgh, PA 15215
412 321.3266

Bender, Brenda
4170 S Arbor Cir, Marietta, GA 30066
404 924.4793

Bender, Cherie
12105 NE Sixth Ave, N Miami, FL 33161
305 891.1629

Bender, Mark
1749 Perrysville Ave, Pittsburgh, PA 15212
412 321.3266

Benedict, Ken
5769 N Foxburrow Cir, Memphis, TN 38115
901 363.3075

Benger, Brent
6201 Sunset Blvd, Hollywood, CA 90028
800 236.4371

Benioff, Carol
3311 Jennings St, S.F., CA 94124
415 467.5014
fax 415 467.3637
page 275

Benjamin, Christine
1697 Bellomy St, Santa Clara, CA 95050
408 243.6987

Bennett, Dianne
c/o Danielle Collignon
200 W 15th St, NYC, NY 10011
212 243.4209

Bennett, James
5821 Durham Rd, Pipersville, PA 18947
201 963.1457

Benny, Mike Illustration
2773 Knollwood Ave, Cameron Park, CA 95682
916 677.9142

Bensen, Ben
800 Montrose Ave, S Pasadena, CA 91030
818 441.1009

Benson, Linda
89 Fifth Ave, NYC, NY 10003
212 627.1554

Bensusen, Sally J
932 S Walter Reed Dr, Arlington, VA 22204
703 979.3931

Beranbaum, Sheryl
617 437.9459
401 737.8591
fax 617 437.6494
pages 310-311

Berendsen & Associates
2233 Kemper Ln, Cincinnati, OH 45206
513 861.1400

Berg, John
110 Cottage St, Buffalo, NY 14201
716 884.8003

Berg, Ron
71 Hewitt Ave, Toronto,
ONT, Canada M6R 1Y4
416 537.4069
fax 416 539.8840
page 197

Berg, Ron
420 Lexington Ave, NYC, NY 10170
212 986.5680
fax 212 818.1246
page 197

Bergendorff, Roger
1010 S Robertson Blvd, L.A., CA 90035
310 652.7322

Bergherr, Mary
2520 W 22nd St, Mpls, MN 55405
612 377.0996

Bergin, Kieran
171 Beech St, Kearny, NJ 07032
212 459.5244

Bergin, Tom Studios
708 E University Blvd, Tucson, AZ 85719
520 884.1618

Berglund, Cindy
5275 E Lake Bch Ct, Shoreview, MN 55126
612 490.5141

Bergman, Eliot
250 W 57th St, NYC, NY 10107
212 397.7330

Berkson, Nina
Two Silver Ave, Toronto,
ONT, Canada M6R 3A2
416 530.1500
fax 416 530.1401
page 18

Bernal, Richard
6239 Elizabeth Ave, St Louis, MO 63139
314 781.8851

Bernstein & Andriulli
60 E 42nd St, NYC, NY 10165
212 682.1490

Bernstein, Joanie-Art Rep
817 Westwood Dr S, Mpls, MN 55416
612 374.3169

Berrett, Randy
716 Montgomery St, S.F., CA 94111
415 433.1222
fax 415 433.9560
page 400

Berrit, Grynan
1125 Landwehr Rd, Northbrook, IL 60062
708 498.8936

Berry, Rick
93 Warren St, Arlington, MA 02174
617 721.5418

Bertram, Bob
837 Pebblefield Ter, Ballwin, MO 63021
314 256.0405

Betz, Karen
7310 47th Ave SW, Seattle, WA 98136
206 932.6554

Betzold, Hal Illustration
404 E Kensington, Mt Prospect, IL 60056
708 590.9675

Bialek, David
230 N Michigan Ave, Chicago, IL 60601
312 368.8777

Bianco, Peter
201 Manning St, Needham, MA 02194
617 444.9077

Bieck, Kathy
5855 Green Valley Cir, Culver City, CA 90230
310 642.2721

Biegel, Michael David
PO Box 428, Allandale, NJ 07401
201 612.1324

Biers, Nanette
123 Willow Ave, Corte Madera, CA 94925
415 927.1531

The Big Pixel
3183 Airway Ave, Costa Mesa, CA 92626
714 433.7400

Bigda, Diane
77 Fuller St, Brookline, MA 02146
617 232.3299

Billout, Guy
225 Lafayette St, NYC, NY 10012
212 431.6350

Bilter, Lori
Nashville, TN
615 297.3930

Binder, Pat
2108 Loch Haven Dr, Dallas, TX 75023
214 596.5275

Binkley, Paul
5855 Green Valley Cir, Culver City, CA 90230
310 642.2721

Birenbaum, Molly
Seven Williamsburg Dr, Cheshire, CT 06410
203 272.9253

Birkey, Randal
635 S Home Ave, Oak Park, IL 60304
708 386.5150

Birkey, Randal
900 W Jackson Blvd, Chicago, IL 60607
312 944.5680

Birmingham, Lloyd
500 Peekskill Hollow Rd,
Putnam Valley, NY 10579
914 528.3207
Extensive experience illustrating for all
major sciences, including natural science
(animals, fish, birds, dinosaurs, etc.),
earth science, medical science,
astronomy, oceanography, and
aerospace for major publishers of
textbooks, encyclopedias and posters.

Birnbaum, M Dianne
17301 Elsinore Cir, Huntington Beach, CA 92647
714 847.7631

Bischel, Mark
112 W Ninth St, Kansas City, MO 64105
816 421.4473

Bishofs, Maris
251-16 Northern Blvd, Little Neck, NY 11363
718 229.7570

Bixby, Mark
925 Elm Grove Rd, Elm Grove, WI 53122
414 785.1940

Bjorck, Liselotte/Betula Prod
PO Box 1625, Morro Bay, CA 93443
805 772.0546

Björkman, Steve
501 Fifth Ave, NYC, NY 10017
212 490.2450
fax 212 697.6828
page 54

BK Communications
1638 Eastern Pky, Louisville, KY 40204
502 459.0295

Black, Dave
c/o Bruck & Moss
333 E 49th St, NYC, NY 10017
212 980.8061

Black, Richard H
205 Foxridge Dr, Dayton, OH 45429
513 293.9001
Specializes in figure portraits, hospital
art. Clients include - Proctor and
Gamble, Frigidaire, General Motors,
Shaw Barton, General Electric,
Masonite, Delco, Grandcor.

BlackDog
239 Marin St, San Rafael, CA 94901
415 258.9663

Blackshear, Ami
220 Elm Cir, Colorado Spgs, CO 80906
719 636.5009

Blackshear, Thomas
220 Elm Cir, Colorado Springs, CO 80906
719 636.5009

Blackwell, Garie
60 E 42nd St, NYC, NY 10165
212 682.1490

Blackwell, Patrick
Pond Rd, PO Box 324, North Truro, MA 02652
508 487.3336

Blair, Dru
22 E 36th St, NYC, NY 10016
212 685.4580

Blake, Marty
PO Box 266, Jamesville, NY 13078
315 492.1332

Blakey, Paul
2910 Caribou Trl, Marietta, GA 30062
404 977.7669

Blanchette, Dan
428 Charleston Dr, Bolingbrook, IL 60440
708 972.0092

Blank, Jerry
1048 Lincoln Ave, San Jose, CA 95125
408 289.9095
fax 408 289.8532
page 320

Blasutta, Mary Lynn
156 Huguenot St, New Paltz, NY 12561
914 256.0830

Blechman, RO
Two W 47th St, NYC, NY 10036
212 869.1630
fax 212 764.4169

Bleck, Linda
642 W Aldine, Chicago, IL 60657
312 281.0286

Blessen, Karen
c/o Vicki Morgan
194 Third Ave, NYC, NY 10003
212 475.0440

Bliss, Jim
25 Drury Ln, Rochester, NY 14625
716 586.6041

Bliss, Phil
22 Briggs Ave, Fairport, NY 14450
716 377.9771

Bliss, Rachel
c/o Vicki Morgan
194 Third Ave, NYC, NY 10003
212 475.0440

Blitt, Barry
34 Lincoln Ave, Greenwich, CT 06830
203 622.2988

Bloch, A Calligraphy & Design
139 E 33rd St, NYC, NY 10016
212 532.3374

Blockey, Gloria
100 Wyndham Cir W,
New Brighton, MN 55112
612 631.2353
fax 612 631.2340
page 405

Bloomer, Charles
820 S Rosemead Blvd, Pasadena, CA 91107
818 796.6959

Blubaugh, Susan M
511 E 81st St, NYC, NY 10028
212 570.6731

Blue Moon Graphics Studio
3100 Carlisle, Dallas, TX 75204
214 871.0085

Blumen, Irina
2265 S Bascom Ave, Campbell, CA 95008
408 377.3872

Boatwright, Phil
2342 Stillwater, Mesquite, TX 75181
214 222.2399

Bobnick, Dick
9801 Dupont Ave S, Bloomington, MN 55431
612 881.1008

Boddy, Joe
5375 Skyway Dr, Missoula, MT 59801
406 251.3587
fax 406 251.3587
page 208

Boehm, Roger
31726 Fourth Ave, South Laguna, CA 92677
714 499.6230

Boer, Jan-Willem
2654 Rodeo Dr NE, Blaine, MN 55449
612 780.4085

Boerger, Andrew
83 Walnut Ave, Corte Madera, CA 94925
415 924.7881

Bohbot, Michel
3823 Harrison St, Oakland, CA 94611
510 547.0667

Bohn Illustration
14 N First Ave, St Charles, IL 60174
708 513.1269

Boie, Chuck
925 Elm Grove Rd, Elm Grove, WI 53122
414 785.1940

Boies, Alex
126 N Third St, Mpls, MN 55401
612 333.2418

Boise, Kathyjean
1233 De Haro St, S.F., CA 94107
415 285.3014

Boldman, Craig
PO Box 18128, Fairfield, OH 45018
513 868.2874

Boles, Terry
8145 Hearthside Rd S, Cottage Grove, MN 55016
612 459.9820

Bolesky, John
921 First Ave W, Seattle, WA 98119
206 281.0960

Boll, Maxine
200 Aquetong Rd, New Hope, PA 18938
215 862.2091
fax 215 862.2641
page 228
Maxine Boll's watercolors appeared in
Bon Appetit, Better Homes & Gardens,
Berlitz, Mattel, The Los Angeles County
Museum, DC Heath, Prudential
Mortgage, The Gap, Land's End, Sayes
International Japan, Paramount
Pictures, American Airlines, Macmillan/
McGraw-Hill and design firms.

Boll, Tom Illustration
9500 Wyoming Ave S, Bloomington, MN 55438
612 942.6119

Bollinger, Peter
232 Madison Ave, NYC, NY 10016
212 889.8777

Bolster, Rob
Seven Hope St, Walpole, MA 02081
508 660.1751

Bolten, Jennifer
7118 Upper River Rd, Prospect, KY 40059
502 228.9427

Bomba, Ron
421 N 36th St, Seattle, WA 98103
206 634.0777

Bond, Bob & Associates
20 Ocean Ter, Lynn, MA 01902
617 595.4201

Bond, Higgins
304 Woodbine St, Teaneck, NJ 07666
201 836.1396

Bonham, Patti
10006 Cedar Creek Dr, Houston, TX 77042
713 977.6522

Bonilla, Michael
4743 Shaunee Creek, Dayton, OH 45415
513 275.7071

Bonk, Christopher
1400 N Elmhurst Rd, Mt Prospect, IL 60056
708 577.5157

Bono, Peter
63 Stark Rd, Columbia, NJ 07832
908 496.8524

Booker, George
5855 Green Valley Cir, Culver City, CA 90230
310 642.2721

Bookmakers Ltd
40 Mouse House Rd, Taos, NM 87571
505 776.5435

Bookwalter, Tom
11440 Oak Dr, Shelbyville, MI 49344
616 672.5756

Booth, Martha Anne
990 Acacia St, Montara, CA 94037
415 728.8332

Boquel, Beth
31 First St, Rumson, NJ 07760
908 842.9162

Borda, Juliette
114 Carnegie Pl, Pittsburgh, PA 15208
412 441.7188

Borge, Rich
459 W 49th St, NYC, NY 10019
212 262.9823

Borowski, Diane
848 Greenwood Ave NE,
Atlanta, GA 30306
404 875.1363 / 800 347.0734
fax 404 875.9733
page 339

Borruso, John
1259 Guerrero St, S.F., CA 94110
415 647.1972

Bory, Lou
108 E 35th St, NYC, NY 10016
212 889.3337

Boscamp, Walt Design Inc
4100 Simonis St, Stevens Point, WI 54481
715 344.4344

Bostic, Alexander
1888 Century Park E, L.A., CA 90067
310 826.1332

Boston, David
Eight Mirlo Ln, Hot Springs Vlg, AR 71909
501 922.2238

Boswick, Steven
331 Oak Cir, Wilmette, IL 60091
708 251.1430

Bote, Tividar
280 Madison Ave, NYC, NY 10016
212 545.9155

Botero, Kirk
847A Second Ave, NYC, NY 10017
212 486.0177

Botzis, Ka
Nine Babbling Brook Ln, Suffern, NY 10901
914 368.8606

Bower, Joel
2164 Elysian Pl, Cincinnati, OH 45219
513 651.9280

Bowers, David
100 Scott Way, Carnegie, PA 15106
412 276.7224

Bowler, Jean
PO Box 1854, Orinda, CA 94563
510 256.9923

Bowles, Bruce Illustration
1045 Sansome St, S.F., CA 94111
415 362.4478
page 144

Bowles, Doug
716 Sanchez St, S.F., CA 94114
415 285.8267
fax 415 285.8268
page 69

Bowles, Doug
10305 Wenonga Ln,
Leawood, KS 66206
913 385.0462
fax 913 384.0445
page 69

Bowman, Eric
11605 SW Terra Linda St,
Beaverton, OR 97005
503 644.1016
page 330

Bowman, Rich
3215 Central, Kansas City, MO 64111
816 756.0925

Bowser, Ken
909 Camellia St, Winter Park, FL 32789
407 644.9888

Boyd, Silvia
3219 Autumn Bridge Ln, Houston, TX 77084
713 578.3971

Boyer-Nelles, Lyn
7482 Cook Rd, Williamsburg, MI 49690
616 267.9267

Boyko, Bill
16 Conrad Ave, Toronto, ONT, Canada M6G 3G5
416 656.6616

Bozzini, James
501 Fifth Ave, NYC, NY 10017
212 490.2450
fax 212 697.6828
page 40

Braddick, Wayne
4331 Dickason, Dallas, TX 75219
214 823.7573

Brady, Elizabeth Illustration
1444 Holbrook St, L.A., CA 90041
213 340.8026

Bragg, Shokie
Five Oklahoma Ave, Wilmington, DE 19803
302 761.9144

Bralds, Braldt
270 Park Ave S, NYC, NY 10010
212 260.6700

Bramsen, David
4376A Cuna Dr,
Santa Barbara, CA 93110
805 683.0912
fax 805 964.5004
Bramsen would hate to waste $50 on
this ad: a bonus good deal awaits caller
#1. All Dave's callers need good service
& fine humorous (or realistic) ink/
watercolor/scratchboard or sprightly-
colored computer illustration.

Brancato, Ron
72 Cascade Dr, Rochester, NY 14614
716 262.4450

Brandon, Bill
137 Fifth Ave, NYC, NY 10010
212 529.3556

Brandt, Kim Wilson
219 Crescent Ave, S.F., CA 94110
415 824.2055 / 718 237.8546
page 432
Vivid colors or bold black and white.
Sizes from billboard to postage stamp.
Clients include: Big Blue Dot, Cartoon
Network, Hallmark, Hal Riney, Harcourt
Brace, NY Times, Penguin, Price
Waterhouse, Sony, Sports Illustrated,
Time, Travel & Leisure, Unicef.

Brandts, Dirk
PO Box 23808, Santa Barbara, CA 93121
805 569.1037

Braswell, Amy
3721 Steve Dr NW, Marietta, GA 30064
404 426.4230

Brauckmann-Towns, Krista
731 N 24th St, Phila, PA 19130
215 232.6666

Braught, Mark
767 N Parkwood Rd, Decatur, GA 30030
404 373.7430

Brault, Gene
2115 Hyperion Ave, L.A., CA 90027
213 664.3034

Braun, David
12104 Greenway Ct, Fairfax, VA 22033
703 352.3659

Braun, Kathy Represents
75 Water St, S.F., CA 94133
415 775.3366

Braun, Marty
265 Pleasant Ave,
Peaks Island, ME 04108
207 766.9726
page 291

Brautigam, Don
211 E 51st St, NYC, NY 10022
212 755.1365

Brawner, Dan
7118 Upper River Rd, Prospect, KY 40059
502 228.9427

Brazeal, Lee Lee
PO Box 141, Chappell Hill, TX 77426
409 277.9926
page 443

Breakey, John
611 Broadway, NYC, NY 10012
212 982.0188
page 215

Breeden, Don
PO Box 5686, Brownsville, TX 78523
210 542.5193

Brennan, Dan Illustration
120 W Illinois St, Chicago, IL 60610
312 822.0887

Brennan, Neil
c/o Bernstein & Andriulli
60 E 42nd St, NYC, NY 10165
212 682.1490

Brenner, Tom
217 E 86th St, NYC, NY 10028
212 427.5632

Brenno, Vonnie
5855 Green Valley Cir, Culver City, CA 90230
310 642.2721

Breuer, Lee
910 Laurens St, Columbia, SC 29201
803 779.9669
fax 803 765.9308
page 190

Brewster, John Creative Services
597 Riverside Ave, Westport, CT 06880
203 226.4724
fax 203 454.9904
pages 433-437

Briant, Edward
58 W 15th St, NYC, NY 10011
212 741.2539

Brice, Jeff
2814 NW 72nd St, Seattle, WA 98117
206 784.1136

Brickman, Robin
32 Ft Hoosac Pl, Williamstown, MA 01267
413 458.9853

Bridewell, Elizabeth
5360 Kester Ave, Sherman Oaks, CA 91411
818 906.7361

Bridges, Gregory
c/o Bernstein & Andriulli
60 E 42nd St, NYC, NY 10165
212 682.1490

Bridy, Dan
280 Madison Ave, NYC, NY 10016
212 545.9155

Briers, Stuart
108 E 35th St, NYC, NY 10016
212 889.3337

Briggs, Harry
PO Box 51266, Pacific Grove, CA 93950
408 393.9433

Brigham, Derek
4512 Harriet Ave S, Mpls, MN 55409
612 827.3431

Brignell, Ian
511 King St W, Toronto, ONT, Canada M5V 1K4
416 581.1075

Brindak, Hermine
Three Lockwood Ave, Old Greenwich, CT 06870
203 698.1732

Bringham, Sherry
1804 Arlington, El Cerrito, CA 94530
510 235.2859

Brissette•Gendron
250 W 57th St, NYC, NY 10107
212 397.7330
fax 212 397.7334
page 244

Bristol, Suzanne
112 Blackburn Ave, Menlo Park, CA 94025
415 324.4235

Britt, Stephanie
PO Box 818, Hanalei, HI 96714
808 828.0069

Britt, Tracy
c/o Barb Hauser
PO Box 421443, S.F., CA 94142
415 647.5660
fax 415 285.1102
page 114
Realistic acrylic paintings from product
to conceptual, technical to stylized. With
airbrush and brush, on paper and
canvas, the only limits are our
imaginations.

Broad, David
100 Golden Hinde, San Rafael, CA 94903
415 479.5505

Broda, Ron
420 Lexington Ave, NYC, NY 10170
212 697.8525

Brodie, Cindy
Six Monterey Ter, Orinda, CA 94563
510 253.9451

Brogan, Walter
49 W 45th St, NYC, NY 10036
212 921.1199

Bronson, Linda
c/o Leighton & Co
Four Prospect St, Beverly, MA 01915
508 921.0887
fax 508 921.0223
page 211

Brook, Elvis
111 NE 42nd St, Miami, FL 33137
305 576.0142

Brooke & Co
4323 Bluffview, Dallas, TX 75209
214 352.9192
fax 214 350.2101
page 443

Brooks, Andrea
99 Bank St, NYC, NY 10014
212 633.1477

Brooks, Nan
770 N Halsted P102, Chicago, IL 60622
312 338.7110

Brooks, Rob
501 Fifth Ave, NYC, NY 10017
212 490.2450
fax 212 697.6828
page 38

Brother, Kelly
5250 Sycamore Grove Ln, Memphis, TN 38120
901 761.4204

Brothers, Barry
1920 E 17th St, Brooklyn, NY 11229
718 336.7540

Broussard, Edwin Scott
43 E Grand Ave, Montvale, NJ 07645
201 391.0226

Brown, Calef
15339 Camarillo St, Sherman Oaks, CA 91403
818 986.6361

Brown, Charley
716 Montgomery St, S.F., CA 94111
415 433.1222

Brown, Charlie & Co
8811 Gaylord, Houston, TX 77024
713 468.8161

Brown, Dan
3815 Falk Rd, Vancouver, WA 98661
360 737.9920
fax 360 737.9920
page 105

Brown, Dan
89 Fifth Ave, NYC, NY 10003
212 627.1554

Brown, Greg
1025 Conkey St, Hammond, IN 46320
219 931.1164

Brown, Mark Kingsley
1234 Orpheus Ave, Leucadia, CA 92024
619 753.5196

Brown, Michael David
932 Hungerford Dr, Rockville, MD 20850
301 762.4474

Brown, Peter D
235 E 22nd St, NYC, NY 10010
212 684.7080

Brown, Rick
16635 Howard Cir, Omaha, NE 68118
402 697.1962

Brown, Rick
4290 Upper Mt Rd, Furlong, PA 18925
215 794.8186

Brown, William L
6704 Westmoreland Ave, Takoma Park, MD 20912
301 270.2014

Brown-Wing, Katherine
Eight Washington St, Jamestown, RI 02835
401 423.2609

Brownson, Matt
9899 Iris St, Westminster, CO 80021
303 423.5240
page 322

Brownson, Matt
1863 S Pearl St, Denver, CO 80210
303 733.0128 / 800 417.5120
fax 303 733.8154
page 322

Bruce, Sandra
13997 Emerald Ct, Grass Valley, CA 95945
916 477.1909

Bruce, Taylor
946 B St, Petaluma, CA 94952
707 765.6744
fax 707 765.0551
page 332

Bruce, Tim
1826 Asheville Pl, Charlotte, NC 28203
704 372.6007

Bruck & Moss
333 E 49th St, NYC, NY 10017
212 980.8061

Bruck, Victoria Vebell
4711 Spicewood Springs Rd, Austin, TX 78759
512 343.8260

Brugger, Bob
1930 Robinson St, Redondo Beach, CA 90228
310 372.0135

Brun, Robert
76 State St, Newburyport, MA 01950
508 462.1948

Bruning, Bill
118 E 26th St, Mpls, MN 55404
612 871.4539

Brunnick, Jeanne
1233 Hermosa Ave, Hermosa Beach, CA 90254
310 798.2771

Bryant Lettering & Design
7305 Kenneth Dr, Richmond, VA 23228
804 262.7133

Bryant, Amy
5521 Greenville Ave,
Dallas, TX 75206
214 696.4950
fax 214 696.6163
page 236

Bryn, Barnard
67 Upper Mountain Ave, Montclair, NJ 07042
201 744.4465

Buchanan, Nigel
111 NE 42nd St, Miami Beach, FL 33137
305 576.0142

Buchs, Thomas
925 Elm Grove Rd, Elm Grove, WI 53122
414 785.1940

Buck & Kane
135 W 41 St, NYC, NY 10036
212 221.8090

Buehner, Mark
2806 S 2000 E, Salt Lake City, UT 84109
801 467.1565

Bull, Michael H
75 Water St, S.F., CA 94133
415 755.3380

Burchard, Michelle
2269 India St, L.A., CA 90039
213 664.5036

Burckhardt, Marc
112 W 41st St, Austin, TX 78751
512 474.9781

Burgard, WC
2785 Heather Way, Ann Arbor, MI 48104
313 971.3014

Burger, Robert
145 Kingwood Stockton Rd, Stockton, NJ 08559
609 397.3737

Burgoyne, John
200 E 78th St, NYC, NY 10021
212 570.9069

Burke, Kevin
4501 Lyons Rd, Miamisburg, OH 45342
513 866.4013

Burke, Leland
675 Drewry St, Atlanta, GA 30306
404 881.8255

Burke, Phillip
1948 Juron Dr, Niagara Falls, NY 14304
716 297.0345

Burkhart, Amelia
63 Hawthorne St, Lenox, MA 01240
413 637.4951

Burleson, Joe
c/o Bernstein & Andriulli
60 E 42nd St, NYC, NY 10165
212 867.8097

Burman, Rob
2100 W Big Beaver Rd, Troy, MI 48084
810 643.6000

Burn, Ted
56 Cliff Dr, Fairhope, AL 36532
205 990.8159

Burnett, Lindy
4424 Power's Ferry Rd,
Atlanta, GA 30327
404 255.8094 / 800 347.0734
fax 404 875.9733
page 342

Burnett, Yolanda
6478 Chestnut Hill Rd, Flowery Branch, GA 30542
404 967.0039

Burns, Charles
210 Brown St, Phila, PA 19123
215 925.7618

Burns, Jim
11 Kings Ridge Rd, Long Valley, NJ 07853
908 813.8718

Burns, Rhonda
13049 Hartsook St, Sherman Oaks, CA 91423
818 789.6949

Burrell, Chris
PO Box 2676, Vineyard Haven, MA 02568
508 696.8257

Burton, Caroline
330 Eighth St, Jersey City, NJ 07302
201 656.2688

Burzynski, Mary
1535 N Western Ave, Chicago, IL 60622
312 227.6755

Busacca, Mark
420 Lexington Ave, NYC, NY 10528
212 986.5680

Bustamante, Gerald
2400 Kettner Blvd, San Diego, CA 92101
619 234.8803
page 29

Buszka-Pollis, Kimberly
PO Box 1665, Ranchos Taos, NM 87557
505 758.0974

Butler, Chris
7018 Redwing Pl, Longmont, CO 80503
303 494.4118

Butler, Nate Studio
PO Box 27470, Albuquerque, NM 87125
505 268.6869

Butler, Paul
5597 Seminary Rd, Falls Church, VA 22041
703 671.4363

Butterfield, Ned
278 Cedar Ave, Islip, NY 11751
516 277.3151

Buttram, Andy
68 E Franklin St, Dayton, OH 45459
513 433.8383

Byram, Stephen
52 68th St, Guttenberg, NJ 07093
201 869.7493

Byrd, Bob
280 Madison Ave, NYC, NY 10016
212 545.9155

Byrne, Robert
6135 Reseda Blvd, Reseda, CA 91335
818 342.3766
page 85

Cabarga, Leslie
258 W Tulpehocken St, Phila, PA 19144
215 438.9954

Cable, Annette
2018 Maryland Ave, Louisville, KY 40205
502 451.4228

Cabossel, Jannine
Rte 19 Box 90-8, Santa Fe, NM 87505
505 983.4099
page 418

Cabry, Cyryl
211 E 89th St, NYC, NY 10128
212 289.5514

Cacy, Michael Studio
537 SE Ash St, Portland, OR 97214
503 233.7715
fax 503 233.0978
page 376
Specialties include realistic airbrush and
traditional mixed media in a variety of
styles. Clients include: Nike, Seiko,
Anheuser-Busch, Microsoft,
National Geographic, Boeing, Speedo,
Mercedes-Benz.

Cadman, Joel
41-15 50th Ave, Sunnyside, NY 11104
718 784.1267

Cagle Design
5353 Hinton Ave, Woodland Hills, CA 91367
818 340.2887

Cain, David
200 W 20th St, NYC, NY 10011
212 633.0258

Cain, Janan
46 Woodside Rd, Riverside, IL 60546
708 447.4208

Cain, Thomas
510 Toluca Dr, Burbank, CA 91505
818 557.1305

Cairns, Brian
58 W 15th St, NYC, NY 10011
212 741.2539

Caldwell, Kirk
1033 Battery, S.F., CA 94111
415 398.7553

Caldwell, Sam
4801 Woodway, Houston, TX 77056
713 850.9030

Calhoun, Dia
731 N 24th St, Phila, PA 19130
215 232.6666

Callanan, Brian
Five Winston Pl, Yonkers, NY 10710
914 779.4120

Callen, Liz
866 UN Plz, NYC, NY 10017
212 644.2020

Calligraphy by Carol Ostrow
2933 N Sheridan Rd, Chicago, IL 60657
312 348.6965

Calligraphy by Domenica
1010 E Lois Ln, Phoenix, AZ 85020
602 395.9786

Calnan, John
49 W 45th St, NYC, NY 10036
212 921.1199

Calver, Dave
70 Stoneham Dr, Rochester, NY 14625
716 383.8996

Camarro, Paul
36 Bank St, Sussex, NJ 07461
201 875.2092

Camp, Barbara
c/o Bernstein & Andriulli
60 E 42nd St, NYC, NY 10165
212 682.1490

Campbell, Denise Hilton
716 Sanchez St, S.F., CA 94114
415 285.8267

Campbell, Jenny
731 N 24th St, Phila, PA 19130
215 232.6666

Campbell, Pamela & Associates
511 Port, Angleton, TX 77515
713 523.5328

Campbell-Boyd, Alice
4838 Milwee, Houston, TX 77092
713 681.3172

Canty, Bill
PO Box 1053, South Wellfleet, MA 02663
508 349.7549

Capalungan, David
780 Monroe Dr NE, Atlanta, GA 30308
404 876.1230

Caporale, Wende
Studio Hill Farm, North Salem, NY 10560
203 226.4724

Carbone, Carol
240 Davjo Dr, Cold Spring, KY 41076
606 781.6766

Carden, Vincent
2308 E Glenoaks Blvd, Glendale, CA 91206
818 956.0807

Carey, Sue Illustration
1700 Bush St, S.F., CA 94109
415 441.7046

Caricatures by Sherry Lane
155 Bank St, NYC, NY 10014
212 675.6224

Carloni, Kurt
1942 W Shore Dr, Delafield, WI 53018
414 646.3356

Carlsen, Jonathon
3000 Chestnut Ave, Baltimore, MD 21211
410 467.9172

Carlson, Frederick H
118 Monticello Dr,
Monroeville, PA 15146
412 856.0982
fax 412 856.0983
page 159

Carlson, Holly Hanes
1256 Vincente Dr, Apt F,
Sunnyvale, CA 94086
415 961.4906
fax 415 961.4906
page 399
Holly combines realistic drawing with a
fanciful style. Her inviting scenes of
flora, fauna, real, and imaginary
characters have been used for
packaging, books, and consumer
products. Clients include Joe Boxer,
Colorbook, and Monterey Aquarium.

Carlson, Jim
118 1/2 N Main St, Galena, IL 61036
815 777.3250

Carlson, Jonathan
853 Broadway, NYC, NY 10003
212 677.9100

Carlson, Lisa
407 14th Ave SW, Rochester, MN 55902
507 252.0311

Carlson, Sue Johnston
1412 Jarvis Dr, Manhattan, KS 66502
913 539.5535
fax 913 539.5535
page 280
Natural science illustration and
cartographic art. Husband and wife
team both formerly on staff with the
National Geographic Society – map
services and design. Computer mapping
and stock illustration available for both
children and adult viewers.

Carmichael, Dennis
307 N Michigan Ave, Chicago, IL 60601
312 704.0500

Carmichael, Dennis
19355 Pacific Coast Hwy, Malibu, CA 90265
310 456.5915

Carnabuci, Anthony
92 Village St, S Easton, MA 02375
508 238.4231

Carpenter, Mia
5855 Green Valley Cir, Culver City, CA 90230
310 642.2721

Carpenter, Michael
2125 NW 72nd St, Seattle, WA 98117
206 784.1136

Carr, Alan
51 Dean St, Brooklyn, NY 11201
718 596.8850

Carr, Barbara
245 E 40th St, NYC, NY 10016
212 370.1663

Carr, Noell
30 E 14th St, NYC, NY 10003
212 675.1015

Carra, Gina
52-25 Skillman Ave, Woodside, NY 11377
718 565.1835

Carrabotta, Vic
5855 Green Valley Cir, Culver City, CA 90230
310 642.2721

Carroll, Jim
Box 233 Albany Tpke, Old Chatham, NY 12136
518 794.8803

Carroll, Justin
1316 Third St, Santa Monica, CA 90401
310 458.7600

Carroll, Michael
538 Belleforte Ave, Oak Park, IL 60302
708 386.6197
page 119

Carroll, Michael
520 N Michigan Ave, Chicago, IL 60611
312 527.0351
fax 312 527.5468
page 119

Carrozza, John
56 Maquan St, Pembroke, MA 02359
617 293.3580
fax 617 293.3580
Published graphic artist illustrator.
Assignments include: children's books,
maps, brochures, newsletters, greeting
cards, textbooks, postcards, computer
and informational graphics. Style:
realistic, conceptual representations of
people and the natural environment
including animals and landscapes.
Samples available.

Carruthers, Roy
270 Park Ave S, NYC, NY 10010
212 260.6700

Carsello Creative Inc
954 W Washington, Chicago, IL 60607
312 733.5709
fax 312 733.5736
page 96

Carson, Jim
11 Foch St, Cambridge, MA 02140
617 661.3321
fax 617 661.3321
page 350

Carson, Lynn
12165 SE Foster Pl, Portland, OR 97266
503 760.8987

Carter, Abby
666 Greenwich St, NYC, NY 10014
212 675.5719

Carter, Bunny
828 Pine Hill Rd, Stanford, CA 94305
415 856.2741

Carter, Mary
c/o Barb Hauser
PO Box 421443, S.F., CA 94142
415 647.5660
fax 415 285.1102
page 115
Computer illustration, Mac or Windows,
from whimsical to stylized realism.

Carter, Mike Illustration Inc
32 Oaken Gateway, Toronto,
ONT, Canada M2P 2A1
416 250.5433
fax 416 250.6919
page 417
Client list includes: Air France, American
Express, Bayer, Coca-Cola, Federal
Express, Ford, Goodyear, IBM, Pillsbury,
and Visa.

Carter, Penny
12 Stuyvesant Oval, NYC, NY 10009
212 473.7965

Carter, Stephanie
921 First Ave W, Seattle, WA 98119
206 281.0960

Cary & Co
666 Banty Ln, Stone Mountain, GA 30083
404 296.9666

Cascardo Art & Design
217 W Huron, Chicago, IL 60610
312 335.8262

Cason, Merrill
21-08 72nd St, Jackson Heights, NY 11370
718 932.6045

Cassano, Rose
863 Carolina St, S.F., CA 94107
415 550.1402

Cassidy, Michael
610 Marine View, Del Mar, CA 92014
619 755.6290

Castellanos, Carlos
13174 80th Ln N, West Palm Beach, FL 33412
407 791.7993

Castelo, Elizabeth
140 N Serrano Ave, L.A., CA 90004
213 389.1746

Castillito, Mark
67 Upper Mountain Ave, Montclair, NJ 07042
201 744.4465

Castillo, Julie
c/o Bernstein & Andriulli
60 E 42nd St, NYC, NY 10165
212 682.1490

Catalano, Sal
114 Boyce Pl, Ridgewood, NJ 07450
201 447.5318

Cathey, Kirsten
1430 W Belmont, Chicago, IL 60657
312 348.8501

Caton, Chip
15 Warrenton Ave, Hartford, CT 06105
203 523.4562

Cavanagh, Tom
119 NW 93rd Ter, Coral Springs, FL 33071
305 753.0336

Cavette, Mike
22840 Jorgenson Ln, Red Bluff, CA 96080
916 528.1930

Ceballos, John
1047 Broadmoor Dr, Napa, CA 94558
707 226.1026

Ceccarelli, Chris
3427 Folsom Blvd, Sacramento, CA 95816
916 455.0569

Celio, Jim
15015 S La Condesa Dr, La Mirada, CA 90638
714 994.1350

Centola, Tom
213 Long Ln, Upper Darby, PA 19082
610 352.5990
fax 610 352.5990
Airbrushed acrylic illustrations for
advertising and publishing. Concept and
design, specializing in book jackets and
paperback covers. Samples available
upon request, including highly realistic,
fantasy, adult novels, juvenile and
young adult, and scientific/medical
textbooks.

Cericola, Anthony
731 N 24th St, Phila, PA 19130
215 232.6666

Cerulli, Frank
281 Mercer St, Stirling, NJ 07980
908 580.1198

Chabrian, Deborah
89 Fifth Ave, NYC, NY 10003
212 627.1554

Champlin, Dale
2405 NW Thurman, Portland, OR 97210
503 225.9687

Chan, Harvey
Two Clinton Pl, Toronto, ONT, Canada M6G 1J9
416 533.6658

Chan, Ron
110 Sutter St, S.F., CA 94104
415 441.4384
fax 415 395.9809
page 1

Chandler, Karen
80 Lattington Rd, Locust Valley, NY 11560
516 671.0388

Chandler, Roger
597 Riverside Ave, Westport, CT 06880
203 226.4724
fax 203 454.9904
page 433

Chapleski, Gerry
Ten E Ontario St, Chicago, IL 60611
312 573.1370

Chapman, Shirley
20 Espada Ct, Fremont, CA 94539
510 792.8986

Chappell, Ellis
111 Madison Ave, Memphis, TX 38103
901 527.0496

Charpentier, Russ
51 Oakwood St, S.F., CA 94110
415 553.8943

Chaves, Leslie
121-12 115th Ave, S Ozone Pk, NY 11420
718 845.4407

Chen, David
2211 Newton Dr, Rockville, MD 20850
301 460.6575
fax 301 460.5351
page 401

Chernishov, Anatoly
Four Willowbank Ct,
Mahwah, NJ 07430
201 327.2377
page 306

Cherry, Jim
341 W Vernon, Phoenix, AZ 85003
602 252.5072
fax 602 252.5073
page 441

Chesak, Lina
2265 Idylwood Station Ln,
Falls Church, VA 22043
703 573.4230

Chesterman, Adriane
89 Fifth Ave, NYC, NY 10003
212 627.1554

Cheung, Phil
2149 Lyon St, S.F., CA 94115
415 921.7140

Chewning, Randy
666 Greenwich St, NYC, NY 10014
212 675.5719

Chezem, Douglas R
3613 Cornell Rd, Fairfax, VA 22030
703 591.5424

Chiaramonte, Vincent
4300 N Narragansett, Chicago, IL 60634
708 670.0912

Chiba, Lisa
4141 NE 63rd Ave, Portland, OR 97218
503 282.5816

Chichoni, Oscar
43 E 19th St, NYC, NY 10003
212 254.4996

ChiD Studios
115 Rumsey Rd, Yonkers, NY 10705
914 963.6997
fax 914 963.6997
Specializing in humorous Illustration,
color and black & white, tight deadlines.
Clientele: Bell Atlantic, 1010 WINS News
Radio, Science Diet Pet Foods, WNEW-
FM Radio, Corinthian Media, Rainbow
Media, Citadel Productions, Boulder
Resources, Halsted Energies.

Chironna, Ron
122 Slosson Ave, Staten Island, NY 10314
718 720.6142

Chislovsky, Carol Design Inc
853 Broadway, NYC, NY 10003
212 677.9100
fax 212 353.0954
pages 124-125, 165

Cho, Young Sook
68 E Franklin St, Dayton, OH 45459
513 433.8383

Chodos-Irvine, Margaret
2814 NW 72nd St, Seattle, WA 98117
206 784.1136
fax 206 784.1171
page 356

Choi, Jae
70 Clark St, Brooklyn, NY 11201
718 237.0216

Chorney, Steve
420 Lexington Ave, NYC, NY 10170
212 986.5680

Chow, Rita
280 Madison Ave, NYC, NY 10016
212 545.9155

Christensen, David
4338 Manchester Pl, Cypress, CA 90630
714 761.3488

Christensen, Wendy
256 Timbertop Rd, New Ipswich, NH 03071
603 878.4251

Christiana, David
731 N 24th St, Phila, PA 19130
215 232.6666

Christiansen, Lee
12 Kings Ln, Chaska, MN 55318
612 448.3912

Christmas, Lawrence
161-34 120th Ave, Jamaica, NY 11434
718 525.6864

Chu, Michael
5009 Woodman Ave, Sherman Oaks, CA 91423
818 788.3835

Chwast, Seymour
215 Park Ave S, NYC, NY 10003
212 674.8080

Ciardiello, Joseph
2182 Clove Rd, Staten Island, NY 10305
718 727.4757

Cieslawski, Steve
420 Lexington Ave, NYC, NY 10170
212 986.5680
fax 212 818.1246
page 195

Cigliano, Bill
501 Fifth Ave, NYC, NY 10017
212 490.2450
fax 212 697.6828
page 46

Claire, Geneviève
200 Aquetong Rd, New Hope, PA 18938
215 862.2091
fax 215 862.2641
page 232
Geneviève Claire's whimsical
watercolors have been used by Rapp
Collins Advertising for Procter &
Gamble, Silver Burdett & Ginn, Global
Finance Magazine, Simon & Schuster,
MacMillan/McGraw Hill Publishers,
Piper Design, Hanes, Kids-R-Us,
Nordstrom, Macy's, Levi's, The Gap and
various fabric design firms.

Clapp, John
4961 Monaco Dr, Pleasanton, CA 94566
510 462.6444

Clar, David Austin
311 Alexander St, Rochester, NY 14604
716 546.4240

Clare, Pam Represents
7535 Bradley Blvd, Wash, DC 20817
301 365.5422
fax 301 365.1653
pages 316-317, 402

Clark Studio
333 N Michigan, Chicago, IL 60601
312 263.3754

Clark, Bradley H
36 Haggerty Hill Rd, Rhinebeck, NY 12572
914 876.2615

Clark, Johnston
1210 Gregory Ave, Wilmette, IL 60091
708 251.2444

Clark, Tim
1256 25th St, Santa Monica, CA 90404
310 453.7613

Clarke, Bob
55 Brook Rd, Pittsford, NY 14534
716 248.8683

Clarke, Greg
844 Ninth St, Santa Monica, CA 90403
310 395.7958

Class Act Design Inc
600 E Higgins Rd, Elk Grove Vlg, IL 60007
708 640.0066

Clayton, Christian
543 N Sycamore Ave, L.A., CA 90036
213 936.8448

Clegg, Dave
3571 Aaron Sosebee Rd, Atlanta, GA 30130
404 255.1430

Cleland, Janet
One Mono Ln, San Anselmo, CA 94960
415 457.1049

Clement, Cameron /
National Graphic Explorer
3422 S Fresno, Ft Smith, AR 72903
501 646.7734
page 127
In AR, OK, KS, MO, TX, or Los Angeles
call Suzanne Craig Represents @ 918
749. 9424. Specializing in handcut
scratchboard illustrations with hi-res
digital output. Finished art provided in
either digital format (3.5" Floppy/44MB
Syquest/Modem) or transparencies
(35mm or 4x5).

Clement, Gary
52 Arlington Ave, Toronto,
ONT, Canada M6G 3K8
416 657.8975

Clement, Rick
2343 London Bridge Dr, Silver Spring, MD 20906
301 598.1689

Clementson, John
11 Kings Ridge Rd,
Long Valley, NJ 07853
908 813.8718
fax 908 813.0076
page 421

Cleveland, Thomas
10730 Glenora Dr, Houston, TX 77065
713 894.6546

Cline, Donna
PO Box 664, Sierra Madre, CA 91025
818 355.9481

Clizia
97 Croton Ave, Ossining, NY 10562
914 762.2009

Clownbank Studio
PO Box 7709, Santa Cruz, CA 95060
408 426.4247

Clubb, Rick Illustrations Inc
310 S Hale St, Wheaton, IL 60187
708 690.5554
fax 708 690.5553
page 382
Rick Clubb paints people. I look for
challenges to achieve a spirit of people
and realism in a painterly execution.
Clients include Tatham RSGG Euro, FCB,
Equinox Adv., Leo Burnett Co., Quaker
Oat Co., Scott Foresman.

Clyne, Dan
20 W Hubbard, Chicago, IL 60610
312 222.1361

Cobane, Russell
1863 S Pearl, Denver, CO 80210
303 733.0128

Cober, Alan E
95 Croton Dam Rd, Ossining, NY 10562
914 941.8696

Cober-Gentry, Leslie
285 Mayfield Dr, Trumbull, CT 06611
203 452.0188

CoConis, Ted
Box 758, Cedar Key, FL 32625
904 543.5720

Cocozza, Chris
Nine Woodbury Pl,
Woodbury, CT 06798
203 263.2061
page 414

Codarcea, Daniela
43 E 19th St, NYC, NY 10003
212 254.4996

Codner, Ellen
1966 W Roselawn, Falcon Heights, MN 55113
612 644.8474

Coe, Laura Design
4918 N Harbor Dr, San Diego, CA 92106
619 223.0909

Cogbill, Sharon
3138 N Seminary, Chicago, IL 60657
312 348.6541

Cohen, Adam
252 W 17th St, NYC, NY 10011
212 691.4074

Cohen, Cindy
PO Box 90, East Setauket, NY 11733
516 751.6531

Cohen, Elisa
1076 S Ogden Dr, L.A., CA 90019
213 933.2500

Cohen, Jim Illustration
107 Miller Rd,
Hawthorn Woods, IL 60047
708 726.8979
page 63

Cohen, M E
357 W 12th St, NYC, NY 10014
212 627.8033
fax 212 627.1167
page 224

Cohen, Santiago
705 Park Ave, Hoboken, NJ 07030
201 420.7275

Cohen, Shari
33522 Heritage Hills Dr,
Farmington Hills, MI 48331
810 661.5005

Cohen, Sharon
20200 Shipley Ter, Germantown, MD 20874
301 540.3466

Colallilo, Giovannina
19 East Dr, Toronto ONT, Canada M6N 2N8
416 604.0057

Colby, Garry
6375 Indian Wells Blvd, Boynton Beach, FL 33437
407 731.1759

Cold Springs Design
1494 Cold Springs Rd,
Pottstown, PA 19464
610 326.8038
fax 610 326.6173
page 370

Cole Studios
847 W Jackson Blvd, Chicago, IL 60607
312 455.0911

Cole, Aaron
108 E 35th St, NYC, NY 10016
212 889.3337

Cole, Dick
716 Montgomery St, S.F., CA 94111
415 433.1222
fax 415 433.9560
page 400

Cole, G William
11440 Oak Dr, Shelbyville, MI 49344
616 672.5756

Cole, Lo
280 Madison Ave, NYC, NY 10016
212 545.9155

Coleman, Gail Simon
54 W Gennessee St, Skaneateles, NY 13152
315 685.3123

Coleman, Woody Presents
490 Rockside Rd, Cleveland, OH 44131
216 661.4222

Colley, Michael
4170 S Arbor Cir, Marietta, GA 30066
404 924.4793

Collicott, Sharleen
201 Ocean Ave, Santa Monica, CA 90402
310 458.6616

Collier, Jan
PO Box 470818, S.F., CA 94147
415 383.9026
fax 415 383.9037
pages 26-30
Barbara Banthien, Gary Baseman, Rich
Borge, Gerald Bustamante, Greg Clarke,
Mitchell Confer, Alex Cro, Rae Ecklund,
Douglas Fraser, Lilly Lee (Lettering),
Michele Manning, Coco Masuda, Jennie
Oppenheimer, Robert Gantt Steele,
Cynthia Torp, Nicholas Wilton.

Collier, John
8329 San Leandro, Dallas, TX 75218
214 324.2879

Collier, Michele
1839 Ninth St, Alameda, CA 94501
510 769.1421

Collignon, Daniele
200 W 15th St, NYC, NY 10011
212 243.4209
pages 6-7, 273

Collins, Brigid
11 Kings Ridge Rd, Long Valley, NJ 07853
908 813.8718

Collins, Daryll
2969 Ensley Ct, Maineville, OH 45039
513 683.9335

Collins, Martha
30166 Chapala Ct, Laguna Niguel, CA 92677
714 495.3664

Collot, Philippe
5855 Green Valley Cir, Culver City, CA 90230
310 642.2721

Colon, Raul
43-C Heritage Dr, New City, NY 10956
914 639.1505

Colquhoun, John
172 Midland Ave, Bronxville, NY 10708
914 779.6965

Colvin, Rob
1351 N 1670 West, Farmington, UT 84025
801 451.6858

Combs, Jonathan
716 Montgomery St, S.F., CA 94111
415 433.1222
fax 415 433.9560
page 400

Commander, Bob
1565 Village Round Dr, Park City, UT 84060
801 649.4356

Comp Art Plus
49 W 45th St, NYC, NY 10036
212 921.1199

Comport, Alan
750 94th Ave N, St Petersburg, FL 33702
813 579.4499

Comport, Sally Wern
750 94th Ave N,
St Petersburg, FL 33702
813 579.4499
fax 813 579.4585
page 345

Comstock, Jacqueline
17 Oakland Ct, Warwick, NY 10990
914 987.8314

Conant, Pat
13 Heritage Ln, Westfield, MA 01085
413 568.3843

Condon, Ken
126 Ashfield Mtn Rd,
Ashfield, MA 01330
413 628.4042
fax 413 628.4043
page 407

Conge, Bob
8600 Giles Rd, Wayland, NY 14572
716 728.3424

Conlon, Jean
461 Broome St, NYC, NY 10013
212 966.9897

Connally, Connie
8827 Kingsley Rd, Dallas, TX 75231
800 408.3647

Connections Unlimited
PO Box 568, Carmel, NY 10512
914 828.7200

Connelly, Gwen Design
840 D Forest, Evanston, IL 60202
312 943.4477

Connelly, Jim
7421 Harmon Ln, Jenison, MI 49428
616 669.5043

Conner, Mona
One Montgomery Pl, Brooklyn, NY 11215
718 636.1527

Connor, Todd
223 Prospect, Seattle, WA 98109
206 282.8558

Connor, Tom
912 President St, Brooklyn, NY 11215
718 230.0391

Conrad, James & Associates
2149 Lyon Ave, S.F., CA 94115
415 921.7140
fax 415 921.3939
page 401

Conrad, Jon
221 W Maple St, Monrovia, CA 91016
818 301.9662

Conran, Kevin
4770 Kester Ave, Sherman Oaks, CA 91403
818 990.0611

Conroy, Lois Bertoli
3326 NE 60th St, Portland, OR 97213
503 288.2938

Consani, Chris
728 33rd St, Manhattan Beach, CA 90266
310 546.6622

Continuity Studios
62 W 45th St, NYC, NY 10036
212 869.4170

Continuity Studios
4710 W Magnolia Blvd, Burbank, CA 91505
818 980.8852

Cook, Richard
617 437.9459
fax 617 437.6494
page 310

Cook, Richard James
153 Thatcher St, Westwood, MA 02090
617 326.1226
page 396
A traditional, painterly approach to the
advertising market servicing a wide
range of clients.

Cook, Steve
731 N 24th St, Phila, PA 19130
215 232.6666

Cook, Timothy
3107 Ravensworth Pl,
Alexandria, VA 22302
703 820.2049
fax 703 820.3521
page 31

Cook, William
3804 E Northern Pky, Baltimore, MD 21206
410 426.1130

Cooley, Gary
2100 W Big Beaver Rd, Troy, MI 48084
810 643.6000

Cooley, Rick
Rt 1 Box 149, Check, VA 24072
703 651.4481

Coonts, Bob Design Group
233 Linden St, Ft Collins, CO 80524
303 493.3181

Copeland, Greg
510 Marquette Ave, Mpls, MN 55402
612 339.0947

Coppin, Steve
101 Yesler Way, Seattle, WA 98104
206 447.1600

Corio, Paul
263 First Ave, NYC, NY 10003
212 228.4630

Cormier, Wil
2251 Oakshade Rd, Bradbury, CA 91010
818 303.6066

Cornelius, Ray-Mel
1526 Elmwood, Dallas, TX 75224
214 946.9405
fax 214 946.5209
Brilliantly colored acrylic paintings
depicting bold, stylized, often fantasy-
oriented figures and elements.

Cornell & McCarthy
2-D Cross Hwy, Westport, CT 06880
203 454.4210

Cornell, Jeff
232 Madison Ave, NYC, NY 10016
212 889.8777

Cornell, Kathleen
737 Milwood Ave, Venice, CA 90291
310 301.8059

Cornerstone Design
49A North Main St, Concord, NH 03301
603 224.8323

Cornner, Haydn
c/o Bernstein & Andriulli
60 E 42nd St, NYC, NY 10165
212 682.1490

Corporate Art Planning
16 W 16th St, NYC, NY 10011
212 645.3490

Corporate Characters
4497 Streets Boro Rd, Richfield, OH 44286
216 659.4626

Corrigan, Paul
4015 E 53rd St, Tulsa, OK 74135
918 749.9424
fax 918 749.9424
page 76

Cosgrove, Dan
203 N Wabash Ave, Chicago, IL 60601
312 609.0050

Cossette, Ann
7850 Chessire Ln N, Maple Grove, MN 55311
612 420.4249

Costantino, FM
13-B Pauline St, Winthrop, MA 02152
617 846.4766

Costantino, Valerie
2037 New Hyde Park Rd,
New Hyde Park, NY 11040
516 358.9121

Cote, Barbara
40 Colonial Village Rd, Rochester, NY 14625
716 383.8338

Côté, Genevieve
Two Silver Ave, Toronto
ONT, Canada M6R 3A2
416 530.1500
fax 416 530.1401
page 21

Couch, Greg
51 Seventh Ave, Brooklyn, NY 11207
718 789.9276

Coughlin, Craig
1500 Bay Rd, Miami Beach, FL 33139
305 531.9122

Coulas, Mick
99 Coleman Ave, Toronto,
ONT, Canada M4C 1P8
416 698.3304
page 136

Coulson, David
1107 Goodman St, Pittsburgh, PA 15218
412 243.7064

Cournoyer, Jacques
200 Aquetong Rd, New Hope, PA 18938
215 862.2091
fax 215 862.2641
page 227
Jacques Cournoyer's conceptual
illustrations highlight articles in
Canadian & U.S. publications such as
Chatelaine, Outdoor Canada,
BusinessWeek, House Beautiful,
Outside Magazine, American Medical
News, The Progressive, America's
Agenda, Bloomberg, L'Actualite,
Strategies, book covers and childrens
books.

Cousineau, Normand
Two Silver Ave, Toronto
ONT, Canada M6R 3A2
416 530.1500
fax 416 530.1401
page 21

Covert, Susan
1134 Pittsford, Honeoye Falls, NY 14472
716 624.9682

Covington, Neverne
405 Central Ave, St Petersburg, FL 33710
813 822.1267

Cowdrey, Richard
Five W Main St, Westerville, OH 43081
614 898.5316

Cox, Bob
4701 Crystal Dr, Columbia, SC 29206
803 790.0208
page 274

Cox, Paul
121 Madison Ave, NYC, NY 10016
212 683.1362

Cox, Teresa
308 Princes St, St Paul, MN 55101
612 290.9158

Cozzolino, Paul
NYC, NY
212 969.8680
page 369

Craft, Diana
413 Creekside, Richardson, TX 75081
214 235.1700

Craft, Kinuko Y, c/o Fran Siegel
515 Madison Ave, Rm 2200, NYC, NY 10022
212 486.9644

Craig, Casey
PO Box 1841, Wimberley, TX 78767
512 847.7008

Craig, Daniel
118 E 26th St, Mpls, MN 55404
612 871.4539

Craig, John
Soldiers Grove, WI
608 872.2371

Craig, Suzanne Represents
4015 E 53rd St, Tulsa, OK 74135
918 749.9424
fax 918 749.9424
pages 76-77, 127

Crampton, Michael
2909 Cole Ave, Dallas, TX 75204
214 871.1316

Crane, Gary
1826 Asheville Pl, Charlotte, NC 28203
704 372.6007

Crawford, Denise Chapman
2716 Albans, Houston, TX 77005
713 663.7377

Crawford, Robert
123 Minortown Rd, Woodbury, CT 06798
203 266.0059

The Creative Advantage
620 Union St, Schenectady, NY 12305
518 370.0312

Creative Capers
60 E 42nd St, NYC, NY 10165
212 682.1490

Creative Force Studio
1235-B Colorado Ln, Arlington, TX 76015
817 467.1013

Creative Freelancers
25 W 45th St, NYC, NY 10036
212 398.9540

Creative Network
100 Wyndham Cir W,
New Brighton, MN 55112
612 631.6353
page 405

Creative Network
12422 Whittington, Houston, TX 77077
713 870.1102

The Creative Resource
12056 Summit Cir, Beverly Hills, CA 90210
310 276.5282

Criss, Keith W Illustration
155 Filbert St, Oakland, CA 94607
510 444.4569

Criswell, Ron
900 W Jackson Blvd, Chicago, IL 60607
312 944.5680
fax 312 421.5948
page 91

Crittenden, Guy
853 Broadway, NYC, NY 10003
212 677.9100

Crittenden, Susan
5914 Lakecrest Dr, Garland, TX 75043
214 226.2196

Crnkovich, Tony
900 W Jackson Blvd, Chicago, IL 60607
312 944.5680

Cro, Alex
PO Box 470818, S.F., CA 94147
415 383.9026
fax 415 383.9037
page 30
My oil paintings are conceived from
memory, live drawings or invented
images. I use paint like eye candy to
seduce the viewer, once I capture your
interest, we can communicate your
product, service, or idea.

Crofut, Bob
Eight New St, Ridgefield, CT 06877
203 431.4304

Croll, Carolyn
666 Greenwich St, NYC, NY 10014
212 675.5719

Cromwell, Janelle
1151 N Fuller Ave, West Hollywood, CA 90046
213 882.6011

Cronin, Brian
58 W 15th St, NYC, NY 10011
212 741.2539

Crowell, James/Michael Nakai
218 Madison Ave, NYC, NY 10016
212 213.5333
Storyboards, comps and animatics
professionally tailored to enhance your
concepts. Please call for portfolio.

Crowson, Lyndon
14318 Towerglen, Houston, TX 77084
713 855.7363

Cruz & Slowik Associates
190 Elm Ave, Hackensack, NJ 07601
201 489.3528
Typographic design and consulting.
Design and production of logos,
brochures and newsletters. Pre-press
and trapping experts.

Cruz, Arthur
871 Hawaii Ave, San Diego, CA 92154
619 575.8279

Cruz, Jose
6321 Bramble Dr, Fort Worth, TX 76133
817 292.2418

Csicsko, David Lee
1727 S Indiana Ave, Chicago, IL 60616
312 663.5300

Cueto, Ruben
PO Box 488, Whittier, CA 90608
310 945.8546

Cuevas, Goerge
4640 NW Seventh St, Miami, FL 33126
305 447.3849

Cumming, Moira Illustration
9754 Parkford Dr, Dallas, TX 75238
214 343.8655

Cummings, Barbara
19261 Red Bluff Dr, Trabuco Canyon, CA 92679
714 858.4912

Cummings, Terrance
210 W 64th St, NYC, NY 10023
212 586.4193

Cuneo, John
1836 Blake St, Denver, CO 80202
303 296.7449

Cunis, Peter
14281 E Kentucky Pl, Aurora, CO 80012
303 751.4865

Cunningham, Dennis
2405 NW Thurman St,
Portland, OR 97210
503 225.9687
fax 503 228.6030
page 141
Blockprint style: linocut & vinylcut.
Book illustration: Empty Creel with
David Godine, Cuisine of the Rain with
Karen Brooks. Advertising: Hewlett-
Packard, Hastings, Humble, Giardini.
Featured in Artists Market. NEA/
WESTAF fellowship winner.

Cunningham, Robert M
45 Cornwall Rd, Warren, CT 06754
203 868.2702

Curl, Steve Illustration
460 Everett Ave, Palo Alto, CA 94301
415 328.3499

Curran, Don
215 Parkland, St Louis, MO 63122
314 965.8672

Curry, Tom
901 W Sul Ross, Alpine, TX 79830
915 837.2311

Curtis, Todd Design
2032 14th St, Santa Monica, CA 90405
310 452.0738

Cusack, Margaret
124 Hoyt St, Brooklyn, NY 11217
718 237.0145

Cusano, Steven R
80 Talbot Ct, Media, PA 19063
610 565.8829

Custodio, Bernard
20103 Baltar St, Canoga Park, CA 91306
818 998.4242

Cutler, Dave
Seven Sunrise Rdg, Florida, NY 10921
914 651.1580

Cutter, David P
c/o Folio
888 Seventh Ave, NYC, NY 10106
212 333.5515

Cyr, Lisa L
PO Box 5754, Manchester, NH 03108
603 626.0043

Czechowski, Alicia
106 Emery St, Portland, ME 04102
207 874.2206

Czeczot, Andrzej
211 E 89th St, NYC, NY 10128
212 289.5514

D'Andrea, Bernard
217 E 86th St, NYC, NY 10028
212 427.5632

D'Antuono, Mike
158 W 29th St, NYC, NY 10001
212 268.9400

Dacey, Bob
7213 Woodchuck Hill Rd, Fayetteville, NY 13202
315 637.4614

Dadds, Jerry
2221 Morton St, Baltimore, MD 21218
410 243.0211
fax 410 243.0215
page 269

Dagne, Gerd
18 Prospect Pl, Hillsdale, NJ 07642
201 666.9479

Dahlquist, Roland
1149 E Village Circle Dr, Phoenix, AZ 85022
602 993.9895

Daigle, Stéphan
501 Fifth Ave, NYC, NY 10017
212 490.2450
fax 212 697.6828
page 57

Dailey, Eileen
4929 Lisette Ave, St Louis, MO 63109
314 832.1335

Daily, Don
57 Academy Rd, Bala Cynwyd, PA 19004
610 664.5729

Daily, Renee Quintal
57 Academy Rd, Bala Cynwyd, PA 19004
610 664.5729

Dale, Robert
41 Union Sq, NYC, NY 10003
212 206.0066

Daley, Joann
420 Lexington Ave, NYC, NY 10170
212 986.5680

Daley, Katie Represents
245 W 29th St, NYC, NY 10001
212 465.2420

Daley, Tom
1320 Paseo San Luis, Sierra Vista, AZ 85635
520 458.0112

Daly, Tom
47 E Edsel Ave, Palisades Park, NJ 07650
201 943.1837

Dammer, Mike
350 W Ontario, Chicago, IL 60610
312 943.4995
page 121

Dammer, Mike
520 N Michigan Ave, Chicago, IL 60611
312 527.0351
fax 312 527.5468
page 121

Damore, Georgan
200 E Delaware, Chicago, IL 60611
312 266.9451
Georgan specializes in stylized high
fashion, beauty, cosmetic, illustration.
Various techniques including airbrush.
Clients include Pierre Cardin, Clairion,
Helene Curtis, BBDO, New York Times.

Daniels & Daniels
14 S Madrid Ct, Newbury Park, CA 91320
805 498.1923

Dannenberg, Thomas
154 Crestwood Rd, Thornhill,
ONT, Canada L4J 1A6
416 731.8038

Danz, David
4680 Demyhig Ln, Placerville, CA 95667
916 622.3218
fax 916 622.4346
page 415

Danz, Sandy
4680 Demyhig Ln, Placerville, CA 95667
916 622.3218
fax 916 622.4346
page 415

Darden, Howard
56 Roosevelt Ave, Butler, NJ 07405
201 492.1273

Darnell, Jim
c/o The Art Source
PO Box 2193, Grapevine, TX 76099
817 481.2212
fax 817 481.2908
pages 74-75
Each of 4 illustrators brings his own
style & experience to your needs.
Further, by combining talents, they can
create almost anything imagined. Digital
pioneers; conventional masters.

Darrow, David
12290 Dormouse Rd, San Diego, CA 92129
800 594.9132

Das Grüp
311 Ave H, Redondo Beach, CA 90277
310 540.5958

Daugavietis, Ruta
5301 N Lakewood, Chicago, IL 60640
312 227.6225

Davanti Media/Denny Lee Thrush
920 W Market St, Lima, OH 45805-2739
419 227.4988
fax 419 224.3921
Agriculture, Consumer, and Industrial
Illustrations. Clients: Cadillac, Girl
Scouts, Huffy Bicycles, John Deere & Co.,
White/New Idea, Time Warner, Vroman
Foods.

David Art Sales
108 E 35th St, NYC, NY 10016
212 889.3337

David, Roy
764 S Front St, Phila, PA 19147
215 468.4296

Davidson, Dennis
43 E 19th St, NYC, NY 10003
212 254.4996

Davis, Allen
43 E 19th St, NYC, NY 10003
212 254.4996

Davis, Dennas
904 Sutton Hill Rd, Nashville, TN 37204
615 386.0444
fax 615 386.0430
page 164

Davis, Jack
108 E 35th St, NYC, NY 10016
212 889.3337

Davis, Jack E
121 Madison Ave, NYC, NY 10016
212 683.1362

Davis, Lambert
4378 Clayford St, San Diego, CA 92117
800 344.8034

Davis, Nancy
58 W 15th St, NYC, NY 10011
212 741.2539

Davis, Nelle
20 E 17th St, NYC, NY 10003
212 807.7737

Davis, Paul Studio
14 E Fourth St, NYC, NY 10012
212 420.8789
fax 212 995.9176
Complete Illustration and design services
for editorial, advertising and corporate
clients. Clients include Time Magazine,
Esquire, Kiplinger's, NY Times, UN,
Amicus Journal, Hewlett-Packard,
Fukuoka City Bank, Honda (Japan),
Benedictine, Harper-Collins, UNITE
(Merged unions).

Davis, Susan
1107 Notley Rd, Silver Spring, MD 20904
301 384.9426

Dawson, Henk
3519 170th Pl NE, Bellevue, WA 98008
206 882.3303

Dawson, John D
c/o Fran Siegel
515 Madison Ave, Rm 2200, NYC, NY 10022
212 486.9644

Day, Brant
575 Station View Run, Lawrenceville, GA 30243
404 963.0731

Day, Burnis C
PO Box 205, Detroit, MI 48231
313 273.2329

Day, Danny
1325-I Caminito Gabaldon, San Diego, CA 92108
619 298.4102

Day, Rob
6059 Ralston Ave, Indpls, IN 46220
317 253.9000

Day, Sam
119 S Main St, Seattle, WA 98104
206 382.7413

Dayal, Antar
968 Estrella Dr, Santa Barbara, CA 93110
805 965.5988

De Amicis, John
35 S Durst Dr, Milltown, NJ 08850
908 249.4937

de la Houssaye, Jeanne
400 N Peters, New Orleans, LA 70130
504 581.2167

De La Hoz, D'Ann
One SE Third Ave, Miami, FL 33131
305 371.9417

De Leon, Cam
4330 Tujunga, Studio City, CA 91604
818 797.8890

de Michiell, Robert
250 W 85th St, NYC, NY 10024
212 769.9192

de Moreta, Linda Represents
1839 Ninth St, Alameda, CA 94501
510 769.1421
fax 510 521.1674
page 185

De Palma, Mary Newell
45 Bradfield Ave, Boston, MA 02131
617 327.6241

de Seve, Peter
25 Park Pl, Brooklyn, NY 11217
718 398.8099

De Vito, Grace
140 Hoyt St, Stamford, CT 06905
203 967.2198

Dean, Bruce
23211 Leonora Dr, Woodland Hills, CA 91367
818 716.5632

Dean, Glenn
501 Fifth Ave, NYC, NY 10017
212 490.2450

Dean, Mike
Ten E Ontario, Chicago, IL 60611
312 573.1370

DeAnda, Ruben
890 Entrada Pl, Chula Vista, CA 91910
619 421.2845

DeanHouston Computer Illustration
2228 Gilbert Ave, Cincinnati, OH 45206
513 221.6622

Dearstyne, John
Ten La Purisima, Santa Margarita, CA 92688
714 589.6447

Dearth, Greg
68 E Franklin St, Dayton, OH 45459
513 433.8383

Dearwater, Andy
5650 Kirby, Houston, TX 77005
713 660.8513

Deas, Michael
708 Toulouse St, New Orleans, LA 70130
504 524.3957

Deaver, Georgia
1045 Sansome St, S.F., CA 94111
415 362.8960

Dedell, Jacqueline Inc
58 W 15th St, NYC, NY 10011
212 741.2539

Deen, Georganne
3834 Aloha St, L.A., CA 90027
213 665.2700

Deeter, Catherine
c/o Fran Siegel
515 Madison Ave, Rm 2200, NYC, NY 10022
212 486.9644

deGrandpre, Patty
233 Hale St, Beverly, MA 01915
508 921.0410

deGroat, Diane
One Bristol Pl, Chappaqua, NY 10514
914 238.4115

Dekle, Merritt
4318 Lafayette St, Marianna, FL 32446
305 576.0142

Del Nero, Jeff
6702 N 11th Ave, Phoenix, AZ 85013
602 336.8997

DeLapine, Jim
398 31st St, Lindenhurst, NY 11757
516 225.1247

Delessert, Etienne
Box 1689, Lakeville, CT 06039
203 435.0061

Delhomme, Jean-Phillipe
c/o Barbara Schlager, Inc
225 Lafayette St, NYC, NY 10012
212 941.1777

Dellorco, Chris
8278 Kirkwood Dr, L.A., CA 90046
213 650.1370

Delmonte, Steve
328 W Delavan Ave, Buffalo, NY 14213
716 883.6086

Deloy, Dee
8166 Jellison St, Orlando, FL 35825
407 273.8365

DeLuz, Tony
c/o Leighton & Co
Four Prospect St, Beverly, MA 01915
508 921.0887
fax 508 921.0223
page 219

DeMarco, Kim
Six E 12th St, NYC, NY 10003
212 675.2023

DeMarco, Susanne
Pine Rd, Neversink, NY 12765
914 985.2936

Demers, Don
61 Tilton Ave, Kittery, ME 03904
207 439.1463

Demorat, Charles
305 Cornelia Dr, Graham, NC 27253
910 229.7359

Dempsey, Paul
1863 S Pearl St, Denver, CO 80210
303 733.0128 / 800 417.5120
fax 303 733.8154
page 323

DeMuth, Roger
4103 Chenago St, Cazenovia, NY 13035
315 655.8599

Deneergaard, Margaret
1335 Fairridge Cir, Atlanta, GA 30060
404 499.8009

DeSantis, Laura
c/o Leighton & Co
Four Prospect St, Beverly, MA 01915
508 921.0887
fax 508 921.0223
page 213

Deschamps, Bob
108 E 35th St, NYC, NY 10016
212 889.3337

Desrocher, Jack
Rte Seven Box 611, Eureka Spgs, AR 72632
501 253.7980

Detwiler, Darius
5018 Fawn Lake, San Antonio, TX 78244
210 662.0603

Devaud, Jacques
1863 S Pearl St, Denver, CO 80210
303 733.0128 / 800 417.5120
fax 303 733.8154
page 327

Dever, Eric
200 Aquetong Rd, New Hope, PA 18938
215 862.2091
fax 215 862.2641
page 231
Eric Dever's portraits on rusty metal and
illustrations on plaster have been
commissioned by the New Yorker,
Harvard Business Review, New York
Magazine, Rodale Press, & Mitsubishi.
His work has been exhibited in galleries
in the U.S. & Europe.

DeVito, Grace
140 Hoyt St, Stanford, CT 06905
203 967.2198

Devlin, Bill
108 E 35th St, NYC, NY 10016
212 889.3337

Dewar, Ken
Two Silver Ave, Toronto
ONT, Canada M6R 3A2
416 530.1500
fax 416 530.1401
page 19

Dey, Lorraine
45 Johnson Ln N, Jackson, NJ 08527
908 928.5510

Di Blasio, Nicholas
207 Commonwealth Ave, Boston, MA 02116
617 266.2650

Di Fate, Vincent
12 Ritter Dr, Wappingers Falls, NY 12590
914 297.6842

Di Marco, Anthony
2948 1/2 Grand Rt St John,
New Orleans, LA 70119
504 948.3128

Diaz, David
6708 Corintia St,
Rancho La Costa, CA 92009
619 438.0070
fax 619 438.0315
page 169

DiCesare, Joe
27 Sterling Pl, Brooklyn, NY 11217
718 398.6686

Dickens, Holly
50 E Bellevue, Chicago, IL 60611
312 280.0777

Dickey, Burrell
4975 Elmwood Dr, San Jose, CA 95130
408 866.0820

Dicks, Jan Thompson
1472 Georgia PL, Gulfportque, MS 39507
601 896.7691

DiComo, Charles
49 W 45th St, NYC, NY 10036
212 921.1199

Didier, Paul
5855 Green Valley Cir, Culver City, CA 90230
310 642.2721

Diebel, John
4503 Pillsbury Ave S, Mpls, MN 55409
612 824.7337

Dierksen, Jane
5384 Shemiran St, La Verne, CA 91750
818 359.7745

Dieterichs, Shelley
Five Plant Ave, St Louis, MO 63119
314 968.4515

Dietz, Jim
165 E 32nd St, NYC, NY 10016
212 686.3514

Dietz, Mike
23962 Dovekie Cir, Laguna Niguel, CA 92677
714 448.0652

Diffenderfer, Ed
32 Cabernet Ct, Lafayette, CA 94549
510 284.8235

Digital Art
3166 E Palmdale Blvd, Palmdale, CA 93550
805 265.8092

Dill, Wally
34019 Oakland, Farmington, MI 48335
313 476.5581

Dillard, Elaine
PO Box 1171, Atlanta, GA 30655
404 255.1430

Dillard, Elaine
PO Box 1171, Atlanta, GA 30655
404 267.8786

Dillon, Kathleen
3710 Murworth Dr, Houston, TX 77025
713 661.5205

Dillon, Tom
599 Rio Grande Cir, Thousand Oaks, CA 91360
805 493.0397

Dimension Creative Artworks
9801 DuPont Ave S, Bloomington, MN 55431
612 884.4045

Dimock Illustration
308 Prince St, St Paul, MN 55101
612 291.7718

Dininno, Steve
553 E Fulton St, Long Beach, NY 11561
516 431.1495

Dinser, John
9308 Merrill Rd, Whitmore Lake, MI 48189
313 449.2336

Dinyer, Eric
5510 Holmes, Kansas City, MO 64110
816 363.4795

Dionisi, Sandra
37 Hanna Ave, Toronto, ONT, Canada, M6K 1W9
416 588.4588

Dismukes, John Taylor
5371 Wilshire Blvd, L.A., CA 90036
213 986.5680

Distinctive CalligraphicStudio
30400 Wolf Rd, Bay Village, OH 44140
216 871.6590

Dixon, Don
2519 Cedar Ave, Long Beach, CA 90806
310 595.8487

Do, Thien Design
1839 Ninth St, Alameda, CA 94501
510 769.1421

Dobrowolski, Chris
153 Pine Grove St, Needham, MA 02194
617 444.7545

Dodeles, Elise
34 Clay St, N Brunswick, NJ 08902
908 821.5299

Dodge, Larry
2100 W Big Beaver Rd, Troy, MI 48084
810 643.6000

Dodge, Sharon & Associates
3033 13th Ave W, Seattle, WA 98119
206 284.4701

Doheny, Dennis
654 Pier Ave, Santa Monica, CA 90405
310 392.4877

Doktor, Patricia
4118 Beck Ave, Studio City, CA 91604
818 769.7321
page 309

Dolby, Karen
307 N Michigan Ave, Chicago, IL 60601
312 855.9336

Dolobowsky, Mena
177 Newtown Tpke, Weston, CT 06883
203 222.1608

Dombrowski, Bob
89 Fifth Ave, NYC, NY 10003
212 627.1554

Domingo, Ray
108 E 35th St, NYC, NY 10016
212 889.3337

Donatelli, Steven
19723 Redwood Rd, Castro Valley, CA 94546
310 281.4724

Donato
381 Park Ave S, NYC, NY 10016
212 889.2400

Donelan, Eric
31 Kensington Cir, Wheaton, IL 60187
708 260.1712

Doney, Todd
26 Elm St, Morristown, NJ 07960
201 292.7572

Doniger, Nancy
109 Eighth Ave, Brooklyn, NY 11215
718 399.8666

Donin, Judi
645 Westmount Dr, L.A., CA 90069
310 659.4344
fax 310 652.9604
Spirited textural brush lettering for
logos, films, headlines, accents. Clients
include Pepsi-Cola Co., Gillette, Columbia
Pictures, Walt Disney Pictures, American
Film Foundation, CBS Records, Patagonia.

Donner, Carol
501 Fifth Ave, NYC, NY 10017
212 490.2450

Donovan's DreamMerchant
437 Engel Ave, Henderson, NV 89015
702 564.3598

Doody, Jim
1010 S Robertson Blvd, L.A., CA 90035
310 652.7322

Doong, Arnold T
15 San Rafael Ave, San Anselmo, CA 94960
415 721.7795

Dorety, Joe
731 N 24th St, Phila, PA 19130
215 232.6666

Dorsey, Bob
Pine Rd, Neversink, NY 12765
914 985.2936

Doty, Eldon
101 Yesler Way, Seattle, WA 98104
206 447.1600

Doucet, Bob
PO Box 961, Cambridge, MA 02140
617 497.7551

Douglas, Tony
49 W 45th St, NYC, NY 10036
212 921.1199

Dovrat
58 W 15th St, NYC, NY 10011
212 741.2539

Dowd, Jason
9322 Olive St Rd, St Louis, MO 63132
314 997.2655

Dowell, Julian
329 Canterbury Rd, Westfield, NJ 07090
908 233.1951

Dowlen, James
PO Box 15152, Santa Rosa, CA 95402
707 579.1535

Downing, Ray
130 W 42nd St, NYC, NY 10036
212 921.8922

Downs, Richard
716 Sanchez St, S.F., CA 94114
415 285.8267

Dragaset, Erik
2658 Santa Ana Ave, Costa Mesa, CA 92627
714 722.9707

Drayton, Richard
PO Box 20053, Sedona, AZ 86341
520 284.9125

Drebelbis, Marsha
8150 Brookriver Dr, Dallas, TX 75247
214 951.0266

Drescher, Henrik
2434 California St, Berkeley, CA 94703
510 883.9616

Dressel, Peggy
11 Rockaway Ave, Oakland, NJ 07436
201 337.2143

Drew, Kim
1617 Taylor Ave N, Seattle, WA 98109
206 281.9298

Drisi Studio
100 W Main St, Glenwood, IL 60425
708 758.5143

Drobek, Carol
1260 Broadway, S.F, CA 94109
415 776.6188

Drucker, Mort
42 Juneau Blvd, Woodbury, NY 11797
516 367.4920

Drummey, Jack
Eight Ninth St, Medford, MA 02155
617 395.2778

Dryden, Jim
1503 Briarknoll Dr, Arden Hills, MN 55112
612 631.8480

Dryden, Patti
5855 Green Valley Cir, Culver City, CA 90230
310 642.2721

Dryden, Rod
5855 Green Valley Cir, Culver City, CA 90230
310 642.2721

D'Souza, Helen
487 Mortimer Ave, Toronto,
ONT, Canada M4J 2G6
416 466.0630

Duarte, Pamela
1758 N Fairfax Ave, L.A., CA 90046
213 874.9509

DuBois, Gérard
211 E 89th St, NYC, NY 10128
212 289.5514
fax 212 987.2855
page 295

DuBois, Tom
13856 Shady Ln, Lockport, IL 60441
708 301.2130

Dubois-Dennis, Françoise
305 Newbury Ln, Newbury Park, CA 91320
805 376.9738

Dubrowski, Ken
845 Moraine St, Marshfield, MA 02050
617 837.3457

Duckworth, Tom
10109 Rain Drop Cir, Granger, IN 46530
219 674.6226

Dudash, C Michael
RR One Box 2803, Moretown, VT 05660
802 496.6400

Dudzinski, Andrzej
54 E 81st St, NYC, NY 10028
212 772.3098

Duffy, Dan
89 Fifth Ave, NYC, NY 10003
212 627.1554

Dugan, Brian
Six Candlewood Rd, Washington, NJ 08888
908 276.0651

Duggan, Lee
3780 Schooner Rdg, Alpharetta, GA 30202
404 664.1609

Duillo, Elaine I
146 Dartmouth Dr, Hicksville, NY 11801
516 681.8820

Duke, Bette
116 W 29th St, NYC, NY 10001
212 967.1393

Duke, Lawrence W
PO Box 421443, S.F., CA 94142
415 647.5660

Duke, William
90 Hilkview Ave, Los Altos, CA 94022
415 949.1344

Dumville, Fritz
22 Edison Ave, Providence, RI 02906
401 861.7629

Dundee, Angela
250 W 57th St, NYC, NY 10107
212 397.7330
fax 212 397.7334
page 254

Dunnahoe, Hugh
2720 S Harbor Blvd, Santa Ana, CA 92704
714 751.4846

Dunnick, Regan
250 W 57th St, NYC, NY 10107
212 397.7330

Dunphy-Becker, Ann
9131 Westview, Houston, TX 77055
713 465.3037

DuPays, Nicky
353 W 53rd St, NYC, NY 10019
212 582.0023 / 212 682.2462
fax 212 582.0090
page 183

DuPont, Lane
597 Riverside Ave, Westport, CT 06880
203 226.4724
fax 203 454.9904
page 435

Durand, Janice Lee
12144 Shadow Ridge Way, Northridge, CA 91326
818 366.7654

Durden, Kirk
50 W 72nd St, NYC, NY 10023
212 877.2390

Duren, Kris
2411 S Raymond, Seattle, WA 98108
206 722.6328

Dusk to Dawn Studio
PO Box 1252, NYC, NY 10011
718 375.2413

Dutko, Deborah
245 Roselle St, Fairfield, CT 06432
203 579.1751

Dverin, Anatoly
c/o Bernstein & Andriulli
60 E 42nd St, NYC, NY 10165
212 682.1490

Dwyer, Yukari
861 N Fourth Ave, Covina, CA 91723
818 331.1797

Dye, Gregory
7952 W Quarto Dr, Littleton, CO 80123
303 933.0340
fax 303 933.0340
page 162
Gregory works in two styles. The first a
painting style that is very conceptual
and somewhat abstract. The second a
contemporary woodcut look. Clients
include IBM, Phillip Morris, McGraw-Hill
Publishing, Coors and American
Express.

Dyen, Don
49 W 45th St, NYC, NY 10036
212 921.1199

Dyer Mutchnick Group Inc
8360 Melrose Ave, L.A., CA 90069
213 655.1800

Dyess, John
703 Josephine Ave, Glendale, MO 63122
314 822.2893

Dykeman, James
738 Peekskill Hollow Rd,
Putnam Valley, NY 10579
914 528.6545

Dykes, John S
17 Morningside Dr S,
Westport, CT 06880
203 222.8150
fax 203 222.8155
page 191

The Dynamic Duo
95 Kings Hwy S, Westport, CT 06880
203 454.4518

Dypold, Pat
429 W Superior, Chicago, IL 60610
312 337.6919

Dzedzy, John
976 Old Huntington Pike,
Huntingdon Vly, PA 19006
215 663.0587

Dzielak, Dennis
350 W Ontario, Chicago, IL 60610
312 642.1241

Eade Creative Svcs
9701 Breckenridge Pl, Gaithersburg, MD 20879
301 963.7335

Eagle, Bruce
14713 Brasswood Blvd, Edmond, OK 73013
405 755.6228

Eagle, Cameron
1911 NW 29th St, Oklahoma City, OK 73106
405 525.6676

Eames, Tim
1104 Canyon Trl, Topanga, CA 90290
310 455.3266

Eastman, Jody
1116 W Philadelphia St, Ontario, CA 91762
909 983.2515

Eastwood, Matthew
28 Shelton St, Covent Gdn, London,
England WC2H 9HP
011 44 171 240 2077
fax 011 44 171 836 0199
page 359

Ebel, Alex
Ten E Ontario, Chicago, IL 60611
312 573.1370

Ebeling, Suzanne
PO Box 2294, Westport, CT 06880
203 454.4346

Eberbach, Andrea
68 E Franklin St, Dayton, OH 45459
513 433.8383

Ebersol, Rob
734 Clairemont Ave, Decatur, GA 30030
404 687.8889

Echevarria, Abe
119 W 23rd St, NYC, NY 10011
212 633.9880

Eckart, Chuck
Ten E Ontario St, Chicago, IL 60611
312 573.1370

Ecklund, Rae
Three Roxanne St, S.F., CA 94549
510 283.6648

Eclectic Styles
PO Box 31, Upper Falls, MD 21156
410 679.3517
"Easily among the best pen and ink
studios around". Catch clients with your
ideas illustrated by us. Clients include
Microsoft, Ingram Micro, and over 150
commissions.

Edgerton, Tom
911 Elizabethan Dr, Greensboro, NC 27410
910 854.2816

Edinjinklian, Teddy
5652 Elmer Ave, N Hollywood, CA 91601
310 390.9595

Edison, Susan Illustration
12700 Hillcrest Rd, Dallas, TX 75230
214 233.8222

Edsey, Steven & Sons
520 N Michigan Ave, Chicago, IL 60611
312 527.0351
fax 312 527.5468
pages 118-123

Edwards, Andrew
353 W 53rd St, NYC, NY 10019
212 582.0023 / 212 682.2462
fax 212 582.0090
page 182

Edwards, Karl
11126 Manhattan Mine Ln,
Nevada City, CA 95959
916 265.5666
fax 916 265.8118
pages 188-189

Edwards, Kate
11126 Manhattan Mine Ln,
Nevada City, CA 95959
916 265.4502
fax 916 265.8118
page 187

Edwards, Kathleen
PO Box 1003, Woodacre, CA 94973
415 488.4546

Edwards, Mona Shafer
3143 Nichols Canyon Rd, L.A., CA 90046
213 876.6662

Edwards, Ron
73-4685 Kohana Iki, Kailua, Kona, HI 96740
818 325.6744

Effler, Jim
353 W 53rd St, NYC, NY 10019
212 682.2462

Egan, Shawn
201 Country Creek, Ballwin, MO 63011
314 227.7770

Ehlert, Lois
866 UN Plz, NYC, NY 10017
212 644.2020

Ehrenfeld, Jane
301 St George St, Farmville, VA 23901
804 392.6190

Eidrigevicius, Stasys
211 E 89th St, NYC, NY 10128
212 289.5514

Eiko, Joni
1317 12th St, Santa Monica, CA 90401
310 395.1761

Einsel, Naiad & Walter
26 S Morningside Dr, Westport, CT 06880
203 226.0709

Eisner-Hess, Viv
63 Littlefield Rd, East Greenwich, RI 02818
401 884.3424

Eldridge, Gary
501 Fifth Ave, NYC, NY 10017
212 490.2450
fax 212 697.6828
page 53

Electric Art Studio
39 Prospect Ave, Pompton Plains, NJ 07444
201 835.3534

Ella Inc
PO Box 201, N Marshfield, MA 02059
617 266.3858

Elliott, JoAnn
Ten Highland Pl, Richardson, TX 75081
214 231.5332

Elliott/Oreman Artists' Rep
25 Drury Ln, Rochester, NY 14625
716 586.6041

Ellis, Jon
1622 Brownsville Rd, Langhorne, PA 19047
215 750.6180

Ellis, Steve
1915 Voorhees Ave,
Redondo Beach, CA 90278
310 792.1888
fax 310 792.1890
page 103

Ellison, Jake
2233 Kemper Ln, Cincinnati, OH 45206
513 861.1400

Ellison, Pauline
c/o Bernstein & Andriulli
60 E 42nd St, NYC, NY 10165
212 682.1490

Ellithorpe, Chris
490 Dover Dr, Roselle, IL 60172
708 924.7938
fax 708 924.7950
page 343

Elmer, Richard
504 E 11th St, NYC, NY 10009
212 598.4024
page 143

Elmore, Larry
490 Rockside Rd, Cleveland, OH 44131
216 661.4222

Eloqui
100 G St, Mt Lake Park, MD 21550
301 334.4086
fax 301 334.4186
pages 278-279

Elsner Illustration
PO Box 5365, Takoma Park, MD 20913
301 585.4347

Elwell, Tristan
188 E 80th St, NYC, NY 10021
212 734.3353

Ely, Creston
279 Black Rock Tpke, Redding Ridge, CT 06876
203 938.8000

Ember, Kathi
666 Greenwich St, NYC, NY 10014
212 675.5719

Emberley, Michael
46 Waltham St, Boston, MA 02118
617 426.1835

Embler, Jennifer Represents
7520 NW Fifth St, Plantation, FL 33317
305 792.4592

Emerson, Carmela
25 W 45th St, NYC, NY 10036
212 398.9540

Endewelt, Jack
50 Riverside Dr, NYC, NY 10024
212 877.0575

England, David
129 Thomas St, Bel Air, MD 21014
410 838.5030

English, M John
4601 Rock Hill Rd, Kansas City, MO 64110
816 931.5648

English, Mark
512 Lakeside Ct, Liberty, MO 64068
816 781.0056

English, Sarah Jane
23 Hapworth Dr, Toronto,
ONT, Canada M9R 3W1
416 247.7336

Enik, Ted
24 Charles St, NYC, NY 10014
212 924.1076

Enos, Randall
11 Court of Oaks, Westport, CT 06880
203 227.7684

Epkes, Greg
3626 Walnut St, Kansas City, MO 64111
816 931.5806

Epstein.Eagle, Barbara
Six Monterey Ter, Orinda, CA 94563
510 253.9451

Epton, Amy Paluch
Chicago, IL 60605
312 663.5595

Erdmann, Dan
3301A S Jefferson Ave, St Louis, MO 63118
314 773.2600

Erickson, Kerne
PO Box 2175, Mission Viejo, CA 92692
714 364.1141

Erika Groeschel Inc
15 E 32nd St, NYC, NY 10016
212 685.3291

Eriksson, Christer
111 E 42nd St, Miami, FL 33137
305 576.0142 / 800 484.8592 code 2787
fax 305 576.0138
page 306

Erlacher, Bill
211 E 51st St, NYC, NY 10022
212 755.1365

Ernster, Scott
12832 Bloomfield St, Studio City, CA 91604
818 753.1504

Escher Illustrations
6630 Lyndale Ave S, Richfield, MN 55423
612 866.8732

Escobedo, Pete
4322 Olcott Ave, East Chicago, IN 46312
219 795.6869 / 219 397.6978

Ettlinger, Doris
Ten Imlaydale Rd, Hampton, NJ 08827
908 537.6322

Eucalyptus Tree Studio
2221 Morton St, Baltimore, MD 21218
410 243.0211
fax 410 243.0215
page 269

Eureka Cartography
654 Pier Ave, Santa Monica, CA 90405
310 392.4877

Evans, Bill
101 Yesler Way, Seattle, WA 98104
206 447.1600

Evans, Jan
23042 Park Sorrento, Calabasas, CA 91302
818 222.5040

Evans, Leslie
17 Bay St, Watertown, MA 02172
617 924.3058

Evans, Melvyn
28 Shelton St, Covent Gdn, London,
England WC2H 9HP
01144 171 240 2077
fax 01144 171 836 0199
page 361

Evans, Robert
716 Montgomery St, S.F., CA 94111
415 433.1222
fax 415 433.9560
page 400

Evans, Shane
4152 McGee St, Kansas City, MO 64111
816 756.1534

Evans, Sharron
Two Harold Ave, S.F., CA 94112
415 239.7024

Everitt, Betsy
582 Santa Rosa, Berkley, CA 94707
510 527.3239

Ewers, Joseph
220 Mill St, Holliston, MA 01746
508 429.6375
A children's illustrator, Joe specializes in
licensed characters. He also has
trade/text credits. Clients include:
Random House, Golden Books, Disney,
CTW, Jim Henson Productions,
McDonald's, Parker Brothers, Little-
Brown, Houghton-Mifflin, Macmillan,
Silver-Burdett, Grolier.

Ewing, Richard
1442 Freeman Ave, Long Beach, CA 90804
310 498.2273

Ezell, Heather
PO Box 710045, Dallas, TX 75371
214 428.7046

Fabbri, Miriam
1334 Burnett St, Berkeley, CA 94702
510 849.1364

Fabricatore, Carol
1123 Broadway, NYC, NY 10010
212 463.8950

Fairman, Dolores
58 W 15th St, NYC, NY 10011
212 741.2539

Falcon Adv Art
1138 W Ninth St, Cleveland, OH 44113
216 621.4327

Falkenstern, Lisa
904 Ravine Rd, Califon, NJ 07830
908 832.5789

Falls, Mark
111 NE 42nd St, Miami, FL 33137
305 576.0142

Famous Frames
5855 Green Valley Cir, Culver City, CA 90230
310 642.2721

Fanning, Jim
67 Upper Mountain Ave, Montclair, NJ 07042
201 744.4465

Faranak
11 Kings Ridge Rd, Long Valley, NJ 07853
908 813.8718

Farber, Joan
1888 Century Park E, L.A., CA 90067
310 826.1332

FarFalla Illustration & Design
12105 NE Sixth Ave, N Miami, FL 33161
305 891.1629

Faricy, Patrick
1110 Town Centre Dr, Eagan, MN 55123
612 687.9717

Farkas, Gabriella
5855 Green Valley Cir, Culver City, CA 90230
310 642.2721

Farley, Andrew
28 Shelton St, Covent Gdn, London,
England WC2H 9HP
011 44 171 240 2077
fax 011 44 171 836 0199
page 363

Farley, David
353 W 53rd St, NYC, NY 10019
212 682.2462

Farley, Malcolm
7625 Quartz St, Golden, CO 80403
303 420.9135

Farnham, Joe
c/o Leighton & Co
Four Prospect St, Beverly, MA 01915
508 921.0887
fax 508 921.0223
page 221

Farquharson, Alexander
16 Adams St, Marlborough, MA 01752
508 485.5739

Farrar, David
4167 Ridgeway Ln, Knoxville, TN 37919
615 588.0624

Farrell, Kevin
5855 Green Valley Cir, Culver City, CA 90230
310 642.2721

Farrell, Rick
3918 N Stevens St, Tacoma, WA 98407
206 752.8814

Farrell, Russ
353 W 53rd St, NYC, NY 10019
212 682.2462

Farrington, Susan
191 Middlesex Ave, Wilmington, MA 01887
508 988.0664

Fasciano, Nicholas
180 Sunset Rd,
Oyster Bay Cove, NY 11771
516 922.7143
fax 516 624.8183
Multi-media two and three dimensional
design and illustration. Clients include
Ammirati & Puris/Lintas, CBS, DDB
Needham Worldwide, Fortune, Museum
of Television & Radio, Sony, Time-Life
Books.

Fasolino, Teresa
270 Park Ave S, NYC, NY 10010
212 260.6700

Fast, Judith
33-68 21st St, L.I.C., NY 11106
718 721.5426
Fine line black & white and full color.
Florals & Foods, Friends & Fiends,
Borders & Beasts (excellent researcher).
Clients include Newsday, Guideposts,
Harper & Row, H.B.J., Atheneum, and
Macmillan.

Fastner & Larson
529 S Seventh St, Mpls, MN 55415
612 338.0959

Faust, Clifford
25 W 45th St, NYC, NY 10036
212 398.9540

Fawell, Tom Illustration
437 Highland Ave, W Chicago, IL 60185
312 231.1771

FeBland, David
670 West End Ave, NYC, NY 10025
212 580.9299

Feldman, Ken & Associates
625 N Michigan, Chicago, IL 60611
312 337.0447

Feldman, Steve
1402 W Jackman St, Lancaster, CA 93534
805 945.5966

Felker, Robert
7118 Upper River Rd, Prospect, KY 40059
502 228.9427

Fell, Dan/Studio Graphex
420 Lexington Ave, NYC, NY 10170
212 986.5680
fax 212 818.1246
page 196

Fellows, Kara
1401 Willow St, Mpls, MN 55403
612 872.4284

Fennimore, Linda
808 West End Ave, NYC, NY 10025
212 866.0279
pages 314-315

Ferentz, Nicole Illustration
1440 N Dayton St, Chicago, IL 60622
312 943.4864

Fernandez, Laura
41 Union Sq W, NYC, NY 10003
212 206.0066

Ferster, Gary
3363 Melendy Dr, San Carlos, CA 94070
415 598.0115

Fiat, Randi & Associates
1727 S Indiana Ave, Chicago, IL 60616
312 663.5300

Fickling, Phillip
1863 S Pearl St, Denver, CO 80210
303 733.0128

Fiedler, Joseph Daniel
250 W 57th St, NYC, NY 10107
212 397.7330
fax 212 397.7334
page 246
I am a painter and professional
illustrator. I was born on June 18, 1953.
That year, in Memphis, Tennessee, Elvis
Presley made his first record. It was the
year of the first television broadcast in
Japan and the initiation of water
fluoridation in the US. It was also the
year that the Rosenbergs were executed
and Art Klokey debuted Gumby on a
segment of the Howdy Doody show.

Field, Ann
2910 16th St, Santa Monica, CA 90405
310 450.6413

Field, Jillian
35093 Sunflower Ln, Squaw Valley, CA 93675
209 332.2832

Field, Lori Nelson
900 W Jackson Blvd, Chicago, IL 60607
312 944.5680

Fields, Gary
30 Allen Dr, Wayne, NJ 07470
201 633.8060

Findley, John
729.G Edgewood Ave NE, Atlanta, GA 30317
404 523.6370

Finewood, Bill
25 Drury Ln, Rochester, NY 14625
716 586.6041

Finger, Ronald
c/o Bernstein & Andriulli
60 E 42nd St, NYC, NY 10165
212 682.1490

Fiore, Peter
89 Fifth Ave, NYC, NY 10003
212 627.1554

Fiore, Peter
40-1906 Newport Pky, Jersey City, NJ 07310
201 222.6369

Firchow, Steve
719 W Wilson, Costa Mesa, CA 92627
714 642.2779

Firehouse 101 Art & Design
492 Armstrong St, Columbus, OH 43215
614 464.0928
page 424

Firestone, Bill
4810 Bradford Dr, Annandale, VA 22003
703 354.0247

Fisch, Paul
5111 Coffee Tree Ln, North Syracuse, NY 13212
315 451.8147

Fischer, Judith
206 N Glenwood, Enid, OK 73703
405 242.6504

Fischler, Scott
1824 West Dr, Clearwater, FL 34615
813 443.7106

Fisher, Bunny
730 N Franklin, Chicago, IL 60610
312 280.1961

Fisher, Carolyn
425 S Black Ave, Bozeman, MT 59715
406 585.2767

Fisher, Jane
1410 W Sunnyside, Chicago, IL 60640
312 271.0465

Fisher, Leonard Everett
Seven Twin Bridge Acres Rd, Westport, CT 06880
203 227.1632

Fisher, Mark
15 Colonial Dr, Westford, MA 01886
508 392.0303
fax 508 392.0304
page 157
"You should see my black and white
work. Call for a booklet".

Fisher, Mike
416 N Columbia St,
Covington, LA 70433
504 892.7557
page 409

Fisher, Randy
PO Box 2193, Grapevine, TX 76099
817 481.2212

Fisher, Shell
3395 San Luis Ave, Carmel, CA 93923
408 625.0130

Fitting, Cynthia
2131 1/2 Pine St, S.F., CA 94115
415 567.3353

Fitz-Maurice, Jeff
731 N 24th St, Phila, PA 19130
215 232.6666

Fitz.Maurice, Karen
731 N 24th St, Philadelphia, PA 19130
215 232.6666

Fitzgerald, Frank
212 E 89th St, NYC, NY 10128
212 722.6793

Fitzgerald, Patrick
Two Milepost Pl, Toronto,
ONT, Canada M4H 1C7
416 429.2512

Fitzhugh, Greg
25 W 45th St, NYC, NY 10036
212 398.9540

Flaherty, David
One Union Sq W, NYC, NY 10003
212 675.2038

Flaming, Jon
2200 N Lamar, Dallas, TX 75202
214 922.9757

Flanders, Shelley
968 Estrella Dr, Santa Barbara, CA 93110
805 682.0020

Flatland
1128 Ocean Park Blvd, Santa Monica, CA 90405
310 394.5204

Fleishman, Michael
247 Whitehall Dr, Yellow Springs, OH 45387
513 767.7955

Fleming, Dean
c/o Bernstein & Andriulli
60 E 42nd St, NYC, NY 10165
212 682.1490

Fleming, Joe
420 Lexington Ave, NYC, NY 10170
212 697.8525

Fleming, Margaret
65 W 55th St, NYC, NY 10019
212 767.0260

Floeter, Nell
c/o Teri O
1045 Diamond NE, Grand Rapids, MI 49503
616 454.1278

Flood, Dick
1603 Sheridan Rd, Champaign, IL 61821
217 352.8356

Florczak, Robert
PO Box 2160, Moorpark, CA 93021
805 529.8111

Florian, Douglas
147.42 Village Rd, Jamaica, NY 61435
718 380.4397

Fluharty, Thomas L
200 Rector Pl, NYC, NY 10280
212 799.6532

Flynn, James
1930 W Newport, Chicago, IL 60657
312 871.4744

Fogle, David
2372 Wooster Rd, Lakewood, OH 44116
216 356.1493

Foley, Tim
1045 Diamond NE, Grand Rapids, MI 49503
616 454.1278

Folio Forums/Vicki Sander
48 Gramercy Park N, NYC, NY 10010
212 420.1333

Forbes, Bart
5323 Montrose Dr, Dallas, TX 75209
214 357.8077

Ford, Terri Illustration
401 N 17th St, San Jose, CA 95112
408 971.2662

Forgus, Rick
8120 E Montebello Ave, Scottsdale, AZ 85250
602 483.7609

Fornalski, Michael
621 River Oaks Pkwy, San Jose, CA 95134
408 434.6434

Forte, Geneva
11805 Cromwell Ave, Cleveland, OH 44120
216 791.6148

Fortin, Pierre
67 Upper Mountain Ave, Montclair, NJ 07042
201 744.4465

Fortuni
2508 E Belleview, Milwaukee, WI 53211
414 964.8088

Foster, Matt
6766 Snowdon Ave,
El Cerrito, CA 94530
510 215.1251
fax 510 215.1257
pages 6-7

Foster, Pat
32 W 40th St, NYC, NY 10018
212 575.6887

Foster, Phil
528 Independence Way, Murfreesboro, TN 37129
615 895.1114

Foster, Stephen
894 Grove St, Glencoe, IL 60022
708 835.2741
fax 708 835.2783
page 210

Foster, Susan
853 Broadway, NYC, NY 10003
212 677.9100

Foster, Teenuh
840 Bricken Pl, St Louis, MO 63122
314 821.2278
fax 314 821.1667
page 419

Foster, Travis
1209 Shelton Ave, Nashville, TN 37216
615 227.0895
fax 615 227.2996
pages 312-313

Fotheringham, Edwin
6049 Sycamore, Seattle, WA 98106
206 706.9481

Fountain, Linda
34 Westwood Dr, East Rochester, NY 14445
716 385.8513

Fournier, Joe
151 N Elmwood, Oak Park, IL 60302
708 848.2756
page 262
"Please, Please, Please, Please, Please,
Please, Please, Please, Please, Please,
Please, Please, Please, Please, Please,
Please look at my page!"

Fowler, Ann
475 Candler St, Atlanta, GA 30307
404 688.4730

Fowler, Eric
417 Beatty St, Trenton, NJ 08611
609 695.4305

Fox Art Inc
8350 Melrose, L.A., CA 90069
213 653.6484

Fox, Bill
2233 Kemper Ln, Cincinnati, OH 45206
513 861.1400

Fox, Brian
29 Massasoit St, Somerset, MA 02725
508 674.0511

Fox, Mark
239 Marin St, San Rafael, CA 94901
415 258.9663

Fox, Rosemary
PO Box 186, Bearsville, NY 12409
914 657.7040

Foxx, Kim
30166 Chapala Ct, Laguna Niguel, CA 92677
714 495.3664

Foy, Lynne/Graphiis
243 Linwood Ave, Newton, MA 02160
617 244.3768

Frampton, Bill
c/o Daniele Collignon
200 W 15th St, NYC, NY 10011
212 243.4209
page 273

Frampton, David
58 W 15th St, NYC, NY 10011
212 741.2539

Francis, John
1665 Logan St, Denver, CO 80203
303 894.8350
fax 303 894.8343
page 372
Specializing in the "blue print" look. An
interesting combination of loose and
technical drawing, focusing with realistic
airbrush art. Clients include; DuPont,
Infiniti, Norelco and AT&T.

Francis, Judy
110 W 96th St, NYC, NY 10025
212 866.7204

Frank, Robert
Nine Babbling Brook Ln, Suffern, NY 10901
914 368.8606

Franke, Phil
420 Lexington Ave, NYC, NY 10170
212 986.5680

Franks, Sylvia
12056 Summit Cir, Beverly Hills, CA 90210
310 276.5282

Fraser, Douglas
250 W 57th St, NYC, NY 10107
212 397.7330
fax 212 397.7334
page 248

Frazier Design
600 Townsend St, S.F., CA 94103
415 863.9613

Frazier, Jim
221 Lakeridge Dr, Dallas, TX 75218
214 340.9972

Freas, Kelly Studios
7713 Nita Ave, West Hills, CA 91304
818 992.1252
fax 818 992.1252
Over 2,000 published prizewinning
illustrations, all media. 50+
International awards. Who's Who
Biographee. Author of 3 books on
illustration. Editorial and advertising.
Clients include NASA, MAD Magazine,
science fiction and fantasy publishers.
See also American Showcase.

Freda, Anthony
222 E Fifth St, NYC, NY 10003
212 529.4990

Fredericks Illustration Inc
9705 S 52nd Ave, Oak Lawn, IL 60453
708 857.8090
fax 708 857.8111
page 404

Frederking, Sarah
433 N Harvey Ave, Oak Park, IL 60302
708 386.6886

Fredrickson, Mark
5093 E Patricia St, Tucson, AZ 85712
520 323.3179

Freelance Hotline
311 First Ave N, Mpls, MN 55401
612 341.4411

Freeman, Laura
208 E 34th St, NYC, NY 10016
212 679.0812

Freeman, Lisa
740 E 52nd St, Ste 8, Indpls, IN 46205
317 920.0068
fax 317 923.9906
I: **Brian Behnke, Calef Brown,**
Barbara Friedman, Todd Graveline,
Susan Kwas, Sara Love, Joseph Mahler,
Susan Moore, Dianne McElwain,
Paul Moschell, Carol O' Malia, Chris
Pyle, Fred Schrier, Matt Wawiorka
P: **Harold Miller**
Calligraphy: **Joan Presslor, Juana Silcox**

Freestyle Studio
PO Box 823554, Dallas, TX 75382
214 319.0555

French, Lisa/L French Illustration
355 Molino Ave, Long Beach, CA 90814
310 434.5277
fax 310 434.5277
Anatomical illustration/other realism for
advertising and editorial purpose.

French, Martin
101 Yesler Way, Seattle, WA 98104
206 447.1600

Frenett, Elaine
1761 Marina Way, San Jose, CA 95125
408 450.1630

Frichtel, Linda
58 W 15th St, NYC, NY 10011
212 741.2539

Fricke, Bill
487 Drum Pt Rd, Brick, NJ 08723
908 477.5482

Fridell, Pat
PO Box 19412, Seattle, WA 98109
206 634.1880

Fried, Janice
459 Ninth St, Brooklyn, NY 11215
718 832.0881

Friedensohn, Shola
31 Lawrence St, Cambridge, MA 02139
617 876.6589

Friedman, Barbara
29 Bank St, NYC, NY 10014
212 242.4951

Friel, Bryan
3914 E Second St, Long Beach, CA 90803
310 439.0107

Friend & Johnson
3624 Oak Lawn Ave, Dallas, TX 75219
214 559.0055

Frisari, Frank
78-11 161st Ave,
Howard Beach, NY 11414
718 848.5007
page 218

Frisari, Frank
c/o Leighton & Co
Four Prospect St, Beverly, MA 01915
508 921.0887
fax 508 921.0223
page 218

Fritch, Diana
28315 Driza, Mission Viejo, CA 92692
714 458.2356

Frith, Amy/ARF Productions
59 Wareham St, Boston, MA 02118
617 423.2212
fax 617 423.2213
page 198

Fritsch, Steve
49 W 45th St, NYC, NY 10036
212 921.1199

Frost, Ralph III
2233 Kemper Ln, Cincinnati, OH 45206
513 861.1400

Frost, Robert
One Winsor Rd, Baldwin, NY 11510
516 623.4764

Frueh, Mark
840 Bricken Pl, St Louis, MO 63122
314 821.2278

Frye, Michael
Rt Seven Box 61A, Alvin, TX 77511
713 523.8444

Fuchs, Bernie
Three Tanglewood Ln, Westport, CT 06880
203 227.4644

Fujimori, Brian
325 W Huron St, Chicago, IL 60610
312 787.6826

Fujisaki, Tuko
NYC, NY
718 789.7472
page 419

Fujisaki, Tuko
San Diego, CA
619 276.0566
page 419

Fuka, Ted
770 N Halsted P102, Chicago, IL 60622
312 338.7110

Fuller, Rocky
2540 Cleinview Ave, Cincinnati, OH 45206
513 281.5312

Fuller, Steve
29 Terry Ave, Schenectady, NY 12303
518 356.1048

Funkhouser, Kristen
716 Sanchez St, S.F., CA 94114
415 285.8267

Furchgott-Scott, Carol
242 Barren Hill Rd, Spring Mill, PA 19428
610 828.3446

Gabbana, Marc
2453 Olive Ct, Windsor, ONT,
Canada N8T 3N4
519 948.2418
fax 519 948.2418
page 393
Realistic & surrealistic representations of
futuristic and sci/fi themes with a strong
emphasis on character, robot, vehicle
and architectural design.

Gabel, Ed
340 Lighthouse Dr, Perrysburg, OH 43551
419 874.3662

Gaber, Brad
4946 Glenmeadow, Houston, TX 77096
713 723.0030

Gadecki, Ted
900 W Jackson Blvd, Chicago, IL 60607
312 944.5680

Gadino, Victor
417 E 90th St, NYC, NY 10128
212 860.8066

Gaetano, Nick
c/o Vicki Morgan
194 Third Ave, NYC, NY 10003
212 475.0440

Gal, Susan
267 Cambridge Ave, Kensington, CA 94708
510 528.9343

Gale, Cynthia
229 E 88th St, NYC, NY 10128
212 860.5429

Galey, Chuck
211 Lea Cir, Jackson, MI 39204
601 373.6426

Galindo, Felipe
509 Cathedral Pky, NYC, NY 10025
212 864.6648

Gall, Chris
c/o Carol Chislovsky Design
853 Broadway, NYC, NY 10003
212 677.9100
page 124

Gallagher, James
462 Bergen St, Brooklyn, NY 11217
718 857.5958

Gallagher, Saelig
3624 Amaryllis Dr, San Diego, CA 92106
619 222.3892

Galloway, Nixon
755 Marine Ave, Manhattan Beach, CA 90266
310 545.7709

Garbett, Paul
RR2, Puslinch, ONT, Canada N0B 2J0
416 431.7034
page 397

Garbot, Dave
11369 SW Winterlake Dr, Tigard, OR 97223
503 579.0663

Garcia, Art
2811 McKinney Ave, Dallas, TX 75208
214 922.9080

Garcia, Manuel
716 Sanchez St, S.F., CA 94114
415 285.8267

Garcia, Stephanie
551 Observer Hwy, Hoboken, NJ 07030
201 963.8089

Garcia, Tom
597 Riverside Ave, Westport, CT 06880
203 226.4724

Gardner Graphics
2453 East Billings, Mesa, AZ 85213
602 844.1956

Gardner, Bonnie
67 Upper Mountain Ave, Montclair, NJ 07042
201 744.4465

Garland, Bill
353 W 53rd St, NYC, NY 10019
212 582.0023 / 212 682.2462
fax 212 582.0090
page 178

Garns, Allen
209 W First Ave, Mesa, AZ 85210
602 835.5769

Garramone, Rich
49 Ridgedale Ave, East Hanover, NJ 07936
201 887.7234

Garre, John & Karen
1321 S Montana Ave, Bozeman, MT 59715
406 585.9804

Garrett, Tom
817 Westwood Dr S, Mpls, MN 55416
612 374.3169

Garrison, Barbara
12 E 87th St, NYC, NY 10128
212 348.6382

Garrity, Dennis
8443 Michael Dr, Boynton Beach, FL 33437
407 734.9414

Garro, Mark
13 Richard St, White Plains, NY 10603
914 946.7499

Garrow, Dan
501 Fifth Ave, NYC, NY 10017
212 490.2450
fax 212 697.6828
page 55

Gartel, Laurence
501 Fifth Ave, NYC, NY 10017
212 490.2450

Gar•th
1131 S Burnside Ave, L.A., CA 90019
213 857.0981

Garvie, Ben
9400 Cedarview Way, Elk Grove, CA 95758
916 683.1171

Gast, Joseph
68 E Franklin, Dayton, OH 45459
513 433.8383

Gaston, Jane
36 Ednam Vlg, Charlottesville, VA 22901
804 295.2755

**Gatlin, Rita Represents
83 Walnut Ave,
Corte Madera, CA 94925
415 924.7881 / 800 924.7881
fax 415 924.7891
page 82**
I: **Don Dudley, Andrew Boerger, Michel
Bohbot, Don Dudley, Tom Hennessy,
Tina Hill, Jack Lutzow, Kathy
McNicholas, Ron Peterson, Mary Ross,
Peter Stallard, Elizabeth Traynor,
Julie Tsuchiya.**
P: **Jackson Vereen**

Gay, Patti
3443 Wade St, Pacifica, CA 90066
310 390.9595

Gaynin, Gail
c/o Vicki Morgan
194 Third Ave, NYC, NY 10003
212 475.0440

Gaz, Stan
58 W 15th St, NYC, NY 10011
212 741.2539

Gazzi, Edward
7930 Sycamore Dr, New Port Richey, FL 34654
813 844.3482

Geary, Rick
701 Kettner Blvd, San Diego, CA 92101
619 234.0514

Gebert, Warren
Two Hunt Ct, Suffern, NY 10901
914 354.2536

Geerinck, Manuel
420 Lexington Ave, NYC, NY 10170
212 697.8525

Gehm, Charles
420 Lexington Ave, NYC, NY 10170
212 697.8525

Geiger, Nancy
178 Willow Cove Ct, Lawrenceville, GA 30244
404 921.6619

Gelb, Jacki
108 E 35th St, NYC, NY 10016
212 889.3337

Geng, Maud
430 Ventura Pl, Vero Beach, FL 32963
407 231.4362

Genova, Joe
c/o Bernstein & Andriulli
60 E 42nd St, NYC, NY 10165
212 682.1490

Genovese, Janell
PO Box 1154, Boston, MA 02205
617 782.3218

George, Jeff
11936 W Jefferson Blvd, Culver City, CA 90230
310 390.8663

George, Nancy
302 N La Brea Ave, L.A., CA 90036
213 655.0998

Geras, Audra
501 Fifth Ave, NYC, NY 10017
212 490.2450

Gergely, Peter
24 Roe Park, Highland Falls, NY 10928
914 446.2367

Gersten, Gerry
177 Newtown Tpke, Weston, CT 06883
203 454.4134

Gettier-Street, Renee
13908 Marblestone Dr, Clifton, VA 22024
703 631.1650

Geyer, Mark
2447 Ridgeway Dr, Atlanta, GA 30360
404 451.4778

Giacobbe, Beppe
c/o Vicki Morgan
194 Third Ave, NYC, NY 10003
212 475.0440

Giannini, Judi
8208 Houston Ct, Takoma Park, MD 20912
301 439.0103

Giannini-Kabilyo Design
68 Harvard St, Cranston, RI 02920
401 781.3441

Gibbons, Anne
125 W 72nd St, NYC, NY 10023
212 724.6979

Gibbs, Michael
Seven W Braddock Rd, Alexandria, VA 22301
703 684.7447

Gibson, Barbara Leonard
3501 Toddsbury Ln, Olney, MD 20832
301 570.9480

**Gibson, Clancy
Two Silver Ave, Toronto,
ONT, Canada M6R 3A2
416 530.1500
fax 416 530.1401
page 20**

**Gibson-Nash, Nancy
15 Autumn Rd, Dedham, MA 02026
617 461.4574
page 128**

Giguere, Ralph
41 Union Sq W, NYC, NY 10003
212 206.0066

Gilbert, Yvonne
666 Greenwich St, NYC, NY 10014
212 675.5719

Gillespie, Mike
6076 Highland Dr, Kaufman, TX 75142
214 962.5365

Gillette, Kathleen
13911 Old Harbor Ln, Marina del Rey, CA 90292
310 821.5441

Gillig, Steve
1836 N Winchester, Chicago, IL 60622
312 482.9535

Gilliland, Tim
2701 Meadowstone Ct, Carrollton, TX 75006
214 416.2687

Gillot, Carol
67 Upper Mountain Ave, Montclair, NJ 07042
201 744.4465

Gilmour, Joni
Ten A Orchard Ter, Salem, NH 03079
603 898.6961

Gin, Byron
Four E Ohio, Chicago, IL 60611
312 935.1707 / 312 944.1130
pages 14-15
Actual linoleum cuts combined with
acrylic and colored pencil. Sensitive and
compelling artwork serving clients as
diverse as Busch Entertainment,
Symantec, Toyota, Forbes, Tyson Foods,
DHL, Sizzler, Inc., Bantam books, Cutty
Sark, Dial, Klar Bruen, Acura,
McDonald's.

Giraud, Jean
6539 Jamieson Ave, Reseda, CA 91335
818 343.9922

Girvin, Tim Design
1601 Second Ave, Seattle, WA 98101
206 623.7808

Gisko, Max
2629 Wakefield Dr, Belmont, CA 94002
415 647.5660

Gitelman, Ellen
101 Tremont St, Boston, MA 02108
617 426.6668

Githens, Doug
770 N Halsted P102, Chicago, IL 60622
312 338.7110

Giurbino, Linda
3848 Los Feliz Blvd, L.A., CA 90027
213 662.9222

Giusti, Robert
270 Park Ave S, NYC, NY 10010
212 260.6700

Glad, Deanna
PO Box 1962, San Pedro, CA 90733
310 831.6274

Gladstone, Dale
32 Havemeyer St, Brooklyn, NY 11211
718 782.2250

Glasbergen, Randy
PO Box 797, Sherburne, NY 13460
607 674.9492
fax 607 674.9492
Clients, accounts include: King Features
Syndicate, Hallmark, Funny Times,
Glamour, Ralston Purina, American
Airlines, IBM. Call for portfolio package.

Glasgow & Associates
448 Hartwood Rd,
Fredericksburg, VA 22406
540 286.2539
fax 540 286.0316
pages 282-283
We offer the total creative solution for
your illustration, animation, or
multimedia needs. Clients include: The
White House, National Geographic,
Compuserve, Xerox, Reader's Digest,
American Medical Association, The
Martin Agency, Addison-Wesley, and
MacMillan McGraw Hill.

Glass, Damian V
102 Cooks Bay Dr, Keswick, ONT, Canada L4P 1M3
905 476.7985

Glass, Randy
716 Montgomery St, S.F., CA 94111
415 433.1222
fax 415 433.9560
page 400

Glassford, Carl
25361 Posada Ln, Mission Viejo, CA 92691
714 768.7288

Glattauer, Ned
343 E 30th St, NYC, NY 10016
212 686.6927

Glazer, Art
Two James Rd, Mt Kisco, NY 10549
914 666.4554

Glazer, Ted
28 Westview Rd, Spring Valley, NY 10977
914 354.1524

Glazier, Garth
353 W 53rd St, NYC, NY 10019
212 682.2462

Gleason, Bob
2981-C 142nd Pl SE, Bellavue, WA 98007
206 643.8084

Glenn, Chris
520 N Michigan, Chicago, IL 60611
312 670.7737

Glick, Ivy & Associates
PO Box 30485,
Walnut Creek, CA 94598
510 944.0304 / 212 869.0214
pages 268-271

Glick, Judith Medical Art Inc
301 E 79th St, NYC, NY 10021
212 734.5268

Gloeckner, Phoebe
PO Box 31682, S.F., CA 94131
510 339.9461

Glover, Ann
1308 Factory Pl/Box 25, L.A., CA 90013
213 623.6203

Glover, Gary
6715 Xana Way, Rancho La Costa, CA 92009
619 471.9453

Gnan, Patrick
731 N 24th St, Phila, PA 19130
215 232.6666
fax 215 232.6585
page 131

Godfrey, Dennis
231 W 25th St, NYC, NY 10001
212 807.0840

Goembel, Ponder
PO Box 762, Riegelsville, PA 18077
610 749.0337

Goethals, Raphaelle
1205 Maclovia St, Santa Fe, NM 87505
505 474.6651

Gold, Albert
6814 McCallum St, Phila, PA 19119
215 848.5568

Gold, Marcy
5157 Floria Way, Boynton Beach, FL 33437
407 737.2569

Goldammer, Ken
116 W Illinois, Chicago, IL 60610
312 836.0143

Goldberg, Janice
77 Carlton St, Toronto, ONT, Canada M5B 2J7
416 410.0848

Goldberg, Richard A
15 Cliff St, Arlington, MA 02174
617 646.1041
fax 617 646.0956
page 106

Goldin, David
111 Fourth Ave, NYC, NY 10003
212 529.5195
fax 212 674.3225
pages 460-461

Goldin, David
c/o Joanne Palulian
NYC, NY
212 581.8338
pages 460-461

Goldin, David
c/o Joanne Palulian
18 McKinley St, Rowayton, CT 06853
203 866.3734
fax 203 857.0842
pages 460-461

Goldman, David Agency
41 Union Sq W, NYC, NY 10003
212 807.6627

Goldsmith, Lloyd
Six Monterey Ter, Orinda, CA 94563
510 253.9451

Goldstein, Elisse Jo
182 E 95th St, NYC, NY 10128
212 534.3594

Goldstein, Gwen Walters
50 Fuller Brook Rd, Wellesley, MA 02181
617 235.8658

Goldstein, Howard
7031 Aldea Ave, Van Nuys, CA 91406
818 987.2837

Goldstrom, Robert
270 Park Ave S, NYC, NY 10010
212 260.6700

Gomberg, Susan
41 Union Sq W, NYC, NY 10003
212 206.0066

Gomez, Ignacio
853 Broadway, NYC, NY 10003
212 677.9100

Gonzales, Chuck
520 N Michigan Ave, Chicago, IL 60611
312 670.7737

Gonzalez, Danilo
324 N Marengo Ave, Alhambra, CA 91801
818 441.2787

Gonzalez, Thomas
848 Greenwood Ave NE,
Atlanta, GA 30306
404 875.1363 / 800 347.0734
fax 404 875.9733
page 344

Goode, Harley
50 W 72nd St, NYC, NY 10023
212 877.2390

Goodell, Brad Illustration
605 Arizona St SE, Albuquerque, NM 87108
505 255.7889

Goodfellow, Peter
11 Kings Ridge Rd, Long Valley, NY 07853
908 813.8718

Goodman, Joan Elizabeth
684 Washington St, NYC, NY 10014
212 255.3134

Goodman, Johanna
222 E 51st St, NYC, NY 10022
212 759.8215

Goodman, Marlene K
625 Ivy Ct, Wheeling, IL 60090
708 255.5772

Goodman, Michael
1922 Windingridge Dr, Richmond, VA 23233
804 741.6577

Goodrich, Carter
100 Angell St, Providence, RI 02906
401 272.6094

Goodridge, James
c/o Bernstein & Andriulli
60 E 42nd St, NYC, NY 10165
212 682.1490

Gordon, Barbara
165 E 32nd St, NYC, NY 10016
212 686.3514

Gordon, TJ
PO Box 4112, Montebello, CA 90640
213 887.8958
page 345

Gordon-Lucas, Bonnie
2233 Kemper Ln, Cincinnati, OH 45206
513 861.1400

Goring, Trevor
5855 Green Valley Cir, Culver City, CA 90230
310 642.2721

Gorman, Ron Automotive Illustration
PO Box 2233, Eugene, OR 97402
503 343.3434

Gorman, Stan
217 Santa Rosa Ct, Laguna Beach, CA 92651
714 733.8071

Gorton, Julia
207 Baldwin St, Glen Ridge, NJ 07028
201 748.6997

Gothard, David
104 Creek Rd, Bangor, PA 18013
610 588.4937

Gottfried Renderings
12655 W Bayaud, Lakewood, CO 80228
303 988.1517

Gradisher, Martha
245 Piermont Ave, S Nyack, NY 10960
914 358.0185

Graham Studios
900 W Jackson Blvd, Chicago, IL 60607
312 944.5680
fax 312 421.5948
page 93

Graham, Corey Represents
Pier 33 N, S.F., CA 94111
415 956.4750

Graham, Ian
1926 Hillcrest Rd, L.A., CA 90068
213 876.1310

Graham, Mariah
PO Box 425, Jeffersonville, NY 12748
914 482.4036

Graham, Mark
19 Hilltop Rd, Port Washington, NY 11050
516 944.7653

Graham, Tom
408 77th St, Brooklyn, NY 11209
718 680.2975

Grahn, Geoffrey
4054 Madison Ave, Culver City, CA 90232
310 838.7824

Grajek, Tim
213 Webber Ave, N Tarrytown, NY 10591
914 332.9704

Grand Pre, Mary
68 E Franklin St, Dayton, OH 45459
513 433.8383

Granner, Courtney
328 N Fifth St, Patterson, CA 95363
209 892.2973

Grant, Collin
5855 Green Valley Cir, Culver City, CA 90230
310 642.2721

Grant, Renee
89 Fifth Ave, NYC, NY 10003
212 627.1554

Grant, Stan
307 N Michigan Ave, Chicago, IL 60611
312 704.0500

Graphic Chart & Map Co Inc
236 W 26th St, NYC, NY
212 463.9354

Graphix
32 Guernsey St, West Roxbury, MA 02132
617 325.8953

Grasso, Mitch
731 N 24th St, Phila, PA 19130
215 232.6666

**Graves, David
84 Main St, Gloucester, MA 01930
508 283.2335
Specializes in expressing movement,
motion, life in machines, animals,
people, buildings, and most other visual
things. Clients include: Disney/Spielberg,
Hasbro Toys, Parker Bros., Met Life,
Boston University Medical School,
Boston Gas, Pacific Gas.**

Graves, Keith
1403 Pinewood Cove, Leander, TX 78641
512 259.8586

Gray, Barbara
150 E 69th St, NYC, NY 10021
212 288.3938

Gray, Lynda/CIA
c/o Bernstein & Andriulli
60 E 42nd St, NYC, NY 10165
212 682.1490

Gray, Steve
Pier Plz / 115 W Torrance Blvd,
Redondo Beach, CA 90277
310 546.2188

Gray, Susan
42 W 12th St, NYC, NY 10011
212 675.2243

Green, Norman
119 W 23rd St, NYC, NY 10011
212 633.9880

**Green, Patti
5222 N Clark St, Chicago, IL 60640
312 275.5895
fax 312 878.6857
page 352**

**Greenberg, Karen L
95 Horatio St, NYC, NY 10014
212 645.7379
fax 212 645.3582
page 305**

Greenberg, Merrill
4175 Park Blvd, Oakland, CA 94602
510 482.0588

**Greenberg, Sheldon
200 Aquetong Rd, New Hope, PA 18938
215 862.2091
fax 215 862.2641
page 229
Sheldon Greenberg's paintings have
been used by The Washington Post
Magazine, Technology Review,
Redbook, National Geographic,
Hallmark, Coach Leatherware, Coca-
Cola USA, Sony Music, CBS
Masterworks, Readers Digest, The New
York Times, Price Waterhouse & in
advertising and design.**

Greenbladt, Mitch
374 Eighth St, Brooklyn, NY 11215
718 369.6005

Greene, Pauline
70 Village Pky, Santa Monica, CA 90405
310 450.4200

Greenstein, Susan
229A Windsor Pl, Brooklyn, NY 11215
718 788.6447

Gregg & Associates
112 W Ninth, Kansas City, MO 64105
816 421.4473

Gregoretti, Rob
41.07 56th St, Woodside, NY 11377
718 779.7913

Gregori, Lee
400 E 56th St, NYC, NY 10022
212 758.1662

Grejniec, Michael
866 UN Plz, NYC, NY 10017
212 644.2020

**Grell, Susi
3375 Ponytrail Dr, Ste 1003,
Mississauga, ONT, Canada L4X 1V8
905 624.0141
fax 905 624.0141
page 336**

Grider, Dick
218 Madison Ave, NYC, NY 10016
212 213.5333

Grief, Gene
114 W 16th St, NYC, NY 10011
212 647.1286

Grien, Anita
155 E 38th St, NYC, NY 10016
212 697.6170

Griesbach/Martucci
58 W 15th St, NYC, NY 10011
212 741.2539

Grieve, Judy
86 Cheryl Shepway, Toronto, ONT,
Canada M2J 4R5
416 502.3874

Griff, Tony
6171 N Sheridan Rd, Chicago, IL 60660
312 465.3702

Griffin, Craig
341 E Catawba Ave, Akron, OH 44301
216 773.9419

Griffith, Robert
250 E Sixth St, St Paul, MN 55101
612 222.1353

Grigsby, David
2401 Hitchcock Dr, Alhambra, CA 91803
818 284.7100
fax 818 289.4510
Color and b&w editorial, portraiture,
advertising and fashion. See samples of
work in GAG Directory of Illustration
#11 and #12.

Grimes, Melissa
901 Cumberland Rd, Austin, TX 78704
512 445.2398

Grimes, Rebecca
936 Stone Rd, Westminster, MD 21158
410 857.1675

Grimwood, Brian/CIA
c/o Bernstein & Andriulli
60 E 42nd St, NYC, NY 10165
212 682.1490

Grinnell, Derek
621A 42nd Ave, S.F., CA 94121
415 221.2820
fax 415 221.2820
page 268

Groff, David
420 N Liberty St, Delaware, OH 43015
614 363.2131

Groover, Susan
980 E Rocksprings Rd,
Atlanta, GA 30306
404 875.5295
page 305

Gross, Alex
1727 La Senda Pl, South Pasadena, CA 91030
818 799.4014

Gross, Susan
532 Cabrillo St, S.F., CA 94118
415 751.5879
fax 415 751.5876
page 205

Grossman, Myron
2027 N Lake Ave, Altadena, CA 91001
818 798.3691

Grossman, Rhoda
716 Sanchez St, S.F., CA 94114
415 285.8267

Grossman, Wendy
355 W 51st St, NYC, NY 10019
212 262.4497
page 89

Grote, Rich
67 Upper Mountain Ave, Montclair, NJ 07042
201 744.4465

Grothman, Lisa
1293 First Ave, #4, NYC, NY 10021
212 794.2627
page 176

Grove, David
382 Union St, S.F., CA 94133
415 433.2100

Grover, Max
PO Box 1935, Port Towsend, WA 98368
206 385.5051

Gryder, Jonas
67 Upper Mountain Ave, Montclair, NJ 07042
201 744.4465

Guarnaccia, Steven
31 Fairfield St, Montclair, NJ 07042
201 746.9785

Gudynas, Peter
11 Kings Ridge Rd, Long Valley, NJ 07853
908 813.8718

Guenzi, Carol Agents
1863 S Pearl St, Denver, CO 80210
303 733.0128 / 800 417.5120
fax 303 733.8154
pages 322-327

Guida, Liisa Chauncy
420 Lexington Ave, NYC, NY 10170
212 986.5680

Guided Imagery
2995 Woodside Rd, Woodside, CA 94062
415 324.0323

Guidice, Rick
Nine Park Ave, Los Gatos, CA 95030
408 354.7787

Guitteau, Jud
501 Fifth Ave, NYC, NY 10017
212 490.2450
fax 212 697.6828
page 42

Gullickson, Vicki
750 94th Ave N, St Petersburg, FL 33702
813 579.4499

Gully, Bethany
791 Tremont St, Boston, MA 02118
617 350.3089

Gumble, Gary
10926 NE 17th St, Bellevue, WA 98004
206 688.1961

Gunion, Jefrey
8100 Harvard Dr, Ben Lomond, CA 95005
408 336.3300

Gunning, Kevin
37 Denison Rd, Middletown, CT 06457
203 347.0688

Gunsaullus, Marty
716 Sanchez St, S.F., CA 94114
415 285.8267

Gurbo, Walter
25 Drury Ln, Rochester, NY 14625
716 586.6041

Gurche, John
Denver, CO
303 370.8365

Gurney, John
261 Marlborough Rd, Brooklyn, NY 11226
718 462.5073

Gurvin, Abe
31341 Holly Dr, Laguna Beach, CA 92677
714 499.2001

Gusay, Charlotte
10532 Blythe, L.A., CA 90064
310 559.0831

Gushock, Mike
313 E Thomas Rd, Phoenix, AZ 85012
602 650.1810
page 440

Gusman, Annie
15 King St, Putnam, CT 06260
203 928.1042

Gustafson, Dale
420 Lexington Ave, NYC, NY 10017
212 986.5680

Gustafson, Glenn
597 Riverside Ave, Westport, CT 06880
203 226.4724
fax 203 454.9904
page 436

Gustafson, Scott
4045 N Kostner Ave, Chicago, IL 60641
312 725.8338

Guy, Edmund
309 Race Track Rd, Hohokus, NJ 07423
201 251.7660

Guyer, Terry Illustration
1125 E Hillsdale Blvd, Foster City, CA 94404
415 570.5502

Guzman, R Designs
21037 Superior St, Chatsworth, CA 91311
818 700.9893

Gwilliams, Scott
501 Fifth Ave, NYC, NY 10017
212 490.2450

Haber-Schaim, Tamar
1870 Beacon St, Brookline, MA 02146
617 738.8883

Hackett, Pat Artist Rep
101 Yesler Way, Seattle, WA 98104
206 447.1600

Hackworth, Alex
1926 Chamdun Way, Chamblee, GA 30341
404 457.9831

Hagel, Mike
520 N Michigan Ave, Chicago, IL 60611
312 527.0351
fax 312527.5468
page 123

Hagel, Mike
11146 Q St, Omaha, NE 68137
402 596.1415
fax 402 596.1418
page 123

Hagen, David
5580 Village Ctr Dr, Centreville, VA 22020
703 830.4208

Hagio, Kunio
125 Table Top Rd, Sedona, AZ 86336
602 282.3574

Hagner, Dirk
27931 Paseo Nicole, San Juan Capistr, CA 92675
619 272.8147

Hahn, Holly
770 N Halsted P102, Chicago, IL 60622
312 338.7110

Halbert, Michael
420 Lexington Ave, NYC, NY 10170
212 986.5680

Hall & Associates
1010 S Robertson Blvd, L.A., CA 90035
310 652.7322

Hall, Bill
1235-B Colorado Ln, Arlington, TX 76015
817 467.1013

Hall, H Tom
1519 Warwick Furnace Rd, Pottstown, PA 19465
610 469.9744

Hall, Joan
155 Bank St, NYC, NY 10014
212 243.6059

Hall, Kate Brennan
301 DeArment Pky, Pittsburgh, PA 15241
412 833.9648

Hallgren, Gary
98 Laurelton Dr, Mastic Beach, NY 11951
516 399.5531

Hallman Studio, Tom
2553 Mill House Rd, Macungie, PA 18062
610 395.5656

Halloran, Pat
2233 Kemper Ln, Cincinnati, OH 45206
513 861.1400

Hally, Greg
911 Victoria Dr, Arcadia, CA 91007
818 574.0288

Halstead, Virginia
4336 Gayle Dr, Tarzana, CA 91356
818 705.4353
fax 818 705.4353
page 79

Hamann, Brad
330 Westminster Rd, Brooklyn, NY 11218
718 287.6086

Hamblin, George
944 Beach Ave,
La Grange Park, IL 60525
708 352.1780
fax 708 352.1783
page 122

Hamblin, George
520 N Michigan Ave, Chicago, IL 60611
312 527.0351
fax 312 527.5468
page 122

Hamblin, Randy
731 N 24th St, Phila, PA 19130
215 232.6666

Hamilton, Ken
16 Helen Ave, West Orange, NJ 07052
201 736.6532

Hamilton, Laurie
333 E Ontario, Chicago, IL 60611
312 944.3970

Hamilton, Meredith
55 W 11th St, NYC, NY 10022
212 243.9490

Hamilton, Pamela
4900 Overland Ave, Culver City, CA 90230
310 837.1784

Hamlin, Janet
529 Ninth St, Brooklyn, NY 11215
718 768.3647

Hammond, Franklin
68 E Franklin St, Dayton, OH 45459
513 433.8383

Hampshire, Michael
320 Bee Brook Rd, Washington, CT 06777
203 868.1011

Hampson, Denman & Tonia
172 N Salem Rd, Ridgefield, CT 06877
203 438.2419

Hamrick, Chuck Illustration/Portrait
1068 Ridgefield Rd, Wilton, CT 06897
203 762.7775

Hancock, Jim
840 Bricken Pl, St Louis, MO 63122
314 821.2278

Hand to Mouse Arts
3700 E 34th St, Mpls, MN 55406
612 724.1172

Hand, Judy
2233 Kemper Ln, Cincinnati, OH 45206
513 861.1400

Hanes, Larry
6108 Faircrest Ct, Cincinnati, OH 45224
513 542.2473

Hankins & Tegenborg
c/o Bernstein & Andriulli
60 E 42nd St, NYC, NY 10165
212 867.8092

Hanley, John Illustration
4803 Wyoming Way, Crystal Lake, IL 60012
815 459.1123

Hanna, Gary
25 W 45th St, NYC, NY 10036
212 398.9540

Hannaford, Joey
505 Page Ave NE, Atlanta, GA 30307
404 378.0668

Hannah, Halstead
1250 Addison #2116, Berkeley, CA 94702
800 742.4225

Hansen, Clint
68 E Franklin St, Dayton, OH 45459
513 433.8383
fax 513 433.0434
pages 10-11

Hansen, Clint
NYC, NY
212 966.3604
pages 10-11

Hanson, Eric
817 S Westwood Dr, Mpls, MN 55416
612 374.3169

Hanson, Jenny Illustration
325 W Huron, Chicago, IL 60611
312 787.6826

Hanson, Jim
777 N Michigan Ave, Chicago, IL 60611
312 337.7770

Hanxleden, Rainer G
1077-42 Santo Antonio Dr, Colton, CA 92324
909 824.8324

Hardebeck, George
2233 Kemper Ln, Cincinnati, OH 45206
513 861.1400

Harder, Vivian
407 Rio Grande NW, Albuquerque, NM 87104
505 243.4000

Hardy, Neil O
Two Woods Grove Rd, Westport, CT 06880
203 226.4446

Harfield, Mark
270 Park Ave S, NYC, NY 10010
212 260.6700

Harlib, Joel Associates Inc
Ten E Ontario, Chicago, IL 60611
312 573.1370
fax 312 573.1445
page 239

Harlin, Greg
17 Pinewood St, Annapolis, MD 21401
410 266.6550

Harmon, Tracy
25 W 45th St, NYC, NY 10036
212 398.9540

Harness, Cheryl
Six Monterey Ter, Orinda, CA 94563
510 253.9451

Harper, Thomas
9192 Russell Ave, Garden Grove, CA 92644
714 530.5215

Harr, Shane
99 Detering St, Houston, TX 77007
713 863.0202

Harrelson, Pam-ela
2707 Beechmont Dr, Dallas, TX 75228
214 321.6061

Harries, Danny
700 Peden St, Houston, TX 77006
713 523.8102

Harrigan, Peggy
900 W Jackson Blvd, Chicago, IL 60607
312 944.5680

Harrington, Bobbi
4042 Thomas St, Oceanside, CA 92056
310 390.9595

Harrington, Glenn
329 Twin Lear Rd, Pipersville, PA 18947
610 294.8104

Harrington, Richard S
3612 Kemp Dr, Endwell, NY 13760
607 748.7806
fax 607 748.2970
page 233

Harris, Gretchen & Associates
5230 13th Ave S, Mpls, MN 55417
612 822.0650
fax 612 822.0358
pages 258-259

Harris, Jennifer
7134 Glendora, Dallas, TX 75230
214 750.4669

Harris, John
11 Kings Ridge Rd,
Long Valley, NJ 07853
908 813.8718
fax 908 813.0076
page 422

Harrison, Sean
1349 Lexington Ave, NYC, NY 10028
212 369.3831

Harrison, William
501 Fifth Ave, NYC, NY 10017
212 490.2450
fax 212 697.6828
page 47

Harritos, Pete
68 E Franklin St, Dayton, OH 45459
513 433.8383

Harston, Jerry
5732 Skyline Dr, Seven Hills, OH 44131
216 741.4722

Hart, Debbie
253 Park St, Morgantown, WV 26505
304 296.0485

Hart, John
5906 N Moore Ave, Portland, OR 97217
504 289.3477

Hart, Thomas
108 E 35th St, NYC, NY 10016
212 889.3337

Hart, Vikki
780 Bryant St, S.F., CA 94107
415 495.4278

Hartland, Jessie
165 William St, NYC, NY 10038
212 233.1413

Hartmann, Daniel
9801 Royal Ln, Dallas, TX 75231
214 340.2299

Hartmann, Robin
3429 Goldenave, Cincinnati, OH 45226
513 871.3560

Harto, David
101 Yesler Way, Seattle, WA 98104
206 447.1600

Hartsock, Marcia
2233 Kemper Ln, Cincinnati, OH 45206
513 861.1400

Hartstock, Marcia
2233 Kemper Ln, Cincinnati, OH 45206
513 861.1400

Harvill, Kitty
3221 Ozark St, Little Rock, AR 72205
501 661.0508

Harwin, Fred
420 Lexington Ave, NYC, NY 10170
212 697.8525

Harwood, John
c/o Bernstein & Andriulli
60 E 42nd St, NYC, NY 10165
212 682.1490

Hasler, Gino
13630 Muscatine St, Arleta, CA 91331
818 782.1736

Hasselle, Bruce
8691 Heil Ave, Westminster, CA 92683
714 848.2924

Hastings, Ian
211 S Riverview Dr, Amherstburg,
ONT, Canada N9V 3R3
519 734.6276
fax 513 734.6276
page 62

Hatton, Enid
46 Parkway, Fairfield, CT 06430
203 259.3789

Hauser, Barb/Another Girl Rep
PO Box 421443, S.F., CA 94142
415 647.5660
fax 415 285.1102
pages 113-117
Nick Backes, Tracy Britt, Mary Carter,
Lawrence W. Duke, Fred Hilliard, Paul
Kratter, Ed Lindlof, Ben Perini, Miro
Salazar, Marty Smith, Wilfred Spoon,
Judy Unger.

Haverfield, Mary
3104 Cornell Ave, Dallas, TX 75205
214 520.2548

Havlicek, Karel
353 W 53rd St, NYC, NY 10019
212 582.0023

Hawk, Richard
7940 Silverton Ave, San Diego, CA 92126
619 549.8499

Hawkes, Kevin
30 Central Ave, Peaks Island, ME 04108
207 766.5153

Hawthorne House Productions
63 Hawthorne St, Lenox, MA 01240
413 637.4951

Hayden, Charles
20 Church St, Montclair, NJ 07042
201 746.3456

Hayden, Chuck
65 W 55th St, NYC, NY 10019
212 767.0260

Hayes, Cliff
PO Box 1239, Chicago Hts, IL 60411
708 755.7115

Hayes, Colin
PO Box 19412, Seattle, WA 98109
206 634.1880
fax 206 632.2024
page 447

Hayes, John
2145 N Dayton, Chicago, IL 60614
312 787.1333

Hayes, Kathy Associates
131 Spring St, NYC, NY 10012
212 925.4340

Hayes, Stephen F
13400 SW Bay Meadows Ct,
Beaverton, OR 97005
503 524.6726
page 138
Blends strong conceptual ability with
rich, painterly style. Old-world,
European influences. Clients: Tyco,
Georgia Pacific, Human Resources
Effectiveness, Whatman Labsales,
Bloomberg Magazine. Awarded
International Association of Business
Communicators Gold Medal. Published
in Communication Arts.

Haymans, Traci
88 Broad Reach Ct, Savannah, GA 31410
912 897.0902

Haynes, Bryan
Two Farmfield Rd, St Albans, MO 63073
314 451.5115

Haynes, Michael
19050 Fox Run, Pacific, MO 63069
314 458.6894

Hays, Diane
1839 Ninth St, Alameda, CA 94501
510 769.1421

Head Productions
267 Wyckoff St, Brooklyn, NY 11217
718 624.1906

Head, Gary
6023 Wyandotte, Kansas City, MO 64113
816 363.3119

Healy, Deborah
72 Watchung Ave, Upper Montclair, NJ 07043
201 746.2549

Heavner, Becky
202 E Raymond Ave, Alexandria, VA 22301
703 683.1544

Hebert, Doug
2929 Briar Park, Houston, TX 77042
713 784.4141

Hecht, Marilyn
15 Philbrick Rd, Newton, MA 02159
617 969.2299

Hedge, Joanne/Artist Representative
1838 El Cerrito Pl, L.A., CA 90068
213 874.1661
fax 213 874.0136
Award-winning traditional and
computer generated illustration.
Realistic, photorealistic, classical, post-
industrial. Animated products, gutsy
heroes, lively kids! Lush, bright, classy
food, flora, fauna! Quaint, charming,
elegant still-lifes, portraits, tableaus!
Maps. Logos. "Period" reproductions.

Heffron, Joe
3825 E 26th St, Mpls, MN 55406
612 729.1774

Hegelson-Moen, Connie
278 Hwy 105, Lake Mills, IA 50450
515 592.5900

Heimann, Jim
8522 National Blvd, Culver City, CA 90232
310 204.0749

Heindel, Robert
211 E 51st St, NYC, NY 10022
212 755.1365

Heine, Mark
921 First Ave W, Seattle, WA 98119
206 281.0960

Heiner, Joe & Kathy
250 W 57 St, NYC, NY 10107
212 397.7330

Heinz, Joel
211 E Ohio, Chicago, IL 60611
312 527.3283

Heinz-Jenkins, Laurie
2405 NW Thurman St, Portland, OR 97210
503 225.9687

Heinze, Mitch
11440 Oak Dr, Shelbyville, MI 49344
616 672.5756

Hejja, Attila
420 Lexington Ave, NYC, NY 10170
212 986.5680

Hellman Associates Inc
1225 W Fourth St, Waterloo, IA 50702
319 234.7055

Helton, Linda
7000 Meadow Lake, Dallas, TX 75214
214 319.7877
fax 214 319.6063
page 160

Hemingway, Ron
5975 Keller Rd, St Louis, MO 63128
314 849.8952

Henderling, Lisa
232 Madison Ave, NYC, NY 10016
212 889.8777

Henderson, David
420 Lexington Ave, NYC, NY 10170
212 986.5680

Henderson, Hayes
815 Burke St, Winston Salem, NC 27103
910 748.1364

Henderson, Louis
22 E 36th St, NYC, NY 10016
212 685.4580

Hendler, Sandra
1823 Spruce St, Phila, PA 19103
215 735.7380

Hendrix, Gina
1966 California Rd, Pomona, KS 66076
913 746.5465

Hendrix, Reggie
5855 Green Valley Cir, Culver City, CA 90230
310 642.2721

Hennessy, Thomas Illustrations
210 Chapman Rd, Mill Valley, CA 94941
415 388.7959

Henrichsen, Ronda
Six Monterey Ter, Orinda, CA 94563
510 253.9451

Henrie, Cary
1659 E Maple Hills Dr, Bountiful, UT 84010
801 298.2044

Henriquez, Celeste
101 Yesler Way, Seattle, WA 98104
206 447.1600

Henry, Doug
353 W 53rd St, NYC, NY 10019
212 682.2462

Henry, Mike
3400 Aurora Ave, Des Moines, IA 50310
515 279.9478

Herbert, Jonathan Computer Illustration
501 Fifth Ave, NYC, NY 10017
212 490.2450
fax 212 697.6828
page 39

Hering, Al
16 Lown Ct, Poughkeepsie, NY 12603
914 471.7326

Herman, Mark
c/o Carol Chislovsky Design
853 Broadway, NYC, NY 10003
212 677.9100
page 124

Herman, Terry
925 Elm Grove Rd, Elm Grove, WI 53122
414 785.1940

Hernandez, Jorge
1200 83rd St, North Bergen, NJ 07047
201 869.9489

Hersey, John Illustration
330 Sir Francis Drake Blvd,
San Anselmo, CA 94960
415 454.0771
page 154

Hertz, Michael
225 W 34th St, NYC, NY 10122
212 239.4835

Herzberg, Tom
4128 W Eddy, Chicago, IL 60641
312 736.1089
Specialist in realistic traditional black
and white pen illustration and
watercolor rendering. Clients include:
The Washington Post, The Chicago
Tribune, Chicago Magazine, World
Book, The Lincoln Park Zoo, The AMA,
and ABA. Call for samples.

Hess, Lydia J
1246 SE 49th St, Portland, OR 97215
503 234.4757
fax 503 233.1330
page 78
Lydia combines the organic qualities of
stylized scratchboard, with the
convenience of a 4/C digital document.
Traditional techniques incorporated into
Photoshop and Freehand. Clients
include: Nike, Lotus Software, Simpson
Paper, The New York Times and Outside
Magazine.

Hess, Mark
270 Park Ave S, NYC, NY 10010
212 260.6700

Hess, Rob
63 Littlefield Rd, East Greenwich, RI 02818
401 885.0331

Hesse, Laura
325 W Huron, Chicago, IL 60611
312 787.6826

Hewgill, Jody
17 Bellwoods Pl, Toronto, ONT, Canada M6J 3V5
416 601.0301

Hewitson, Jennifer Illustration
1145 Wotan Dr, Encinitas, CA 92024
619 944.6154

Hewitt, Margaret
c/o Liz Sanders Agency,
714 495.3664
fax 714 495.0129
pages 260-261

Hewitt, Margaret
144 Soundview Rd,
Huntington, NY 11743
516 427.1404
fax 516 427.0948

Heyer, Carol
925 E Ave De Los Arboles,
Thousand Oaks, CA 91360
805 492.3683
Specializes in: Children's Books, Science
Fiction, Fantasy Art, Mystery, Religious.
Clients include: TSR, Inc., Ideals, F.X.
Schmid, Sovereign Media, Dell
Magazines. Awards: Prints Regional
Design Annual, IRA/CBC Favorite
Children's Paperbacks, SCBWI Magazine
Merit Award.

Hicks, Brad
3739 Bluff Pl, San Perdo, CA 90731
310 832.2471

Hicks, Richard
127 Peachtree St, Atlanta, GA 30303
404 659.0919

High, Richard
420 Lexington Ave, NYC, NY 10170
212 697.8525

Hildebrand, Sheryl
2115 Marywood Dr, Royal Oak, MI 48073
810 589.7916

Hill, Charlie
7412 Meridian Hills Ct, Indpls, IN 46260
317 257.5417

Hill, Michael
353 W 53rd St, NYC, NY 10019
212 682.2462

Hill, Roger
63A Yorkville Ave, Toronto,
ONT, Canada M5R 1B7
416 923.5933
fax 416 920.4546
page 44

Hill, Roger
501 Fifth Ave, NYC, NY 10017
212 490.2450
fax 212 697.6828
page 44

Hill, Tina Lee
837 W Gregory Blvd, Kansas City, MO 64114
816 361.9827

Hill, Tracy
831 E Belmont, Phoenix, AZ 85020
602 997.7357

Hilliard, Fred
5425 Crystal Springs NE, Bainbridge Is, WA
98110
206 842.6003

Hillman, Betsy
Pier 33 North, S.F., CA 94111
415 391.1181

Himsworth, Jim
731 N 24th St, Phila, PA 19103
215 232.6666

Hines, Jordan
1844 Los Encantos Ct, Los Gatos, CA 95030
408 379.6444

Hines, Norman
719 Flint Way, Sacramento, CA 95818
916 444.6553

Hinlicky, Gregg
158 W 29th St, NYC, NY 10001
212 268.9400

Hinton, Hank
302 N La Brea, L.A., CA 90036
213 655.0998

Hirashima, Jean
166 E 61st St, NYC, NY 10021
212 593.9778

Hirokawa, Masami
3144 W 26th Ave, Denver, CO 80211
303 458.1381

Hirschfeld, Al
122 E 95th St, NYC, NY 10028
212 534.6172

Hitch, David
11 Kings Ridge Rd,
Long Valley, NJ 07853
908 813.8718
fax 908 813.0076
page 422

HK Portfolio
666 Greenwich St, NYC, NY 10014
212 675.5719

Hobbs, Pamela
4222 18th St, S.F., CA 94114
415 255.8080

Hobson, Ken
Three Pineburr Ct, Greensboro, NC 27455
910 282.7789

Hoch & Associates
101 N Wacker Dr, Chicago, IL 60606
312 689.8077

Hodges, Jeanette
12401 Bellwood Rd, Los Alamitos, CA 90720
310 431.4343

Hodges, Ken
12401 Bellwood Rd, Los Alamitos, CA 90720
310 431.4343

Hoey, Peter
1715 15th St, Wash, DC 20009
202 234.2110

Hoff, Terry
1525 Grand Ave, Pacifica, CA 94044
415 359.4081

Hofflund, Sylvia
909 Loma Ave, Long Beach, CA 90804
310 439.4175

Hoffman, Gene
1811 12th St, Greeley, CO 80631
303 351.7991

Hoffman, Kate
PO Box 224, Ft Collins, CO 80522
303 493.1492

Hofkin, Bonnie
NYC, NY
212 581.8338
pages 454-455

Hofkin, Bonnie
18 Mckinley St, Rowayton, CT 06953
203 866.3734
fax 203 857.0842
pages 454-455

Hofmann, Ginnie
108 E 35th St, NYC, NY 10016
212 889.3337

Hofmekler, Ori
1965 Broadway, NYC, NY 10023
212 496.6100

Hogan, Barb
1917 Chase Common Dr, Norcross, GA 30071
404 409.8664

Hogan, Jamie
265 Pleasant Ave,
Peaks Island, ME 04108
207 766.9726
page 290

Hogan, Shannon
715 Marco Pl, Venice, CA 90291
310 821.8131

Hoggan, Pat
Six Monterey Ter, Orinda, CA 94563
510 253.9451

Hogue, Michael
4015 E 53rd St, Tulsa, OK 74135
918 749.9424
fax 918 749.9424
page 77

Hohmann, Pam
2100 W Big Beaver Rd, Troy, MI 48084
810 643.6000

Hokanson/Cichetti
c/o Fran Siegel
515 Madison Ave, Rm 2200, NYC, NY 10022
212 486.9644

Holbrook, Heather
44 Laird Dr, Toronto,
ONT, Canada M4G 3T2
416 467.7098
fax 416 422.0031
page 385

Holder, Jimmy
1507 Columbia Dr, Glendale, CA 91205
818 244.6707

Holewski, Jeff
67 Upper Mountain Ave, Montclair, NJ 07042
201 744.4465

Holladay, Reggie
7395 NW 51st St, Lauderhill, FL 33319
305 749.9031

Holland, Brad
96 Greene St, NYC, NY 10012
212 226.3675

Holland, Gary
Six Monterey Ter, Orinda, CA 94563
510 253.9451

Holland, Mary & Co
6638 N 13th St, Phoenix, AZ 85014
602 263.8990
fax 602 277.0680
pages 328-331

Holley, Jason
852 Monterey Rd, S Pasadena, CA 91030
818 403.0152

Holm, John
353 W 53rd St, NYC, NY 10019
212 582.0023 / 212 682.2462
fax 212 582.0090
pages 177

Holmberg, Irmeli
280 Madison Ave, NYC, NY 10016
212 545.9155

Holmes, Craig
17 SE Third, Portland, OR 97214
503 235.6878

Holmes, David/CIA
c/o Bernstein & Andriulli
60 E 42nd St, NYC, NY 10165
212 682.1490

Holmes, Matthew
8412 Gaylor Way,
Carmichael, CA 95608
916 944.7270
fax 916 944.3830
page 271

Holmes, Nigel
544 Riverside Ave, Westport, CT 06880
203 226.2313
fax 203 222.9545
page 110
Explanation graphics of all kinds:
charts, pictorial maps, diagrams.

Holmgren, Jean
1348 Pidgeon Roost Rd, Byhalia, MS 38611
601 838.5501

Holton Art & Design
1512 W Jonquil Ter, Chicago, IL 60626
312 973.6429

Hom, Check
65 W 55th St, NYC, NY 10019
212 767.0260

Homad, Jewell
c/o Richard Salzman
716 Sanchez St, S.F., CA 94114
415 285.8267

Home Grown Studio
119 N Fourth St, Mpls, MN 55401
612 341.2855

Hong, Min Jae
54 Points of View, Warwick, NY 10990
914 986.8040
fax 914 987.1002
page 206

Hooks, Mitchell
89 Fifth Ave, NYC, NY 10003
212 627.1554

Hooper, Ward P
3000 N Lakeharbor Ln, Boise, ID 83703
208 853.4313

Hopkins, Chris
5018 Sound Ave, Everett, WA 98203
206 347.5613

Hopson, Melissa
2400 McKinney, Dallas, TX 75201
214 747.3122
fax 214 720.0080
page 185

Horjus, Peter
3647 India St, San Diego, CA 92103
619 299.0729

Horne, Daniel
381 Park Ave S, NYC, NY 10016
212 889.2400

Horne, Doug
3435 E Turney Ave, Phoenix, AZ 85018
602 553.8438
page 328

Hornyak, Steve
625 Danube Way, Costa Mesa, CA 92626
714 556.0147

Horridge, Peter/CIA
c/o Bernstein & Andriulli
60 E 42nd St, NYC, NY 10165
212 682.1490

Horusiewicz, Maria
2022 Jones St, S.F., CA 94133
415 928.0457

Hossan, Carole
1122 N Ogden Dr, West Hollywood, CA 90046
213 656.4804

Hoston, Jim
420 Clinton Ave, Brooklyn, NY 11238
718 230.7908

Hot Art
10890 Gold Hill Dr, Grass Valley, CA 95945
916 477.5077

Hot Dog Studios
17-06 Pheasant Hollow Dr, Plainsboro, NJ 08536
609 275.7471

Hotchkiss, Robin
731 N 24th St, Phila, PA 19130
215 232.6666

Houle, Harrison
702 California Ave, Venice Beach, CA 90291
310 822.5587

Hovland, Gary
698 West End Ave, NYC, NY 10025
212 222.9107

Howard, John H
270 Park Ave S, NYC, NY 10010
212 260.6700

Howard, Kim
Six Monterey Ter, Orinda, CA 94563
510 253.9451

Howard, Linda
4045 Lansdowne Ave, Cincinnati, OH 45236
513 891.1967

Howe, Philip
540 First Ave S, Seattle, WA 98104
206 682.3453

Howell, Troy
58 Dobson Ln, Falmouth, VA 22405
703 373.5199

Howell, Van
Box 812, Huntington, NY 11743
516 424.6499

Hrabe, Curt
684 Pleasant Ave, Highland Park, IL 60035
708 432.4632

Hranilovich, Barbara
3422 Ridgefield Rd, Lansing, MI 48906
517 321.2917

Hsu, Deja
3586 Mound Ave, Ventura, CA 93003
805 644.3027

Huber, Cathy Lundeen
1503 Briarknoll Dr, Arden Hills, MN 55112
612 631.8480

Huber, Greg
2409 Clark Ln, Redondo Beach, CA 90278
310 374.8325

Huerta, Catherine
337 W 20th St, NYC, NY 10011
212 627.0031

Huerta, Gerard
54 Old Post Rd, Southport, CT 06490
203 256.1625

Huey, Kenneth
460 N 39th St, Seattle, WA 98103
206 632.3759

Huffaker, Sandy
60 Laurel Ave, Kingston, NJ 08528
609 252.0267

Huffman, Elise A
1473 Redwood Dr, Santa Cruz, CA 95060
408 423.6012

Hugg, Martin
718 Park Ave, Hoboken, NJ 07030
201 420.6304

Hughes Design Group
202 Mill Wharf Plz, Scituate, MA 02066
617 545.0740

Hughes, Marianne
731 N 24th St, Phila, PA 19130
215 232.6666

Hughes, Ralph
6003 Calhoun Dr, Fredericksburg, VA 22407
703 786.5420

Huhn, Tim
324 Acacia St, Altadena, CA 91001
818 791.1287

Huling, Phil
938 Bloomfield St, Hoboken, NJ 07030
201 795.9366

Hull, Cathy
165 E 66th St, NYC, NY 10021
212 772.7743

Hull, John
353 W 53rd St, NYC, NY 10019
212 582.0023

Hull, Richard
Pine Rd HCR, Neversink, NY 12765
914 985.2936

Hull, Scott Associates
68 E Franklin St, Dayton, OH 45459
513 433.8383
fax 513 433.0434
pages 10-11

Hull, Scott Associates
NYC, NY
212 966.3604
pages 10-11

Hulsey, Kevin
666 Bantry Ln, Stone Mtn, GA 30083
404 296.9666

Hume, Kelly
PO Box 10878, Bainbridge, WA 98110
206 780.9000

Hummel, Jim
3023 Delta Rd, San Jose, CA 95135
408 270.2349
fax 408 270.2349
page 408

Humor Associates
21-16 28th St, L.I.C., NY 11105
718 204.6184

Humphries, Michael
11241 Martha Ann Dr, Rossmoor, CA 90720
310 493.3323

Hungry Dog Studio
1361 Markan Ct, Atlanta, GA 30306
404 872.7496

Hunt, Robert
107 Crescent Rd, San Anselmo, CA 94960
415 459.6882

Hunt, Scott
Six Charles St, NYC, NY 10014
212 924.1105

Hunter, Nadine
PO Box 307/80 Wellington Ave, Ross, CA 94957
415 456.7711

Hurd, Jane
351 Pacific St, Brooklyn, NY 11217
212 556.5167

Hussar, Michael
1076 S Ogden Dr, L.A., CA 90019
213 933.2500

Huston, Lance
2958 Greenwich Rd, Glendale, CA 91206
818 956.7021

Hutchison, Bruce
135 Lester Dr, Portland, ME 04103
508 872.4549

Huxtable, John
24548 Tesoro Way, Ramona, CA 92065
619 788.2070

Huynh, Si
921 First Ave N, Seattle, WA 98119
206 281.0960

Huyssen, Roger
54 Old Post Rd, Southport, CT 06490
203 256.9192

Hyde, Bill
751 Matsonia, Foster City, CA 94404
415 345.6955

Hyman, Miles
250 W 57th St, NYC, NY 10107
212 397.7330

Hynes, Robert
5215 Muncaster Mill Rd, Rockville, MD 20855
301 926.7813

Iannaccone, Cynthia
Nine Sandcastle Dr, Rochester, NY 14622
716 288.0868

Ibusuki, James
13053 Beaver St, L.A., CA 91342
818 362.9899

Icard, Reid
1826 Asheville Pl, Charlotte, NC 28203
704 372.6007

Ickert, Tom
354 E 83rd St, NYC, NY 10028
212 794.9723

Icon Graphics Inc
34 Elton St, Rochester, NY 14607
716 271.7020
fax 716 271.7029
page 167

Igarashi, Satoru
NYC, NY
212 741.3848

Ilic, Mirko
652 Hudson St, NYC, NY 10014
212 645.8180

Illustrated Alaskan Moose
Five W Main St, Westerville, OH 43081
614 898.5316

The Independent Pencil
76 State St, Newburyport, MA 01950
508 462.1948

Ingemanson, Donna
82 Central Ave, Braintree, MA 02184
617 848.2012

Ingram, Fred
737 SE Sandy Blvd, Portland, OR 97214
503 235.6885
pages 72-73

The Ink Tank
Two W 47th St, NYC, NY 10036
212 869.1630

Inman, EW
2149 N Kenmore Ave, Chicago, IL 60614
312 525.4955

Innes, Grant
Two Silver Ave, Toronto,
ONT, Canada M6R 3A2
416 530.1500
fax 416 530.1401
page 22

Inouye, Carol
200 Aquetong Rd, New Hope, PA 18938
215 862.2091

Integrity Creations
2433 Cambridge, High Ridge, MO 63049
314 677.4858

Iofin, Michail/GRAPHIKCO
318 21st Ave, S.F., CA 94121
415 386.1984
fax 415 386.1984
page 207

Irwin, Liz
RD One Box 1133, Monhton, PA 19540
610 856.5140

Isip, Jordin
44 Fourth Pl, Brooklyn, NY 11231
718 624.6538

Ito, Joel
505 NW 185th St, Beaverton, OR 97006
503 690.5378

Ivens, Rosalind
156 Prospect Park W, Brooklyn, NY 11215
718 499.8285

The Ivy League of Artists
156 Fifth Ave, NYC, NY 10010
212 243.1333

Iwamoto, Jessica
301 E 75th St, NYC, NY 10021
212 988.9623

Izold, Donald
20475 Bunker Hill Dr, Cleveland, OH 44126
216 333.9988

Izquierdo, Abe Marketing Dsgn
213 W Institute Pl, Chicago, IL 60610
312 787.9784

Jaben, Seth
NYC, NY
212 673.5631
page 199

Jackson, Barry
4118 Beck Ave, Studio City, CA 91604
818 769.7321
page 308

Jackson, Jeff
250 W 57th St, NYC, NY 10107
212 397.7330

The Jacobsen Studio
97 Manzanita Dr, Solvang, CA 93463
805 688.4272

Jacobsen, Ken
1458 W 33rd St, Mpls, MN 55408
612 823.4662

Jacobson, Rick
41 Union Sq W, NYC, NY 10003
212 206.0066

Jacobus, Tim
381 Park Ave S, NYC, NY 10016
212 889.2400

Jaekel, Susan
409 Alberto Way, Los Gatos, CA 95032
408 354.1555

Jake
28 Shelton St, Covent Gdn, London,
England WC2H 9HP
01144 171 240 2077
fax 01144 171 836 0199
page 360

Jakesevic, Nenad
165 E 32nd St, NYC, NY 10016
212 686.3514

Jambor, Nancy
2545 Winfield Ave, Mpls, MN 55422
612 544.6387

James, Bill
420 Lexington Ave, NYC, NY 10170
212 986.5680

James, Bob
68 E Franklin St, Dayton, OH 45459
513 433.8383

James, Odie
49 W 45th St, NYC, NY 10036
212 921.1199

James, Patrick
1452 W 37th St, San Pedro, CA 90731
310 519.1357

Jamieson, Doug
41.08 43rd St, Sunnyside, NY 11104
718 392.0782

Janovitz, Marilyn
41 Union Sq W, NYC, NY 10003
212 727.8330
fax 212 627.2524
Simple, whimsically expressive 'Animal
Characters' lend softsell charm to adult
and children's products/services alike.
Clientele: Avon, Godiva, Nyquil, CTW,
Gear, Hyperion, Newbridge, North
South Books.

Janovsky Illustration
310 E Waltann Ln, Phoenix, AZ 85022
602 863.1633

Janssen, Kim
200 W 51st Ter, Kansas City, MO 64112
816 561.0590

Jareaux, Robin
28 Eliot St, Boston, MA 02130
617 524.3099
fax 617 524.5151
page 111

Jarecka, Danuta
114 E Seventh St, NYC, NY 10009
212 353.3298
page 214

Jarecka, Danuta
c/o Leighton & Co
Four Prospect St, Beverly, MA 01915
508 921.0887
fax 508 921.0223
page 214

Jaroszko, Mike
353 W 53rd St, NYC, NY 10019
212 582.0023 / 212 682.2462
fax 212 582.0090
page 180

Jarvis, David Studio
2533 Chattahoochee Cir, Roswell, GA 30075
404 993.0955

Jarvis, Nathan Young
13307 Park Hills Dr, Grandview, MO 64030
800 765.0617

Jasin, Mark Design
3333 Blake St, Denver, CO 80205
303 295.2728

Jasinski, Terry
20 W Hubbard, Chicago, IL 60610
312 222.1361

Jasper, Jackie
165 E 32nd St, NYC, NY 10016
212 686.3514

Jastrzebski, Zbigniew T
Chicago, IL 60605
312 663.5595

Jauniskis, Ramune
210 Hillside Ave, Needham, MA 02194
617 444.1185
page 368

Javier Romero Design Group
24 E 23rd St, NYC, NY 10010
212 420.0656
fax 212 420.1168
page 287

Jaynes, Bill
12200 Montecito, Seal Beach, CA 90740
310 596.3316

JB Illustration
7726 Noland Rd, Lenexa, KS 66216
913 962.9595

Jeffery, Megan
769 Daniels Farm Rd, Trumbull, CT 06611
203 261.6034

Jeffries, Shannon
1905 Kalorama Rd, Wash, DC 20009
202 234.8958

Jenne, ER
210 N Higgins, Missoula, MT 59802
406 543.5535

Jenny Illustrations
25512 Via Inez Rd, San Juan Capistr, CA 92675
714 443.9603

Jensen, Brian
420 N Fifth St, Mpls, MN 55401
612 339.7055
fax 612 339.8689
page 439

Jermann, Paul
165 N Sycamore Ave, L.A., CA 90036
213 934.4557

Jessell, Tim
c/o Bernstein & Andriulli
60 E 42nd St, NYC, NY 10165
212 682.1490

Jester, Thomas
4309 Belleview Ave, Kansas City, MO 64111
816 753.3134

Jett & Associates
7118 Upper River Rd, Prospect, KY 40059
502 228.9427

Jette, Blaise
12480 SE Wiese Rd, Boring, OR 97009
503 658.7070
fax 503 658.3960
page 99

Jetter, Frances
390 West End Ave, NYC, NY 10024
212 580.3720

Jew, Flora
Six Monterey Ter, Orinda, CA 94563
510 253.9451

Jew, Robert
1770 E Sonoma Dr, Altadena, CA 91001
818 797.6141

Jill Norvell Calligraphy
2123 Cabots Point Ln, Reston, VA 22091
703 264.0600

Jinks, John
27 W 20th St, NYC, NY 10003
212 675.2961

John & Wendy
385 Graham Ave, Brooklyn, NY 11211
718 349.9638

Johnson Reps
1643 W Swallow, Fort Collins, CO 80526
303 223.3027

Johnson, Al
4170 S Arbor Cir, Marietta, GA 30066
404 924.4793

Johnson, Audean
89 Fifth Ave, NYC, NY 10003
212 627.1554

Johnson, Bob
75 Water St, S.F., CA 94133
415 775.3366

Johnson, Brook
Brook Trout Studio, Columbus, OH 43206
800 2.TROUT2

Johnson, Cathy
c/o Bernstein & Andriulli
60 E 42nd St, NYC, NY 10165
212 682.1490

Johnson, Celia
108 E 35th St, NYC, NY 10016
212 889.3337

Johnson, David
299 South Ave, New Canaan, CT 06840
203 966.3269

Johnson, Diane
130 S Kainer Ave, Barrington, IL 60010
708 382.4634

Johnson, Evelyne
201 E 28th St, NYC, NY 10016
212 532.0928

Johnson, Gary
654 Pier Ave, Santa Monica, CA 90405
310 392.4877

Johnson, Lonni Sue
357 West End Ave, NYC, NY 10024
212 873.7749

Johnson, Meredith
5855 Green Valley Cir, Culver City, CA 90230
310 642.2721

Johnson, Osie
2233 Kemper Ln, Cincinnati, OH 45206
513 861.1400

Johnson, Richard/ActualReality
197 Judson Rd, Fairfield, CT 06430
203 254.2413

Johnson, Rick
One S 608 Lambert Rd, Glen Ellyn, IL 60137
708 790.0084

Johnson, Rose
6638 N 13th St, Phoenix, AZ 85014
602 263.8990

Johnson, Scott
10 South Trail, Orinda, CA 94563
510 254.1635

Johnson, Stephen
81 Remsen St, Brooklyn, NY 11201
718 237.2352

Johnston, Scott
244 Ninth St, S.F., CA 94103
415 621.2992

Johnston, Suzy
39 Cranfield Rd, Toronto, ONT,
Canada M4B 3H6
416 285.8905

Johnston, WB
476 College Ave, Winnipeg, MB R2W 1M8
204 582.1686

Johnstone, Anne
77 Liberty Ave, Sommerville, MA 02144
617 666.8120
page 334

Joly, David
15 King St, Putnam, CT 06260
203 928.1042

Jones, Barry
4630 Timberline Rd, Walnutport, PA 18088
610 767.3696

Jones, Buck
4313 65th St, Des Moines, IA 50322
515 278.0379

Jones, Catherine
PO Box 6309, Santa Fe, NM 87502
505 986.8629

Jones, Dan
716 Sanchez St, S.F., CA 94114
415 285.8267
fax 415 285.8268
page 66

Jones, Jan
2232 N Halsted, Chicago, IL 60614
312 929.1851

Jones, Jeff Illustration
7011 N 22nd Way, Phoenix, AZ 85020
602 331.4599
fax 602 331.4799
page 329
For spots that work, ask: Kraft Foods,
Bass Shoes, Ralston Purina, Coors, DuPont,
British Airways, Time Warner or me.

Jones, John Michael
25 Mine St, Flemington, NJ 08822
908 735.4391

Jones, Mary
211 E Ohio, Chicago, IL 60611
312 527.3283

Jones, Michael
1944 N Wilmot, Chicago, IL 60647
312 278.4652

Jones, Michael Scott
1944 N Wilmot, Chicago, IL 60647
312 278.4652

Jones, Randy
153 N 84th St, Seattle, WA 98103
206 782.4348

Jones, Robert
89 Fifth Ave, NYC, NY 10003
212 627.1554

Jones, Steve
654 Pier Ave, Santa Monica, CA 90405
310 392.4877

Jonke, Tim
88 Jefferson Ln, Chicago, IL 60107
708 213.3994

Jordan, Polly
29 Warren Ave, Somerville, MA 02143
617 776.0329

Jorgensen, Donna/Annie Barrett
PO Box 19412, Seattle, WA 98109
206 634.1880
fax 206 632.2024
pages 445-447

Joyce, Tony
853 Broadway, NYC, NY 10003
212 677.9100

Joyner, Eric
227 Kentucky St, Petaluma, CA 94952
707 769.1344

Joyner, Ginny
Six Walnut St, Burlington, VT 05401
802 865.9565

Juhasz, Victor
270 Park Ave S, NYC, NY 10010
212 260.6700

Jung, Rodney
67-14 108th St, Forest Hills, NY 11375
718 544.4278

Just, Alan
520 SW Sixth, Portland, OR 97204
503 228.5853
fax 503 221.4296
page 104

Just, Hal
155 E 38th St, NYC, NY 10016
212 697.6170

Justice Studios Inc
1700 Madison Rd, Cincinnati, OH 45206
513 861.1400

Justinsen, Lars
420 Lexington Ave, NYC, NY 10170
212 697.8525

Jutton, Paul
226 Greeley St, Rochester, NY 14609
716 482.4761

K & K Studios
510 Marquette Ave, Mpls, MN 55402
612 339.0947

Kabaker, Gayle
NYC, NY
212 581.8338
pages 458-459

Kabaker, Gayle
18 McKinley St, Rowayton, CT 06853
203 866.3734
fax 203 857.0842
pages 458-459

Kachik, John
3000 Chestnut Ave, Baltimore, MD 21211
301 467.7916

Kaczman, James
16 Acron Rd, Brookline, MA 02146
617 738.9924
fax 617 738.1585
page 222

Kaczman, James
c/o Leighton & Co
Four Prospect St, Beverly, MA 01915
508 921.0887
fax 508 921.0223
page 222

Kahl, David
551 Observer Hwy, Hoboken, NJ 07030
201 963.7975

Kahn, Jill
4317 Cornelia Cir, Mpls, MN 55435
612 925.1699

Kaji, Nobu
703 Market St, S.F., CA 94103
415 543.4886

Kalish, Lionel
108 E 35th St, NYC, NY 10016
212 889.3337

Kalish, Renee
203 N Wabash, Chicago, IL 60601
312 704.0010

Kalman, Maira
59 W 12th St, NYC, NY 10011
212 735.5577

Kaloustian, Rosanne
208.19 53rd Ave, Bayside, NY 11364
718 428.4670

Kamel, Kathy
806 Hartzell St, Pacific Palisade, CA 90272
310 459.3341

Kamin, Vincent & Associates
111 E Chestnut, Chicago, IL 60611
312 787.8834

Kammerer, Ann
925 Elm Grove Rd, Elm Grove, WI 53122
414 785.1940

Kanai, Kiyoshi
115 E 30th St, NYC, NY 10016
212 679.5542

Kanayama, Nobee
4300 N Narragansett, Chicago, IL 60634
708 670.0912

Kane, John
4300 N Narragansett, Chicago, IL 60634
708 670.0912

Kane, Jude
Nine W Bridge St, New Hope, PA 18938
215 862.0392

Kaneda, Shirley
96 Grand St, NYC, NY 10013
212 226.2670

Kanelous, George
8020 Grenfell St, Kew Gardens, NY 11415
212 688.1080

Kann, Victoria
7118 Upper River Rd, Prospect, KY 40059
502 228.9427

Kanner, Catherine
572 Radcliffe Ave, Pacific Palisade, CA 90272
310 454.7675

Kantor, Barbara
336 Ninth Ave, NYC, NY 10001
212 564.3607

Kaplan, Kari
4901 Broadway, San Antonio, TX 78209
210 822.1336

Kaplan, Mark
374 Fifth St, Brooklyn, NY 11215
718 832.2317

Karapelou, John
731 N 24th St, Phila, PA 19130
215 232.6666

Karas, G Brian
4126 N 34th St, Phoenix, AZ 85018
602 956.5666

Karchin, Steve
211 E 51st St, NYC, NY 10022
212 755.1365

Karl, Kevin
12437 Court Dr, Sunset Hills, MO 63127
314 966.0903

Karpinski, John Eric
PO Box 112, Fredonia, WI 53021
414 692.9354

Karst, Max
320 Tenth St, Suite 3,
Kirkland, WA 98033
206 828.4218
fax 206 828.9457
page 234

Kascht, John
407-A Fourth St SE, Wash, DC 20003
202 546.9527

Kasnot Medical Illustration
9228 N 29th St, Phoenix, AZ 85028
602 482.6501

Kastaris, Harriet & Associates
3301 A S Jefferson St, St Louis, MO 63118
314 773.2600

Kastaris, Rip
3301 A S Jefferson St, St Louis, MO 63118
314 773.2600

Kasun, Mike
405 N Wabash Ave, Chicago, IL 60611
312 321.1336

Katayama, Mits
PO Box 19412, Seattle, WA 98109
206 634.1880
fax 206 632.2024
page 446

Kato, RM
638 S Marengo Ave, Pasadena, CA 91106
818 356.9990

Katsulis, Tom
43 E Ohio St, Chicago, IL 60611
312 527.2244

Katz, Steve
39 Buccaneer St,
Marina Del Ray, CA 90292
310 821.5042
page 425

Kaufman, Donna
3044 Orange Ave, La Crescenta, CA 91214
818 248.7022

Kaufman, Mark
135 W 41st St, NYC, NY 10036
212 221.8090

Kay, Stanford
427 Third St, Brooklyn, NY 11215
718 965.2231

Kearin, Alan
69 Engert Ave, Brooklyn, NY 11222
718 388.6037

Keats, Adrienne Calligraphy
980 Ashbury St, S.F., CA 94117
415 759.5678
Hand-lettering in a variety of
calligraphic styles...Specializing in
personalized invitation designs,
stationery, awards, announcements,
menus and headlines. Call for
information, promo or price list.

Keeter, Susan
666 Greenwich St, NYC, NY 10014
212 675.5719

Kehl, Richard
PO Box 19412, Seattle, WA 98109
206 634.1880

Keleny, Earl
c/o Fran Siegel
515 Madison Ave, Rm 2200, NYC, NY 10022
212 486.9644

Keller, Merle
5855 Green Valley Cir, Culver City, CA 90230
310 642.2721

Keller, Steve
108 E 35th St, NYC, NY 10016
212 889.3337

Kelley, Barbara
280 Madison Ave, NYC, NY 10016
212 545.9155

Kelley, Gary
301 1/2 Main St, Cedar Falls, IA 50613
319 277.2330

Kelley, Patrick
4239 Westchester Dr, Grand Rapids, MI 49546
616 949.0925

Kelley, Susan
301 Claremont Ave, Long Beach, CA 90803
310 434.5843

Kelly, Joan
203 W 107th St, NYC, NY 10025
212 865.0692

Kelly, Rita M
1439 W Sapphire Dr, Hoffman Estates, IL 60195
708 202.8013

Kendall, Brad
217 Slater Ave, Providence, RI 02906
401 351.8017

Kennedy, Anne
666 Greenwich St, NYC, NY 10014
212 675.5719

Kennedy, Dean
Denver, CO 80210
303 733.0128
fax 303 733.8154
page 326

Kennedy, Kelly
1025 Idaho Ave, Santa Monica, CA 90403
310 394.2239

Kennedy, Victor
514 Meadowfield Ct, Lawrenceville, GA 30243
404 339.0345

Kennevan, Steve
2401 Thorndyke Ave, Seattle, WA 98199
206 285.7758

Kern, Michael
449 Santa Fe Dr, Encinitas, CA 92024
619 481.6512

Kest, Kristin
666 Greenwich St, NYC, NY 10014
212 675.5719

Ketler, Ruth Sofair
101 Bluff Ter, Silver Springs, MD 20902
301 593.6059
fax 301 593.1236
page 171

Kettler, Al
1420 Prince St, Alexandria, VA 22314
703 548.8040

Kiefer, Alfons
420 Lexington Ave, NYC, NY 10170
212 986.5680
fax 212 818.1246
page 195

Kihlstrom, Chris
890 Saratoga Rd, Berwyn, PA 19312
610 296.0353

Kilberg, James
8418 Naylor Ave, L.A., CA 90045
310 215.0092

Kilian, Tim
PO Box 19412, Seattle, WA 98109
206 634.1880

Kimball, Anton
820 SE Sandy Blvd, Portland, OR 97214
503 234.4777
fax 503 234.4687
page 364

Kimber, Murray
853 Broadway, NYC, NY 10003
212 677.9100

Kimble, David
220 N Highland, Marfa, TX 79843
915 729.4802

Kimche, Tania
137 Fifth Ave, NYC, NY 10011
212 529.3556

Kimura, Hiro
237 Windsor Pl, Brooklyn, NY 11215
718 788.9866

King, Greg
200 Aquetong Rd, New Hope, PA 18938
215 862.2091
fax 215 862.2641
page 230
Greg King completed assignments in his
pen & ink woodcut style for Hallmark,
Addison Wesley, IBM, Silver Burdett,
Qualex Corporation, Prentice Hall,
Oregon Beer Company and Frito-Lay,
Pizza Inn, Pepsi-Cola, Pepto Bismol,
Stolichnaya Vodka through national
advertising agencies.

King, JD
PO Box 91, Stuyvesant Falls, NY 12174
518 822.0225
fax 518 822.0957
page 276

King, Patty
1337 Honey Trl, Walnut Creek, CA 94596
510 938.7474

Kirchoff/Wohlberg Inc
866 UN Plz, NYC, NY 10017
212 644.2020

Kirk, Daniel
c/o Bernstein & Andriulli
60 E 42nd St, NYC, NY 10165
212 682.1490

Kirk, Rainey
11440 Oak Dr, Shelbyville, MI 49344
616 672.5756

Kirkland, James Ennis
234 Nimitz Ave, Redwood, CA 94061
415 366.2898

Kirkman, Rick
2432 W Peoria Ave, Phoenix, AZ 85061
602 997.6004

Kirsch Represents
122 S Oneida Ave, Rhinelander, WI 54501
213 651.3706

Kitchell, Joyce
2755 Eagle St, San Diego, CA 92103
619 291.1378

Kittelberger, Eric
2960 Stockton St, Akron, OH 44314
216 753.8334

Kiuchi, Tatsuro
37 Overlook Ter, NYC, NY 10033
212 781.7845

Kiwak, Barbara
165 E 32nd St, NYC, NY 10016
212 686.3514

Klanderman, Leland
3286 Ivanhoe, St Louis, MO 63139
314 781.7377

Klare, Tom
PO Box 370561, San Diego, CA 92137
619 565.6167

Klauba, Douglas C
1728 N Damen, Chicago, IL 60647
312 384.4676
fax 312 384.4643
page 256

Kleber, John
Chicago, IL
312 663.5300

Klein, David
408 Seventh St, Brooklyn, NY 11215
718 788.1818

Klein, Hedy
11-56 76th Dr, Forest Hills, NY 11375
718 793.0246
page 95
Conceptual humor/watercolor and line.
Advertising and editorial clients include:
Burson-Marsteller, Grey Advertising,
J.Walter Thompson/Brouillard
Communications, Johnson & Johnson,
Life Savers, Rubbermaid, Sandoz
Pharmeceuticals, United Cerebral Palsy,
Ad Age/Creativity, Family Circle,
Prevention, Macmillan, Scholastic.

Klein, Jane
1635 E 22nd St, Oakland, CA 94606
510 535.0495
fax 510 535.0437
pages 399, 418-419
I: Holly Hanes Carlson, Jannine
Cabossel, Tuko Fujisaki, Chris Peterson,
Paul Young
P: Christian Peacock Photography

Klein, Michael S
22 Edgewood Rd, Madison, NJ 07940
201 765.0623

Klimt, Bill & Maurine
15 W 72nd St, NYC, NY 10023
212 799.2231

Kline, Michael
1106 S Dodge, Wichita, KS 67213
316 264.4112
page 448

Kline, Sandy Art Rep
1816 Banks, Houston, TX 77098
713 522.1862

Klioze-Hughes, Marcia
2409 Andorra Pl, Reston, VA 22091
703 620.4922

Kliros, Thea
60 E 42nd St, NYC, NY 10165
212 682.1490

Klobucar, Nancy
2226 Brier Ave, L.A., CA 90039
213 660.1454

Klug, David
2304 James St, McKeesport, PA 15132
412 754.5584

Kluglein, Karen
37 Cary Rd, Great Neck, NY 11021
212 684.2974

Kluskowski, Darryl
703 W Linden St, Stillwater, MN 55082
612 430.2303

Knaack, Jennifer
427 Hazel St, Oshkosh, WI 54901
414 426.2639

Knaak, Dale
809 N Eighth St, Sheboygan, WI 53081
414 457.1915

Knabel, Lonnie S
8506 Suburban Dr, Orlando, FL 32829
407 381.4226
fax 407 381.0585
Lonnie is a realistic illustrator.
SPECIALTY: People within settings. Exact
likenesses are guaranteed, including
any age, race, or gender. CLIENTS:
Disney, Martin Marietta, Harcourt Brace,
Harper Collins, Viking USA, Prentice
Hall, MCI, Hasbro Inc.

Knable, Ellen & Associates
1233 S La Cienega Blvd, L.A., CA 90035
310 855.8855

Knaff, Jean-Christian
430 Ventura Pl, Vero Beach, MA 32963
407 231.4362

Knecht, Cliff
309 Walnut Rd, Pittsburgh, PA 15202
412 761.5666

Knier, Maria
553 N Wisconsin St,
Port Washington, WI 53074
414 284.3449
fax 414 284.3449
page 365
Conscious collaged conceptual
communication and continuous careful
control counterbalanced with contrasting
crazy contra-cerebral creativity.

Knowles, Philip
847A Second Ave, NYC, NY 10017
212 486.0177

Knox, Berney
11440 Oak Dr, Shelbyville, MI 49344
616 672.5756

Knutsen, Jan
5120 Minnaqua Dr, Golden Valley, MN 55422
612 529.7410

Kocar, George
24213 Lake Rd, Bay Village, OH 44140
216 871.8325

Kocon, John
14 S Halstead St, Allentown, PA 18103
610 770.7550

Koeffler, Ann Represents
5015 Clinton St, L.A., CA 90004
213 957.2327
fax 213 957.1910
pages 316-317

Koegel, Jeff
210 Eighth St, Huntington Beach, CA 92648
714 969.1775

Koehli, Urs
853 Broadway, NYC, NY 10003
212 477.8811

Koelsch, Michael
232 Madison Ave, NYC, NY 10016
212 889.8777

Koerber, Nora
2408 Paloma St, Pasadena, CA 91104
818 791.1953

Koester, Michael
490 Rockside Rd, Cleveland, OH 44131
216 661.4222

Kohler, Keith
3503 Stonewall Pl, Atlanta, GA 30339
404 436.8664

Kolacz, Jerzy
51 Camden St, Toronto, ONT,
Canada M5V 1V2
416 362.1913 / 800 730.8945
fax 416 362.6356
page 153

Kolb, Kathleen
229 Berkely St, Boston, MA 02116
617 266.3858

Kolosta, Darrel
PO Box 2715, Oakland, CA 94602
510 530.5917

Kong, Emilie
11169 Weddington St, Ste 25,
North Hollywood, CA 91601
818 762.5471
fax 818 762.0551
Illustrator/Designer expert in licensed
cartoon characters in b&w and full
color, also new characters designed for
style guides. Clients include The Walt
Disney Co., Warner Brothers,
Ogilvy/Mather, Leisure Concepts and
Dentsu of America.

Konz, Stephen
2837 NW 71st St, Seattle, WA 98117
206 783.4147

Koralik Associates
900 W Jackson Blvd, Chicago, IL 60607
312 944.5680
fax 312 421.5948
pages 90-93
I: **Andy Miller, Ron Wojkovich, Robert**
Lawson, Ron Criswell, Ted Gadecki,
Peggy Harrigan, Ken Tiessen, Andy Zito,
Joe McDermott, Michele Noiset, Karen
Kuchar, Bob Scott, Randal Birkey, Tont
Crnkovich, Rosanne Percivalle, Salem
Kreiger, Joann Daley, Myron Grossman,
Terri Starrett, Chuck Ludeke, Graham
Studios, Lori Nelson Field, Susan Edison,
Jim Lange, Tom Price, Eileen Robinette.

Kordic, Stanka
3301 N Park Blvd, Cleveland Hts, OH 44118
216 321.3009

Kordic, Vladimir
490 Rockside Rd, Cleveland, OH 44131
216 951.4026

Koren, Edward
Pond Vlg, Brookfield, VT 05036
802 276.3103

Koriewicz, Maria
2022 Jones St, S.F., CA 94133
415 928.0457

Korn, Pamela
PO Box 521, Canadensis, PA 18325
717 595.9298

Korody, Jamie/FEP Inc
350 E Rustic Rd, Santa Monica, CA 90402
310 459.9984

Kortendick, Susan
2611 Eastwood Ave, Evanston, IL 60201
708 864.6062

Koslow, Howard
1592 Goldspire Rd, Toms River, NJ 08755
908 473.1847

Kossin, Sanford
25 W 45th St, NYC, NY 10036
212 398.9540

Koster, Aaron
Two Yeoman Way, Englishtown, NJ 07726
908 536.2815

Kotik, Kenneth
Nine Last Chance Ct,
St Peters, MO 63376
314 441.1091
page 374

Kotzky, Brian
89 Fifth Ave, NYC, NY 10003
212 627.1554

Koury, Jennifer
19 Crystal Springs Rd, San Mateo, CA 94402
310 640.8258

Kovalcik, Terry
80 Eighth Ave, NYC, NY 10011
212 620.7772

Kowalski, Mike
3033 13th Ave W, Seattle, WA 98119
206 284.4701

Kowitt, Holly
405 N Wabash, Chicago, IL 60611
312 321.1336

Koz-Art
22214 Greekview Dr, Gaithersburg, MD 20882
301 921.6345

Kozmiuk, Michael
353 W 53rd St, NYC, NY 10019
212 682.2462

Kramer, Dave
3100 Carlisle, Dallas, TX 75204
214 871.0080

Kramer, Moline
654 Pier Ave, Santa Monica, CA 90405
310 392.4877

Kramer, Peter
c/o Bernstein & Andriulli
60 E 42nd St, NYC, NY 10165
212 682.1490

Krantz, Kathy
Pine Rd HCR, Neversink, NY 12765
914 985.2936

Kratter, Paul
c/o Barb Hauser
PO Box 421443, S.F., CA 94142
415 647.5660
fax 415 285.1102
page 116
Realistic acrylic and watercolor paintings.
All subjects with a specialty in wildlife.

Kraus, James F / Art Guy Studios
195 W Canton St, Boston, MA 02116
617 437.1945
pages 24-25

Kreiger, Salem
91 Park Ave, Hoboken, NJ 07030
201 963.3754

Krejca, Gary
1203 S Ash Ave, Tempe, AZ 85281
602 829.0946

Krepel, Dick
211 E 51st St, NYC, NY 10022
212 755.1365

Kress, Kurt
735 Pearl St, Laguna Beach, CA 92651
714 494.5101

Kressley, Michael
67 Brookside Ave, Boston, MA 02130
617 522.5132

Kretschmann, Karin
1052 Laura St, Casselberry, FL 32707
407 699.6919

Kretzschmar, Art
67 Upper Mountain Ave, Montclair, NJ 07042
201 744.4465

Kriegshauser, Shannon
12421 W Grafelman Rd, Hanna City, IL 61536
309 565.7110

Krimzer, Herb
1125 Landwehr Rd, Northbrook, IL 60062
708 498.8936

Krizmanic, Tatjana
250 Spinnaker Dr, Halifax, NS,
Canada B3N 3E4
902 477.2117

Krogle, Robert
10835 W Cougar Gulch Rd,
Coeurd'aleine, ID 83814
800 653.6536

Krommes, Beth
310 Old Street Rd, Peterborough, NH 03458
603 924.8790

Kronen, Jeff
5855 Green Valley Cir, Culver City, CA 90230
310 642.2721

Krovatin, Dan
Three Woodbury Rd, Trenton, NJ 08638
609 895.1634

Krudop, Walter Lyon
246 W 73rd St, NYC, NY 10023
212 769.3819

Krueger, Brian
2233 Kemper Ln, Cincinnati, OH 45206
513 861.1400

Kubinyi, Laszlo
108 E 35th St, NYC, NY 10016
212 889.3337

Kuchar, Karen
900 W Jackson Blvd, Chicago, IL 60607
312 944.5680

Kuehnel, Peter & Associates
30 E Huron Plz, Chicago, IL 60611
312 642.6499

Kueker, Donald L
829 Ginger Wood Ct, Manchester, MO 63021
314 225.1566

Kuhn, Grant M
233 Bergen St, Brooklyn, NY 11217
718 596.7808

Kulihin, Victor
714 Sheridan Ave, Plainfield, NJ 07060
908 757.4678

Kulman, Andrew
58 W 15th St, NYC, NY 10011
212 741.2539

Kung, Lingta
420 Lexington Ave, NYC, NY 10170
212 697.8525

Kunze, Helen
1800 S Maple, Carthage, MO 64836
417 359.5233
page 192

Kuper, Peter
250 W 99th St, NYC, NY 10025
212 864.5729

Kupper, Ketti
151 Southworth St, Milford, CT 06460
203 874.7082

Kurlansky, Sharon
192 Southville Rd, Southborough, MA 01772
508 872.4549

Kurrasch, Toni
1928 N Beverly Glen, L.A., CA 90077
310 474.1776

Kurtz, Mara
322 Central Park W, NYC, NY 10025
212 666.1453
fax 212 666.1454
Collages by hand based on original
images, photo illustrations, hand-tinted
photographs. Regularly, New York
Times Magazine Styles page. Also, Body
Shop, Family Life, Metropolis. Awards:
AIGA, Creativity, Graphis, Print, Society
of Illustrators, SPD.

Kustera, Carter
One Orchard St, NYC, NY 10002
212 226.1541

Kwan, Jonny C
2762 Vista Arroyo Dr, Camarillo, CA 93010
805 491.3731

Kwong, Amy
PO Box 23803, Pleasant Hill, CA 94523
510 687.4053

Kylberg, Virginia
14 Midhill Dr, Mill Valley, CA 94941
415 332.7443

Kyllo, James
PO Box 222946, Carmel, CA 93922
408 625.6176

L'Hommedieu, Arthur
578 11th St, Brooklyn, NY 11215
718 499.7339

La Fever, Greg
68 E Franklin St, Dayton, OH 45459
513 433.8383

La Fleur, Dave
9121 E 79th S, Derby, KS 67037
316 788.0253

Laan, Cor
414 Crest Dr, Redwood City, CA 94062
415 365.0953

Labadie, Ed
2402 W Jefferson St, Boise, ID 83702
208 388.0411

Labbe, Jeff M
218 Princeton Ave, Claremont, CA 91711
909 621.6678

Labbe, John
97 Third Ave, NYC, NY 10003
212 529.2831

Lachapelle Representation Ltd
420 E 54th St, NYC, NY 10022
212 838.3170

Lack, Don
216 Sunnyside Rd, Temple Terrace, FL 33617
813 989.0079

Lackner, Paul
422 Second St SE, Waverly, IA 50677
319 352.5689

Lackow, Andy
135 Mamanasco Rd, Ridgefield, CT 06877
203 431.7980

LaCuesta, Karen
495 Carolina St, S.F., CA 94107
415 863.4969

Lada, Elizabeth
c/o Bruck&Moss
333 E 49th St, NYC, NY 10017
212 980.8061

Ladas, George
157 Prince St, NYC, NY 10012
212 673.2208

Ladden, Randee
7445 N Rockwell St, Chicago, IL 60645
312 761.6288

Laden, Nina
1517 McLendon Ave NE,
Atlanta, GA 30307
404 371.0052
Award-winning author/illustrator of
children's books:
The Night I Followed The Dog
Private I. Guana
Pastel, other media. Call for samples.

LaFave, Kim
121 Lyall Ave, Toronto, ONT,
Canada M4E 1W6
416 691.3242
fax 416 691.4113
page 202
Mediums include: scratchboard,
watercolour, pen & ink, and acrylic.
Clients include: Bates, BBDO, Ogilvy &
Mather, MacLaren: LINTAS; American
Express, Digital, Everfresh Beverages,
Lever Brothers, National 4 H Council,
Noranda, Royal Trust, and U.S. Mint

Lafrance, Laurie
c/o Vicki Morgan
194 Third Ave, NYC, NY 10003
212 475.0440

Laird, Campbell
162 E 23rd St, NYC, NY 10010
212 505.5552

Laish, James
55 Charles St W, Toronto, ONT,
Canada M5S 2W9
416 921.1709

Lally, Michelle
345 California Dr, Burlingame, CA 94010
310 556.1439

LaMantia Studio
820 W Howe St, Bloomington, IN 47403
812 332.2667

Lamar, Laura
302 23rd Ave, S.F., CA 94121
415 750.1333

Lambase, Barbara
5400 Calle De Arboles, Torrance, CA 90503
310 373.4993

Lambert, John
1911 E Robin Hood Ln, Arlington Hts, IL 60004
708 392.6349

Lambrenos, Jim
12 Salem Ct, Atco, NJ 08004
609 768.0580

Lamut, Sonja
165 E 32nd St, NYC, NY 10016
212 686.3514

Lander, Ben Dann
4212 Linden Hill Blvd, Mpls, MN 55410
612 927.9095
page 405

Landers, Roberta Holmes
Six Monterey Ter, Orinda, CA 94563
510 253.9451

Landon, Lucinda
26 Tucker Hollow Rd, North Scituate, RI 02857
401 647.7346

Lane, Patricia
54 Preston Rd, Somerville, MA 02143
617 776.4150

Lane, Robert
6711 East Ave, Chevy Chase, MD 20815
301 215.6674

Lane, Tammie
413 Independence Pl, Aspen, CO 81611
303 925.9213

Lang, Donna Illustration
564 Madrone Ave, Sunnyvale, CA 94086
408 730.8511

Lange, Andrew
213 Fairmont Ave, Hackensack, NJ 07601
201 646.9210

Lange, Jim
900 W Jackson Blvd, Chicago, IL 60607
312 944.5680

Langenderfer, Tim
Ten E Ontario St, Chicago, IL 60611
312 573.1370

Langer, DC
77 Pond Ave, Brookline, MA 02146
617 566.6644

Langer, Jean-Claude
716 Sanchez St, S.F., CA 94114
415 285.8267

Langley, Sharon Artist Representative
4300 N Naragansett, Chicago, IL 60634
708 670.0912

Langley, Stephanie
PO Box 19412, Seattle, WA 98109
206 634.1880
fax 206 632.2024
page 445

Langley, William A
300 Tyler St, Pittsfield, MA 01201
413 443.8108

Langsdorf, Henrik
167 Ave A, NYC, NY 10009
212 505.8713

Languedoc, Patricia
850 Highlands Dr, Santa Barbara, CA 93109
805 962.4072

Lanino, Deborah
170 W 23rd St, NYC, NY 10011
212 366.7212

Lapinski, Joe
853 Broadway, NYC, NY 10003
212 677.9100

LaPorte, Michele
579 Tenth St, Brooklyn, NY 11215
718 499.2178

Lapsley, Bob Studio
2430 Glen Haven Blvd, Houston, TX 77030
713 667.4393

Lardy, Philippe
478 W Broadway, NYC, NY 10012
212 473.3057

Larkin, Mary
220 E 57th St, NYC, NY 10022
212 832.8116

Larsen, Tracy
920 SE Third Ter, Lees Summit, MO 64063
816 524.6949

Larson, Gary
4900 Main St, Kansas City, MO 64112
816 932.6713

Larson, Ron
940 N Highland Ave, L.A., CA 90038
213 465.8451

Larson, Seth
1435 Wagar Ave, Lakewood, OH 44107
216 228.2172

Lasher, Mary Ann
c/o Bernstein & Andriulli
60 E 42nd St, NYC, NY 10165
212 682.1490

Laslo, Rudy
89 Fifth Ave, NYC, NY 10003
212 627.1554

Laub, Rolf
4101 Greenbriar, Houston, TX 77098
713 522.9873

Laumann, Scott
402 Avenida Adobe, Escondido, CA 92029
619 743.3910

Lautenslager, Peter
Eight Maple St, Pittsford, NY 14534
716 264.1340

Lavaty, Frank & Jeff
217 E 86 St, NYC, NY 10022
212 355.0910

Lawrence, John
c/o Bernstein & Andriulli
60 E 42nd St, NYC, NY 10165
212 682.1490

Lawson, Robert
900 W Jackson Blvd, Chicago, IL 60607
312 944.5680

Lax Syntax
19 Los Amigos Ct, Orinda, CA 94563
510 253.3131

Lazarus, Robin/Medical Illustration Co
814 Edgewood Dr, Westbury, NY 11590
516 338.0636

Leah, Bonnie Lettering & Design
19351 Sunray Ln, Huntington Beach, CA 92648
800 538.4718

Leary, Catherine
11936 W Jefferson Blvd, Culver City, CA 90230
310 390.8663

Lebbad, James A
24 Independence Way, Titusville, NJ 08560
609 737.3458

Lebel, Ed
5626 Del Ridge Way, Seattle, WA 98106
206 722.4694

Lebenson, Richard
253 Washington Ave, Brooklyn, NY 11205
718 857.9267

Lebo, Narda
911 Thomasson, New Hope, PA 75208
215 862.2091

Lederman, Marsha
107 N Columbus St, Arlington, VA 22203
703 243.5636

Lee, Bill
792 Columbus Ave, NYC, NY 10025
212 866.5664

Lee, Bryce
158 W 29th St, NYC, NY 10001
212 268.9400

Lee, Dom
666 UN Plz, NYC, NY 10017
212 644.2020

Lee, Eric JW
c/o Bernstein & Andriulli
60 E 42nd St, NYC, NY 10165
212 953.7088

Lee, Fran
1911 W Winona, Chicago, IL 60640
312 769.6566

Lee, Jared D
2942 Hamilton Rd, Lebanon, OH 45036
513 932.2154

Lee, Lace
2233 Kemper Ln, Cincinnati, OH 45206
513 861.1400

Lee, Michael
5855 Green Valley Cir, Culver City, CA 90230
310 642.2721

Lee, Paul
5818 1/2 N Figueroa, L.A., CA 90042
213 257.5618

Lee, Steve
200 W 51st Ter, Kansas City, MO 64112
816 561.0590

Lee, Tim
1715 Brantford Dr, Atlanta, GA 30084
404 938.8829

Leech, Dorothy
1024 Sixth Ave, NYC, NY 10018
212 354.6641

Leech, Jeanine
6347 Helen St, Library, PA 15129
412 854.6917

Leech, Kent
716 Montgomery St, S.F., CA 94111
415 433.1222
fax 415 433.9560
page 400

Leer, Rebecca
440 West End Ave, NYC, NY 10024
212 595.5865

Lefebvre, Renae
206 N First St, Mpls, MN 55401
612 332.2361

Leff, Jerry Associates
420 Lexington Ave, NYC, NY 10170
212 697.8525
page 28

Lefkowitz, Mark
132 Oakhill Dr, Sharon, MA 02067
617 784.5293

Lehman, Connie
218 S Banner St, Elizabeth, CO 80107
303 646.4638

Lehmen/Dabney
1431 35th Ave S, Seattle, WA 98144
206 325.8595

Lehner & Whyte Inc
Eight-Ten S Fullerton Ave, Montclair, NJ 07042
201 746.1335

Leib, Vikki
101 Yesler Way, Seattle, WA 98104
206 447.1600

Leigh, LeeAnn
2304 Rosemary, Simi Valley, CA 93065
805 527.8955

Leighton & Co
Four Prospect St, Beverly, MA 01915
508 921.0887
fax 508 921.0223
pages 211-223
I: **Steve Atkinson, John Breakey, Linda**
Bronson, Tony DeLuz, Laura DeSantis,
Robert Evans, Joe Farnham, Frank
Frisari, Daruta Jarecka, James Kaczman,
Lisa Manning, Steve Meek, Scott Nash,
Bruce Sanders, Rod Savely, August Stein,
Steve Stankiewicz, Jennifer Thermes.

Leiner, Alan
353 W 53rd St, NYC, NY 10019
212 682.2462

Leister, Bryan
202 E Raymond Ave, Alexandria, VA 22301
703 683.1544

Leleu, Lisa
25 W 45th St, NYC, NY 10036
212 398.9540

Lemant, Albert
666 Greenwich St, NYC, NY 10014
212 675.5719

Lempa, Mary Flock
194 Olmsted, Riverside, IL 60546
708 447.4454

Lendway, Andy
731 N 24th St, Phila, PA 19130
215 232.6666
fax 215 232.6585
page 132

Lengyel, Kathy
2306 Jones Dr, Dunedin, FL 34698
813 734.1382

Lensch, Chris
209 Ford St, Golden, CO 80401
303 279.8304
fax 303 278.6446
page 413

Leon, Karen
154-01 Barclay Ave, Flushing, NY 11355
718 461.2050

Leon, Thomas
314 N Mission Dr, San Gabriel, CA 91775
818 458.7699

Leonard, Alex
67 Upper Mountain Ave, Montclair, NJ 07042
201 744.4465

Leonardo, Todd
1625 Purdue St, San Leonardo, CA 94579
510 351.3815

Leong, Shelton
580 Washington, S.F., CA 94111
415 362.8280

Leopold, Susan
250 W 57th St, NYC, NY 10107
212 397.7330
fax 212 397.7334
page 241

Lesh, David
5693 N Meridian St, Indpls, IN 46208
317 253.3141
fax 317 255.8462
pages 456-457

Lesh, David
18 McKinley St, Rowayton, CT 06853
203 866.3734
fax 203 857.0842
pages 456-457

Lesh, David
NYC, NY
212 581.8338
pages 456-457

Lessard, Marie
4641 Hutchison, Montreal, QU, Canada H2V 4A2
514 272.5696

Lesser, Ron
420 Lexington Ave, NYC, NY 10170
212 697.8525

Lester, Michelle
15 W 17th St, NYC, NY 10011
212 989.1411

Lester, Mike
17 E Third Ave, Rome, GA 30161
706 234.7733

Letostak, John
7801 Fernhill Ave, Parma, OH 44129
216 885.1753

Levin, Arnie
23 Glenlawn Ave, Seacliff, NY 11579
516 676.1228

Levin, Sergio
67 Upper Mountain Ave, Montclair, NJ 07042
201 744.4465

Levine, Bette
c/o Bernstein & Andriulli
60 E 42nd St, NYC, NY 10165
212 682.1490

Levine, Laura
444 Broome St, NYC, NY 10013
212 431.4787

Levine, Lucinda
2604 Connecticut Ave NW, Wash, DC 20008
202 667.5365

Levine, Marsha
PO Box 456/Rambler Rd, Lincolndale, NY 10540
914 248.4639

Levine, Ned
301 Frankel Blvd, Merrick, NY 11566
516 378.8122

Levinson, David
86 Parson Rd, Clifton, NJ 07012
201 614.1627

Levinson, Jason
11625 Sun Cir Way, Columbia, MD 21044
410 720.1004

Levirne, Joel
203 Mountain Ave, Hawthorne, NJ 07506
212 727.9277

Lewis, HB
16 Canonchet Rd, Hope Valley, RI 02832
401 539.8761

Lewis, Maribeth
838 Cedar St, #G, Alameda, CA 94501
510 521.9715
fax 510 521.9715
Advertising illustration, comps, storyboards, color or B&W. Acrylics, markers, colored pencil, pen & ink and coquille. Call today to receive samples of past work for your files!

Lewis, Maurice
353 W 53rd St, NYC, NY 10019
212 582.0023

Lewis, Ray
4575 Murat Ct, San Diego, CA 92117
619 270.9680

Lewis, Stacey
225 S 18th St, Phila, PA 19103
215 545.5614

Leyonmark, Roger
3476 S Creek Rd, Hamburg, NY 14075
716 648.0335

Liaw, Anson
39 Cranfield Rd, Toronto, ONT,
Canada M4B 3H6
416 285.8905

Lickona, Cheryl
210 E 63rd St, NYC, NY 10021
212 688.2562

Lieberman, Ron
109 W 28th St, NYC, NY 10001
212 947.0653

Liepke, Skip
30 W 72nd St, NYC, NY 10023
212 724.5593

Ligasan, Darryl
151 E 31st St, NYC, NY 10016
212 889.5020

Lilie, Jim
110 Sutter St, S.F., CA 94104
415 441.4384
fax 415 395.9809
page 1

Lilly, Don
2031 N Maple St, Burbank, CA 91505
818 843.2565

Lindgren & Smith
250 W 57th St, NYC, NY 10107
212 397.7330
fax 212 397.7334
pages 241-254

Lindgren & Smith
Chicago, IL
312 819.0880
pages 241-254

Lindgren & Smith
S.F., CA
415 788.8552
pages 241-254

Lindgren, Cindy
4957 Oliver Ave S, Mpls, MN 55409
612 929.0657

Lindholm, Anders
c/o Bernstein & Andriulli
60 E 42nd St, NYC, NY 10165
212 682.1490

Lindlof, Ed
603 Carolyn Ave, Austin, TX 78705
512 472.0195

Ling, Lauren
309 Walnut Rd, Pittsburgh, PA 15202
412 761.5666

Link
Two Silver Ave, Toronto, ONT,
Canada M6R 3A2
416 530.1500
fax 416 530.1401
pages 18-23

Linley, Michael Illustration
1504 W First Ave, Columbus, OH 43212
614 486.2921

Lippman, Miriam
159 President St, Brooklyn, NY 11231
718 722.7465

Lisker, Emily
PO Box 781, Woonsocket, RI 02895
401 762.2502

Litman, Bruce
1514 Magee Ave, Phila, PA 19149
215 744.7442

Litterio, Ray
67 Upper Mountain Ave, Montclair, NJ 07042
201 744.4465

Little Apple Art
409 Sixth Ave, Brooklyn, NY 11215
718 499.7045

Little, Ed
112 Wewaka Brook Rd, Bridgewater, CT 06752
203 350.6523

Littmann, Barry
57 Overlook Dr, Hackettstown, NJ 07840
908 850.4405

Litzinger, Roseanne
Six Monterey Ter, Orinda, CA 94563
510 253.9451

Liu Illustration
2724 Muscatello St, Orlando, FL 32837
407 438.3685

Livingston, Francis
19 Brookmont Cir, San Anselmo, CA 94960
415 456.7103

Livingston, Lourdes
240 Scott St, S.F., CA 94117
415 252.7449

Lloyd, Mary Anne
147 Wolcott St, Portland, ME 04102
207 773.4987
fax 207 773.5362
page 129
Clients include MS Magazine, The New York Times, Nickelodeon Cable Television, Stride Rite Corp. and Timex

LM Pollack Studios
3319 SW First Ave, Portland, OR 97201
503 228.1658

Lochray, Tom
3225 Oakland Ave S, Mpls, MN 55407
612 823.7630

Locke, Gary
1005 Woodruff Bldg, Springfield, MO 65806
417 866.2885

Locke, John Studios
15 E 76th St, NYC, NY 10021
212 288.8010

Lulu
4645 Colfax Ave S, Mpls, MN 55409
612 825.7564
pages 6-7, 304, 418

Lund, David
14721 Bear Creek Ln NE, Woodinville, WA 98072
206 881.3609

Lund, Jonathan
709 Wellesley Ave, Akron, OH 44303
216 864.1762

Lundeen, Cathy
Mpls, MN
612 343.0432

Lundgren, Tim
165 E 32nd St, NYC, NY 10016
212 686.3514

Lunsford, Annie
515 N Hudson St, Arlington, VA 22201
703 527.7696

Lutler, Peggy
13 N Fourth Ave, Winneconne, WI 54986
414 582.8666

Lutnicki, Ann
17417 Comet Cir, Mpls, MN 55345
612 475.1746

Lutzow, Jack A
83 Walnut Ave, Corte Madera, CA 94925
415 924.7881

Lux, Frank & Associates Inc
20 W Hubbard, Chicago, IL 60610
312 222.1361

Lyall, Dennis
89 Fifth Ave, NYC, NY 10003
212 627.1554

Lyhus, Randy
4853 Cordell Ave, Bethesda, MD 20814
301 986.0036
page 64

Lyles, L Kelly
5029 26th Ave SW, Seattle, WA 98106
206 937.2058

Lynch, Alan Artists
11 Kings Ridge Rd,
Long Valley, NJ 07853
908 813.8718
fax 908 813.0076
pages 420-423
Martin Andrews, Michael Armson,
Azpiri, Colin Backhouse, Peter Brown,
Amy Burch, Jim Burns, Nigel
Chamberlain, John Clementson, Brigid
Collins, Elaine Cox, Gordon Crabb,
Merritt Dekle, Gavin Dunn, Les Edwards,
Max Ellis, Faranak, Peter Goodfellow,
Peter Gudynas, John Harris, Matilda
Harrisson, Wendy Hoile, Philip Hood,
John Howe, Stephen Lavis, Diana
Leadbetter, Andy Lovell, Diane Lumley,
Paul McLaughlin, Milo Manara, Edward
Miller, Monica, Terry Oakes, Mark
Oldroyd, Harvey Parker, Liane Payne,
Miguel Angelo Prado, Tony Roberts, Luis
Royo, Vincente Segrelles, Philip Stanton,
Lee Stannard, Brian Sweet, Len
Thurston, Daniel Torres, Jenny Tylden-
Wright, Jim Warren, Tim White, David
Williams, Tracey Wilson, Rosemary
Woods, Janet Woolley, Paul Wright

Lynch, Andrea
5521 Greenville Ave, Dallas, TX 75206
214 369.6990
page 236

Lynch, Bob
138 W 25th St, Baltimore, MD 21218
410 366.6535
fax 410 366.6535
page 403

Lynch, Jeff
420 Lexington Ave, NYC, NY 10170
212 986.5680

Lynn, Kathy
330 W Springfield Ave, Phila, PA 19118
215 242.9165

Lyons, Claudia
39 Starbuck Dr,
Sausalito, CA 94965-9716
415 383.2876
Highly detailed realistic illustrations
including the areas of food, high tech,
people, automotive, animals and
product illustration.

Lytle, John
PO Box 5155, Sonora, CA 95370
209 928.4849

Lyubner, Boris
9015 Flint Way, Park City, UT 84098
801 649.2129
fax 801 649.8803
pages 58-59

Ma, Tom
Eight Wells Hill Ave, Toronto, ONT,
Canada M5R 3A6
416 535.9178

Mably, Greg
52 Saguenay Ave, Toronto, ONT,
Canada M5N 2Y7
416 784.3576

Macanga, Steve
20 Morgantine Rd, Roseland, NJ 07068
201 403.8967

MacDonald, Greg
PO Box 19412, Seattle, WA 98109
206 634.1880

MacDonald, John
PO Box 355,
Cherry Valley, NY 13320-0355
607 264.3699
fax 607 264.3699
B&W and color scratchboard: Macintosh
equipped. Clients include Citibank, General
Electric, The Wall Street Journal, The
Washington Post, Money Magazine, The
Los Angeles Times, National Geographic
Society, and American Heritage.

MacDonald, Ross
189 Franklin St, NYC, NY 10013
212 966.2446

Maceren, Jude
92 Kossuth St, Piscataway, NJ 08854
908 752.5931

Mach, Steven
87 E Elm, Chicago, IL 60611
312 280.0071

Maclachlan, Neil
45 Earswich Dr, Toronto, ONT,
Canada M1E 1C7
416 269.8141
fax 416 269.8959
page 395

MacLeod, Ainslie
111 Third Ave, NYC, NY 10003
212 533.9045

MacLeod, Lee
Rte Seven Box 129.3, Sante Fe, NM 87505
505 982.8744

MacNeill & Macintosh
74 York St, Lambertville, NJ 08530
609 397.4631
fax 609 397.9082
page 377

MacNicol, Gregory
732 Chestnut St, Santa Cruz, CA 95060
408 459.0880

Madan, Dev
2814 NW Golden Dr, Seattle, WA 98117
206.789.2601

Madcap Creations
777 Silver Spur Rd, Rolling Hills Es, CA 90274
310 544.4825

Maddock Douglas
257 N West Ave, Elmhurst, IL 60126
708 279.3939

Maddox, Kelly
2513 Wilson Woods Dr, Decatur, GA 30033
404 315.0377

Madill, Warren
28 Shelton St, Covent Gdn, London,
England WC2H 9HP
011 44 171 240 2077
fax 011 44 171 836 0199
page 360

Maffia, Daniel
236 S Dwight Pl, Englewood, NJ 07631
201 871.0435

Magadia, Farley
13984 Hubbard St, Sylmar, CA 91342
818 365.5794

Magee, Alan
Rte 68 Box 132, Cushing, ME 04563
207 354.8838

Maggard III, John P
102 Marian, Terrace Park, OH 45174
513 248.1550

Magiera, Rob
520 N Michigan Ave, Chicago, IL 60611
312 527.0351

Magovern, Peg
Pier 33 N, S.F., CA 94111
415 956.4750

Magsig, Steve
2100 W Big Beaver Rd, Troy, MI 48084
810 643.6000

Mahan, Benton
PO Box 66, Chesterville, OH 43317
419 768.2204

Mahon, Rich
L.A., CA
310 396.1213

Mahoney, JF
1170 Camelia St, Berkeley, CA 94702
510 524.5795

Mahoney, Katherine
60 Hurd Rd, Belmont, MA 02178
617 868.7877
page 209

Mahoney, Kit Hevron
2682 S Newport St, Denver, CO 80224
303 757.0689
fax 303 757.0689
page 373
Kit specializes in representational
illustration and paintings rendered
primarily in pastel. In addition to
illustration, her skills include graphic
design and computer-based imaging.

Mahoney, Patricia
Pier 33 N, S.F., CA 94111
415 956.4750

Mahoney, Ron
353 W 53rd St, NYC, NY 10019
212 582.0023 / 212 682.2462
fax 212 582.0090
page 182

Maioresco, Daniela Wanda
510 Main St, NYC, NY 10044
212 838.2509

Mair, Jacqueline/CIA
c/o Bernstein & Andriulli
60 E 42nd St, NYC, NY 10165
212 682.1490

Maisner, Bernard
108 E 35th St, NYC, NY 10016
212 889.3337

Majlessi, Heda
1616 Summit Ave, Seattle, WA 98122
206 323.2694

Mak, Kam
369 Sackett St, Brooklyn, NY 11231
718 624.6173

Mallouf, Christine
4206 Franklin Ave, L.A., CA 90027
213 664.4674

Maloney, Tom
307 N Michigan Ave, Chicago, IL 60601
312 704.0500
fax 312 704.0501
pages 162-165, 402

Maloney, Vicki
2965 Mary St, Coconut Grove, FL 33133
305 567.0311

Mamrose, Sharon
9598 Leatherwood Ln, Douglasville, GA 30135
404 949.6349

Manasse, Michèle
200 Aquetong Rd, New Hope, PA 18938
215 862.2091
fax 215 862.2641
pages 225-232
Mike Reagan, Terry Widener, Maxine
Boll, Sheldon Greenberg, Eric Dever,
Greg King, Carol Inouye, Geneviève
Claire, Jacques Cournoyer.

Manchess, Greg
7910 C Moulins Dr, Dayton, OH 45459
513 439.5990

Manda, Antonia
6215 SE 22nd St, Portland, OR 97202
503 236.5826

Mandel, Bette
265 E 66th St, NYC, NY 10021
212 737.5062

Manders, John
6058 Stanton Ave, Pittsburgh, PA 15206
412 362.6580

Mandio, Meridee
5855 Green Valley Cir, Culver City, CA 90230
310 642.2721

Mandrachio, Richard
2275 Sutter, S.F., CA 94115
415 921.5938

Mangiat, Jeff
420 Lexington Ave, NYC, NY 10017
212 986.5680

Manna, Connie
49 Old Stage Coach Rd, Andover, NJ 07821
201 786.7409

Mannes, Don
345 E 76th St, NYC, NY 10021
212 288.1392

Manning, Lisa
12 Ledge Ln, Gloucester, MA 01930
508 927.9990
fax 508 927.9991
page 223

Manning, Lisa
c/o Leighton & Co
Four Prospect St, Beverly, MA 01915
508 921.0887
fax 508 921.0223
page 223

Manning, Michele
PO Box 470818, S.F., CA 94147
415 383.9026
fax 415 383.9037
page 28
As an impressionist, I have learned to
see and capture vibrant light and
sensuous color with my pastels,
bringing energy and excitement to
applications such as Kellogg's
packaging, United travel brochures,
Purina and NBA posters.

Mantel, Richard
250 W 57th St, NYC, NY 10107
212 397.7330

Manton, Helen
99 Pleasant St, Plainville, MA 02762
508 695.5862

Manus, Charles
490 Rockside Rd, Cleveland, OH 44131
216 661.4222

Manyoky, Lisa
308 Crescent Ave, Mercerville, NJ 08619
609 890.6645

Marchese, Carole
PO Box 806, Southport, CT 06490
203 226.4535

Marci, Anita
23-C Hillside Ter, White Plains, NY 10601
914 328.7897

Marconi, Gloria
2525 Musgrove Rd, Silver Spring, MD 20904
301 890.4615

Marden, Phil
28 E 21st St, NYC, NY 10010
212 260.7646

Mardon, Allan
108 E 35th St, NYC, NY 10016
212 889.3337

Marelich, Jeffrey Illustrator
3251 Countryside Dr, San Mateo, CA 94403
415 578.8635

Margeson, John
1030 Aoloa Pl, Kailua, HI 96734
808 262.7980
page 165

Margolis, Don
4300 N Narragansett, Chicago, IL 60634
708 670.0912

Margolis, Don
4300 N Narragansett, Chicago, IL 60634
708 670.0912

Marguerita
Seven E 17th St, NYC, NY 10003
212 741.1172

Margulies, Robert
561 Broadway, NYC, NY 10012
212 219.9621

Marie, Rita & Friends
405 N Wabash, Chicago, IL 60611
312 222.0337

Marinsky, Jane
63 Cleveland Ave, Buffalo, NY 14222
716 881.3138

Marion, Kate
85 Columbus Ave, Greenfield, MA 01301
413 774.4862

Mark, Jamie
4170 S Arbor Cir, Marietta, GA 30066
404 924.4793

Mark, Mona
155 E 38th St, NYC, NY 10016
212 697.6170

Mark, Roger Illustration
353 W 53rd St, NYC, NY 10019
212 682.2462 / 212 582.0023
fax 212 582.0090
page 180

Mark, Steve
3516 Arbor Ln, Minnetonka, MN 55305
612 938.4255

Marlena Agency
211 E 89th St, NYC, NY 10128
212 289.5514
fax 212 987.2855
pages 292-301
Cyryl Cabry, Andrzej Czeczot, Gerard
Dubois, Stasys Eidrigevicius, Craig Frazier,
Scott McKowen, Marc Mongeau, Josee
Morin, Tomek Olbinski, Istvan Orosz,
Victor Sadowski, Ferruccio Sardella,
Waldemar Swierzy, Paul Zwolak.

Marr, Dan
26 Juanita Way, S.F., CA 94127
415 564.2096

Marrero, Carlos A
4900 N Marine Dr, Chicago, IL 60640
312 769.1147

Marsh, Cynthia
4434 Matilija Ave, Sherman Oaks, CA 91423
818 789.5232

Marsh, Dilleen
Pine Rd HCR, Neversink, NY 12765
914 985.2936

Marsh, James
c/o Bernstein & Andriulli
60 E 42nd St, NYC, NY 10165
212 682.1490

Marshall, Craig
425 Hugo St, S.F., CA 94122
415 661.5550

Marten, Ruth
Eight W 13th St, NYC, NY 10011
212 645.0233

Martens & Keifer
853 Broadway, NYC, NY 10003
212 677.9100

Martha Productions
11936 W Jefferson Blvd, Culver City, CA 90230
310 390.8663

Martin, Don
PO Box 1330, Miami, FL 33243
305 665.2376

Martin, Doug
39 Cranfield Rd, Toronto, ONT,
Canada M4B 3H6
416 285.8905

Martin, Gregory S
1307 Greenlake Dr, Cardiff, CA 92007
619 753.4073

Martin, JF
43364 N Gadsden Ave,
Lancaster, CA 93534
800 360.0019
page 238

Martin, John
501 Fifth Ave, NYC, NY 10017
212 490.2450
fax 212 697.6828
page 45

Martin, Karen
25 Drury Ln, Rochester, NY 14625
716 586.6041

Martin, Larry
5402 Carbine Cir, Austin, TX 78736
512 263.2095

Martin, Lyn
PO Box 51972, Knoxville, TN 37950
615 588.1760

Martin, Richard
PO Box 268, Wantagh, NY 11793
516 377.3844

Martinez, Heriberto Viera
144-53 38th Ave, Flushing, NY 11354
718 463.8501

Martinez, John
165 Hudson St, NYC, NY 10016
212 941.0482

Martinez, Sergio
43 E 19th St, NYC, NY 10003
212 254.4996

Martinot, Claude
1133 Broadway, NYC, NY 10010
212 229.2249

Martis, Michael W
612 SE Spring, Des Moines, IA 50315
515 285.8122
fax 515 287.6483
page 204

Marton, Charles
5139 14th Ave S, Gulfport, FL 33707
813 321.8870

Marturello, Mark
13899 Summit Dr, Clive, IA 50325
515 284.8343

Maruyama, Sen T
1307 Scott Rd, Burbank, CA 91504
818 559.6554

Maschler, Lorraine
1310 Brenda Ct, Upland, CA 91786
909 949.2458

Masi Graphica
4244 N Bell Ave, Chicago, IL 60618
312 478.6337

Masla, Robert
165 E 32nd St, NYC, NY 10016
212 686.3514

Maslen, Barbara
55 Bayview Ave, Sag Harbor, NY 11963
516 725.3121

Maslov, Norman
879 Florida St, S.F., CA 94110
415 641.4376

Mason, Brick
349 E 14th St, NYC, NY 10003
212 777.4297

Mason, Marietta & Jerry
3825 E 26th St, Mpls, MN 55406
612 729.1774
fax 612 729.0133
page 348

Massicotte, Alain
1121 W St Catherine, Montreal, QU H3B 4J5
514 843.4169

Mastrorocco, Diane
200 W 90th St, NYC, NY 10024
212 362.0103

Masuda, Coco
300 E 51st St, NYC, NY 10022
212 753.9331
pages 26-27

Matcho, Mark
529 E 13th St, NYC, NY 10009
212 529.1318
fax 212 529.4077
page 289

Mate, Michael
1863 S Pearl, Denver, CO 80210
303 733.0128

Matheis, Shelley
534 E Passaic Ave, Bloomfield, NJ 07003
201 338.9506

Matijczyk, Matthew
Eight Laurel Ave, Kittery, ME 03904
207 439.4775

Matsick, Anni
1000 Bayberry Dr, State College, PA 16801
814 234.4752

Matson, Marla Represents
341 W Vernon, Phoenix, AZ 85003
602 252.5072
fax 602 252.5073
pages 402-403, 440-442

Matsu Illustration
318 Beaconsfield Blvd, Beaconsfield,
QUE, Canada H9W 4A8
514 630.6704
page 35

Matsu Illustration
501 Fifth Ave, NYC, NY 10017
212 490.2450
fax 212 697.6828
page 35

Matsuyoshi, Akio
PO Box 1150, NYC, NY 10276
212 865.8469

Mattelson, Marvin & Judy
37 Cary Rd, Great Neck, NY 11021
212 684.2974

Matthews, Bonnie
100 Tuscany Rd, Baltimore, MD 21210
410 243.3514

Matthews, Lu
547 Mt Hermon Rd, Ashland, VA 23005
804 798.9144

Matthews, Pete
PO Box 18128, Fairfield, OH 45018
513 868.2874

Matthews, Scott
7530 Ethel Ave, St Louis, MO 63117
314 647.9899

Mattingly, David B
1112 Bloomfield St, Hoboken, NJ 07030
201 659.7404

Mattos, John
1546 Grant Ave, S.F., CA 94133
415 397.2138

Maughan, William
1451 Gordon Dr, Napa, CA 94558
707 254.7967

Mauterer, Erin
51 Ascot Dr, Ocean, NJ 07712
800 258.9287

Maxx Madcap c/o Funny Bone
3625 Colfax Ave S, Mpls, MN 55409
612 827.4148

May, Darcy
6006 Carversville Rd, Doylestown, PA 18901
215 297.5395

May, Melinda
834 Moultrie St, S.F., CA 94110
415 648.2376

May, Melinda
3443 Wade St, L.A., CA 90066
310 390.9595

Mayabb, Darrell D
10180 W 73 Pl, Arvada, CO 80005
303 420.7200

Maydak, Michael
2780 Wild West Trl, Cool, CA 95614
916 889.8118

Mayer, Bill
240 Forkner Dr, Decatur, GA 30030
404 378.0686
fax 404 373.1759
pages 264-265

Mayforth, Hal
RR1 Box 4135, Montpelier, VT 05602
802 229.2716

Mayor, Barbara
12916 Greenwood Rd, Minnetonka, MN 55343
612 938.8061

Mayor, Philip
655 Kelton Ave, L.A., CA 90024
310 824.1120

Mayse, Bert
18043 Brooknoll, Houston, TX 77084
713 859.7148

Mazzella, Mary Jo
98 Youngblood Rd, Montgomery, NY 12549
914 361.1765

Mazzetti, Alan
834 Moultrie St, S.F., CA 94110
415 647.7677

McAdams, Barbara
779 San Bruno Ave, S.F., CA 94107
415 821.1379
fax 415 821.1379
page 107
Specializes in lettering design (hand-
done logotypes, film & book titles) and
graphic illustration done with style,
humor and a solid design eye. Clients
include Disney Pictures, MGM, "The
Simpsons", KQED-TV, Zondervan
Publishing.

McAfee, Elizabeth
67 Upper Mountain Ave, Montclair, NJ 07042
201 744.4465

McAfee, Steve
15 W Main St, Buford, GA 30518
404 932.6565

McAllister, Chris
27639 Fireweed Dr, Evergreen, CO 80429
303 674.4154

McBride, Bridget
32925 NE Old Parrett Mtn Rd,
Newberg, OR 97132
503 537.9324

McCaffrey, Peter
141 Second Ave, NYC, NY 10003
212 677.4155

McCall, Paul
5801 W Henry St, Indpls, IN 46241
317 241.8890

The McCann Co
4113 Rawlins, Dallas, TX 75219
214 526.2252

McCarthy, Helen
5855 Green Valley Cir, Culver City, CA 90230
310 642.2721

McCauley, Adam
2400 Eighth Ave, Oakland, CA 94606
510 832.0860

McClain, Lynn
4323 Bluffview Blvd, Dallas, TX 75209
214 352.9192

McClelland, Cam
3422 S Fresno St, Ft Smith, AR 72903
501 646.7734
fax 501 646.7734
page 76

McCollum, Sudi
3244 Cornwall Dr, Glendale, CA 91206
818 243.1345

McConnell McNamara & Co
182 Broad St, Wethersfield, CT 06109
203 563.6154

McConnell, James
PO Box 232, Bangor, CA 95914
800 672.2282

McConnell, Jim
Six Monterey Ter, Orinda, CA 94563
510 253.9451

McCord, Kathi
Pine Rd, Neversink, NY 12765
914 285.2936

McCormack, Daphne
43 Glebeholme Blvd, Toronto, ONT,
Canada M4J 1S3
416 466.3028
fax 416 466.3028
page 346

McCracken, Bev
757 Cricket Ln, Perrysburg, OH 43551
419 874.2751

McDaniel, Jerry
155 E 38th St, NYC, NY 10016
212 697.6170

McDermott, Joe
420 Jeffrey Dr, Lincoln, NE 68505
402 488.5799

McDermott, Teri
38 W 563 Koshare Trl, Elgin, IL 60123
708 888.2206

McDonald, Jerry
180 Clipper St, S.F., CA 94114
415 824.1377

McDonald, Jim
5703 E Evans Dr, Scottsdale, AZ 85254
602 494.0747

McDonald, Mercedes
1459 Athenour Ct, San Jose, CA 95120
408 268.0662

McDonnell, Patrick
1839 Ninth St, Alameda, CA 94501
510 769.1421

McDonnell, Pete
111 New Montgomery St, S.F., CA 94105
415 957.1290

McElhaney, Gary L
8104 Peaceful Hill Ln, Austin, TX 78748
512 282.5743

McElmurry, Jill
5827 Sacramento Ave,
Dunsmuir, CA 96025
916 235.0532
fax 916 235.4113
page 234

McElroy, Darlene
3723 Birch, Newport Beach, CA 92660
714 252.1147
fax 714 252.1260
page 101

McElwee, Jo Ellen
3800 Wood Trail, Mason, OH 45040
513 398.1778
Animal illustration. Clients include
Cincinnati Zoo, Society of Illustrators 36.

McEntire, Larry
c/o Fran Siegel
515 Madison Ave, Rm 2200, NYC, NY 10022
212 486.9644

McFadden, Constance
One Lloyd Ave Pl, Latrobe, PA 15650
412 532.2920

McFarren, Mathew
1553 Platte St, Denver, CO 80202
303 458.7445

McGaw, Laurie
RR 2, Shelburne, ONT, Canada L0N 1S6
519 925.5134
page 394

McGillivray, Jinx
4025 Campbell St, Kansas City, MO 64110
816 531.6034

McGinty, Mick
954 Quail Hollow Cir, Dakota Dunes, SD 57049
605 232.3536

McGovern, Michael
89 Fifth Ave, NYC, NY 10003
212 627.1554

McGovern, Preston
157 E Third St, NYC, NY 10009
212 982.8595

McGowan, Daniel
101 Yesler Way, Seattle, WA 98104
206 447.1600

McGrath, Judy & Associates
809 Forest Ave, Evanston, IL 60202
708 866.8568

McGuire, Richard
45 Carmine St, NYC, NY 10014
212 627.9464

McGurl, Michael
14 Garbosa Rd, Santa Fe, NM 87505
505 466.6889
fax 505 466.8253
page 41

McGurl, Michael
501 Fifth Ave, NYC, NY 10017
212 490.2450
fax 212 697.6828
page 41

McIndoe, Vince
250 W 57th St, NYC, NY 10107
212 397.7330
fax 212 397.7334
page 245

McIntosh, Guy
2233 Kemper Ln, Cincinnati, OH 45206
513 861.1400

McIntosh, Mark
391 Broadway, Costa Mesa, CA 92627
714 642.7445

McInturff, Steve
4828 Ridgewood Rd W, Springfield, OH 45503
513 342.0754

McKay, Craig
15 Parkway, Cincinnati, OH 45216
513 821.8052

McKeever, Michael
3475 Southwood Ct, Davie, FL 33328
305 476.6884

McKelvey, David
125 W 77th St, NYC, NY 10024
212 799.6532

McKelvey, Shawn
353 W 53rd St, NYC, NY 10019
212 682.2462

McKenzie, Dave
1888 Century Park E, L.A., CA 90067
310 826.1332

McKenzie, Norma
43 Mandalay Rd, South Weymouth, MA 02190
617 335.1603

McKie, Roy
165 E 32nd St, NYC, NY 10016
212 686.3514

McKiernan Studio Inc
1850 Redondo Ave, Long Beach, CA 90804
310 985.1441

McKissick, Stewart
250 Piedmont Rd, Columbus, OH 43214
614 262.3262

McKowen, Scott
211 E 89th St, NYC, NY 10128
212 289.5514
fax 212 987.2855
page 298

McLaren, Chesley
228 W 82nd St, NYC, NY 10024
212 496.1505

McLaughlin, Paul
11 Kings Ridge Rd, Long Valley, NJ 07853
908 813.8718

McLean & Friends
559 Dutch Valley Rd NE, Atlanta, GA 30324
404 881.6627

McLean, Wilson
270 Park Ave S, NYC, NY 10010
212 260.6700

McLoughlin, Wayne
501 Fifth Ave, NYC, NY 10017
212 490.2450
fax 212 697.6828
page 51

McMacken Graphics
19481 Franquelin Pl, Sonoma, CA 95476
707 996.5239

McMacken, David
c/o Bernstein & Andriulli
60 E 42nd St, NYC, NY 10165
212 682.1490

McMahon, Bob
7260 Apperson St, Tujunga, CA 91042
818 352.9990

McMahon, Brad
1949 S Manchester Ave, Anaheim, CA 92802
714 733.0489

McMahon, Brian
1535 N Western Ave, Chicago, IL 60622
312 227.6755

McMahon, Mike
1826 Asheville Pl, Charlotte, NC 28203
704 372.6007

McMillan, Ken
137 Fifth Ave, NYC, NY 10010
212 529.3556

McMullan, James
207 E 32nd St, NYC, NY 10016
212 689.5527

McNeel, Richard
140 Hepburn Rd, Clifton, NJ 07012
201 779.0802

McOwan, Alex
5855 Green Valley Cir, Culver City, CA 90230
310 642.2721

McShane, David
12 Lees Ave, Collingswood, NJ 08108
609 858.1567

McShane, Frank
432 Tulpehocken Ave, Elkins Park, PA 19027
215 572.7707

McWilliams, Julie
5915 Hobart St, Pittsburgh, PA 15217
412 421.3138

Meacham, PJ
685 Stratford Green,
Avondale Est, GA 30002
404 299.5842
fax 404 299.5842
page 172

Meadows, Laura
1863 S Pearl, Denver, CO 80210
303 733.0128

Meaker, Mike
11936 W Jefferson Blvd, Culver City, CA 90230
310 390.8663

Medbery, Sherrell
6409 Lone Oak Dr, Bethesda, MD 20817
202 223.2127

Medical Art Co/Marcia Hartsock
2142 Alpine Pl, Cincinnati, OH 45206
513 221.3868

Medici, Raymond
16 Hawthorne St, Boston, MA 02131
617 323.0842

Medlock, Scott
11522 N Poema Pl, Ste 201
Chatsworth, CA 91311
818 341.6207
fax 818 341.6207
page 156

Medoff, Jack
14 Hillside Rd S, Weston, CT 06883
203 454.3199
A Joke
A hamburger walks into a bar and
orders a beer. The bartender says,
"Sorry, we don't serve...food". If you
like the joke you'll like my funny
drawings.

Mee, Piri
1036 Locust St, Pasadena, CA 91106
818 405.0626

Meek, Genevieve
6207 Orchid Ln, Dallas, TX 75230
214 363.0680
fax 214 692.9337
page 77

Meek, Steve Inc
743 W Buena, Chicago, IL 60613
312 477.8055
page 216
Steve creates line drawings in a flat,
graphic yet elegantly descriptive style. A
few of his clients are: Amoco, Book-of-the-
Month Club, Cahners, Helene Curtis, Men's
Health, Prudential, Scholastic and Subaru.

Meek, Steve Inc
c/o Leighton & Co
Four Prospect St, Beverly, MA 01915
508 921.0887
fax 508 921.0223
page 216

Meers, Tony
89 Fifth Ave, NYC, NY 10003
212 627.1554

Meier, Melissa
3033 13th Ave W, Seattle, WA 98119
206 284.4701

Meiklejohn
28 Shelton St, Covent Gdn, London,
England WC2H 9HP
011 44 171 240 2077
fax 011 44 171 836 0199
pages 359-363
Europe's leading illustration group is
based in London, England but holds
portfolios in New York City for rapid
despatch across the States.
I: Christine Berrington, Cathy Brear, Alex
Callaway, Alan Case, Alan Cracknell,
Paul Cross, Edmond Davis, Matt
Eastwood, Melvyn Evans, Andrew
Farley, Brian Fitzgerald, Danny Flynn,
Dave Foster, Giannelli, David Griffiths,
Bernard Gudynas, Mark Guilfoyle, Steve
Gulbis, Clare Harris, David Hensley,
Chris Hiett, David Holmes, Jake, Brian
James, Martin Johnson, Wendy Jones,
Pete Kelly, Jack Kelsey, Elizabeth Kerr,
Joanna Kerr, Nick Kobyluch, Robin
Koni, Kiki Lewis, Liddell, Robert Loxston,
Barry Macey, James Macfarlane, Gavin
Macleod, Hugh Macleod, Warren Madill,
Michael Mascaro, Gavin McBain, Fiona
McCosh, Petar Mesel, Naylor Faulkner,

Bonnie Ogden, Roger O' Reilly, Irvine Peacock, David Penfound, Zig Peterson, Christine Pilsworth, Steve Read, Gavin Reece, Corinna Reetz, Leigh Roberts, Paul Sample, Nigel Sandor, Piers Sanford, Ian Saxton, Paul Schofield, Phil Schramm, Steve Sellick, Paul Sheldon, Wendy Sinclair, Penny Sobr, Clive Stevens, Sarah Symonds, Dave Thompson, Paula Vine, Garry Walton, Trevor Webb, Gary West, Matt Westrup, Gareth Williams, Pamela Wilson, Jonathan Wood

Meisel, Paul
666 Greenwich St, NYC, NY 10014
212 675.5719

Melia, Paul
3121 Atherton Rd, Dayton, OH 45409
513 294.0669

Mellet, Fanny Berry
155 E 38th St, NYC, NY 10016
212 697.6170

Mellett Illustration
1480 McFarland Rd, Pittsburgh, PA 15216
412 563.4131

Mellon, David
5500 Village Green, L.A., CA 90016
213 299.9111

Melodia, Barbara
1141 Bernal Ave, Burlingame, CA 94010
415 343.7331

Melrath, Susan Illustration
3100 Jackson Ridge Ct,
Phoenix, MD 21131
410 785.0797
fax 410 785.1196
page 303

Meltzoff, Stanley
128 Grange Ave, Fair Haven, NJ 07704
908 747.4415

Menchin, Scott
640 Broadway, NYC, NY 10012
212 673.5363

Mendelsson, Jonny
125 W 77th St, NYC, NY 10024
212 799.6532

Mendola Ltd
West Coast
503 236.2645
pages 194-198

Mendola Ltd
420 Lexington Ave, NYC, NY 10170
212 986.5680
fax 212 818.1246
pages 194-198

Meredith, Bret
4645 Colfax Ave S, Mpls, MN 55409
612 825.7564

Merewether, Patrick C
1836 Blake St, Denver, CO 80202
303 296.8857

Merrell, David
811 Lake Rd, Guthrie, OK 73044
405 282.8157
fax 405 282.8157
page 77

Merrell, Patrick
80 Eighth Ave, NYC, NY 10011
212 620.7777

Merrill, Abby
850 Park Ave, NYC, NY 10021
212 772.6853

Merrill, Karen
18551 Cocqui Rd, Apple Valley, CA 92307
619 242.4635

Merrill, Laurance
18551 Cicqui Rd, Apple Valley, CA 92307
619 242.4635

Merscher, Heidi
PO Box 295, Arroyo Hondo, NM 87513
505 776.1333

Messi, Enzo
41 Union Sq W, NYC, NY 10003
212 206.0066

Meyer, Bill
101 Yesler Way, Seattle, WA 98104
206 447.1600

Meyer, Gary
21725 Ybarra Rd,
Woodland Hills, CA 91364
818 992.6974
fax 818 992.4538
page 430

Meyer, Jeff
1427-A N Hawley Rd, Milwaukee, WI 53208
414 476.6161

Meyer, Jim
1010 Lake St NE, Hopkins, MN 55343
612 938.0058
page 263

Meyer, Karen
PO Box 191, Saratoga Spgs, NY 12866
518 581.0310

Meyers, Kristine
5262 Butterwood Cir, Orangevale, CA 95662
916 989.2450

Meyers, Mike
5319 Ramsdell Ave, La Crescenta, CA 91214
818 248.6386

Meza, John
3417 Faircrest Dr, Anaheim, CA 92804
714 827.8841

Michail Iofin, GRAPHIKCO
318 21st Ave, S.F., CA 94121
415 386.1984
fax 415 386.1984
page 207

Micich, Paul
c/o Bernstein & Andriulli
60 E 42nd St, NYC, NY 10165
212 682.1490

MicroColor Inc
2345 Broadway, Ste 728,
NYC, NY 10024
212 787.0500
fax 212 787.6740
MicroColor provides computer illustration, multimedia and web site services to the country's most demanding designers. Illustration includes architectural and technical drawings, identity, maps, and signage. For a complimentary portfolio on Macintosh disk, please call or fax.

Middendorf, Frances
337 E 22nd St, NYC, NY 10010
212 473.3586

Middendorf, Nikki
200 E 28th St, NYC, NY 10016
212 683.2848
page 366

Middlechild Studio
2970 N Sheridan, Chicago, IL 60657
312 404.2112

Mike Carter Illustration Inc
32 Oaken Gateway, Toronto, ONT,
Canada M2P 2A1
416 250.5433
fax 416 250.6919
page 425

Milam, Larry
3530 SE Hawthorne, Portland, OR 97214
503 236.9121

Milbourn, Patrick
89 Fifth Ave, NYC, NY 10003
212 627.1554

Miles, Chris
160 Garfield Pl, Brooklyn, NY 11215
718 499.1656

Milgrim, David
Eight Gramercy Pk S, NYC, NY 10003
212 673.1432
page 112

Milicic, Michael
PO Box 3343, NYC, NY 10163
212 223.8057

Mille, Mark
133 W Pittsburgh Ave, Milwaukee, WI 53204
414 278.8400

Millea, Kristen
617 437.9459
fax 617 437.6494
page 311

Miller, Andy
900 W Jackson Blvd, Chicago, IL 60607
312 944.5680

Miller, Claudia Artist's Unltd
6679 NW 24th Ter, Boca Raton, FL 33496
407 995.9444

Miller, Dave
20 W Hubbard, Chicago, IL 60610
312 222.1361

Miller, Edward
11 Kings Ridge Rd, Long Valley, NJ 07853
908 813.8718

Miller, Jane
1260 Day Valley Rd, Aptos, CA 95003
408 684.1593
page 427

Miller, Kristen
1540 Creek Run Trl, Excelsior, MN 55331
612 470.2284

Miller, Maxine
2110 Holly Dr, L.A., CA 90068
213 461.1091

Miller, Paul
2022 Marlee Ln, Green Bay, WI 54304
414 494.2211

Miller, Russell
1618 Idylwild Dr, Prescott, AZ 86301
520 778.6527

Miller, Star
Houston, TX
713 888.0510
page 281

Miller, Verlin
731 N 24th St, Phila, PA 19130
215 232.6666

Millicent, Mark
5855 Green Valley Cir, Culver City, CA 90230
310 642.2721

Mills, Elise
150 E 79th St, NYC, NY 10021
212 794.2042

Milnazik, Kim
73-2 Drexelbrook Dr, Drexel Hill, PA 19026
610 259.1565

Milot, Rene
501 Fifth Ave, NYC, NY 10017
212 490.2450
fax 212 697.6828
page 48

Ming-Yi, Yang
43-10 Kissena Blvd, Flushing, NY 11355
718 463.2733

Minshull, Steve & Assoc
Overland Park, KS
913 341.6090
page 438

Minnefex Inc
3100 California St NE, Mpls, MN 55418
612 788.7308

Minor, Wendell
15 Old North Rd, Washington, CT 06793
203 868.9101

Mintz, Margery
Nine Cottage Ave, Sommerville, MA 02144
617 623.2291

Misconish, David
175 D Peachtree Hills Ave, Atlanta, GA 30305
404 231.9711

Mission House Artworks
RR One Box 2803, Moretown, VT 05660
802 496.6400

Mitchell, Anastasia
3610 Novick Dr, Madison, WI 53704
608 246.8319

Mitchell, Kurt
3004 W 66, Chicago, IL 60629
312 476.4429

Mitsui, Glenn
1512 Alaskan Way, Seattle, WA 98101
206 682.6221

Miyake, Yoshi
PO Box 959, Ridgefield, CT 06877
203 438.8386

Miyamoto, Mas
Six Monterey Ter, Orinda, CA 94563
510 253.9451

Mjolsness, Jane
300 First Ave, Mpls, MN 55401
612 338.5481

MKG Graphics
625 Ivy Ct, Wheeling, IL 60090
708 255.5772

MLH Illustrations
34057 Emily Way, Rancho Mirage, CA 92270
619 328.9554

Moffet, Maureen
121 Lyall Ave, Toronto, ONT,
Canada M4E 1W6
416 691.3242
fax 416 691.4113
page 202
Agent for illustrators Kim LaFave, Brian
Deines, Joe Brunato, and Murray
Tonkin, whose mediums include: oils,
scratchboard, watercolour, pen & ink,
acrylic, pencil crayon, airbrush and
computer.

Mojher, Michael
781 Mojave Trl, Maitland, FL 32751
407 644.9615

Molina, Luis
307 N Michigan, Chicago, IL 60601
312 704.0500

Moline, Robin
4908 First Ave S, Mpls, MN 55409
612 825.7115

Moline-Kramer, Bobbie
654 Pier Ave, Santa Monica, CA 90405
310 392.4877

Molloy, Jack
817 Westwood Dr S, Mpls, MN 55416
612 374.3169

Monahan, Leo
101 Yesler Way, Seattle, WA 98104
206 447.1600

Mondok, Wayne
27 Renault Crescent, Weston, ONT,
Canada M9P 1J2
416 249.2676
page 390

Mongeau, Marc
211 E 89th St, NYC, NY 10128
212 289.5514
fax 212 987.2855
pages 300-301

Monkey Tree Studios
3854 N Ridgeway, Chicago, IL 60618
312 463.9971

Monley, Jerry
2100 W Big Beaver Rd, Troy, MI 48084
313 643.6000

Monroe, Chris
3825 E 26th St, Mpls, MN 55406
612 729.1774

Montagano, David
211 E Ohio, Chicago, IL 60611
312 527.3283
fax 312 527.9091
pages 316-317, 426

Montague, Desmond
4185 Wheelwright Cres, Mississauga, ONT,
Canada L5L 2X4
905 820.4921

Monteiro, Marcos
731 N 24th St, Phila, PA 19130
215 232.6666

Monteleone, John
305 Lattingtown Rd, Lattingtown, NY 11560
516 674.8834

Montes de Oca, Ivette
212 Fifth Ave, NYC, NY 10010
212 683.7000

Montgomery, MK
5746 Cazaux Dr, L.A., CA 90068
707 829.2135

Montibon, Roy
1440 Veteran Ave, L.A., CA 90024
310 478.0954

Montiel, David
453 Fourth St, Brooklyn, NY 11215
212 929.3659

Montoliu, Raphael
223 S Francisca Ave, Redondo Beach, CA 90277
310 798.2516

Montoya, Priscilla
1863 S Pearl St, Denver, CO 80210
303 733.0128

Moonlight Press Studio
362 Cromwell Ave, Ocean Breeze, NY 10305
718 979.9695

Moonstruck Pictures
229 Berkely St, Boston, MA 02116
617 266.3858

Moore, Chris
c/o Bernstein & Andriulli
60 E 42nd St, NYC, NY 10165
212 682.1490

Moore, Cyd
1139 Harvard Rd, Berkley, MI 48072
810 542.8883

Moore, Helene
9011 Skyline Blvd, Oakland, CA 94611
510 530.4366

Moore, Larry
1635 Delaney St, Orlando, FL 32806
407 648.0832

Moore, Lois
55 Plover Hill Rd, Ipswich, MA 01938
508 356.2796

Moore, Stephen
1077 Country Creek Dr, Lebanon, OH 45036
513 932.4295

Moores, Jeff
PO Box 521, Canadensis, PA 18325
717 595.9298

Mora, Francisco
45 N Allen Ave, Pasadena, CA 91106
818 449.0356

Moraes, Greg Studio
7536 Ogelsby Ave, L.A., CA 90045
310 641.8556

Morales Studio
PO Box 1763, Bloomfield, NJ 07003
201 676.8187

Morales-Denney, Elizabeth
Six Monterey Ter, Orinda, CA 94563
510 253.9451

Moran, Michael
39 Elmwood Rd, Florham, NJ 07932
201 966.6229

Mordan, CB
5317 W 201st Ter, Stilwell, KS 66085
913 897.1141

Morecraft, Ron
97 Morris Ave, Denville, NJ 07834
201 625.5752

Morenko, Michael
255 W Tenth St, NYC, NY 10014
212 627.5920

Moreton, Daniel
866 UN Plz, NYC, NY 10017
212 644.2020

Morgan, Jacqui
692 Greenwich St, NYC, NY 10014
212 463.8488

Morgan, Len
67 Upper Mountain Ave, Montclair, NJ 07042
201 744.4465

Morgan, Leonard E
730 Victoria Ct, Bolingbrook, IL 60440
708 739.7705

Morgan, Michele
2646 DuPont Dr, Irvine, CA 92715
714 722.1026

Morgan, Vicki Associates
194 Third Ave, NYC, NY 10003
212 475.0440
fax 212 353.8538
pages 4-5
Karen Blessen, Rachel Bliss, Nicholas
Gaetano, Beppe Giacobbe, Laurie
LaFrance, William Low, Richard Parisi,
Joyce Patti, Joanie Schwarz, Kirsten
Soderlind, Dahl Taylor, (Steam)
Willardson + Assoc., Kris Wiltse, Bruce
Wolfe, Wendy Wray.

Morgan, Wendy/Network Studios
Five Logan Hill Rd, Northport, NY 11768
516 751.5609

Morgen, Barry
253 W 73rd St, NYC, NY 10023
212 595.6835

Morin, Josee
211 E 89th St, NYC, NY 10128
212 289.5514

Morris, Brian T
2419 Mayhew Dr, Indpls, IN 46227
317 881.9657

Morris, Burton
400 Noble St, Pittsburgh, PA 15232
412 682.7963
fax 412 682.7964
pages 316-317

Morris, Don
848 Greenwood Ave NE, Atlanta, GA 30306
404 875.1363

Morrison, Don
155 E 38th St, NYC, NY 10016
212 697.6170

Morrison, Pat
1512 Crittenden St NW, Wash, DC 20011
202 723.1824

Morrow, Skip
123 Ware St, Wilmington, VT 05363
802 464.5523

Morse, Bill
731 N 24th St, Phila, PA 19130
215 232.6666
fax 215 232.6585
page 134

Morse, Deborah
Six Monterey Ter, Orinda, CA 94563
510 253.9451

Morse, Tony
5624 Kales Ave, Oakland, CA 94618
510 658.5899
fax 510 658.5899
page 270

Morser, C Bruce
108 E 35th St, NYC, NY 10016
212 889.3337

Mortensen, Cristine
514 Bryant St, Palo Alto, CA 94301
415 321.4787

Morton, Ann
1420 E Berridge Ln, Phoenix, AZ 85014
602 248.8055

Moser, Barry
155 Pantry Rd, N Hatfield, MA 01066
413 247.5433

Moser, Mary Magdalen
2106 73rd St, Kenosha, WI 53143
414 654.7758

Moses, Duff
5855 Green Valley Cir, Culver City, CA 90230
310 642.2721

Moskowitz, Marion Represents
315 E 68th St, NYC, NY 10021
212 517.4919

Moss, Geoffrey
315 E 68th St, NYC, NY 10021
212 517.4919

Motzkus, Roger
889 W Huntington Dr, Arcadia, CA 91007
818 447.8293

Mowry, Ken Graphics Inc
2621 Iman Dr, Raleigh, NC 27615
919 676.5644
Information illustration and design. Full
range of illustrated maps, graphs, and
diagrams rendered digitally with
precision and creative flair. Advertising,
corporate and editorial.

Mozley, Peggy
17914 Hillcrest Rd, Dallas, TX 75252
214 248.2704

Mudgett, Diana
26 Mudgett St, NYC, NY 10011
212 242.6313

Mueller, Derek
920 Galvin Dr, El Cerrito, CA 94530
510 527.7971

Mueller, Ellen
314 11th St, Petaluma, CA 94952
707 778.6221
page 170

Mueller, Kate
912 Linwood Ave, St Paul, MN 55105
612 292.0462

Mueller, Pete
643 Eighth Pl, Hermosa Beach, CA 90254
310 379.7791

Mukai, Denis/Flatland
1128 Ocean Park Ave, Santa Monica, CA 90405
310 394.5204

Mull, Christy
3182 Holly Mill Run, Atlanta, GA 30062
404 255.1430

Mulligan, Donald
418 Central Park W, NYC, NY 10025
212 666.6079

Munck, Paula
58 W 15th St, NYC, NY 10011
212 741.2539

Munro Goodman
405 N Wabash, Chicago, IL 60611
312 321.1336
fax 312 321.1350
page 256

Munro Goodman
NYC, NY
212 691.2667
fax 212 633.1844
page 256, 345

Muns, Marjorie
501 Obispo Ave, Long Beach, CA 90814
310 438.2165

Munson, Donald
235 W 76th St, NYC, NY 10023
212 595.1014

Murawski, Alex
108 E 35th St, NYC, NY 10016
212 889.3337

Murphy's Art
9708 Robert Jay Way, Ellicott City, MD 21042
410 750.7222

Murphy, Charley
4146 Pillsbury Ave S, Mpls, MN 55409
612 827.8166

Murphy, Mark
309 Walnut Rd, Pittsburgh, PA 15202
412 761.5666

Murphy, Patricia Beling
71 Indian Head Rd, Framingham, MA 01701
508 820.7751

Murray, Barbara
23 Oakdale Ct, Sterling, VA 20165
703 450.9634

Murray, Robert
11228 E Laurel Ln, Scottsdale, AZ 85259
602 860.0535

Murray, Tom
153 Henry St, S.F., CA 94114
415 863.8292
fax 415 863.8292
page 285
Specializes in humorous illustration and
caricature. Watercolor and ink, color
and b&w. Clients: The San Francisco
Chronicle, Infoworld, The Washington
Post, Los Angeles Magazine, The San
Francisco Giants, and the University of
California.

Muse, Pete Illustration
2334 Highland Hts, Carrollton, TX 75007
214 307.8975

Muslusky, Kim
9420 Activity Rd, San Diego, CA 92126
619 693.7380

Myer, Andy
731 N 24th St, Phila, PA 19130
215 232.6666

Myers, David
228 Bleecker St, NYC, NY 10014
212 989.5260

Myers, Lisa L
794 Ralph McGill Blvd, Atlanta, GA 30312
404 577.6333

Myers, Robert
2632 Second St, Santa Monica, CA 90405
310 396.7303

Mysakov, Leonid
280 Madison Ave, NYC, NY 10016
212 545.9155

Myshka, Christine
One Gentore Ct, Edison, NJ 08820
908 754.1138

Nachreiner Boie Art Factory
925 Elm Grove Rd, Elm Grove, WI 53122
414 785.1940

Nachreiner, Tom
925 Elm Grove Rd, Elm Grove, WI 53122
414 785.1940

Nacht, Merle
374 Main St, Wethersfield, CT 06109
203 563.7993

Nadine Represents
80 Wellington Ave/PO Box 307, Ross, CA 94957
415 456.7711

Nagata, Mark
1948 Leavenworth St, S.F., CA 94133
415 922.6612

Nahigian, Alan
33-08 31st Ave, L.I.C., NY 11106
718 274.4042

Najaka, Marlies Merk
241 Central Park W, NYC, NY 10024
212 580.0058

Nakai, Michael/James Crowell
218 Madison Ave, NYC, NY 10016
212 213.5333
Storyboards, comps and animatics
professionally tailored to enhance your
concepts. Please call for portfolio.

Nakamura, Joel
221 W Maple Ave, Monrovia, CA 91016
818 301.0177

Nam, Peter W
2027 Powell St, S.F., CA 94133
415 397.7084

Napoleon Art
460 W 42nd St, NYC, NY 10036
212 967.6655

Nascimbene, Yan
250 W 57th St, NYC, NY 10107
212 397.7330
fax 212 397.7334
page 250
Half-Italian, half-French, Yan
Nascimbene lives in California with his
Mexican-American wife, Moroccan
daughter and Franco-American son.
The last of his award-winning books,
"A Day in September", is published by
Creative Editions in Mankato,
Minnesota.

Nash, Nancy Gibson
15 Autumn Ln, Dedham, MA 02026
617 461.4574
page 128

Nash, Scott
c/o Leighton & Co
Four Prospect St, Beverly, MA 01915
508 921.0887
fax 508 921.0223
page 212

Nass, Rick
731 N 24th St, Phila, PA 19130
215 232.6666

Nasta, Vincent
250 W 57th St, NYC, NY 10107
212 397.7330

Nathan, Charlotte
6516 Cookson Ct, Fair Oaks, CA 95628
916 965.5622

Nation, Tate
719 Bradburn Dr, Mt Pleasant, SC 29464
803 884.9911

Nau, Steven
731 N 24th St, Phila, PA 19130
215 232.6666
fax 215 232.6585
page 130

Naugle, Diane
1839 Ninth St, Alameda, CA 94501
510 769.1421

Nayduch, John
65 W 55th St, NYC, NY 10019
212 767.0260

Nazz, James
41 Union Sq, NYC, NY 10003
212 366.5684

Nees, Susan
450 McDuffie Dr, Athens, GA 30605
706 543.3985

Neider, Alan
597 Riverside Ave, Westport, CT 06880
203 226.4724

The Neis Group
PO Box 174/11440 Oak Dr,
Shelbyville, MI 43944
616 672.5756
fax 616 672.5757
pages 107-109

Nelsen, Randy
1863 S Pearl St, Denver, CO 80210
303 733.0128 / 800 417.5120
fax 303 733.8154
page 324

Nelson, Bill
107 E Cary St, Richmond, VA 23219
804 783.2602

Nelson, Craig
c/o Bernstein & Andriulli
60 E 42nd St, NYC, NY 10165
212 682.1490

Nelson, Donna Kae
4300 N Narragansett, Chicago, IL 60634
708 670.0912

Nelson, Jerry
3033 13th Ave W, Seattle, WA 98119
206 284.4701

Nelson, John
Pier 33 N, S.F., CA 94111
415 956.4750

Nelson, John Killian
5855 Green Valley Cir, Culver City, CA 90230
310 642.2721

Nelson, Lynne Illustrator
910 J St, Salida, CO 81201
719 539.8660

Nelson, R Kenton
12 S Fair Oaks, Pasadena, CA 91105
818 792.5252

Nelson, Will
716 Montgomery St, S.F., CA 94111
415 433.1222
fax 415 433.9560
page 400

Nenzione, Gabriele
320 Bee Brook Dr, Washington, CT 06777
203 868.1011

Neski, Peter
315 E 68th St, NYC, NY 10021
212 737.2521

Nessim, Barbara & Associates
63 Greene St, NYC, NY 10012
212 219.1111

Neubecker, Robert
395 Broadway, NYC, NY 10013
212 219.8435

Neumann, Ann
78 Franklin St, Jersey City, NJ 07307
201 420.1137

The Newborn Group
270 Park Ave S, NYC, NY 10010
212 260.6700

Newell, Claudia
151 First Ave, NYC, NY 10003
212 969.0795

Newman, B Johansen
45 South St, Needham, MA 02192
617 449.2767
page 158
Barbara loves truly tacky people, places
and chotchkas. If you want characters
who came of age with Lucy and
Ovaltine call her for a good time. Your
mother's rec room is her specialty.

Newman, Carole
1119 Colorado Ave, Santa Monica, CA 90401
310 394.5031

Newman, Kevin
1128 Ocean Park Blvd, Santa Monica, CA 90405
310 394.0322

Newsom, Carol
420 Lexington Ave, NYC, NY 10170
212 986.5680

Newsom, Tom
420 Lexington Ave, NYC, NY 10170
212 986.5680

Newstart Art
8166 Jellison St, Orlando, FL 32825
407 273.8365

Newton, Richard
501 Fifth Ave, NYC, NY 10017
212 490.2450

Nez, John
320 Bee Brook Dr, Washington, CT 06777
203 868.1011

Nicholls, Calvin
48 Bond St, Lindsay, ONT, Canada K9V 3R2
705 878.1640

Nichols, Garry
1449 N Pennsylvania St, Indpls, IN 46202
317 637.0250

Nichols, James
18 Old Creek Rd, S.F., CA 94952
707 762.4455

Nicholson, Norman
132 Leona Ct, Alamo, CA 94507
510 837.0695

Nickel, David
679 S Reed Ct, Lakewood, CO 80226
303 935.2239

Nicodemus, Stephen
1839 Ninth St, Alameda, CA 94501
510 769.1421

Nigash, Chuck
2259 El Empino Dr, La Habra Hts, CA 90631
310 697.7626

Niklewicz, Adam
26 Great Quarter Rd, Sandy Hook, CT 06482
203 270.8424

Nimoy, Nancy
10534 Clarkson Rd, L.A., CA 90064
310 202.0773

Ning, Amy
30166 Chapala Ct, Laguna Niguel, CA 92677
714 495.3664

Nishibeppu, Mariko
4325 Franklin Ave, L.A., CA 90027
213 665.8747

Nishinaka, Jeff
c/o Bernstein & Andriulli
60 E 42nd St, NYC, NY 10165
212 682.1490

Nitta, Kazushige
41 Union Sq W, NYC, NY 10003
212 807.6627

Nitto, Tomio
51 Camden St, Toronto, ONT, Canada M5V 1V2
416 362.1913

Nixon, Marian
1514 W Henderson, Chicago, IL 60657
312 472.2279
page 161
Bright, beautiful, and bold watercolors;
loose impressions, tight imitations: —
food, clothing, scenes, products,
patterns/fabrics, furniture, nature — all
sorts of things. (Also a professional
graphic designer, so I understand the
concept of deadlines.)

Nixon, Tony
7210 Robinson, Overland Park, KS 66204
913 384.5444

No Steroids Studios
1409 N Alta Vista Blvd, L.A., CA 90046
213 850.8209

Nobens, CA Illustration
3616 Rhode Island Ave S, St Louis Park, MN 55426
612 935.9130

Noble, Steven
47 Andreas Cir, Novato, CA 94945
415 897.6961
fax 415 892.4449
page 383
A portfolio will be furnished upon
request and additional samples can be
seen in the American Showcase Vol. 19.
Clients: Bank of America, World Savings
& Loan Association, Metropolitan
Transportation Commission, Rockwell
International, Inglenook, and Ampex.

Noche, Mario
7118 Upper River Rd, Prospect, KY 40059
502 228.9427

Noiset, Michele
900 W Jackson Blvd, Chicago, IL 60607
312 944.5680

Noll, Cheryl Kirk
19 Hooker St, Providence, RI 02908
401 861.5869

Noonan, Julia
19 Stuyvesant Oval, NYC, NY 10009
212 505.9342

Norby, Carol H
112 S Main, Alpine, UT 84004
801 756.1096

Norcia, Ernest
224 Engle Dr, Wallingford, PA 19086
610 566.2868

Nordmann, Suzanne
1100 Meredith Ln, Plano, TX 75093
214 930.7302

Norlien, Kim
11808 Van Buren St, Blaine, MN 55434
612 767.9276

Norman, Marty
Five Radcliff Blvd, Glen Head, NY 11545
516 671.4482
Cartoonist and illustrator whose "101
Uses For A Dead Angel" was recently
published by St. Martin's Press. Pen and
ink, color and hi-contrast computer art.
Clients include NatWest Bank, Merrill
Lynch, CBS Sports, Macmillan, The N.Y.
Times and The Washington Post.

North, Ann
PO Box 17024, Irvine, CA 92713
714 501.5055

Northeast, Christian
48 Abell St, Toronto, ONT, Canada M6J 3H2
416 538.0400

Norwell, Jeff
63A Yorkville Ave, Toronto, ONT, Canada M5R 1B7
416 928.1010

Notarile, Chris
420 Lexington Ave, NYC, NY 10170
212 986.5680

Notmot, Nik
353 W 53rd St, NYC, NY 10019
212 682.2462

Novak, Bob
6878 Fry Rd, Middleburg Hts, OH 44130
216 234.1808
page 398

Novak, Tony Illustration
5010 Idaho Ave, Nashville, TN 37209
615 385.4368

Nowicki, Lori
33 Cogswell Ave,
Cambridge, MA 02140
617 497.5336
pages 316-317

Nunley, Vivian
3952 N Sheridan, Chicago, IL 60613
312 929.2115

O'Brien, James Illustration
430 First Ave N, #410, Mpls, MN 55401
612 579.5582
fax 612 928.9281
Media include computer, watercolor,
acrylic, scraperboard. Clients include
BusinessWeek, Smart Money, MacUser,
Macworld, PC World, Family PC, and
Computer Life Magazines: Adobe
Systems, Target Stores, University of
Minnesota, Musicland Group.

O'Brien, Tim
480 13th St, Brooklyn, NY 11215
718 832.1287

O'Connell, Kathy
1494 Cold Springs Rd,
Pottstown, PA 19464
610 326.8038
fax 610 326.6173
page 370

O'Connell, Mitch
6425 N Newgard, Chicago, IL 60626
312 743.3848
page 163

O'Connell, Robin Ghelerter
3044 Paula Dr, Santa Monica, CA 90405
310 452.4168

O'Connor, Cathy Christy
PO Box 477, Pocono Lake, PA 18347
717 646.8739

O'Connor, Jeff
4300 N Narragansett, Chicago, IL 60634
708 670.0912

O'Donnell, William
3159 Byrnes Mill Rd, Eureka, MO 63025
314 677.5592

O'Friel, Patty
1112 N Hoyne, Ste 2, Chicago, IL 60622
312 384.3496
fax 312 384.3496
page 281
Clients include: 7-Eleven, Pepsi, United
Airlines, DiscoverCard. In Texas, represented by Star Miller at (713) 888-0510.

O'Grady, Beth
161 Fourth St, Hoboken, NJ 07030
201 653.3901

O'Leary, Christopher
250 W 57th St, NYC, NY 10107
212 397.7330
fax 212 397.7334
page 253

O'Leary, Daniel
89 Fifth Ave, NYC, NY 10003
212 627.1554

O'Malia, Carol
235 Burgess Ave, Westwood, MA 02090
617 769.7138

O'Malley, Kevin
Nine Babbling Brook Ln, Suffern, NY 10901
914 368.8606

O'Neal, Patrick studiO
234 32nd Pl, Hermosa Beach, CA 90254
310 379.9010

O'Neil, Sharron
409 Alberto Way, Los Gatos, CA 95032
408 354.3816

O'Neill, Fran
PO Box 990716, Boston, MA 02199
617 267.9215
page 304

O'Regan, Bernice
95 Bergen St, Brooklyn, NY 11201
718 243.2824

O'Shaughnessy Studio
2519 Columbia Dr, Costa Mesa, CA 92626
714 545.1663

O'Shea, Kevin
828 S Lawson Rd, Camano Island, WA 98292
360 387.7669

O'Sullivan, John
20 Neck Hill Rd, Mendon, MA 01756
508 473.2310

Oakes, Jim
6638 N 13th St, Phoenix, AZ 85014
602 263.8990

Oakes, Terry
11 Kings Ridge Rd, Long Valley, NJ 07853
908 813.8718

Oakley, Mark
849 Bricken Pl, St Louis, MO 63122
314 821.2278

Oaks, Jim
1863 S Pearl St, Denver, CO 80210
303 733.0128

Oasis Studio
118 E 26th St, Mpls, MN 55404
612 871.4539

Ochagavia, Carlos
217 E 86th St, NYC, NY 10028
212 355.0910

Ochsner, Dennis Co
701 Galer St, Seattle, WA 98109
206 286.9249

Oetinger, Bill
7315 Fircrest Ave, Sebastopol, CA 95472
707 823.9807

Ogai, Masaaki
Haiku, HI 96708
310 826.1332
fax 310 284.3290
page 86

Ogburn, Greg
1826 Asheville Pl, Charlotte, NC 28203
704 372.6007

Ogden, Robin Represents
3722 W 50th St, Mpls, MN 55410
612 925.4174
fax 612 925.2135
page 263
I: Dianne Bennett (cut paper), Bob
Brugger (humorous), Jan Evans (B/W &
watercolor), Kelly Hume (logo/lettering),
Jim Meyer (woodcuts).

Oh, Jeffrey
Six Challenger Ct, Baltimore, MD 21234
410 661.6064
page 381

Olbinski, Rafal
137 Fifth Ave, NYC, NY 10010
212 529.3556

Olbinski, Tomek
211 E 89th St, NYC, NY 10128
212 289.5514

Oldroyd, Mark
11 Kings Ridge Rd,
Long Valley, NJ 07853
908 813.8718
fax 908 813.0076
page 423

Olds, Scott
2100 W Big Beaver Rd, Troy, MI 48084
810 643.6000

Oliver, Mindy
1001 S Alfred St, L.A., CA 90035
310 556.1439

Olivere, Ray
65 W 55th St, NYC, NY 10019
212 767.0260

Olivia
3723 Birch, Newport Beach, CA 92660
714 252.1147
fax 714 252.1260
page 101

Olivieri, Teofilo
1001 Willow Ave, Hoboken, NJ 07030
201 413.0046
page 257

Olmstead, David Mayo
1300 Nicollet Mall, Mpls, MN 55403
612 339.2112
fax 612 339.2233
page 255

Olson, Erik
221 W Maple St, Monrovia, CA 91016
818 303.2455

Olson, Rik
749 Circle Ct S, S.F., CA 94080
415 589.4392

Olson, Stan
817 Westwood Dr S, Mpls, MN 55416
612 374.3169

One Lonely Knight Art Svc
20423 Napa St, Canoga Park, CA 91306
818 341.7138

Oppenheimer, Jennie
220 Alta Ave, Lagunitas, CA 94938
415 488.1047

Orosz, Istvan
211 E 89th St, NYC, NY 10128
212 289.5514
fax 212 987.2855
page 294

Ortega, Jose
131 Charlie Parker Pl, NYC, NY 10009
212 228.2606
fax 212 228.2807
page 8 - 9

Ortiz, Jose Luis
66 W 77th St, NYC, NY 10024
212 877.3081

Osborn, Jacqueline
827 Viejo Rastro, Santa Fe, NM 87505
505 989.4948

Osborn, Steve
67 Upper Mountain Ave, Montclair, NJ 07042
201 744.4465

Osher, Glynnis
19 Stuyvesant Oval, NYC, NY 10009
212 505.9342

Oshidari, Houmann
Hand Carved Lettering in Stone,
Lexington, MA 02173
617 862.1583

Osiecki, Lori
123 W Second St, Mesa, AZ 85201
602 962.5233
fax 602 962.5233
page 353

Osser, Stephanie
150 Winding River Rd, Needham, MA 02192
617 237.1116

Otnes, Fred
211 E 51st St, NYC, NY 10022
212 755.1365

Otteson, Gary
200 51st Ter, Kansas City, MO 64112
816 561.0590

Ottinger, John
1291 Sunkist Cir, Corona, CA 91720
909 279.7758

Otto, Brian
840 Bricken Pl, St Louis, MO 63122
314 821.2278

Oudekerk, Doug
2003 Goodrich Ave, St Paul, MN 55105
612 884.8083

Overacre, Gary
3802 Vineyard Trace, Marietta, GA 30062
404 973.8878

Ovies, Joe
853 Broadway, NYC, NY 10003
212 677.9100

Owens, James
3000 Chestnut Ln, Baltimore, MD 21211
410 243.0324

Owens, Jim
25 W 45th St, NYC, NY 10036
212 398.9540

Ownbey, Scott
5855 Green Valley Cir, Culver City, CA 90230
310 642.2721

Oxborough, Paul G
8133 Julianne Ter, Mpls, MN 55427
612 544.5345

Pace, Julie
PO Box 491, Sky Forest, CA 92385
909 337.0731

Paciulli, Bruno
125 W 77th St, NYC, NY 10024
212 799.6532

Pack, John
2342 N Fillmore, Arlington, VA 22207
703 243.4024

Packer, Neil/CIA
c/o Bernstein & Andriulli
60 E 42nd St, NYC, NY 10165
212 682.1490

Page, Frank
5315 Oakdale Ave, Woodland Hills, CA 91364
818 346.0816

Page, Splash
1125 Landwehr Rd, Northbrook, IL 60062
708 498.8936

Page.Trim, Debra
156 Putnam St, Hartford, CT 06106
203 247.8282

Pagowski, Filip
113 W 106th St, NYC, NY 10025
212 662.3601

Paillot, Jim
4907 Holly, Kansas City, MO 64112
816 561.8045
fax 816 561.6201
page 452

Pakula, Joani
918 NE 109th Ter, Kansas City, MO 64155
816 734.4344

Paladin Freelance Professional
875 N Michigan Ave, Chicago, IL 60611
312 654.2600

Palencar, John Jude
249 Elm St, Oberlin, OH 44074
216 774.7312

Pallas, Brent
395 South End Ave, NYC, NY 10280
212 912.1117

Palmer, Gary
1826 Asheville Pl, Charlotte, NC 28203
704 372.6007

Palmer, Jan
666 Greenwich St, NYC, NY 10014
212 675.5719

Palmer, Tom
40 Chicasaw Dr, Oakland, NJ 07436
201 337.8638

Palombo, Lisa A
89 Fifth Ave, NYC, NY 10003
212 627.1554

Pals, Dan
PO Box 66, Prairie City, IA 50228
515 994.3263

Palulian, Dick
18 McKinley St, Rowayton, CT 06853
203 866.3734
fax 203 857.0842
page 463

Palulian, Dick
NYC, NY
212 581.8338
page 463

Palulian, Joanne
18 McKinley St, Rowayton, CT 06853
203 866.3734
fax 203 857.0842
pages 454-464

Palulian, Joanne
NYC, NY
212 581.8338
pages 454-464

Pansini, Tom
16222 Howland Ln, Huntington Beach, CA 92647
714 847.9329

Paperny, Vladimir
1375 Kelton Ave, L.A., CA 90024
310 444.7883

Papitto, Aurelia
300 Commercial St, Boston, MA 02109
617 742.3108
page 407

Paragraphics
427 Third St, Brooklyn, NY 11215
718 965.2231

Paraskevas, Michael
250 W 57th St, NYC, NY 10107
212 397.7330

Pardini, Patricia
88 Lexington Ave, NYC, NY 10016
212 683.2010

Pardue, Jack
2307 Sherwood Hall Ln, Alexandria, VA 22306
703 765.2622

Pardy, Cindy
c/o Daniele Collignon
200 W 15th St, NYC, NY 10011
212 391.1830

Parios Studio
65 W 55th St, NYC, NY 10019
212 767.0260

Parisi, Richard
c/o Vicki Morgan
194 Third Ave, NYC, NY 10003
212 475.0440

Park, Darcie
2461 Roswell Ave, Long Beach, CA 90815
310 985.0506

Park, Elliott
PO Box 2193, Grapevine, TX 76099
817 481.2212
fax 817 481.2908
pages 75

Park, WB
110 Park Ave S, Winter Park, FL 32789
407 644.1553

Parke, Steven
3233 O'Donnel St, Baltimore, MD 21224
410 675.9087

Parker, Curtis
1946 E Palomino Dr, Tempe, AZ 85284
602 820.6015

Parker, Earl
67 Upper Mountain Ave, Montclair, NJ 07042
201 744.4465

Parker, Edward
58 W 15th St, NYC, NY 10011
212 741.2539

Parkey Design
310 Bryant Ave, Cincinnati, OH 45220
513 961.4105

Parmenter, Wayne
309 Walnut Rd, Pittsburgh, PA 15202
412 761.5666

Parnell, Miles
597 Riverside Ave, Westport, CT 06880
203 226.4724
fax 203 454.9904
page 437

Parrow, Neal
5855 Green Valley Cir, Culver City, CA 90230
310 642.2721

Parry, Ivor
280 Madison Ave, NYC, NY 10016
212 779.1554

Parson, Nan
353 W 53rd St, NYC, NY 10019
212 682.2462

Parsons, Jennifer
251 Steilen Ave, Ridgewood, NJ 07450
201 652.7122

Partners by Design
11240 Magnolia Blvd,
N Hollywood, CA 91601
818 509.0555
page 186

Partners by Design
353 W 53rd St, NYC, NY 10019
212 582.0023 / 212 682.2462
fax 212 582.0090
page 186

Pascual, Linda
49 W 45th St, NYC, NY 10036
212 921.1199

Passarelli, Charles
6769 Villas Dr E, Boca Raton, FL 33433
407 750.9960

Passey, Kim
115 Hurlbut, Pasadena, CA 91105
818 441.4384

Pastrana, Robert M
473 A Riverdale Dr, Glendale, CA 91204
818 548.6083

Pate, Judith Arlene
1614 Hillhaven Rd, Brown Summit, NC 27214
910 656.3738

Pate, Martin
32 Wesley St, Newnan, GA 30263
404 251.5286

Pate, Randy
PO Box 2160, Moorpark, CA 93021
805 529.8111

Paterson, Diane
866 UN Plz, NYC, NY 10017
212 644.2020

Patkau, Karen
980 Broadview Ave, Ste 203,
Toronto, ONT, Canada M4K 3Y1
416 461.9747
fax 416 461.0382
page 391
All types of intriguing papers - colored,
patterned, textured, preprinted, or
recycled; go into the making of my
collage illustrations. Any paper, or even
material; may be used to enhance your
specific concept or product.

Patrick, John
68 E Franklin, Dayton, OH 45459
513 433.8383

Patrick, Pamela
c/o Bruck & Moss
333 E 49th St, NYC, NY 10017
212 982.6533

Patrick, Tom
4726 Fairmont Ave, Kansas City, MO
64112
816 531.4853
page 438

Patti, Joyce
c/o Vicki Morgan
194 Third Ave, NYC, NY 10003
212 475.0440

Patton, Edd
905 W 29th, Austin, TX 78705
512 478.3338

Paulsen, Larry
c/o Bernstein & Andriulli
60 E 42nd St, NYC, NY 10165
212 682.1490

Pavey, Jerry
9903 Markham St, Silver Springs, MD 20901
212 889.8777

Pavlovits, Ivan
5855 Green Valley Cir, Culver City, CA 90230
310 642.2721

Payne, Adair
5921 E Inca, Mesa, AZ 85205
602 641.7345

Payne, CF
121 Madison Ave, NYC, NY 10016
212 683.1362

Payne, Liane
11 Kings Ridge Rd, Long Valley, NJ 07853
908 813.8718

Payne, Scott
49 W 45th St, NYC, NY 10036
212 921.1199

Payne, Tom
19 Stuyvesant Oval, NYC, NY 10009
212 505.9342

Peake, Kevin
8930 SW 95th St, Miami, FL 33176
305 271.5219
page 307

Peavey, Gail
One S 608 Lambert Rd, Glen Ellyn, IL 60137
708 790.0084

Pechanec, Vladimir M
67 Upper Mountain Ave, Montclair, NJ 07042
201 744.4465

Peck's Builders Art
17865 Sky Park Cir, Irvine, CA 92714
714 261.6233

Peck, Beth
Rte Five Box 220B, Menomonie, WI 54751
715 235.8886

Peck, Everett
716 Sanchez St, S.F, CA 94114
415 285.8267

Peck, Marshall
3443 Wade St, L.A., CA 90066
310 390.9595

Peck, Scott
2701 Thorndale, Plano, TX 75074
214 422.7438
page 321
Humorous illustration, comic art, or
whatever you want to call it. Full color,
spot color, black & white. Clients include
Ogilvy & Mather, DDB Needham
Worldwide, The Walt Disney Company,
American Airlines, Pepsi and Frito-Lay.

Peck, Virginia
34 Erie Ave, Newton, MN 02161
617 558.7014

Pedersen, Judy
Seven West St, Warwick, NY 10990
914 987.1090

Peebles, Peter
89 Fifth Ave, NYC, NY 10003
212 627.1554

Peery, Joe
999 Greenwood Ave, Atlanta, GA 30306
404 874.3518

Pegasus Design
13831 NW Fwy, Houston, TX 77040
713 690.7878

Pelavin, Daniel
80 Varick St, NYC, NY 10013
212 941.7418

Peled, Einat
c/o Schneidman
62-28 Cromwell Cres, Rego Park, NY 11374
718 275.6549

Pelo, Jeffrey
501 Fifth Ave, NYC, NY 10017
212 490.2450
fax 212 697.6828
page 52

Pema Brown Ltd
Pine Rd HCR, Neversink, NY 12765
914 985.2936

Pembroke, Richard
353 W 53rd St, NYC, NY 10019
212 682.2462

Pen Station
11661 W Bluemound Rd, Milwaukee, WI 53226
414 771.3181

Penberthy, Mark
47 Greene St, NYC, NY 10013
212 219.2664

Penca, Gary
8335 NW 20th St, Coral Springs, FL 33071
305 752.4699

Pendleton, Roy
28 Pimlico Dr, Commack, NY 11725
516 543.0003

Peng, Leif
731 N 24th St, Phila, PA 19130
215 232.6666

Pennington, Jack
8882 Woodsman, Washington, MI 48094
203 226.4724

Penny & Stermer Group
19 Stuyvesant Oval, NYC, NY 10009
212 505.9342

Pentleton, Carol
685 Chestnut Hill Rd, Chepachet, RI 02814
401 568.0275

Pepera, Fred
Ten E Ontario, Chicago, IL 60611
312 573.1370

Pepper, Bob
157 Clinton St, Brooklyn, NY 11201
718 875.3236

Pepper, Brenda
157 Clinton St, Brooklyn, NY 11201
718 875.3236

Pepper, Missy Representative
166 S Park, S.F., CA 94107
415 543.6881

Percivalle, Rosanne
132 W 21st St, NYC, NY 10011
212 727.9158

Perez, Vincent Studio
1279 Weber St, Alameda, CA 94501
510 521.2262

Perini, Ben
PO Box 421443, S.F., CA 94142
415 647.5660
fax 415 285.1102
page 113
Acrylic paintings from realistic to
surreal. Traditional brush and airbrush.

Perkins, Ken
5938 W 41st Ave, Denver, CO 80212
303 422.2557

Pertile, Paula
419 22nd Ave, S.F., CA 94121
415 668.7156

Pesek, Marjorie E
603 Orchid Ave,
Corona Del Mar, CA 92625
714 721.9805
page 84
Marjorie has a unique style of paper
mosaic, where her pallet consists of
patterns, colors and texture cut out of
magazines. You can see more of
Marjorie's work in CIB '92-'95 and
American Showcase '96.

Petan, Greg
c/o Bernstein & Andriulli
60 E 42nd St, NYC, NY 10165
212 682.1490

Petersen, Chris
1635 E 22nd St, Oakland, CA 94606
510 535.0495

Petersen, Don
3451 Guido St, Oakland, CA 94602
510 482.3808

Peterson, Chris
1630 N Main St, Walnut Creek, CA 94596
510 942.0257

Peterson, Julie
Six Monterey Ter, Orinda, CA 94563
510 253.9451

Peterson, Ron
2350 Taylor St, S.F., CA 94133
415 776.3833

Peterson, Stephanie
PO Box 605, Westport, CT 06881
203 227.9396

Peterson, Zig
28 Shelton St, Covent Gdn, London,
England WC2H 9HP
011 44 171 240 2077
fax 011 44 171 836 0199
page 363

Petrauskas, Kathy
1660 N LaSalle, Chicago, IL 60614
312 642.4950
fax 312 642.6391
page 173

Petrucci, Sam
275 Newbury St, Boston, MA 02116
617 267.0618

Petruzzi, Rosemary E
Nine Meadow Ave, Woodbury, CT 06798
203 266.9196

Petter, Noel
1716 Hillside Dr, Glendale, CA 91208
213 245.5455

Pflumm, Kristin
401 Miguel St, S.F., CA 94131
415 550.8057

PG Representatives
E Main St, Ware, MA 01082
413 967.9855

Phalen, Mary Jo
405 N Wabash Ave, Chicago, IL 60611
312 321.1336

Philbrook, Diana
20927 Wolfe Way,
Woodland Hills, CA 91364
818 348.4255
fax 818 887.6372
With a fashion background, Diana
specializes in "people art"...including
children and teens with a flair for
expression and action. Book illustration,
fashion and portraits too.

Philippidis, Evangelia
68 E Franklin St, Dayton, OH 45459
513 433.8383

Phillips, Chet
6527 Del Norte, Dallas, TX 75225
214 987.4344

Phillips, Jared
67 Upper Mountain Ave, Montclair, NJ 07042
201 744.4465

Phillips, Laura
c/o Bernstein & Andriulli
60 E 42nd St, NYC, NY 10165
212 682.1490

Phillips, Liz
2508 E Belleview, Milwaukee, WI 53211
414 964.8088

Phillipson, Andrew
27375 Brighton Dr, Valencia, CA 91354
805 297.8529

**Photo Group, The Creative Source
2512 E Thomas Rd, Phoenix, AZ 85016
602 381.1332
Photo Group represents graphic
illustrations in brush and ink: pen and
ink drawings: photorealism, technical
and medical illustrations: and
watercolor and oil paintings.**

Photocom/Melanie Spiegel
3005 Maple Ave, Dallas, TX 75201
214 720.2272

Picardi, Valerie
13-17 Laight St, NYC, NY 10013
212 219.0014

Picasso, Dan
817 Westwood Dr S, Mpls, MN 55416
612 374.3169

Pickard, Ann
Pier 33 N, S.F., CA 94111
415 956.4750

Pierazzi, Gary
13997 Emerald Ct, Grass Valley, CA 95945
916 477.1950

Piersanti, Robert
6040 Blvd E, W New York, NJ 07093
201 854.0603

Pietrobono, Janet
Five Spring St, Mt Kisco, NY 10549
914 666.4730

Pietzsch, Steve
9802 B Hundred Oaks Cir, Austin, TX 78750
512 331.8755

Pifko, Sigmund
108 E 35th St, NYC, NY 10016
212 889.3337

Piland Goodell Inc
24 Greenway Plz, Houston, TX 77046
713 965.0453

Pinaha, Bob
24 Patton Dr, Sayreville, NJ 08872
908 257.3228

Pincus, Harry
160 Ave of the Americas, NYC, NY 10013
212 925.8071

Pinkney, Brian
41 Furnace Dock Rd, Croton, NY 10520
914 271.5238

Pinkney, Brian J
444 Henry St, Brooklyn, NY 11231
718 643.0342

Pinkney, Debbie
309 Walnut Rd, Pittsburgh, PA 15202
412 761.5666

Pinkney, Jerry
41 Furnace Dock Rd, Croton, NY 10520
914 271.5238

Pippo, Louis
56 Westminster Rd, Yorktown Heights, NY 10598
914 245.8267

Pirman, John
330 W 76th St, NYC, NY 10023
212 721.9787

Pitts, Ted
68 E Franklin St, Dayton, OH 45459
513 433.8383

Piven, Hanoch
310 W 22nd St, NYC, NY 10011
212 691.5133

Pizzo, Robert
288 E Devonia Ave, Mt Vernon, NY 10552
914 664.4423

Pizzo, Susan
288 E Devonia Ave, Mt Vernon, NY 10552
914 664.4423

Plank, Michael
5833 Monrovia, Shawnee Mission, KS 66216
913 631.7021

Platz III, H Rusty
15922 118th Pl NE, Bothell, WA 98011
206 488.9171

Plunkert, David
3647 Falls Rd, Baltimore, MD 21211
410 235.7803

Podevin, Jean-Francois
5812 Newlin Ave, Whittier, CA 90601
310 945.9613

Pohle, Peter
3748 Lakspur Dr, Loveland, CO 80538
303 663.7353

Poje, Elizabeth
1001 S Alfred St, L.A., CA 90035
310 556.1439

Polfus, Roberta
226 N Lombard, Oak Park, IL 60302
708 383.3651

Polkinghorne, Sharron
856 Fifth St, Manhattan Beach, CA 90266
310 379.7323

**Pollack, Scott
78 Hidden Ridge Dr, Syosset, NY 11791
516 921.1908
fax 516 921.2383
page 302**

**Pomerantz, Lisa
731 N 24th St, Phila, PA 19130
215 232.6666
fax 215 232.6585
page 133**

Ponte, Don
101 Hill Rd, Glen Ellen, CA 95442
707 935.6535

**Poole, Colin
353 W 53rd St, NYC, NY 10019
212 582.0023 / 212 682.2462
fax 212 582.0090
page 185**

Popadics, Joel
336 Viviney St, Elmwood Pk, NJ 07407
201 794.1860

Pope, Kevin
3735 Cleve Butcher Rd, Bloomington, IN
47401
812 824.6949
fax 812 824.6111
page 81

Popeo, Joanie
230 Arriba Dr, Sunnyvale, CA 94086
415 964.1733

Porazinski, Rob
2218 N Newland, Chicago, IL 60635
312 745.9005

Porfirio, Guy
4101 E Holmes, Tucson, AZ 85711
602 881.7708

Porter, John
302 Hickory Rd, Washington Grove, MD 20880
301 921.0545

Porter, Pat
28 W 69th St, NYC, NY 10023
212 799.8493

Porter, Walter
4010 W El Camino del Cerro, Tucson, AZ 85745
602 743.9821

Portraits & Caricatures
2613 NE Garfield St, Mpls, MN 55418
612 789.5650

Posey, Pam
2763 College Blvd, Oceanside, CA 92056
619 724.3566

Potts, Carolyn & Associates Inc
Four E Ohio, Chicago, IL 60611
312 944.1130 / 312 935.1707
fax 312 988.4236
pages 14-17
I: John Craig, Byron Gin, Stacey Previn,
Rhonda Voo, Julia LaPine, Karen Bell,
Joe Ovies, Susan Nees, Leslie Wolf, Greg
Huber, Jack Slattery, Nathan Y. Jarvis,
Joyce Kitchell
P: Alan Kaplan, Todd Haiman, Craig van
der Lende, Douglas Walker, Paul
Goirand, Ralph Daniel
Lettering: Joe Plume

Powditch Associates
30954 Pobo Cyn, Aroura, CA 91301
818 707.6274

Powell, Andrew
212 Third Ave N, Mpls, MN 54401
612 349.6611

Powell, Polly
2319 J St, Sacramento, CA 95816
916 444.1646

Powell, Rick
104 W Arden Cir, Norfolk, VA 23505
804 440.1723

Powell, Tana
531 Hugo St, S.F., CA 94122
415 759.6453

Powell, Victor
5112 Trew Ct, El Paso, TX 79924
915 755.3729

Powers, Teresa
6010 Wilshire Blvd, L.A., CA 90036
213 931.7449

Pozzatti, Illica/Hirons & Co
117 E Sixth St, Bloomington, IN 47408
812 331.7500

Prapas, Christine
12480 SE Wiese Rd, Boring, OR 97009
503 658.7070
fax 503 658.3960
pages 78, 98-105
Brian Battles, Dan Brown, Steve Ellis,
Lydia Hess, Kelly Hume, Blaise Jette,
Alan Just, Jeff Labbe, Darlene McElroy,
Mick McGinty, Craig Nelson, Joe Saputo,
Shelly Shaffer, Charles Varner, Madeline
Vasquez, Elsa Warnick, Brad Weinman,
Mike Wepplo, Leslie Winter-Gorsline.

Pratt, Pierre
Two Silver Ave, Toronto, ONT,
Canada M6R 3A2
416 530.1500
fax 416 530.1401
page 23

Pratt, Russell E
171 Ogden Ave, Jersey City, NJ 07307
201 222.2887

The Pred Group
10012 Perry Dr, Overland Park, KS 66212
913 438.7733

Prentice, Vicki Associates Inc
1888 Century Park E, L.A., CA 90067
310 826.1332
fax 310 284.3290
pages 84-87

Prescott, Richard
1506 Georgia Ave, W Palm Beach, FL 33401
407 832.1056

Preslicka Studio
7730 Grinnell Way, Lakeville, MN 55044
612 432.2166

Preston, Jeff
6182 Sydney Dr, Huntington Beach, CA 92647
714 898.7288

Preuitt, Clayton
420 S Detroit St, L.A., CA 90036
213 965.8285

Pribble, Holly
7428 W 57th St, Summit, IL 60501
708 458.0387

Pribble, Laurie
653 Pomfret Rd, Hampton, CT 06247
203 455.0811

Price, Heather
921 First Ave W, Seattle, WA 98119
206 281.0960

Price, Tom
900 W Jackson Blvd, Chicago, IL 60607
312 944.5680

Primary Colors
311 First Ave N, Mpls, MN 55401
612 338.7033

Primeau, Chuck
404 Main St, Pine Meadow, CT 06061
203 738.3229

Prince, Kevin
24436 Ward St, Torrance, CA 90505
310 375.9232

Pritchett, Karen
309 Walnut Rd, Pittsburgh, PA 15202
412 761.5666

Pritchett, Tom
247 W Tenth St, NYC, NY 10014
212 688.1080

Pro Art
2008 Polaris, N St Paul, MN 55109
612 770.7011

Proulx, Art
353 W 53rd St, NYC, NY 10019
212 582.0023 / 212 682.2462
fax 212 582.0090
page 184

Prud'Homme, Jon
1119 Colorado Ave, Santa Monica, CA 90401
310 394.5031

Pryor, Robert
1198 Pacific Coast Hwy, Seal Beach, CA 90740
310 597.6161

Przewodek, Camille
522 E D St, Petaluma, CA 94952
707 762.4125

Puckett, David
16 Prairie Falcon, Aliso Viejo, CA 92656
714 837.4417

Pulver, Harry Jr
105 Meadow Lane N, Mpls, MN 55422
612 377.1797

Punchatz, Don Ivan
2605 Westgate Dr, Arlington, TX 76015
817 469.8151

Punin, Nikolai
161 W 16th St, NYC, NY 10011
212 727.7237
fax 212 620.4056
page 305

Purdom, Bill
2805 Oleander Dr, Wilmington, NC 28403
910 763.1208

Purse, Brad
381 Park Ave S, NYC, NY 10016
212 889.2400

Pushpin Group
215 Park Ave S, NYC, NY 10003
212 674.8080

Pyle, Charles
946 B St, Petaluma, CA 94952
707 765.6734

Pyle, Chris
770 E 73rd St, Indpls, IN 46240
317 255.1197

Pyner, Marcia
89 Fifth Ave, NYC, NY 10003
212 627.1554

Queen of Arts
12325 S 90th Ave, Palos Park, IL 60464
708 361.0679

Quidley, Peter T
490 Rockside Rd, Seven Hills, OH 44131
216 661.4222

Quinlan, Stephen Illustration Ltd
1957 Creston Pl, Burlington, ONT,
Canada L7P 2Y5
416 485.8277
fax 416 485.8277
page 392

Quon, Mike Design Office
568 Broadway, NYC, NY 10012
212 226.6024

Rabin, Bill & Associates
680 N Lake Shore Dr, Chicago, IL 60611
312 944.6655

Rabl, Lorraine
629 Glenwood Ave, Teaneck, NJ 07666
201 836.4283
page 97

Rachko, Barbara
1311 W Braddock Rd, Alexandria, VA 22302
703 998.7496

Radenich, Mike
RR Two, Holt, MO 64048
913 631.1949

Radigan, Robert
742 Pyrula, Sanibel Island, FL 33957
813 472.0910

Radmilovich, Joanne
2405 NW Thurman, Portland, OR 97210
503 225.9687

Rae, Ron
2100 W Big Beaver Rd, Troy, MI 48084
313 643.6000

Ragland, Greg
2500 Lucky John Dr, Park City, UT 84060
801 645.9232

Raglin, Tim
250 W 57th St, NYC, NY 10107
212 397.7330

Ramage, Alfred
Five Irwin St, Winthrop, MA 02152
617 846.5955

Ramin, Linda
6239 Elizabeth Ave, St Louis, MO 63139
314 781.8851

Ramirez, Roberto
1410 W First St, Winston-Salem, NC 27101
910 722.5113

Ramos, Ruben
4300 N Narragansett, Chicago, IL 60634
708 670.0912

Ramsay - In The Black Inc
1128 Smith St, Honolulu, HI 96813
808 537.2787
fax 808 533.6690
Ramsay specializes in quill and ink
landmark depiction. Clients include
Rockresorts, Sheraton Corp., Westin
International, Hasegawa Komuten, PPG
Industries. To commission fine art with
commercial applications, contact Russ
Sowers at Ramsay Galleries.

Ramune
210 Hillside Ave, Needham, MA 02194
617 444.1185
page 368

Rancorn, Chuck
750 94th Ave N, St Petersburg, FL 33702
813 579.4499

Randazzo, Anthony
353 W 53rd St, NYC, NY 10019
212 682.2462

Random Arts
2617 E Hedrick Dr, Tucson, AZ 85716
602 881.8882

Raphael & Bolognese
53 Irving Pl, NYC, NY 10003
212 228.5219

Rapp, Gerald & Cullen
108 E 35th St, NYC, NY 10016
212 889.3337

Rappaport, Jill
11454 Elbert Way, San Diego, CA 92126
619 566.6247

Rashid, Mai Gebara
93 86th St, Brooklyn, NY 11209
718 833.1982

Raszka, Brian
1385 Clay St, #26, S.F., CA 94109
415 673.4479
page 288

Rawson, Jon M
1368 Waterside Dr, Bollingbrook, IL 60440
815 838.4462

Ray, Dennis Paul
681 Woodcrest Ct, Corona, CA 91719
909 371.4655

Rayevsky, Robert
716 Sanchez St, S.F., CA 94114
415 285.8267
fax 415 285.8268
page 67

Raymond, Victoria
94 Mercer St #1, Jersey City, NJ 07302
201 332.8343

Rea, Tracy
3301A S Jefferson Ave, St Louis, MO 63118
314 773.2600

Reactor
51 Camden St, Toronto, ONT,
Canada M5V 1V2
416 703.1913 / 800 730.8945
fax 416 703.6356
pages 150-155
Represents: **Jamie Bennett, Roxanna
Bikadoroff, Federico Botana, Shelley
Browning, Blair Drawson, Henrik
Drescher, Louis Fishauf, Bob Fortier, Gail
Geltner, Carolyn Gowdy, Margaret
Hathaway, John Hersey, Tom Hunt,
Huntley/Muir, Jeff Jackson, Jerzy Kolacz,
Ross MacDonald, James Marsh, Simon
Ng, Tomio Nitto, Alain Pilon, Stephanie
Power, Bill Russell, Fiona Smyth, Jean
Tuttle, Maurice Vellekoop, Tracey Wood,
Rene Zamic, Andreas Zaretzki.**

Reagan, Mike
200 Aquetong Rd, New Hope, PA 18938
215 862.2091
fax 215 862.2641
page 226
**Mike Reagan specializes in maps. His
clients include The New Yorker, BBDO
South, Sports Illustrated, Harvard Business
Review, Audubon, Outside Magazine, FCB
Advertising, DDB Needham, DC Heath,
Addison Wesley, National Geographic and
various design firms.**

Recker, Mary Jo Illustration
23 Aberdeen Dr, Middletown, OH 45042
513 420.9157

Redgrafix Design/Illustration Studio
Dralene "Red" Hughes
19750 W Observatory Rd,
New Berlin, WI 53146
414 542.5547
fax 414 542.5322
page 416
**"Promotional Rescuing" your creative
needs: Creative consulting, concepts,
design, illustration, production,
character development, animation, 3D,
photo manipulation & retouching,
copywriting and multi-media! Computer
and traditional creative! Concepts to
finish...or anything in between!**

Rediger, Deborah
4819 W Stanford Ave, Dallas, TX 75209
214 357.9980

Redline Illustrations
222 E Fifth St, NYC, NY 10003
212 529.4990

Reece, Gavin
28 Shelton St, Covent Gdn, London,
England WC2H 9HP
01144 171 240 2077
fax 01144 171 836 0199
page 362

Reed, Chris
17 Edgewood Rd, Edison, NJ 08820
908 548.3927

Reed, David
2233 Kemper Ln, Cincinnati, OH 45232
513 861.1400

Reed, Elizabeth
101 Yesler Way, Seattle, WA 98104
206 447.1600

Reed, Judy
1808 Manning Ave, L.A., CA 90025
310 474.7701

Reed, Mike
666 Greenwich St, NYC, NY 10014
212 675.5719

Reed, Susie
2175 Francisco Blvd, San Rafael, CA 94901
415 456.8267

Reed, William
1206 N Clinton, Dallas, TX 75208
214 942.3446

Reese, Eric
1850 Redondo Ave, Long Beach, CA 90804
310 985.3192

Reese, Garrett Illustration
52 W Huron, Chicago, IL 60610
312 335.1137

Reetz, Corinna
28 Shelton St, Covent Gdn, London,
England WC2H 9HP
01144 171 240 2077
fax 01144 171 836 0199
page 361

Rehbein, Richard
643 Newark Ave, Kenilworth, NJ 07033
908 241.0743

Reich, Allen J
64 S Parker Dr, Wesley Hills, NY 10952
914 354.3202

Reid, Andrew
924 Lincoln Rd, Miami Beach, FL 33139
305 531.7338

Reilly, Donald
211 Newtown Tpk, Wilton, CT 06897
203 834.0067

Reilly, Kerry Reps
1826 Asheville Pl, Charlotte, NC 28203
704 372.6007
page 345

Reiner, Annie
10532 Blythe, L.A., CA 90064
310 559.0831

Reingold, Alan
155 E 38th St, NYC, NY 10016
212 697.6170

Reinhardt, Dorothy
466 Melrose Ave, S.F., CA 94127
415 584.9369

Reinman, Mick
5855 Green Valley Cir, Culver City, CA 90230
310 642.2721

Reisch, Jesse
135 Elinor Ave, Mill Valley, CA 94041
415 388.8704

Renard Represents
501 Fifth Ave, NYC, NY 10017
212 490.2450
fax 212 697.6828
pages 32-57, 271

Renaud, Carol
2830 W Leland, Chicago, IL 60625
312 583.2681

Renaud, Phillip
2830 W Leland, Chicago, IL 60625
312 583.2681

Rendeiro, Charlene
643 Santa Clara Ave, Venice, CA 90291
310 396.8308

Rendon, Maria
6997 Perris Hill Rd, San Bernardino, CA 92404
909 889.8979

Renlie, Frank
500 Aurora Ave N, Seattle, WA 98109
206 682.1203

Renshaw, Jennifer
137 E Marshall Ave, Langhorne, PA 19047
215 752.2003

Renwick
405 N Wabash Ave, Chicago, IL 60611
312 222.0337

Reott, Paul
731 N 24th St, Phila, PA 19130
215 232.6666

Rep Art
Seattle, WA
206 467.9156
page 412

Reppel, Aletha
905 W 29th St, Austin, TX 78705
512 478.0853
fax 512 478.5123
page 76

Reyes, Ed
454 W 36th St, NYC, NY 10018
212 967.6756

Reynolds, Bill
5248 W 106th St, Bloomington, MN 55437
612 831.0398

Reynolds, Gene
71 Thompson St, NYC, NY 10012
212 431.3072

Rhodes, Barbara Illustration
6739 Cantil St, Rancho La Costa, CA 92009
619 929.1049

Rhyne, Paulette
2075 S University Blvd, Denver, CO 80210
303 871.9166

Ricceri, David
505 Court St, Brooklyn, NY 11231
718 852.8987

Riccio, Frank
420 Lexington Ave, NYC, NY 10170
212 986.5680

Rich, Anna
1821 Chelsea St, Elmont, NY 11003
516 352.5025

Richards, Kenn
Three Elwin Pl, E Northport, NY 11731
516 499.7575

Richards, Linda
420 Lexington Ave, NYC, NY 10170
212 986.5680

Richardson, James Craque
PO Box 3962, Long Beach, CA 90803
310 439.8098

Richardson, Jeff
2400 McKinney Ave, Dallas, TX 75201
214 747.3122

Richter, Andrea
Seven Trout Way, Salisbury, MA 01952
508 462.0527

Rider, Mike
c/o Bernstein & Andriulli
60 E 42nd St, NYC, NY 10165
212 682.1490

Riding, Lynne
280 Madison Ave, NYC, NY 10016
212 545.9155

Ridley, Dave
Seven Flintlock Rd, Norwalk, CT 06850
203 866.5865

Riedy, Mark
68 E Franklin St, Dayton, OH 45459
513 433.8383

Riegel, Margaret
160 E Third St, NYC, NY 10009
212 254.8240

Rieser, Bonnie
934 NE 33rd St, Portland, OR 97232
503 452.2210

Rieser, William
405 N Wabash, Chicago, IL 60611
312 222.0337

Rigie, Mitchell
41 Union Sq W, NYC, NY 10003
212 807.6627

Rigsby Design Inc
5650 Kirby Dr, Houston, TX 77005
713 660.6057

Riley Illustration
155 W 15th St, NYC, NY 10011
212 989.8770

Riley, Frank
108 Bamford Ave, Hawthorne, NJ 07506
201 423.2659

Risko, Robert
155 W 15th St, NYC, NY 10011
212 255.2865

Risser Digital Studio
5330 W Electric Ave, Milwaukee, WI 53234
800 747.7371
Two Quantel graphic paint boxes with
3D Contour upgrade. High resolution
Isomet drum scanner. LVT 8 x 10 film
recorder. Macintosh, Silicon graphics
and Pentium support stations via in-
house network. Photo murals and
lamination to 6 x 30 feet.

Ritscher, Paul
9386 S Harpeth Rd, Nashville, TN 37221
615 646.9832

Ritta, Kurt Studio
66 Willow Ave, Hoboken, NJ 07030
201 792.7422

Rivers, Larry
405 E 13th St, NYC, NY 10003
212 475.4532

Rivoche, Paul
Two Silver Ave, Toronto ONT, Canada M6R 3A2
416 530.1500

Rixford, "Puppets"
308 W 97th St, NYC, NY 10025
212 865.5686

RKB Studios Inc
420 N Fifth St, Mpls, MN 55401
612 339.7055
fax 612 339.8689
page 439

Robbins, David
2814 NW 72nd St, Seattle, WA 98117
206 784.1136

Roberts, Eva
540 Erbes Rd, Thousand Oaks, CA 91362
805 495.2266

Roberts, Peggi
13075 N 75th Pl, Scottsdale, AZ 85260
602 991.8568

Roberts, Ray
c/o Bernstein & Andriulli
60 E 42nd St, NYC, NY 10165
212 682.1490

Roberts, Scott
Six N Main St, Bel Air, MD 21014
410 879.3362
fax 410 879.3362
page 240

Robertson, Chris
3708 Watseka, L.A., CA 90034
310 836.8968

Robinette, Ilene Illustration
120 W Illinois, Chicago, IL 60610
312 527.1805

Robinson, Aminah Brenda L
791 Sunbury Rd, Columbus, OH 43219
614 252.4771

Roche, Diann Represents
200 W 51st Ter, Kansas City, MO 64112
816 561.0590

Roda, Bot
78 Victoria Ln, Lancaster, PA 17603
717 393.1406

Rodgers, Joel
709 Carroll St #2R, Brooklyn, NY 11215
800 439.9217
page 286

Rodorigo, Sandro
23-17 33rd St, Astoria, NY 11105
718 274.2764

Rodriguez, Francisco
3286 Ivanhoe, St Louis, MO 63139
314 781.7377

Rodriguez, Robert
501 Fifth Ave, NYC, NY 10017
212 490.2450
fax 212 697.6828
page 37

Roehr, KE
230 Babcock St, Brookline, MA 02146
617 566.1137

Rogers, Adam
414 W Pender St, Vancouver, BC,
Canada V6B 1T5
604 684.6826

Rogers, Buc
Ten E Ontario, Chicago, IL 60611
312 573.1370
fax 312 573.1445
page 239

Rogers, Lilla
Six Parker Rd, Arlington, MA 02174
617 641.2787

Rogers, Nip
848 Greenwood Ave,
Atlanta, GA 30306
404 875.1363 / 800 347.0734
fax 404 875.9733
page 340

Rogers, Nip
212 S Front St, Phillipsburg, PA 16866
814 342.6572
page 340

Rogers, Paul
405 N Wabash, Chicago, IL 60611
312 222.0337

Rogers, Randy
1212 N Post Oak, Houston, TX 77055
713 688.0637
fax 713 688.9988
page 348

Rohani, Michael Sours
424 Third Ave, Edmonds, WA 98020
206 771.2905

Rohr, Dixon
155 W 68th St, NYC, NY 10023
212 580.4065

Rohrer, Neal
725 17th St, Kenosha, WI 53140
414 551.7233

Roldan, Jim
141 E Main St, E Hampstead, NH 03826
603 382.1686

Roman, Barbara J
345 W 88th St, NYC, NY 10024
212 362.1374

Roman, Irena
369 Thomas Clapp Rd, PO Box 571,
Scituate, MA 02066
617 545.6514

Roman, John
369 Thomas Clapp Rd, PO Box 571,
Scituate, MA 02066
617 545.6514

Rombola, John
3804 Farragut Rd, Brooklyn, NY 11210
212 645.8000

Romero, Javier Design Group
24 E 23rd St, NYC, NY 10010
212 420.0656
fax 212 420.1168
page 287

Root, Kimberly Bulcken
58 W 15th St, NYC, NY 10011
212 741.2539

Root, Lynn Green
4449 Wedgewood St, Jackson, MS 39211
601 366.5780

Roper, Marty
6115 Brookside Blvd, Kansas City, MO 64113
816 361.8589

Rosandich, Dan
PO Box 410, Chassell, MI 49916
906 482.6234

Rosas, Wilfredo
60 63rd St, W New York, NJ 07093
201 854.8142

Rosborough, Tom
3825 E 26th St, Mpls, MN 55406
612 729.1774

Rosch, Brucie
256 Hansen Ave, Albany, NY 12208
518 459.3261

Rosco, Delro
89 Fifth Ave, NYC, NY 10003
212 627.1554

Rose, David
1623 N Curson Ave, L.A., CA 90046
213 876.0038

Rose, Peggy J
53 Sonora Way, Corte Madera, CA 94925
415 924.6485

Rosen, Jake
34 Bal Harbour, St Louis, MO 63146
314 432.0941

Rosen, Jonathan
408 Second St, Brooklyn, NY 11215
718 499.3911

Rosenbaum, Jon & Georgina
597 Riverside Ave, Westport, CT 06880
203 226.4724

Rosenberg, Ben Killen
3734 SE Stephens, Portland, OR 97214
503 230.7735
page 140
Monoprints in black and white or with
watercolor. Subjects ranging from
animals to objects and portraits. Bold
style for editorial, advertising.

Rosenberg, Ken
9710 E Lemon Ave, Arcadia, CA 91007
818 574.1631

Rosenhouse, Irwin
256 Mott St, NYC, NY 10012
212 226.2848

Rosenthal, Marc
Eight Rte 66, Malden Bridge, NY 12115
518 766.4191

Rosenthal, Marshal M
231 W 18th St, NYC, NY 10011
212 807.1247

Rosenthal, Roberta
182 E 210th St, Bronx, NY 10467
718 881.8024

Rosenwald, Laurie
54 W 21st St, NYC, NY 10010
212 675.6707

Rosenworld
54 W 21st St, NYC, NY 10010
212 675.6707

Rosner, Meryl
25 W 45th St, NYC, NY 10036
212 398.9540

Ross, Barry
12 Fruit St, Northampton, MA 01060
413 585.8993

Ross, Bill
602 Davidson Rd, Nashville, TN 37205
615 352.3729

Ross, Gregory Lettering
315 Springfield Ave, Summit, NJ 07901
908 277.2800

Ross, Ian
375 Riverside Dr, NYC, NY 10025
212 932.7707

Ross, Larry
53 Fairview Ave, Madison, NJ 07940
201 377.6859

Ross, Mary
S.F., CA
415 924.7881 / 800 924.7881
fax 415 924.7891
page 82

Ross, Richard
545 Eighth Ave, NYC, NY 10018
212 330.0411

Ross, Scott
731 N 24th St, Phila, PA 19130
215 232.6666

Rosser, Toby
Four Main St, Purdys, NY 10578
914 277.1064

Rossi, Pamela
908 Main St, Evanston, IL 60602
708 475.2533

Rossiter, Nan
353 W 53rd St, NYC, NY 10019
212 682.2462

Rotblatt, Steven
19508 Turtle Ridge Ln, Northridge, CA 91326
818 831.3908

Roth, Arnold
157 W 57th St, NYC, NY 10019
212 333.7606

Roth, Robert
420 Lexington Ave, NYC, NY 10170
212 697.8525

Roth, Roger
7227 Brent Rd, Upper Darby, PA 19082
610 352.3235
page 203

Rother, Sue
19 Brookmont Cir, San Anselmo, CA 94960
415 454.3593

Rothman, Sharon
112 Elmwood Ave, Bogota, NJ 07603
201 489.8833

Roundy, Laine
42 Buttonball Dr, Sandy Hook, CT 06482
203 426.9531

Rouner, Elizabeth
339 Chestnut St, St Paul, MN 55102
612 298.0059

Rowe, Charles
133 Aronimink Dr, Newark, DE 19711
302 738.0641

Rowe, Greg Alan
900 E First St, L.A., CA 90012
213 626.6563

Rowe, John
316 Mellow Ln, La Can Flintrdge, CA 91011
818 790.2645

Roy, Doug
Six Monterey Ter, Orinda, CA 94563
510 253.9451

Royo, Luis
11 Kings Ridge Rd,
Long Valley, NJ 07853
908 813.8718
fax 908 813.0076
page 423

Rubin, Ken
4140 Arch Dr, Studio City, CA 91604
818 508.9028

Rudd, Greg
Pine Rd HCR, Neversink, NY 12765
914 985.2936

Rudnak, Theo
501 Fifth Ave, NYC, NY 10017
212 490.2450
fax 212 697.6828
page 36

Ruegger, Rebecca
Bruck & Moss
333 E 49th St, NYC, NY 10017
212 982.6533

Ruff, Donna
18 Crockett St, Rowayton, CT 06853
203 866.8626

Rugh, Doug Illustration
37 Gosnold Rd, Woods Hole, MA 02543
508 548.6684
fax 508 457.6394
page 410

Ruscha, Paul
940 N Highland Ave, L.A., CA 90038
213 856.0008

Rush, John
123 Kedzie St, Evanston, IL 60202
847 869.2078

Russell, Bill
51 Camden St, Toronto, ONT,
Canada M5V 1V2
416 362.1913 / 800 730.8945
fax 416 362.6356
page 155

Russell, David M
823 Seamaster, Houston, TX 77062
713 488.2302

Russell, Mike
427 First St, Brooklyn, NY 11215
718 499.3436

Russo, Anthony
51 Fogland Rd, Tiverton, RI 02878
401 624.9184

Rusynyk, Kathy
2309 Twp Rd, Jeromesville, OH 44840
419 368.3664

Rutherford, John
563 Ocean, Ferndale, CA 95536
707 786.4055

Ryan, Cheri
PO Box 19412, Seattle, WA 98109
206 634.1880

Ryan, Terry
8020 Grenfell St, Kew Gardens, NY 11415
212 688.1080

Rybka, Stephen
3119 W 83rd St, Chicago, IL 60652
312 737.1981

Ryden, Mark
221 W Maple, Monrovia, CA 91016
818 355.5047

S.F. Society of Illustrators
690 Market St, S.F., CA 94104
415 399.1681

Sabanosh, Michael
433 W 34th St, NYC, NY 10001
212 947.8161

Sabella, Jill
2607 Ninth Ave W, Seattle, WA 98104
206 285.4794

Sabin, Tracy
13476 Ridley Rd, San Diego, CA 92129
619 484.8712

Sachs, Jenny
157 E 32nd St, NYC, NY 10016
212 684.0565

Sacks, Cal
721-B Heritage Vlg, Southbury, CT 06488
203 262.1427

Sadowski, Victor
211 E 89th St, NYC, NY 10128
212 289.5514
fax 212 987.2855
page 299

Saffold, Joe
501 Fifth Ave, NYC, NY 10017
212 490.2450
fax 212 697.6828
page 50

Sagerman, Robert
283 Swan Ct, Manhasset, NY 11030
718 384.8591

Saint James, Synthia
PO Box 27683, L.A., CA 90027
213 464.8381
fax 818 558.5613
Saint James specializes in book covers (over
30 including Alice Walker and Terry
McMillan), children's picture books (6 to
date), as well as major commissions including
Essence Magazine, Kayser-Roth/Maybelline,
and the House of Seagram.

Sakahara, Dick
28826 Cedar Bluff Dr, Rancho Palos, CA 90274
310 541.8187

Saksa, Cathy
280 Madison Ave, NYC, NY 10016
212 545.9155

Salazar, Miro
363 Southport Way, Vallejo, CA 94591
707 552.3649
fax 707 552.3649
page 117
Scratchboard and pen & ink
illustrations. Black and white or color.

Salazar, Miro
c/o Barb Hauser
PO Box 421443, S.F., CA 94142
415 647.5660
fax 415 285.1102
page 117

Salentine, Katherine
2022 Jones St, S.F., CA 94133
415 928.0457

Salerno, Steven
250 W 57th St, NYC, NY 10107
212 397.7330
fax 212 397.7334
page 251

Salina, Joseph
2255 B Queen St E, Toronto, ONT,
Canada M4E 1G3
416 699.4859

Salk, Lawrence
19029 Sprague St, Tarzana, CA 91356
818 776.1992

Salmela, Don
24262 E Typo Drive NE, Stacy, MN 55079
612 884.4045

Salmon, Paul
5826 Jackson's Oak Ct, Burke, VA 22015
703 250.4943

Salvati, Jim
6600 Royer Ave, West Hills, CA 91307
818 348.9012

Salvatore, Rosemary McGuirk
244 North Ave, New Rochelle, NY 10801
914 833.1689

Salzman, Richard W
London, England
44 0171 636 7141
pages 66-69, 156

Salzman, Richard W
L.A., CA
310 276.4298
pages 66-69, 156

Salzman, Richard W
Chicago, IL
312 252.2244
pages 66-69, 156

Salzman, Richard W
716 Sanchez St, S.F., CA 94114
415 285.8267
fax 415 285.8268
pages 66-69, 156

Salzman, Richard W
NYC, NY
212 997.0115
pages 66-69, 156

Samanich, Barbara
1126 S Ash Ave, Tempe, AZ 85281
602 966.3070

Sammel, Chelsea
482 South St, Hollister, CA 95023
408 636.7443

Sams, BB
PO Box A, Social Circle, GA 30279
404 464.2956

Samul, Cynthia
15 Pacific St, New London, CT 06320
203 442.5695

Sancha, Jeremy/CIA
c/o Bernstein & Andriulli
60 E 42nd St, NYC, NY 10165
212 682.1490

Sanchez, Carlos
3301A S Jefferson Ave, St Louis, MO 63118
314 773.2600

Sanchez, Michael
457 Nevada St, S.F., CA 94110
415 641.1791

Sanders, Bruce
c/o Leighton & Co
Four Prospect St, Beverly, MA 01915
508 921.0887
fax 508 921.0223
page 220

SANDERS/TIKKANEN
Westford, MA
508 692.9800
fax 508 392.5899
page 220
Technical, scientific and descriptive
product illustration, charts/graphs.
Airbrush and computer illustration.

Sanders, Liz Agency
30166 Chapala Ct,
Laguna Niguel, CA 92677
714 495.3664
fax 714 495.0129
pages 260-261

Sandford, John
Pine Rd HCR, Neversink, NY 12765
914 985.2936

Sandro, Cindy
834 Briarcliff Rd, Atlanta, GA 30306
404 872.7193

Sands, Trudy Artist Rep
1350 Chemical St, Dallas, TX 75207
214 905.9037

Sanfilippo, Margaret
261 Hamilton Ave, Palo Alto, CA 94301
415 322.2057

Sanford, Piers
28 Shelton St, Covent Gdn, London,
England WC2H 9HP
01144 171 240 2077
fax 01144 171 836 0199
page 362

Sanford, Steve
41 Union Sq W, NYC, NY 10003
212 243.6119

Sano, Kazuhiko
105 Stadium Ave, Mill Valley, CA 94941
415 381.6377
page 49

Sano, Kazuhiko
501 Fifth Ave, NYC, NY 10017
212 490.2450
fax 212 697.6828
page 49

Sanson, Jeff
1212 N Post Oak, Houston, TX 77055
713 688.0637

Santa Lucia, Francesco
420 Lexington Ave, NYC, NY 10170
212 986.5680

Santoleri, Ray
153 Cortelyous Ln, Somerset, NJ 08873
908 297.9116

Santoliquido, Dolores R
60 W Broad St, Mt Vernon, NY 10552
914 667.3199

Saputo, Joe
737 Milwood Ave, Venice, CA 90291
310 301.8059

Sardella, Ferruccio
211 E 89th St, NYC, NY 10128
212 289.5514
fax 212 987.2855
pages 296-297

Sargent, Claudia Karabaic
15-38 126th St, College Point, NY 11356
718 461.8280

Sasaki, Goro
c/o Bernstein & Andriulli
60 E 42nd St, NYC, NY 10165
212 682.1490

Sasaki, Yutaka
101 Yesler Way, Seattle, WA 98104
206 447.1600

Sauck Illustration
5401 Martin Ln, Hanover Park, IL 60103
708 837.6114
fax 708 837.8337
Mark Sauck specializes in air brush art,
commercial and editorial. Clients include
Gottlieb, Nike, Premier Gaming, Leo
Burnett, Stargate, JWT-CBS.

Sauer, Jennifer
5855 Green Valley Cir, Culver City, CA 90230
310 642.2721

Saunders, Rob
34 Station St, Brookline, MA 02146
617 566.4464
fax 617 739.0040
page 142
Conceptualist with a personal,
whimsical style in editorial, advertising,
corporate media. Numerous years
experience, clients from Fortune 500.
Member Graphic Artists Guild.

Sava, Judy
6180 14th St, Sacramento, CA 95831
916 427.3441

Savely, Rod
Four Prospect St, Beverly, MA 01915
508 921.0887

Sawyer, Scott Illustration
573 Mission St, S.F., CA 94105
415 227.0539

Sayles Graphic Design
308 Eighth St, Des Moines, IA 50309
515 243.2922

Scanlan, David
1600 18th St,
Manhattan Beach, CA 90266
310 545.0773
fax 310 545.7364
page 375
"Stylized Realism" art rendered in
watercolor dyes with airbrush, colored
pencil, and brush; with or without black
pen and ink. Also, B/W line art (thin line,
fat line, lots of lines or few lines, etc.)

Scanlan, Peter
65 Arthur St, Ridgefield Park, NJ 07660
201 807.1881

Scardova, Jaclyne
17 Redwood Rd, Fairfax, CA 94930
415 721.0707

Scarpulla, Caren
2832 Waverly Dr, L.A., CA 90039
213 913.2458

Schaffer, Amanda
445 Hanson Ln, Ramona, CA 92065
619 788.0388

Schagun, David
43-49 Tenth St, L.I.C., NY 11101
718 472.5530

Schechter, Martin
34 Bedford Rd, Katonah, NY 10536
914 232.7267

Scherman, John
310 E 12th St, NYC, NY 10003
212 473.7237

Scheuer, Lauren
77 Pierce Rd, Watertown, MA 02172
617 924.6799
page 88

Scheuer, Phil
126 Fifth Ave, NYC, NY 10011
212 620.0728

Schiettino, Joe
49 W 45th St, NYC, NY 10036
212 921.1199

Schill, George
629 Tartan Dr, Monroeville, PA 15146
412 761.5666

Schilling, John
8507 137th NE, Redmond, WA 98052
206 867.1074

Schindler, Steven D
155 Bethlehem Pike, Phila, PA 19118
215 242.9739

Schiwall, Linda
280 Madison Ave, NYC, NY 10016
212 545.9155

Schleinkofer, David
420 Lexington Ave, NYC, NY 10170
212 986.5680

Schmehl, Brad
381 Park Ave S, NYC, NY 10016
212 889.2400

Schmid, Paul
2702 Walnut Ave SW, Seattle, WA 98116
206 938.4516

Schmidt, Chuck
1715 Ramona Ave, S Pasadena, CA 91030
213 256.0815

Schmidt, Urs
41 Union Sq, NYC, NY 10010
212 206.0066

Schneider, Douglas
9016 Danube Ln, San Diego, CA 92126
619 695.6796

Schneider, RM
597 Riverside Ave, Westport, CT 06880
203 226.4724
fax 203 454.9904
page 434

Schneidman, Jared
16 Parkway, Katonah, NY 10536
914 232.1499

Schofield, Glen
25 W 45th St, NYC, NY 10036
212 398.9540

Schofield, Mark
1201 First Ave S, Seattle, WA 98134
206 623.9539

Scholl, Heather
223 Prospect, Seattle, WA 98109
206 282.8558

Schongut, Emanuel
247 Main St, PO Box 247,
Mountain Dale, NY 12763
914 434.8964

Schreer, Jason
4588 Vernon Dr, Marbleton, GA 30059
404 819.8670

Schreiber, Dana
36 Center St, Collinsville, CT 06022
203 693.6688

Schroeder, Michael
5801 La Vista Ct, Dallas, TX 75206
214 821.9834

Schudlich, Stephen
2717 N Wilson, Royal Oak, MI 48073
810 362.3992

Schuett, Stacey
PO Box 15, Duncans Mill, CA 95430
707 632.5123

Schulenburg, Paul
24 Captain Connolly Rd, Brewster, MA 02631
508 385.8845

Schumacher, Michael
101 Yesler Way, Seattle, WA 98104
206 447.1600

Schumaker, Ward
466 Green St, S.F., CA 94133
415 398.1060

Schumann & Co
2472 Bolsover St, Houston, TX 77005
713 523.8444

The Schuna Group
1503 Briar Knoll Dr, Arden Hills, MN 55112
612 631.8480

Schuster, Rob
2233 Kemper Ln, Cincinnati, OH 45206
513 861.1400

Schwab, Michael
501 Fifth Ave, NYC, NY 10017
212 490.2450
fax 212 697.6828
pages 32-33

Schwartz, Daniel
48 E 13th St, NYC, NY 10016
212 683.1362

Schwartz, Judith
231 E Fifth St, NYC, NY 10003
212 777.7533

Schwartz, Sara
130 W 67th St, NYC, NY 10023
212 877.4162

Schwarz, Joanie
c/o Vicki Morgan
194 Third Ave, NYC, NY 10003
212 475.0440

Schwarze, Evan
104 S Home Ave, Oak Park, IL 60302
708 445.0154

Schweigert, Carol
Nine Lanwood Pl, Charlestown, MA 02129
617 242.3901

Schweitzer, David
405 N Wabash Ave, Chicago, IL 60611
312 321.1336

Schwinger, Larry
89 Fifth Ave, NYC, NY 10003
212 627.1554

Scible, Betsy Gosheff
3161 Gosheff Ln, Gambrills, MD 21054
410 451.2855

Scientific Illustration West
PO Box 1025, Camarillo, CA 93011
805 484.7533

Scott, Bob
4108 Forest Hill Ave, Richmond, VA 23225
804 232.1627

Scott, Freda
1015-B Battery St, S.F., CA 94111
415 398.9121
fax 415 398.6136
pages 6-7, 235

Scott, Jack
899 S Plymouth Ct, Chicago, IL 60605
312 922.1467

Scott, Maren
Pine Rd HCR, Neversink, NY 12765
914 985.2936

Scratchy Studio
PO Box 990716, Boston, MA 02199
617 267.9215
page 304

Scribner, Joanne
N 3314 Lee, Spokane, WA 99207
509 484.3208
Specializes in people/children's book
covers. Illustrated most all covers for
"Beverly Cleary" by Dell Publishing,
which became the largest selling series
of children's paperbacks in publishing
history. Currently doing entire "Danger
Guys" series for Harper Collins.

Scrofani, Joseph
353 W 53rd St, NYC, NY 10019
212 582.0023 / 212 682.2462
fax 212 582.0090
page 179

Scudder, Brooke
6390 Hillegass Ave, Oakland, CA 94618
510 652.9246

Scullin, Maureen
109 W Hanover Ave, Randolph, NJ 07869
201 895.8858

Seabaugh, Max
302 23rd Ave, S.F., CA 94121
415 750.1373

Seabrook, Alexis
167 Long Lots Rd, Westport, CT 06880
203 259.4113

Seaholm, Eric
1311 Harold, Houston, TX 77006
713 526.4250

Sealock, Rick
112 C 17th Ave NW, Calgary, AB,
Canada T2M 0M6
403 276.5428

Seaver, Jeff
130 W 24th St, NYC, NY 10011
212 741.2279

Secker, Peter T
PO Box 1160, Wayne, IL 60184
708 289.1700

Seibold, J Otto
S.F., CA
415 558.9115

Seiffer, Alison
305 Canal St, NYC, NY 10013
212 941.7076

Seigel, Fran
515 Madison Ave, NYC, NY 10022
212 486.9644

Sekine, Hisashi
Three Crested Butte Cir, Laguna Niguel, CA 92677
714 363.0705

Selby, Andrea
280 Madison, NYC, NY 10016
212 545.9155

Selby, Bob
159 Lyman St, Pawtucket, RI 02860
401 725.3327

Sell Inc
333 N Michigan Ave, Chicago, IL 60601
312 578.8844
fax 312 578.8847
pages 269, 345, 443

Selman, Larry
381 Park Ave S, NYC, NY 10016
212 889.2400

Selwyn, Paul
PO Box 201, N Marshfield, MA 02059
617 266.3858

Senn, Oscar
1532 Riverside Ave, Jacksonville, FL 32204
904 358.1445

Setterlund, Theresa
6847 Leyland Park Dr, San Jose, CA 95120
408 997.1053

Shadle, Kathlyn
101 Yesler Way, Seattle, WA 98104
206 447.1600

Shaffer, Shelly
HC 30 Box 1025, Sedona, AZ 86336
602 282.6303

Shaller, Bernice
10101 Grosvner Pl, Rockville, MD 20852
301 897.9495

Shannon, Bill Illustration
6800 Milikin Rd, Middletown, OH 45044
513 777.5418

Shannon, David
1328 W Morningside Dr, Burbank, CA 91506
818 563.6763

Shannon/Avery
327 E 89th St, NYC, NY 10128
212 831.5650

Shap, Sandra
853 Broadway, NYC, NY 10003
212 677.9100

Sharp, Bruce
2814 NW 72nd St, Seattle, WA 98117
206 784.1136

Sharp, Chris
156 Ludlow St, NYC, NY 10002
212 505.0649
page 277

Sharpe & Associates
25 W 68th St, NYC, NY 10023
212 595.1125

Sharpe & Associates
7536 Ogelsby Ave, L.A., CA 90045
310 641.8556

Sharpshooter Creative Rep
Toronto, ONT
416 703.5300
page 395

Shaul, Wendy
7556 Rio Mondego Dr, Sacramento, CA 95831
916 429.0288

Shaw, Barclay
170 East St, Sharon, CT 06069
203 364.5974

Shax, Sy
49 W 45th St, NYC, NY 10036
212 921.1199

Shay, RJ/Studio X
3301 S Jefferson Ave,
St Louis, MO 63118
314 773.9989
fax 314 773.6406
page 450

Sheban, Chris
1807 W Sunnyside Ave, Chicago, IL 60640
312 271.2720

SHEd
924 Lincoln Rd, Miami Beach, FL 33139
305 531.7338

Shed, Greg
716 Sanchez St, S.F., CA 94114
415 285.8267

Sheehy, Michael
c/o Bernstein & Andriulli
60 E 42nd St, NYC, NY 10165
212 682.1490

Shega, Marla
4401 Edinburg Ln,
Hanover Park, IL 60103
708 830.4745
fax 708 830.4745
Marla specializes in detailed, realistic
illustrations, whether it's B&W stipple or
full color. Clients include AT&T, Turner
Publishing, Inc., McDonald's and Wendy's.

Shekut, Linda
PO Box 928, Mt Prospect, IL 60056
708 806.0661

Sheldon, Paul
232 Madison Ave, NYC, NY 10016
212 889.8777

Shelly, Jeff
1202 N Harper Ave, L.A., CA 90046
213 654.7368 / 800 318.3244
fax 213 654.8146
page 358

Shelly, Roger
716 Montgomery St, S.F., CA 94111
415 433.1222

Shema, Bob
600 N Bishop Ave, Dallas, TX 75208
214 946.6569

Shephard, Tom
490 Rockside Rd, Cleveland, OH 44131
216 661.4222

Sheridan, Brian
145 Main St, Ossining, NY 10562
914 941.1738

Shigley Illustration
17696 Montero Rd, San Diego, CA 92128
619 451.1101

Shimamoto, Michiko
165 E 32nd St, NYC, NY 10016
212 686.3514

Shinnick, Margie
220 12th Ave, S.F., CA 94118
415 221.4208
fax 415 221.4208
page 431

Shires, Jeremy
49 W 45th St, NYC, NY 10036
212 921.1199

Shoemaker, Doug
5009 Excelsior Blvd, Mpls, MN 55416
612 925.1745

Shoffner, Terry
11 Irwin Ave, Toronto, ONT, Canada M4Y 1L1
416 967.6717

Shohet, Marti
125 W 77th St, NYC, NY 10024
212 799.6532

Shooting Star
1178 Broadway, NYC, NY 10001
212 447.0666

Shooting Star
1441 N McCadden Pl, Hollywood, CA 90028
213 469.2020

Short, Kevin A
34562B Via Catalina, Capistrano Beach, CA
92624
714 240.6979

Shultz, David
1863 S Pearl St, Denver, CO 80210
303 733.0128

SI International
43 E 19th St, NYC, NY 10003
212 254.4996

Siboldi, Carla
Ten Bloomfield Rd, Burlingame, CA 94010
415 344.5069

Sibthorp, Fletcher
58 W 15th St, NYC, NY 10011
212 741.2539

Siciliano, Gerald
Nine Garfield Pl, Brooklyn, NY 11215
718 636.4561

Sicoransa, John Storyboards
280 First Ave, NYC, NY 10009
212 674.0541

Siegel, Estelle
74 Laurel Hollow Ct, Edison, NJ 08820
908 753.9722

Siegel, Mark
97 Spring St, Watertown, MA 02172
617 923.9021

Sigal, Anya
7455-5 Shadyglade, N Hollywood, CA 91605
714 458.9597

Signorino, Slug
PO Box 387, Michigan City, IN 46360
219 879.5221

Silent Sounds Studio
Five Irwin St, Winthrop, MA 02152
617 846.5955

Sillen, Florence
55 W 11th St, NYC, NY 10011
212 243.9490

Silva, Simon
3197 N G St, San Bernardino, CA 92405
909 883.7901

Silvers, Bill
420 Lexington Ave, NYC, NY 10170
212 986.5680

Silvestri, Lorraine
122 Plimpton St, Walpole, MA 02081
508 668.0111
fax 508 668.0111
page 351

Simard, Remy
666 Greenwich St, NYC, NY 10014
212 675.5719

Simeone, Lauren E
855 Windsor-Perrineville Rd, Hightstown, NJ 08520
609 426.4490

Simon, Alex
49 W 45th St, NYC, NY 10036
212 921.1199

Simon, Arline
119 Morris St, Yonkers, NY 10705
914 963.6906

Simon, William
9431 Bonhomme Woods, St Louis, MO 63132
314 993.3522

Simonetti, Sally
1541 N Laurel, L.A., CA 90046
213 654.3729

Simpson, Jet
500 N Michigan, Chicago, IL 60611
312 661.1717

Simson, Orenthal James
Prisoner #3245936-634
LA, CA
800-SPRING ME

Sinclair, Valerie
501 Fifth Ave, NYC, NY 10017
212 490.2450
fax 212 697.6828
page 34

Singer, Alan D
3021 Elmwood Ave, Rochester, NY 14618
716 473.4115

Singer, Phillip
731 N 24th St, Phila, PA 19130
215 232.6666

Singleton, Bill
809 W Wedwick, Tuscon, AZ 85706
520 294.1667

Sipp, Geo
2720 Margaret Mitchell Dr NW,
Atlanta, GA 30327
404 352.9840

Sirrell, T
768 Red Oak Dr, Bartlett, IL 60103
708 213.9003

Sisco, Sam
Eight Sixth St, Toronto, ONT, Canada M8V 2Z9
416 251.5938

Siu, Peter
Four E Ohio, Chicago, IL 60611
312 944.1130

Skeen Studio
1908 Elderleaf Dr, Dallas, TX 75232
214 337.3528

Skeen, Keith D
3228 Prairie Dr, Deerfield, WI 53531
414 423.3020

Skelton, Steve
3205 Fifth St, Boulder, CO 80304
303 546.0117

Sketch Pad Studio
2605 Westgate Dr, Arlington, TX 76015
817 469.8151

Skidmore Inc
2100 W Big Beaver Rd, Troy, MI 48084
810 643.6000

Skillins, Gunar
Seven Wheelright Way, Smithtown, NY 11787
516 724.4877

Skinner, Cortney
32 Churchill Ave, Arlington, MA 02174
617 648.2875

Sklut-Lettire, Meryl
721 Pleasant Valley Way, W Orange, NJ 07052
201 669.8078

SKM Designs
351 Spruce St, Paynesville, MN 56362
612 243.3964

Skrzelowski, David
2233 Kemper Ln, Cincinnati, OH 45206
513 861.1400

Slack, Chuck
Nine Cambridge Ln, Lincolnshire, IL 60069
708 948.9226

Slackman, Chas B
320 E 57th St, NYC, NY 10022
212 758.8233

Slaske, Steve
PO Box 92314, Milwaukee, WI 53202
414 442.1022

Slater, Tim
67 Upper Mountain Ave, Montclair, NJ 07042
201 744.4465

Slattery, Jack
14814 Heritage Wood Dr, Houston, TX 77082
713 558.2246

Slemons, Jeff
2555 Walnut St, Denver, CO 80205
303 298.0807

Sloan, Michael
458 Eighth St, Brooklyn, NY 11215
718 788.5437
fax 718 499.8958
page 145

Sloan, Richard
4300 N Narragansett, Chicago, IL 60634
708 670.0912

Sloan, William A
236 W 26th St, NYC, NY 10001
212 463.7025

Slonim, David
232 South St, Chesterfield, IN 46017
317 378.6511

Smalley, Guy
5340 Date Palm St, Cocoa, FL 32927
407 639.0936
fax 407 633.1539
Stylized humorous illustrations. Works
in conventional or electronic media. See
Directory of Illustration #12 for samples.

Smallish, Craig
777 N Michigan Ave, Chicago, IL 60611
312 337.7770

Smith, Doug
121 Madison Ave, NYC, NY 10016
212 683.1362

Smith, E Silas
14303 Sandown Ct, Poway, CA 92064
619 748.7142

Smith, Eileen Fitzgerald
809 E 41st St, Savannah, GA 31401
912 233.3786

Smith, Elwood H
Two Locust Grove Rd, Rhinebeck, NY 12572
914 876.2358

Smith, Gary
67 Upper Mountain Ave, Montclair, NJ 07042
201 744.4465

Smith, JA
5455 Rosa, St Louis, MO 63109
314 832.1381

Smith, James Nol
Rte Two, Box 107, Unicoi, TN 37692
615 743.3883

Smith, Jere
2814 NW 72nd St, Seattle, WA 98117
206 784.1136
fax 206 784.1171
page 357

Smith, John
2208 Apache Ln, Woodridge, IL 60517
708 910.3583

Smith, John C
101 Yesler Way, Seattle, WA 98104
206 447.1600

Smith, Kirk Richard
492 Armstrong St, Columbus, OH 43215
614 464.0928
page 424

Smith, Laura
6545 Cahuenga Ter, Hollywood, CA 90068
213 467.1700

Smith, Mark T
235 E 22nd St, NYC, NY 10010
212 679.9485

Smith, Owen
135 Prospect Park SW, Brooklyn, NY 11218
718 788.5528

Smith, Polly Represents
1005 Sansome St, S.F., CA 94111
415 989.6501

Smith, Raymond E
602 Willow Ave, Hoboken, NJ 07030
201 653.6638

Smith, Rick
1236 Tranquilla, Dallas, TX 75218
214 321.6264

Smith, Susan
537 Chestnut St, Needham, MA 02192
617 449.7761

Smith, Theresa
666 Greenwich St, NYC, NY 10014
212 675.5719

Smith, Vernon
2125 Cruger Ave, Bronx, NY 10462
718 822.7303

Smith-Griswold, Wendy
Nine Babbling Brook Ln, Suffern, NY 10901
914 368.8606

Smola, Jim
94 Maple Hill Ave, Newington, CT 06111
203 665.0305

Smythe, Danny
405 N Wabash, Chicago, IL 60611
312 222.0337

Snave, Karen/Big Nasty Redhead
812 W Van Buren, Chicago, IL 60607
312 421.5137

Sneberger, Dan
c/o Fran Siegel
515 Madison Ave, Rm 2200, NYC, NY 10022
212 486.9644

Sneed, Brad
5112 W 72nd St, Prairie Village, KS 66208
913 362.6699

Snider, Jackie & Steve
RR Seven Hwy 30, Brighton, ONT,
Canada K0K 1H0
613 475.4551
pages 388-389

Snodgrass, Steve
770 N Halsted P102, Chicago, IL 60610
312 338.7110

Snyder, Deborah Artist Rep
5321 W 62nd St, Edina, MN 55436
612 922.3462

Snyder, Teresa
25727 Mountain Dr, Arlington, WA 98223
360 435.8998

Soder, Dan
2110 McCullough Ave, San Antonio, TX 78212
512 732.7858

Soderlind, Kirsten
c/o Vicki Morgan
194 Third Ave, NYC, NY 10003
212 475.0440

Sogabe, Aki
3319 170th St NE, Bellevue, WA 98008
206 881.7412

Soileau, Hodges
350 Flax Hill Rd, Norwalk, CT 06854
203 852.0751

Sokolowski, Ted
RD Two Box 408, Lake Ariel, PA 18436
717 937.4527

Soldat & Associates
307 N Michigan Ave, Chicago, IL 60601
312 201.9662

Sollenberger, Terry Lee
3820 CR 603B, Burleson, TX 76028
817 561.9191

Solomon, Debby
143 Greene St, NYC, NY 10012
212 473.0060
fax 212 473.7163
page 83

Solomon, Gary
6236 Teesdale Ave, N Hollywood, CA 91606
818 508.9381

Solomon, Richard
121 Madison Ave, NYC, NY 10016
212 683.1362

Soltis, Linda DeVito
PO Box 462, Woodbury, CT 09798
203 263.4019

Solway, Chuck
101 Yesler Way, Seattle, WA 98104
206 447.1600

Somers, Paul
333 N Michigan Ave, Chicago, IL 60601
312 553.9888

Somerville, Kevin
67 Upper Mountain Ave, Montclair, NJ 07042
201 744.4465

Sonneville, Dane & Associates Inc
67 Upper Mountain Ave, Montclair, NJ 07042
201 744.4465

Soos, Erne
2469 Pine Ave, Long Beach, CA 90806
310 424.5765

Sorel, Madeline
140 Jaffray St, Brooklyn, NY 11235
718 646.8404

Sorren, Joe
2125 NW Glisan, Portland, CA 97210
503 295.3670

Soukup, James
Rte One Box 207, Seward, NE 68434
402 643.2339

Soule, Robert
15229 Baughman Dr, Silver Spring, MD 20906
301 598.8883

Sours, Michael
1350 Chemical St, Dallas, TX 75207
214 748.8663

South, Randy
360 Ritch St, S.F., CA 94107
415 512.9010

Southern Draw
5025 Arapaho Rd, Addison, TX 75248
214 387.5667

Spacek, Peter
43 Murray St, NYC, NY 10007
212 962.7383
fax 212 571.4705
page 453

Spain, Valerie
83 Franklin St, Watertown, MA 02172
617 923.1989
fax 617 923.1989
page 147
Valerie is a collage artist. She uses a
variety of techniques, found images and
text to create unique illustrations.
Satisfied clients include: Bloomberg
Financial Markets, Boston Globe
Magazine, Nynex and Wang
Corporation.

Spalenka, Greg
21303 San Miguel St, Woodland Hls, CA 91364
818 992.5828

Sparacin, Ernest
3111 Cole Ave, Dallas, TX 75204
214 855.5405

Sparkman, Gene
PO Box 644-15 Bradley Ln,
Sandy Hook, CT 06482
203 426.0061

Spaulding, Kevin
5855 Green Valley Cir, Culver City, CA 90230
310 642.2721

Spear, Charles
456 Ninth St, Hoboken, NJ 07030
201 798.6466

Specker, Lou
5510 Penway Ct, Cincinnati, OH 45239
512 326.9015

Spector, Joel
Three Maplewood Dr, New Milford, CT 06776
203 355.5942

Spectrum Studio
206 N First St, Mpls, MN 55401
612 332.2361

Speers, Pauline Cilmi
5393 SE Bulman Ave, Port Orchard, WA
98366
206 871.2800
page 306

Speidel, Sandra
616 1/2 West St, S.F., CA 94952
707 765.1151

Spencer, Joe
11201 Valley Spring Ln, Studio City, CA 91602
818 760.0216

Spencer, Mary
7816 Connie Dr, Huntington Beach, CA 92648
714 848.4954

Spencer, Torrey
11201 Valley Spring Ln, Studio City, CA 91602
818 505.1124

Spengler, Ken
2668 17th St, Sacramento, CA 95818
916 441.1932
page 380

Spengler, Margaret
2668 17th St, Sacramento, CA 95818
916 441.1932

Spiegelman, Art
27 Greene St, NYC, NY 10013
212 226.0146

Spiers, Herbert
43 E 19th St, NYC, NY 10003
212 254.4996

Spilsbury, Simon/CIA
c/o Bernstein & Andriulli
60 E 42nd St, NYC, NY 10165
212 682.1490

Spina-Dixon, Debra
5617 Ocean View Dr,
Oakland, CA 94618
510 652.6909
page 235

Spino, Pete
3050 Kellogg St, San Diego, CA 92106
619 225.9476

Splash Page
4300 N Narragansett, Chicago, IL 60634
708 670.0912

Spollen, Chris
362 Cromwell Ave, Ocean Breeze, NY 10305
718 979.9695

Spoon, Wilfred
773 Castro St, S.F., CA 94114
415 282.8479
page 113
Lighthearted illustrations in pen & ink,
watercolor and colored pencil.

Spoon, Wilfred
c/o Barb Hauser
PO Box 421443, S.F., CA 94142
415 647.5660
fax 415 285.1102

Sposato, John
43 E 22nd St, NYC, NY 10010
212 477.3909

Spotted Dog Creative
32925 NE Old Parrett Mtn Rd,
Newberg, OR 97132
503 537.9324

Springer, Sally
Creek View Dr, Millsboro, DE 19966
302 945.9423

Sprouls, Kevin
One Schooner Ln, Sweetwater, NJ 08037
609 965.4795

Spurll, Barbara
366 Adelaide St E, Toronto, ONT,
Canada M5A 3X9
416 594.6594
fax 416 601.1010
page 386

Square Moon
Six Monterey Ter, Orinda, CA 94563
510 253.9451

Squire, Terry
4233 Mountainbrook Rd, Apex, NC 27502
919 772.1262

St Clair, Linda
7028 Wabash Cir, Dallas, TX 75214
214 328.6662

Staake, Bob
726 S Ballas Rd, St Louis, MO 63122
314 961.2303

Stabin, Victor
84-21 Midland Pky, Jamaica, NY 11432
718 658.6842

Stabler, Barton
419 Tremont Ave, Westfield, NJ 07090
908 789.7415

Stagg, James
272 Bay Vista Cir, Sausalito, CA 94965
415 332.7856

Stahl, Nancy
470 W End Ave, NYC, NY 10024
212 362.8779

Stallard, Peter
1863 S Pearl St, Denver, CO 80210
303 733.0128 / 800 417.5120
fax 303 733.8154
page 325

Stammen, Jo Ellen
RR One 4163A, Camden, ME 04843
207 236.0729

Stanford, Walter
1826 Asheville Pl, Charlotte, NC 28203
704 372.6007

Stankciewicz, Steve
Four Prospect St, Beverly, MA 01915
508 921.0887

Stanley, Tom
1741 Prospect, Santa Barbara, CA 93103
805 687.1223

Starrett, Terri
900 W Jackson Blvd, Chicago, IL 60607
312 944.5680
fax 312 944.5948
page 90

Stark, Emma
1209 Reynolds, Bryan, TX 77803
409 779.0722

Starr, Jim
138 W 25th St, Baltimore, MD 21218
410 889.0703
fax 410 889.5498
page 402
Jim enjoys working in several styles including black and white graphics, color graphics, woodcut, scratchboard, pen and ink, and pastel. His scratchboard style is represented in this CIB. Please call Jim to see his portfolio.

Stasolla, Mario
37 Cedar Hill Ave, South Nyack, NY 10960
914 353.3086

Steadman, Broeck
89 Fifth Ave, NYC, NY 10003
212 627.1554

Steadman, Ralph
c/o Sobol Weber
146 E 19th St, NYC, NY 10013
212 420.8585

Steam Inc
c/o Vicki Morgan
194 Third Ave, NYC, NY 10003
212 475.0440

Stearney, Mark
621 S Plymouth Ct, Chicago, IL 60605
312 360.9033
fax 312 360.9034
pages 12-13

Steele, Mark
686 Massachusetts Ave, Cambridge, MA 02139
617 491.5678

Steele, Marlene
2233 Kemper Ln, Cincinnati, OH 45206
513 861.1400

Steele, Robert Gantt
250 W 57th St, NYC, NY 10107
212 397.7330

Stefanski, Janice
2022 Jones St, S.F., CA 94133
415 928.0457
fax 415 775.6337
page 381

Stehrenberger, Michiko
NYC, NY
718 797.4557
fax 718 797.4557
page 80
Takes pride in creating unusual characters and images (humorous people, animals, celebrity caricatures) ranging from full-color paintings to line art and other media. Possible uses include posters, picture books, developmental sketching and design. Clients include Hyperion Books, Miramax Films, Entertainment Weekly, Playboy. [Art Center BFA/Honors]

Stein, August
c/o Leighton & Co
Four Prospect St, Beverly, MA 01915
508 921.0887
fax 508 921.0223
page 217

Steinberg, James
41 Fruit St, Worcester, MA 01609
508 792.0372

Steiner, Joan
Bate Rd, Craryville, NY 12521
518 851.7199

Steirnagle, Michael
2116 Rock Glen, Escondido, CA 92026
619 736.4015

Stentz, Nancy
PO Box 19412, Seattle, WA 98109
206 634.1880

Stepanek, Mike
1014 S Scoville, Oak Park, IL 60304
708 848.9479

Stergulz, Richard
625 W 17th Pl, Tempe, AZ 85281
602 921.0037

Stermer, Dugald
600 The Embarcadero, S.F., CA 94107
415 441.4384

Sterrett, Jane
160 Fifth Ave, NYC, NY 10010
212 929.2566

Stevens, Daryl
1310 Clinton St, Nashville, TN 37203
615 327.9627
fax 615 327.0227
page 378
High impact, bold lines, dynamic composition, vivid color and texture characterize Daryl's style. Specializing in conceptual illustration from kids to corporate subjects, Daryl has the creativity and versatility to visualize anything you can imagine.

Stevens, Georgiann
4727 E Warner Rd, Phoenix, AZ 85044
602 496.9658

Stevens, Heidi
22 Tenth St, Petaluma, CA 94952
707 769.1252
fax 707 769.1252
page 333

Stevens, Robin
410 N Michigan Ave, Chicago, IL 60611
312 689.3442
page 375

Stevenson, Dave
733 Owl Dr, Vacaville, CA 95687
707 447.5720

Stewart, Don
117 W Green Ct, Greensboro, NC 27407
910 854.2769

Stewart, JW
250 W 57th St, NYC, NY 10107
212 397.7330
fax 212 397.7334
pages 242-243

Stiglich, Joyce
727 Forest Glen Ct, Maitland, FL 32751
407 644.5294
page 109

Stiles, Geoff
PO Box 31, Upper Falls, MD 21156
410 679.3517

Still, Wayne Anthony
67 Upper Mountain Ave, Montclair, NJ 07042
201 744.4465

Stillman, Susan
25 Alexander Ave, White Plains, NY 10606
914 682.3771

Stilwell, Jim
108 Palomino Cir, Boca Raton, FL 33487
407 994.8511

Stine, Christopher
731 SE 41st St, Portland, OR 97214
503 238.1820

Stirnweis, Shannon
31 Fawn Pl, Wilton, CT 06897
203 762.7058

Stock, Jeffrey
30 Doaks Ln, Marblehead, MA 01945
617 639.8384

Stokes, Fiona
6248 Goshen St, Simi Valley, CA 93063
805 584.1775

Stone, Sylvia
24 Prudence Dr, Stamford, CT 06907
203 322.2634

Storey, Barron
Nine Kramer Pl, S.F., CA 94133
415 986.4086

Storozuk, Walter
25 W 45th St, NYC, NY 10036
212 398.9540

Storyboards Inc
4052 Del Rey Ave, Venice, CA 90292
310 305.1998

Stout, Tim
Ten E Ontario, Chicago, IL 60611
312 573.1370

Strang, Helen
14618 Tyler Foote Blvd, Nevada City, CA 95959
916 292.3433

Straub, Matt Illustration
207 Ave B, NYC, NY 10009
212 995.9359

Strebel, Carol
2930 Hackberry St, Cincinnati, OH 45206
513 281.6837

Street, Suzanne C
3106 Robinhood St, Houston, TX 77005
713 666.3409

Strelecki, Karen
848 Greenwood Ave NE,
Atlanta, GA 30306
404 875.1363 / 800 347.0734
fax 404 875.9733
page 341

Stromoski, Rick
19 Stuyvesant Oval, NYC, NY 10009
212 505.9342

Stroster, Maria
2057 N Sheffield Ave, Chicago, IL 60614
312 525.2081

Struthers, Doug
6453 Southpoint Dr, Dallas, TX 75248
214 931.0838

Stuart, Walter
716 Sanchez St, S.F., CA 94114
415 285.8267
fax 415 285.8268
page 68

Stubbs, Elizabeth
27 Wyman St, Arlington, MA 02174
617 646.0785

Stubbs, Tommy
4628 Mossburg Ct, Atlanta, GA 30066
404 924.2382

Studio D Inc
7026 SW 106th Pl, Miami, FL 33173
305 371.9417

Studio G Inc
755 Marine Ave, Manhattan Beach, CA 90266
310 545.7709

Studio Macbeth
232 Madison Ave, NYC, NY 10016
212 889.8777

Studio MD
1512 Alaskan Way, Seattle, WA 98101
206 682.6221

Studio West Inc
1005 W Franklin Ave, Mpls, MN 55405
612 871.2900

The Studio
216 E 45th St, NYC, NY 10017
212 661.1363

Stuhmer, Robert
49 W 45th St, NYC, NY 10036
212 921.1199

Sturman, Sally Mara
195 Prospect Pl, Brooklyn, NY 11238
718 857.6743

Sturtz, Donald
758 Hacienda Ave, Campbell, CA 95008
408 370.7106

Stutzman, Laura
100 G St, Mt Lake Park, MD 21550
301 334.4086
fax 301 334.4186
pages 279

Stutzman, Mark
100 G St, Mt Lake Park, MD 21550
301 334.4086
fax 301 334.4186
pages 278

Succinct Ink
5442 E Flower St, Phoenix, AZ 85018
602 840.5635

Sucher, Laurie
6718 N Newgard, Chicago, IL 60626
312 764.2692

Suchit, Stu
284 Fourth St, Jersey City, NJ 07302
201 963.3011
page 56

Suchit, Stu
501 Fifth Ave, NYC, NY 10017
212 490.2450
fax 212 697.6828
page 56

Sudavicius, Dalia
5619 Burdette St, Omaha, NE 68104
402 556.5842

Suggs, Margaret Anne
678 Sunnybrook Dr, Decatur, GA 30033
404 329.0166

Suhrie, Rhonda
12056 Summit Cir, Beverly Hills, CA 90210
310 276.5282

Sullivan & Associates
3805 Maple Ct, Marietta, GA 30066
404 971.6782

Sullivan, Dave
101 Monmouth St, Brookline, MA 02146
617 277.0921

Sullivan, Don
912 S Telluride St, Aurora, CO 80017
303 671.9257
fax 303 752.3037
page 406

Sullivan, Suzanne Hughes
30 Summit St, Eastchester, NY 10707
914 961.6077

Sumichrast, Jozef
501 Fifth Ave, NYC, NY 10017
212 490.2450

Summers, Mark
12 Milverton Close, Watertown,
ONT, Canada LOR 2H3
905 689.6219

Sumpter, Will & Associates
1728 N Rock Springs Rd, Atlanta, GA 30324
404 874.2014

Susan Tracy Illustrative Dsgn
2031 State St, Santa Barbara, CA 93105
805 687.8014

Sutherland, Kelly Stribling
1208 San Gabriel Dr, Denton, TX 76205
817 382.1253

Swales, Scott
1019 Main St, Phoenix, NY 13135
315 695.4519

Swan, Joan
111 NE 42nd St, Miami, FL 33137
305 576.0142 / 800 484 8592 code 2787
fax 305 576.0138
page 307

Swan, Sara
770 N Halsted P102, Chicago, IL 60622
312 338.7110

Swan, Susan Illustration
83 Saugatuck Ave, Westport, CT 06880
203 226.9104

Swanson, James
15 Richmond Ave,
La Grange Park, IL 60525
708 352.3081
fax 708 352.3082
page 65

Swarts, Jeff
308 S Cedar St, Danville, OH 43014
614 599.6516
fax 614 599.6516
page 367
A versatile illustrator with 18 years of
professional experience, Jeff focuses on
outdoor and organic themes; product,
editorial and spot illustration.

Sweat, Lynn
218 Case St, W Granby, CT 06090
203 693.9449

Sweeney, Jerry
1644 Beryl Dr, Pittsburgh, PA 15227
412 884.5704

Sweeny, Glynis
346 W Webster St, Ferndale, MI 48220
716 633.4679

Sweet, Brian
11 Kings Ridge Rd, Long Valley, NJ 07853
908 813.8718

Sweet, Melissa
280 Madison Ave, NYC, NY 10016
212 545.9155

Sweet, Ron Represents
716 Montgomery St, S.F., CA 94111
415 433.1222
fax 415 433.9560
page 400

Sweny, Stephen
3121 Hollywood Dr, Decatur, GA 30033
404 299.7535

Swerdlow, Trina
PO Box 23987, Pleasant Hill, CA 94523
510 687.6499

Swierzy, Waldemar
211 E 89th St, NYC, NY 10128
212 289.5514

Swift, Elvis
817 S Westwood Dr, Mpls, MN 55416
612 374.3169

Swift, Michael
5855 Green Valley Cir, Culver City, CA 90230
310 642.2721

Switlik, Mark
502 W Jackson St, Phoenix, AZ 85003
602 254.7840

Sylvada, Peter
2026 #D Montgomery Ave, Cardiff, CA 92007
619 436.6807

Syme, Hugh
3868 S Spiceland Rd, New Castle, IN 47362
317 529.0978

Szpura, Beata
48-02 69th St, Woodside, NY 11377
718 424.8440

Szumowski, Tom
221 Bigelow St, Marlboro, MA 01752
508 480.8757

Taback, Simms
270 Park Ave S, NYC, NY 10010
212 260.6700

Tachiera, Andrea
7416 Fairmount Ave, El Cerrito, CA 94530
510 525.3484

Tagel, Peggy
666 Greenwich St, NYC, NY 10014
212 675.5719

Taglianetti, Clare
731 N 24th St, Phila, PA 19130
215 232.6666

Takagi, Michael
23 NW Greenwood Ave,
Bend, OR 97701
503 385.3263
fax 503 385.8877
page 412

Talalla, Doug
4616 Grand Ave S, Mpls, MN 55409
612 827.0032

Talaro, Lionel
22 E 36th St, NYC, NY 10016
212 685.4580

Talcott, Julia Illustration
74 Elmhurst Rd, Newton, MA 02158
617 964.6556
fax 617 964.6556
page 146

Taleporos, Plato
333 E 23rd St, NYC, NY 10010
212 689.3138

Tamara
3490 Piedmont Rd #1200, Atlanta, GA 30305
404 262.1209

Tamura, David
412 N Midland, Upper Nyack, NY 10960
212 686.4559

Tanaka, Lynn
4018 W 44th St, Edina, MN 55424
612 926.8923

Tanenbaum, Robert
5505 Corbin Ave, Tarzana, CA 91356
818 345.6741

Tanhauser, Gary
716 Sanchez St, S.F., CA 94114
415 285.8267

Tank, Darrel
716 Montgomery St, S.F., CA 94111
415 433.1222

Tanovitz, Ron
6300 Estates Dr, Oakland, CA 94611
510 339.0182

Tarabay, Sharif
597 Riverside Ave, Westport, CT 06880
203 226.4724

Taranovic, Lydia
280 Madison Ave, NYC, NY 10016
212 545.9155

Tarlofsky, Malcolm
PO Box 786, Glen Allen, CA 95442
707 833.4442

Tate, Clarke
301 Woodford St, PO Box 339, Gridley, IL 61744
309 747.3388

Taugher, Larry
903 Montello St, Hood River, OR 97031
800 386.5905

Taulman, Derek
4331 Dickason, Dallas, TX 75219
214 880.0888

Tauss, Herbert
South Mountain Pass, Garrison, NY 10524
914 424.3765

Tavonatti, Mia
440 Bolero, Newport Beach, CA 92663
714 646.6596

Taxali, Gary
1589 Lovelady Crescent, Mississauga, ONT,
Canada L4W 2Y9
905 625.1079

Taylor, C Winston
17008 Lisette St, Granada Hills, CA 91344
818 363.5761

Taylor, Dahl
c/o Vicki Morgan
194 Third Ave, NYC, NY 10003
212 475.0440

Taylor, Joseph
2117 Ewing Ave, Evanston, IL 60201
708 328.2454
fax 708 328.2485
page 426

Teach, Buz
2501 11th Ave, Sacramento, CA 95818
916 454.3556

Team Design
1809 Seventh Ave, Seattle, WA 98101
206 623.1044

Teare, Brad
89 Fifth Ave, NYC, NY 10003
212 627.1554

Tedesco, Michael
120 Boerum Pl, Brooklyn, NY 11201
718 237.9164

Teebken, Tim
716 Sanchez St, S.F., CA 94114
415 285.8267

Teisher, Ann
977 Via Del Monte, Palos Verdes, CA 90274
310 375.0575

Ten, Arnie
37 Forbus St, Poughkeepsie, NY 12601
914 485.8419

Tenorio, Juan
426 Himrod St, Brooklyn, NY 11237
718 366.2904

Tenret, Carla Calligraphy & Design
623 Cornell Ave, Albany, CA 94706
510 526.7545
fax 510 526.6234
Carla is a lettering artist specializing in the calligraphic and book arts. She delights in designing 'one-of' artists' books in addition to the myriad lettering needs small and large as needed by her clients.

Tenud, Tish
3427 Folsom Blvd,
Sacramento, CA 95816
916 455.0569
fax 916 451.6037
page 201

Teodecki, William
731 N 24th St, Phila, PA 19130
215 232.6666

Teri O
1045 Diamond NE, Grand Rapids, MI 49503
616 454.1270

Terreson, Jeffrey
66 Hack Green Rd, Pound Ridge, NY 10576
914 764.4897

Terry, Emerson
511 Wyoming St, Pasadena, CA 91103
213 681.4115

Tessler, John
1409 R St, Sacramento, CA 95814
916 443.9080

Thacker, Kat
280 Madison Ave, NYC, NY 10016
212 545.9155

Thatcher, David
5309 Halifax Ave S, Edina, MN 55424
612 922.6874

The Studio/Lynne Tucker & Co
2001 S Barrington, L.A., CA 90025
310 996.6767
fax 310 996.6766
The Studio specializes in computer production, advertising, and graphic design, supporting advertising agencies nationwide and clients directly. Our client list includes: Chiat/Day, Ketchum Communications, Sachs/Finley, Hyundai Motor Corporation, Crystal Cruises and Princess Cruises.

Thermes, Jennifer
Five Wendover Rd, Newtown, CT 06470
203 270.0539

Thibodeau, Michael
85 1/2 Third Pl, Brooklyn, NY 11215
718 797.4104

Thiesen, Jim
381 Park Ave S, NYC, NY 10016
212 889.2400

Thole, Cathleen
353 W 53rd St, NYC, NY 10019
212 682.2462

Thomas, Melanie
Ten Bonnie Brae, Hinsdale, IL 60521
708 850.9825

Thomas, Rod
16 Grasmere Rd, Needham, MA 02194
617 449.0480
page 166

Thomas, Troy
1247 Portage Ln, Woodstock, IL 60098
815 338.9455

Thomas-Bradley Illustration & Design
411 Center St, Gidley, IL 61744
309 747.3266

The Thompson Brothers
331 W Stone Ave, Greenville, SC 29609
803 241.0810

Thompson, Art
39 Prospect Ave, Pompton Plains, NJ 07444
201 835.3534

Thompson, Darren
116 W Illinois, Chicago, IL 60610
312 472.7504
fax 312 472.7508
page 411
Editorial humor/watercolor and ink.
Clients: Chicago Tribune, Good
Housekeeping, GQ, Midwest Living,
Oxford University Press, Philadelphia
Enquirer, Playboy.

Thompson, Emily
433 W 43rd St, NYC, NY 10036
212 245.2543

Thompson, George
433 W 43rd St, NYC, NY 10036
212 245.2543

Thompson, Jay
3536 E Thompson St, Phila, PA 19134
215 634.2936

Thompson, John M
118 Parkview Ave, Weehawken, NJ 07087
201 865.7853

Thompson, M Kathryn
333 Cascade Dr, Fairfax, CA 94930
415 459.8835

Thompson, Marina
31 Willow Rd, Nahant, MA 01908
617 581.5808

Thompson, Richard
3504 N 21st St, Arlington, VA 22207
703 516.0354

Thompson, Thierry
212 Dorchester Ln, Alamo, CA 94507
510 210.0155

Thomson, Bill
325 W Huron, Chicago, IL 60611
312 787.6826

Thomson, Rick
1015 N 11th St, Boise, ID 83702
208 384.5205

Thomssen, Kate
1336 Scheffer Ave, St Paul, MN 55116
612 698.9129

Thorn, Dick
353 W 53rd St, NYC, NY 10019
212 682.2462

Thornburgh, Bethann
1673 Columbia Rd NW, Wash, DC 20009
202 667.0147

Thornley, Blair
1251 University Ave, San Diego, CA 92103
619 299.3874

Thorpe, Peter
254 Park Ave S, NYC, NY 10010
212 477.0131

Those 3 Reps
2909 Cole Ave, Dallas, TX 75204
214 871.1347
fax 214 880.0337
pages 316-317

Thrun, Thomas
36 Cory Rd, Flanders, NJ 07836
201 927.7316

Thrush, Denny Lee/Davanti Media
920 W Market St, Lima, OH 45805
419 227.4988
Agriculture, Consumer, and Industrial
Illustrations. Clients: Cadillac, Girl Scouts,
Huffy Bicycles, John Deere & Co., White/
New Idea, Time Warner, Vroman Foods.

Thurston, Russell Studio
2315 W Huron, Chicago, IL 60612
312 235.6257

Tiani, Alex
9401 Ivy Ridge Pl, Charlotte, NC 28269
704 599.0414

Tibbles, Jean-Paul
c/o Bernstein & Andriulli
60 E 42nd St, NYC, NY 10165
212 682.1490

Tiessen, Ken
900 W Jackson Blvd, Chicago, IL 60607
312 944.5680

Tiffany Represents
2000 Second Ave, Seattle, WA 98121
206 441.7701
fax 206 441.3022
page 255

Tilley, Debbie
2051 Shadetree Ln, Escondido, CA 92029
619 432.6282

Tillinghast, David
1003 Diamond Ave, Pasadena, CA 91030
818 403.0991

Tim Gabor
1426 S Jackson St, Seattle, WA 98144
206 860.0089

Timmons, Bonnie
NYC, NY
212 581.8338
page 462

Timmons, Bonnie
18 McKinley St, Rowayton, CT 06853
203 866.3734
fax 203 857.0842
page 462

Timmons, Bonnie
109 Springdell Rd,
Coatesville, PA 19320
610 380.0292
fax 610 380.0479
page 462

Tinkelman, Murray
75 Lakeview Ave W, Peekskill, NY 10566
914 737.5960

Tipton, Beth
840 Bricken Pl, St Louis, MO 63122
314 821.2278

Tise, Katherine
200 E 78th St, NYC, NY 10021
212 570.9069

Tobin, Nancy
Six Monterey Ter, Orinda, CA 94563
510 253.9451

Tocchet, Mark J
225 Weldy Ave, Oreland, PA 19075
215 885.1292

Tocco, Douglas
27542 Newport, Warren, MI 48093
810 755.2729

Toelke, Cathleen
PO Box 487, Rhinebeck, NY 12572
914 876.8776

Tofanelli, Mike
1100 Howe Ave, Sacramento, CA 95825
916 927.4809
fax 916 927.4809
page 335
Mike creates stylized humorous and
editorial illustration with people and
animals as main subject matter. Clients
include Cellular One, Cahners
Publishing, California Journal, Detroit
Free Press Magazine, Variety,
McDonald's, and McGraw-Hill.

Tom, Jack
135 Lazy Brook Rd, Monroe, CT 06468
203 452.0889

Tomas, Luis
7373 Scottsdale Civic Ctr, Scottsdale, AZ 85251
602 947.4614

Tomasulo, Patrick
76 Howard St, Dumont, NJ 07628
201 385.4350

Tomlinson, Richard
319 E 24th St, NYC, NY 10010
212 685.0552

Tonal Values
37 Nokomis Ave,
San Anselmo, CA 94960
415 457.3695 / 800 484.8520 code 1464
fax 415 457.6051
page 305-307

Tonal Values
111 NE 42nd St, Miami, FL 33137
305 576.0142 / 800 484.8592 code 2787
fax 305 576.0138
page 305-307

Tonkin, Tom
353 W 53rd St, NYC, NY 10019
212 682.2462

Toomer, George Sr
3923 Cole Ave, Dallas, TX 75204
214 522.1171
fax 214 528.3588
pages 174-175

Toos, Andrew
50 Bullymuck Rd, New Milford, CT 06776
203 350.3718

Torline, Kevin
2233 Kemper Ln, Cincinnati, OH 45206
513 861.1400

Torp, Cynthia
250 W 57th St, NYC, NY 10107
212 397.7330

Torres, April
106 Covina, Long Beach, CA 90803
310 434.2041

Torres, Carlos
60 Hagen Ave, N Tonawanda, NY 14120
212 831.5650

Torres, Cecilia
1156 Western Ave, Glendale, CA 91201
818 243.0501

Torres, Daniel
11 Kings Ridge Rd, Long Valley, NJ 07853
908 813.8718

Tosch, Jaime R
8732 Fair Oaks Blvd, Carmichael, CA 95608
916 944.2097

Towner, Bob
5855 Green Valley Cir, Culver City, CA 90230
310 642.2721

Trachok, Cathy
1120 Tropical Ave, Pasadena, CA 91107
818 351.1635

Trang, Winson
15 Mill Valley Rd, Phillips Ranch, CA 91766
909 397.9898

Traynor, Elizabeth
702 Nottingham Rd,
Wilmington, DE 19805
302 658.6637
page 338

Treadway, Todd
778 S Swadley St, Lakewood, CO 80228
303 763.9288

Tremlett, Mark
111 NE 42nd St, Miami, FL 33137
305 576.0142

Trimpe, Susan & Co
2717 Western Ave, Seattle, WA 98121
206 728.1300
page 72-73

Trondsen, Bob
49 W 45th St, NYC, NY 10036
212 921.1199

Trondsen, Robert O
36 Lake Rd, Salisbury Mills, NY 12577
914 496.8795

Trout, Brook
211 E Whittier St, Columbus, OH 43206
614 449.2640

Trout, Cary Michael
739 Bryant St, S.F., CA 94107
415 896.5275

Truxaw, Richard
6404 W 125th St, Overland Park, KS 66209
913 338.4224

Tucker, Ezra
325 W Huron, Chicago, IL 60611
312 787.6826

Tucker, Greg
c/o Carol Chislovsky Design
853 Broadway, NYC, NY 10003
212 677.9100
page 125

Tuke, Joni
325 W Huron, Chicago, IL 60610
312 787.6826

Tull, Bobbi
6103 Beachway Dr, Falls Church, VA 22041
703 998.9292

Turgeon, Jim
405 N Wabash Ave, Chicago, IL 60611
312 644.1444

Turgeon, Pol
250 W 57th St, NYC, NY 10107
212 397.7330
fax 212 397.7334
page 247

Turk, Melissa/Artist Network
Nine Babbling Brook Ln, Suffern, NY 10901
914 368.8606

Turk, Stephen
927 Westbourne Dr, L.A., CA 90069
310 788.0682

Turner, Clay
320 S Boston Ave, Tulsa, OK 74103
918 745.9256

Turner, Ray
Pier 33 N, S.F., CA 94111
415 956.4750

Turner, Tracy
1727 S Indiana Ave, Chicago, IL 60616
312 663.5300

Turtel, Jason
574 Leheigh Ln, Woodmere, NY 11598
516 569.5437

Tusan, Stan
Six Monterey Ter, Orinda, CA 94563
510 253.9451

Tuttle, Jean
145 Palisade St, Dobbs Ferry, NY 10522
914 693.7681
fax 914 693.8123
page 150

Ty Methfessel
920 1/4 N Formosa Ave, L.A., CA 90046
213 850.7957

Tylden-Wright, Jenny
11 Kings Ridge Rd,
Long Valley, NJ 07853
908 813.8718
fax 908 813.0076
page 420

Tyrrell, Robert
Ten E Ontario St, Chicago, IL 60611
312 573.1370

Udave, Consuelo
3203 19th St, Bremerton, WA 98312
206 792.1017

Uhl, David Illustration Studio
1501 Boulder St, Denver, CO 80211
303 455.3535
fax 303 455.1603
pages 70-71

Ulay, Ayse
146 S Michigan Ave, Pasadena, CA 91106
818 796.4615

Ulrich, George
666 Greenwich St, NYC, NY 10014
212 675.5719

Ulriksen, Mark
841 Shrader St, S.F., CA 94117
415 387.0170

Ulve, Kirsten
770 N Halsted P102, Chicago, IL 60622
312 338.7110

Unger, Elaine
23650 Via Beguine, Valencia, CA 91355
805 259.2174

Unger, Judy J
19600 Ballinger St,
Northridge, CA 91324
818 701.9030
page 113
Photorealistic food and product illustration
for advertising and design with a specialty
in product labels. Primarily dye with
acrylic and colored pencil.

Unger, Judy
c/o Barb Hauser
PO Box 421443, S.F., CA 94142
415 647.5660
fax 415 285.1102
page 113

Unruh, Jack
716 Montgomery St, S.F., CA 94111
415 433.1222
fax 415 433.9560
page 400

Uram, Lauren
838 Carroll St, Brooklyn, NY 11215
718 789.7717

Urbanovic, Jackie/Cartoonist
420 N Fifth St, Mpls, MN 55401
612 673.9323
Jackie specializes in children's work, in
a variety of styles, mostly lighthearted.
Clients include Scholastic, Inc.,
Silver, Burdett & Ginn, Cultural Toys.
See CIB ads 1993, 1994.

Utley, Tom
490 Rockside Rd, Cleveland, OH 44131
216 661.4222

Uyehara, Elizabeth
135 Prospect Park SW, Brooklyn, NY 11218
718 788.5528

Vaccarello, Paul
1030 N State, Chicago, IL 60610
312 664.2233

Vainisi, Jennine
58 Middagh St, Brooklyn, NY 11201
718 858.4914

Valenti, Lisa
231 73rd St, Brooklyn, NY 11209
718 680.2223
fax 718 680.6080
Atmospheric pastel & ink renderings
with an elegant line quality. Women
and their world is a speciality: retro
subjects a favorite. Lisa also does
handlettering. Clients include AT&T and
Haagen - Dazs.

Valk, Tinam
280 Madison Ave, NYC, NY 10016
212 545.9155

Valko, Diane
235 S Beach Blvd, Anaheim, CA 92804
714 826.3440

Vallejo, Boris
Ten E Ontario, Chicago, IL 60611
312 573.1370

Valley, Gregg
128 Thomas Rd, McMurray, PA 15317
412 941.4662
fax 412 941.3490
page 126

Van Amerongen, Jerry
2533 Washburn Ave S, Mpls, MN 55416
612 374.9574

Van Dusen, Chris
37 Pearl St, Camden, ME 04843
207 236.2961

The Van Noy Group
19750 S Vermont Ave, Torrance, CA 90502
310 329.0800

Van Ryzin, Peter
c/o Bernstein & Andriulli
60 E 42nd St, NYC, NY 10165
212 867.8092

Van Seters, Kim
1202 Lessie Ct, Marietta, GA 30066
404 425.5707

van Valkenburgh, Sherilyn
102 Sidney Green St, Chapel Hill, NC 27516
919 968.1496

Vance, Steve
11936 W Jefferson Blvd, Culver City, CA 90230
310 390.8663

Vann, Bill Studio
1706 S Eighth St, St Louis, MO 63104
314 231.2322

Vanselow, Holly
1677 Tenth St, Sarasota, FL 34236
813 364.8866

Varah, Monte
c/o Carol Chislovsky Design
853 Broadway, NYC, NY 10003
212 677.9100
page 124

Vargo Bockos
500 N Michigan, Chicago, IL 60611
312 661.1717

Vargo, Kurt
94 New Monmouth Rd, Middletown, NJ 07748
908 671.8679

Vasconcellos, Daniel
225 Old Washington St,
Pembroke, MA 02359
617 829.8815
fax 617 829.8867
page 149

Vasquez, Madeline
3627 Niblick Dr, La Mesa, CA 91941
619 465.8683

Vass, Rod
353 W 53rd St, NYC, NY 10019
212 582.0023 / 212 682.2462
fax 212 582.0090
page 181

Vaughan, Jack
1826 Asheville Pl, Charlotte, NC 28203
704 372.6007

Vaughn, Rob
600 Curtiss Pky, Miami Springs, FL 33166
305 885.1292

Vella, Ray
20 N Broadway Bldg I-240,
White Plains, NY 10601
914 997.1424

Vellekoop, Maurice
51 Camden St, Toronto, ONT, Canada H2V 4K2
416 362.1913

Veltfort, Anna
16 W 86th St, NYC, NY 10024
212 877.0430

Ventura, Andrea
2785 Broadway, NYC, NY 10025
212 932.0412

Ventura, Marco
58 W 15th St, NYC, NY 10011
212 741.2539

Verbitsky, Alexander
45 Tiemann Pl, NYC, NY 10027
212 663.9219

Verkaaik, Ben
217 E 86th St, NYC, NY 10028
212 355.0910

Vermont, Hillary Designs
218 E 17th St, NYC, NY 10003
212 674.3845

Verougstraete, Randy
13012 Queensgate Rd, Midlothian, VA 23113
804 379.7986

Verzaal, Dale
331 W Smoke Tree Rd, Gilbert, AZ 85233
602 813.2528

Vetromile, Alfred
776 W Clear Creek Way, Tucson, AZ 85737
520 797.2669

Vibbert, Carolyn
1015 Battery St, S.F., CA 94111
415 398.9121

Vidinghoff, Carol M
11 Lloyd Rd, Watertown, MA 02172
617 924.4846

Villa, Roxana
16771 Addison St, Encino, CA 91436
818 906.3355

Villani, Ron
Ten E Ontario St, Chicago, IL 60611
312 573.1370

Vincent, Benjamin
3100 Carlisle, Dallas, TX 75204
214 871.0080

Vincent, Wayne
957 N Livingston St, Arlington, VA 22205
703 532.8551

Vinton, Will Studios
1400 NW 22nd Ave, Portland, OR 97210
503 225.1130

Virnig, Janet
2532 Kipling Ave S, Mpls, MN 55416
612 926.5585

Visionary Art Resources
1440 Veteran Ave, L.A., CA 90024
310 478.0954

Vismara, Paul
3521 N Wilton, Chicago, IL 60657
312 248.7084
fax 312 248.7505
page 272

Viss, Troy
4914 35th St, San Diego, CA 92116
619 230.1809

Visser, Karen
1979 Yonge St, Toronto, ONT, Canada M4S 1Z6
416 484.3779

Visual Logic
724 Yorklyn Rd, Hockessin, DE 19707
302 234.5707

Vitale, Stefano
250 W 57th St, NYC, NY 10107
212 397.7330
fax 212 397.7334
page 252

Vitsky, Sally Jo
4116 Bromley Ln, Richmond, VA 23221
804 359.4726

Viviano, Sam
25 W 13th St, NYC, NY 10011
212 242.1471

Vivit, Jerry
5855 Green Valley Cir, Culver City, CA 90230
310 642.2721

Vizbar, Milda
55 Bethune St, NYC, NY 10014
212 675.6293

von Buhler, Cynthia
16 Ashford St, Boston, MA 02134
617 783.2421

Von Haeger, Arden
416 Ramble Wood Cir, Nashville, TN 37221
615 646.7022

Von Kap-Herr, Victoria
1344 Lake Breeze Dr, Wellington, FL 33414
407 791.3345

Von Schmidt, Eric
859 N Hollywood Way, Burbank, CA 91505
818 559.1490

von Ulrich, Mark
One Union Sq W, NYC, NY 10003
212 989.9325
pages 60-61

Voo, Rhonda
Four E Ohio, Chicago, IL 60611
312 935.1707 / 312 944.1130
page 16
Cut paper that's joyful, spirited,
spontaneous, colorful, sophisticated,
graphic, impactful...but above all, FUN!! A
West Coast sensibility that spans all
borders. Clients: Pepsi, Disney, IBM, Bonne
Bell, Mattel, 3M, The Gap, American
Express, NBC, Random House, MCI.

Voss, Tom Illustration
632 McDonald Ln, Escondido, CA 92025
619 747.3946
page 87

Voss, Tom Illustration
1888 Century Park E, L.A., CA 90067
310 826.1332
fax 310 284.3290
page 87

Voth, Greg
67 Eighth Ave, NYC, NY 10014
212 807.9766

Voth, Pam
67 Upper Mountain Ave, Montclair, NJ 07042
201 744.4465

Voyajou, Diana
381 Park Ave S, NYC, NY 10016
212 889.2400

W.E.T. Studios
750 Second St, S.F., CA 94107
415 764.1992

W/C Studio
750 94th Ave N, St Petersburg, FL 33702
813 579.4499

Wack, Jeff
3614 Berry Dr, Studio City, CA 91604
818 508.0348

Waddell, Jan
Six Yule Ave, Toronto, ONT, Canada M6S 1E8
416 762.3961

Wagner, Brett
12056 Summit Cir, Beverly Hills, CA 90210
310 276.5282

Wagner, Marijke Paquay
1085 Hickory View Cir, Camarillo, CA 93012
805 987.1123

Wagoner, Jae
654 Pier Ave, Santa Monica, CA 90405
310 392.4877

Waldrep, Richard L
15804 Ensor Mill Rd, Sparks, MD 21152
410 472.2328

Waldron, Sarah Illustration
24 Western Ave, Petaluma, CA 94952
707 778.0848

Walker, John
4423 Wilson Ave, Downers Grove, IL 60515
708 963.8359

Walker, Lawrence
1740 W 120th St, L.A., CA 90047
213 777.5526

Walker, Norman
211 E 51st St, NYC, NY 10022
212 755.1365

Wall, Pam
c/o Bernstein & Andriulli
60 E 42nd St, NYC, NY 10165
212 682.1490

Wallace, Janet
PO Box 6495, Malibu, CA 90264
310 285.3028

Waller, Charles
35 Bethune St, NYC, NY 10014
212 989.5843

Walton, Brenda
14 Midway Ct, Sacramento, CA 95817
916 452.8977

Walton, Matt
7525 State Ln, Kansas City, MO 64114
816 363.6269

Ward, John
20 Birch St, Saranac Lake, NY 12983
518 891.4534

Ward, Keith
1717 N Marshall, Milwaukee, WI 53202
414 277.0733

Ward, Sam
6829 Murray Ln, Annandale, VA 22003
703 256.8313

Ward, Thomas
27 Granada Ave, Long Beach, CA 90803
310 987.5244

Ware, Richard Pattin
339 First Ave, NYC, NY 10003
212 673.9102

Warfield, DL
325 W Huron, Chicago, IL 60610
312 787.6826

Warhola, James
86 Spring St, Kingston, NY 12401
914 339.0082

Wariner, David
1826 Asheville Pl, Charlotte, NC 28203
704 372.6007

Warnick, Elsa
636 NW 20th, #7, Portland, OR 97209
503 228.2659
fax 503 228.2659
page 444
Please see my page in this book, and in
all prior CIB, (1990-1996) for both color
and one color water illustration, from
maps to botanical to conceptual images.

Warren, Dave
2233 Kemper Ln, Cincinnati, OH 45206
513 861.1400

Warren, Jim
11 Kings Ridge Rd,
Long Valley, NJ 07853
908 813.8718
fax 908 813.0076
page 423

Warren, Valerie
14 E Fourth St, NYC, NY 10012
212 505.5366

Warshaw Blumenthal
104 E 40th St, NYC, NY 10016
212 867.4225
fax 212 867.4154
Representing 25 different artist styles.
Our talents range from Tight to Loose:
Fashion to Display: Realistic to Cartoon:
Traditional to Computer. We are known
for Speed, Quality, and Reliability. Call
us at 212-867-4225

Warshaw/Humorous Design
800 Hinman Ave, Evanston, IL 60202
708 866.6667

Warter, Fred
PO Box 598, Los Olivos, CA 93441
805 686.5727

Washington, Dick
22727 Cielo Vista, San Antonio, TX 78255
210 698.1409

Wasserman, Amy L
PO Box 135, Northampton, MA 01061
413 586.0307
fax 413 586.0083
page 198
Amy is a collage illustrator with a
national client base which includes Time
& Smithsonian. She can also be reached
via e-mail: CutNPaced@aol.com

Wasson, Cameron
1118 Sir Francis Drake Blvd, Kentfield, CA 94904
415 455.8874

Waterhouse, Charles
67 Dartmouth St, Edison, NJ 08837
908 738.1804

Watford, Wayne
11936 W Jefferson Blvd, Culver City, CA 90230
310 390.8663

Watkinson, Brent
c/o Bernstein & Andriulli
60 E 42nd St, NYC, NY 10165
212 682.1490

Watson & Spierman Productions
524 Broadway, NYC, NY 10012
212 431.4480

Watson, Neil
22 E 36th St, NYC, NY 10016
212 685.4580

Watts, Mark
2004 Par Dr, Doylestown, PA 18901
215 343.8490

Watts, Sharon
201 Eastern Pky, Brooklyn, NY 11238
718 398.0451
page 449

Watts, Stan
353 W 53rd St, NYC, NY 10019
212 682.2462

Watts-Clark, Cynthia
36 Haggerty Hill Rd, Rhinebeck, NY 12572
914 876.2615

Wawiorka, Matt
5209 83rd St, Kenosha, WI 53142
414 697.9495

Wax, Wendy
322 E 55th St, NYC, NY 10022
212 371.6156

Weakley, Mark
105 N Alamo Rd, San Antonio, TX 78205
210 222.9543

Weast & Weast
1215 18th St, Sacramento, CA 95814
916 441.4231

Weaver, Mike
2927 W 43rd Ave,
Kansas City, KS 66103
913 432.5078
page 267

Weber, Mark
113 E 29th St, Erie, PA 16504
814 453.2050
Mark produces bold, expressive work
that is ideal for all forms of visual
communication.

Weber, Richard/Webwork Illustration
229 W Illinois, Chicago, IL 60610
312 802.5343

Weber, Tricia/The Weber Group
125 W 77th St, NYC, NY 10024
212 799.6532
pages 316-317

Webster & Associates
1445 Fern Pl, Vista, CA 92083
818 889.9131

Weems, Alexandra
200 E 94th St, NYC, NY 10028
212 369.6907

Wehrman, Richard
247 N Goodman St, Rochester, NY 14607
716 271.2280

Wehrman, Vicki
25 Drury Ln, Rochester, NY 14625
716 586.6041

Weiman, Jon
88 Wyckoff St, Brooklyn, NY 11201
718 855.8468

Weiner, Mark
164 E 37th St, NYC, NY 10016
212 696.1792

Weinman, Brad
310 E Santa Anita, Burbank, CA 91502
818 843.2249
fax 818 843.3008
page 98

Weinstein, Ellen
One Sq W, NYC, NY 10003
212 675.4360

Weinstein, Morey
807 Larkwood Dr, Greensboro, NC 27410
910 854.5161

Weisser, Carl Silhouettes
38 Livingston St, Brooklyn, NY 11201
718 834.0952

Welkis, Allen
25 W 45th St, NYC, NY 10036
212 398.9540

Weller, Charles
35 Bethune St, NYC, NY 10014
212 989.5843

Weller, Don
654 Pier Ave, Santa Monica, CA 90405
310 392.4877

Wells, Karen Represents
14027 Memorial Dr, Ste 125,
Houston, TX 77079
713 293.9375
fax 713 293.9375*
pages 346-349
/: Randy Rogers, Stephen Wells, Jeff
Sanson, Daphne McCormack, Dean
Williams, Kay Salem, Denise Chapman
Crawford.

Wells, Peter/Square Dogs Illustration
405 N Wabash Ave, Chicago, IL 60611
312 321.1336

Wells, Stephen
14027 Memorial Dr, Ste 125,
Houston, TX 77079
713 293.9375
fax 713 293.9375*
page 349

Wells, Susan & Associates
5134 Timber Trl NE, Atlanta, GA 30342
404 255.1430
fax 404 255.3449
page 185

Welty, Allyn
Ten Sea Ter, Dana Pt, CA 92629
714 489.5523

Wendt, Bobbi
152 Mississippi, S.F., CA 94107
415 487.2160

Wennekes, RH
1801 S Michigan Ave, Chicago, IL 60606
312 829.8853

Wenngren, Anders
450 Sixth Ave, NYC, NY 10011
212 353.1248

Wenzel, David
666 Greenwich St, NYC, NY 10014
212 675.5719

Wepplo, Mike
Ten Ranch Creek Ct, Pomona, CA 91766
909 865.5056

Werblun, Steve
5855 Green Valley Cir, Culver City, CA 90230
310 642.2721

Werner, Jerry
PO Box 133, Sisters, OR 97759
503 549.9130

Wesen, Michele
405 E 56th St, NYC, NY 10022
212 308.2422

West End Studios
2121 Cloverfield Blvd, Santa Monica, CA 90404
310 264.1717

West, Jeffery Design
736 N 17th, San Jose, CA 95112
408 971.0504

Westbrook, Eric
2830 27th St NW, Wash, DC 20008
202 328.8593

Westerfield, David
3525 W Peterson Ave, Chicago, IL 60659
312 588.4995

Westermeyer, Todd
2233 Kemper Ln, Cincinnati, OH 45206
513 861.1400

Westphal, Ken
325 W Huron St, Chicago, IL 60610
312 787.6826

Wet Paint
1684 Grand Ave, St Paul, MN 55105
612 698.6431

Wetmore, Barry
1840 Hanscom Dr, South Pasadena, CA 91030
213 254.5438

Wexler, Ed
4701 Don Pio Dr, Woodland Hills, CA 91364
818 888.3858

Whatley, Adam
4016 Jaffna Cove, Austin, TX 78749
512 891.9111

Wheatley-Maxwell, Misty
2233 Kemper Ln, Cincinnati, OH 45206
513 861.1400

Wheaton, Liz
16780 Dry Creek Ct, Morgan Hill, CA 95037
408 776.1325

Wheeler, Jody
375 South End Ave, NYC, NY 10280
212 775.1484

Whelan, Michael
23 Old Hayrake Rd, Danbury, CT 06811
203 792.8089

Whelan, Patrick James
490 S Coast Hwy, Laguna Beach, CA 92651
714 494.8175

Whipple, Rick
PO Box 2193, Grapevine, TX 76099
817 481.2212
fax 817 481.2908
pages 74

White Picket Studio
95 North Main, Petersham, MA 01366
508 724.8810

White, Bill
11712 Riviera Pl NE, Seattle, WA 98125
206 367.8003

White, Caroline
126 Ashfield Mountain Rd, Ashfield, MA 01330
413 628.4042

White, Eric
1142 Castro St, S.F., CA 94114
415 821.3839

White, Jim
6231 Forest Ave, Hammond, IN 46324
219 932.6394

White, John
PO Box 174/11440 Oak Dr,
Shelbyville, MI 49344
616 672.5756
fax 616 672.5757
page 108

White, John
1826 Asheville Pl, Charlotte, NC 28203
704 372.6007

White, Roger
160 West End Ave, NYC, NY 10023
212 362.1848

Whitesides, Kim
501 Fifth Ave, NYC, NY 10017
212 490.2450
fax 212 697.6828
page 43

Whiting, Jim
773 S Nardo, Solana Beach, CA 92075
619 755.7449

Whitlatch, Terryl
804 Arlington Way, Martinez, CA 94553
510 228.7675

Whitley, Gary
2405 NW Thurman, Portland, OR 97210
503 225.9687

Whitney, Jack
6239 Elizabeth Ave, St Louis, MO 63139
314 781.8851

Wickart, Mark Illustration
6293 Surrey Ridge Rd, Lisle, IL 60532
708 369.0164
fax 708 369.4004
page 193

Wickstrom, Richard Inc
209 Marion Ave, Mill Valley, CA 94941
415 383.5498

Wickstrom, Shari
5855 Green Valley Cir, Culver City, CA 90230
310 642.2721

Widener, Terry
200 Aquetong Rd, New Hope, PA 18938
215 862.2091
fax 215 862.2641
page 225

Widener, Terry
2215 Old McGarrah Rd,
McKinney, TX 75070
214 540.2360
fax 214 540.2462
page 225
Terry Widener's bold styles have been
published in Travel & Leisure, Playboy
Magazine, The New York Times, Sports
Illustrated, Avon Books, U.S. News & World
Report, Discover Magazine, HarperCollins
Publishers, Kiplinger's, Random House,
American Airlines, Northern Telecom,
design & advertising agencies.

Wieland, Don
420 Lexington Ave, NYC, NY 10170
212 986.5680
fax 212 818.1246
page 194

Wiemer, Dan
3825 E 26th St, Mpls, MN 55406
612 729.1774

Wiens, Carl
2255B Queen St E, Toronto, ONT,
Canada M4E 1G3
416 699.1670
page 387

Wiggins, Bryan
229 Berkely St, Boston, MA 02116
617 266.3858

Wilcox, David
270 Park Ave S, NYC, NY 10010
212 260.6700

Wild Onion Studio
431 S Dearborn, Chicago, IL 60605
312 663.5595

Wiley, David Artist Representative
282 Second St, S.F., CA 94105
415 442.1822

Wiley, Paul
320 W 37th St, NYC, NY 10018
212 224.3118

Wilgus, David
60 E 42nd St, NYC, NY 10165
212 682.1490

Wilgus, Robin
1826 Asheville Pl, Charlotte, NC 28203
704 372.6007

Wilkinson, Corey
855 Joyce Ave, Melrose Park, IL 60164
708 562.2512
page 371

Wilkinson, Joel
39 Blair St, Greenville, SC 29607
803 235.4483

Willardson & Associates
c/o Vicki Morgan
194 Third Ave, NYC, NY 10003
212 475.0440

The Williams Group
1270 W Peachtree St, Atlanta, GA 30309
404 873.2287 / 800 847.5101
page 438

Williams, Carolyn
680 S Federal, Chicago, IL 60605
312 427.2189

Williams, Dean
1817 E Ocean Blvd,
Long Beach, CA 90802
310 436.5352
page 347

Williams, Garry
7045 California Ave, Hammond, IN 46323
219 844.8002

Williams, Jack
PO Box 34464, Richmond, VA 23234
804 796.4797

Williams, Jim
2233 Kemper Ln, Cincinnati, OH 45206
513 861.1400

Williams, Kurt Alan
680 S Federal, Chicago, IL 60605
312 427.2189

Williams, Lorraine
36 Plaza St, Brooklyn, NY 11238
718 638.7203

Williams, Ron
7310 Bennington Dr, Dallas, TX 75214
214 348.6505

Williams, Susan
221 W Elmood Pl, Mpls, MN 55419
612 824.6103
fax 612 824.2896
page 200
Digital Illustration with a brush style.
MAC or PC files for print, video, home
pages or interactive media.

Williams, Tim
520 Country Glen Ct, Alpharetta, GA 30202
404 475.3146

Williams, Toby
82 Fifers Ln, Boxborough, MA 01719
508 263.8106
fax 508 263.4056
page 148

Williams/Marucchi
712 Sycamore Dr, Decatur, GA 30033
404 378.8326

Williamson, Bruce
2101 Stonegate, Carrollton, TX 75010
214 394.3791

Williamson, James
175 E 91st St, NYC, NY 10128
212 427.9801

Willoughby, Ann
602 Westport Rd, Kansas City, MO 64111
816 561.4189

Wilson, Bill
405 N Wabash Ave, Chicago, IL 60611
312 222.0377

Wilson, Lee
5855 Green Valley Cir, Culver City, CA 90230
310 642.2721

Wilson, Lin
1258 Cornelia, Chicago, IL 60657
312 275.7172

Wilson, Phil
309 Walnut Rd, Pittsburgh, PA 15202
412 761.5666

Wilson, Russ
1420 Flagler Ave, Jacksonville, FL 32207
904 398.0018

Wilson, Ty
Seven Cornelia St, NYC, NY 10014
212 627.5703

Wilson, Will
5511 Knollview Ct, Baltimore, MD 21228
410 455.0715

Wilson-Brandt, Kim
219 Crescent Ave, S.F., CA 94110
415 824.2055

Wilson-Zumbo Illustration
301 N Water St, Milwaukee, WI 53202
414 271.3388

Wilton, Nicholas
220 Alta Ave, Algunitas, CA 94938
415 488.4710

Wiltse, Kris, c/o Vicki Morgan
194 Third Ave, NYC, NY 10003
212 475.0440

Wimmer, Mike / I Do Art Inc
3905 Nicole Cir, Norman, OK 73072
405 329.0478

Winborg, Larry
731 N 24th St, Phila, PA 19130
215 232.6666
fax 215 232.6585
page 135

Wind Tunnel/Mitch Hyatt
201 Stewart St, Carmi, IL 62821
618 382.3331

Winger, Jody
1117 Xerxes Ave S, Mpls, MN 55405
612 377.4838
fax 612 377.7505
page 258

Wink, David
1391 Willivee Dr, Decatur, GA 30033
404 325.4895

Winn-Lederer, Ilene
986 Lilac St, Pittsburgh, PA 15217
412 421.8668

Winners, Margo/Winning Designs
15421 Rushmoor Ln, Huntington Beach, CA 92647
714 373.2040

Winston, Jeannie
2549 Patricia Ave, L.A., CA 90064
310 837.8666

Winter, David
Chicago, IL
312 527.3900
page 379

Winter, David
903 W Gunnison, Chicago, IL 60640
312 275.9529
page 379

Winter-Gorsline, Leslie
7683 SW Leslie St, Portland, OR 97223
503 245.8464
fax 503 245.2474
page 102

Winterbauer, Michael
1220 Lyndon St, South Pasadena, CA 91030
818 799.4998

Winterbottom, Jill
5855 Green Valley Cir, Culver City, CA 90230
310 642.2721

Wintermute
5113 Pastura Pl NW, Albuquerque, NM 87107
505 344.8220

Winters, Greg
2139 Pinecrest Dr, Altadena, CA 91001
818 798.7666

Winters, Paula
402-545 SE 12 St, Dania, FL 33004
305 927.9735

Wisenbaugh, Jean
250 W 57th St, NYC, NY 10107
212 397.7330
fax 212 397.7334
page 249
Creative concepts compulsively rendered.

Wisniewski, Jim
520 N Michigan, Chicago, IL 60611
312 527.0351
fax 312 527.5468
page 120

Witmer, Keith
PO Box 0472, Los Gatos, CA 95031
408 356.1415

Witschonke, Alan
68 Agassiz Ave, Belmont, MA 02178
617 484.8023

Witte, Michael
108 E 35th St, NYC, NY 10016
212 889.3337

Wofford, Terry
15951 E El Lago Blvd, Fountain Hills, AZ 85268
602 837.9821

Wohnoutka, Michael
216 Lake Ave N, Spicer, MN 56288
612 796.5749

Wojkovich, Ron
900 W Jackson Blvd, Chicago, IL 60607
312 944.5680
fax 312 421.5948
page 93

Woksa, Marshall
203 School Ave, Rochelle, IL 61068
815 562.3702
page 94

Wokuluk, Jon
1301 S Westgate Ave, L.A., CA 90025
310 473.5623

Wolf, Elizabeth
3717 Alton Pl NW, Wash, DC 20016
202 686.0179

Wolf, Leslie
Four E Ohio St, Chicago, IL 60611
312 944.1130 / 312 935.1707
page 17
Whimsical, warm and wonderful. Pen &
ink illustrations of animals, vegetables,
and folkss of all shapes and sizes.
Clients include: McDonald's, Kellogg's,
United Airlines, Kraft, Sears, Blue Cross
Blue Shield, Ameritech, Amoco, NiGas,
Kohler, Houghton Miflin, Scott
Foresman, etc.

Wolf, Paul
7118 Upper River Rd, Prospect, KY 40059
502 228.9427

Wolf-Hubbard, Marcie
1507 Ballard St,
Silver Spring, MD 20910
301 585.5815
fax 301 585.5060
page 284

Wolfe, Bruce
c/o Vicki Morgan
194 Third Ave, NYC, NY 10003
212 475.0440

Wolfe, Deborah
731 N 24th St, Phila, PA 19130
215 232.6666
fax 215 232.6585
pages 130-135, 269

Wolff, Ashley
98 Cortland, S.F., CA 94110
415 826.7345

Wolff, Punz
457 Herkimer Ave, Haworth, NJ 07641
201 385.6028

Wolnick, James
22028 1/2 Covello St, Canoga Park, CA 91303
818 716.7366

Wong, Benedict Norbert
450 Sansome St, S.F., CA 94111
415 781.7590

Wong, Joshua
37 King St, NYC, NY 11375
212 691.0762

Wood Ronsaville Harlin Inc
17 Pinewood St, Annapolis, MD 21401
410 266.6550

Wood, Clare
16 Heusted Dr, Old Greenwich, CT 06870
203 698.1113

Wood, Rob
17 Pinewood St, Annapolis, MD 21401
410 266.6550

Wood, Tracey
51 Camden St, Toronto, ONT,
Canada M5V 1V2
416 362.1913 / 800 730.8945
fax 416 362.6356
page 151

Wooden, Lenny
49 W 45th St, NYC, NY 10036
212 921.1199

Woods, Paul
414 Jackson St, S.F., CA 94111
415 399.1984

Woods, Rosemary
11 Kings Ridge Rd,
Long Valley, NJ 07853
908 813.8718
fax 908 813.0076
page 421

Woodward, Joanne
24820 Perkins Rd, Harvard, IL 60033
815 943.0409

Woodward, Teresa
544 Paseo Miramar, Pacific Palisade, CA 90272
310 459.6737

Woolley, Janet
11 Kings Ridge Rd,
Long Valley, NJ 07853
908 813.8718
fax 908 813.0076
page 420

Worcester, Mary
2670 Marshland Rd,
Wayzata, MN 55391
612 449.4850
fax 612 449.8975
page 259

Workman, June Illustration
419 Mason St, #200,
Vacaville, CA 95688
707 447.5247
June's illustrations can be viewed in
Airbrush Action II - The Best New
Airbrush Illustration compiled by
Rockport Publishers with Airbrush
Action Magazine. Her illustrations have
a style that combines realism with
multidimensional effects.

Worley, Zoe
222 E 82nd St, NYC, NY 10028
212 288.2011
fax 212 734.8261
page 168

Worth Representing
102 E 22nd St, NYC, NY 10010
212 979.0339

Wray, Greg
40681 Via Diamante, Murrieta, CA 92562
909 696.3560

Wray, Wendy
c/o Vicki Morgan
194 Third Ave, NYC, NY 10003
212 475.0440

Wright, Bob Creative Group
Carnegie Pl, Rochester, NY 14607
716 271.2280

Wright, Jane Chambless
Nine Babbling Brook Ln, Suffern, NY 10901
914 368.8606

Wright, Jonathan
Ten E Ontario, Chicago, IL 60611
312 573.1370

Wright, Ted
3286 Ivanhoe, St Louis, MO 63139
314 781.7377

Wrobel, Cindy
415 Alta Dena, St Louis, MO 63130
314 721.4467

Wu, Benjamin
654 Pier Ave, Santa Monica, CA 90405
310 392.4877

Wu, Leslie
36 Harwood Ln, East Rochester, NY 14445
716 385.3722

Wuerker, Matt
2405 NW Thurman, Portland, OR 97210
503 225.9687

Wunderlich, Dirk
5110 Biloxi Ave, North Hollywood, CA 91601
818 763.4848

Wunsch, Marjory
78 Washington Ave, Cambridge, MA 02140
617 492.3839

Wynne, Bob
4881 Topanga Cyn Blvd,
Woodland Hills, CA 91364
818 710.1559

Xavier, Roger
23200 Los Codona Ave, Torrance, CA 90505
310 373.7049

Yaccarino, Dan
250 W 57th St, NYC, NY 10107
212 397.7330

Yalowitz, Paul
3416 Baugh Dr, New Port Richey, FL 34655
813 372.9444

Yamada, Kenny
1360 Reynolds Ave, Irvine, CA 92714
714 724.9236

Yamashita, Taro Hiroshi
211 E 53rd St, NYC, NY 10022
212 753.3242

Yang, James
41 Union Sq W, NYC, NY 10003
212 807.6627

Yanish, Mary
3887 Bostwick St, L.A., CA 90063
213 263.6040

Yankus, Marc
570 Hudson St, NYC, NY 10014
212 242.6334

Yardley, Joanna
48 Ward Ave, Northampton, MA 01060
413 586.9253

Ybarra, Frank
1230-A E Jackson St,
Phoenix, AZ 85034
602 252.4235
fax 602 254.8178
page 442

Yealdhall, Gary
138 W 25th St, Baltimore, MD 21218
410 889.5361

Yearington, Tim
4709 Northwoods Dr, Woodlawn, ONT,
Canada KoA 2Mo
613 832.0879

Yee, Josie
155 W 15th St, NYC, NY 10011
212 206.1260

Yemi
Seven E 14th St, NYC, NY 10003
212 627.1269

Yiannis, Vicki
159 W Fourth St, NYC, NY 10014
212 242.0077

Yoe, Craig
97 Croton Ave, Ossining, NY 10562
914 734.4756
pages 318-319

Young, Bob
1003 Diamond Ave, S Pasadena, CA 91030
818 441.8955

Young, Eddie
520 N Michigan Ave, Chicago, IL 60611
312 527.0351

Young, Mary O'Keefe
62 Midchester Ave, White Plains, NY 10606
914 949.0147

Young, Paul
PO Box 344, Champaign, IL 61824
217 398.1923

Young, Ted
7261 NW 35th St, Lauderhill, FL 33319
305 749.1092

Young, Timothy
420 Lexington Ave, NYC, NY 10017
212 986.5680

Younger, Heidi
58 W 15th St, NYC, NY 10011
212 741.2539

Youssi, John
17 N 943 Powers Rd, Gilberts, IL 60136
708 428.7398

Yuill, Peter
7202 Oxford Rd, Baltimore, MD 21212
410 583.9619

Yule, Susan Hunt
176 Elizabeth St, NYC, NY 10012
212 226.0439

Zabowski, Lulu
4645 Colfax Ave S, Mpls, MN 55409
612 825.7564
pages 6-7, 304, 418

Zacharow, Christopher
109 Waverly Pl, NYC, NY 10011
212 460.5739

Zahnd, Mark
7010 Leesburg Rd, Charlotte, NC 28215
704 563.6244

Zamchick, Gary
56 Hillside Ave, Tenafly, NJ 07670
201 568.3727

Zamic, Rene
51 Camden St, Toronto, ONT,
Canada M5V 1V2
416 362.1913 / 800 730.8945
fax 416 362.6356
page 152

Zammarchi, Robert Illustration
32 Rugg Rd, PO Box 1147, Boston, MA 02134
617 787.9513

Zampier, A Brian/abz art
4435 E Patterson Rd, Dayton, OH 45430
513 320.5406

Zann, Nicky
155 W 68th St, NYC, NY 10023
212 724.5027

Zarins, Joyce Audy
19 Woodland St, Merrimac, MA 01860
508 346.8994

Zeines, Bruce
103 Albemarle Rd, Brooklyn, NY 11218
718 972.7256

Zellin, Lisa
153 Diamond St, Brooklyn, NY 11222
212 978.2291

Zherdin, Boris
91 Washington Ave, Leonardo, NJ 07737
908 291.8226

Zick, Brian
1233 S La Cienega Blvd, L.A., CA 90035
310 855.8855

Zielinski, John
411 N Fourth Ave, Maywood, IL 60153
708 343.7733
page 118

Zielinski, John
520 N Michigan Ave, Chicago, IL 60611
312 527.0351
fax 312 527.5468
page 118

Ziering, Barbara
5855 Green Valley Cir, Culver City, CA 90230
310 642.2721

Ziering, Bob
108 E 35th St, NYC, NY 10016
212 889.3337

Zimmerman, Jerry
80 Eighth Ave, NYC, NY 10011
212 620.7774

Zimmerman, Robert
704 252.9689
R_Zimm@aol.com
pages 2-3

Zingarelli, Mark
101 Yesler Way, Seattle, WA 98104
206 447.1600

Zingone, Robin
280 Madison Ave, NYC, NY 10016
212 545.9155

Zito, Andy
135 S LaBrea Ave, L.A., CA 90036
213 931.1182

Zlowodzka, Joanna
144 W Tenth St, NYC, NY 10014
212 620.7981

Zolotnitsky, Elena
13 Windy Cliff Pl, Cockeyesville, MD 21303
410 683.0437

Zuba, Bob
105 W Saylor Ave, Plains, PA 18705
717 824.7399

Zudeck, Darryl
35 W 92nd St, NYC, NY 10025
212 663.9454

Zumbo, Matt
301 N Water St, Milwaukee, WI 53202
414 277.9541

Zwarenstein, Alex
425 Riverside Dr, NYC, NY 10025
212 866.4478

Zwicker, Sara Mintz
98 Stetson St, Braintree, MA 02184
617 848.8962
Specializing in details - via pencil or
crowquill. Illustrated the Old Farmer's
Almanac Gardening Calendar, and
articles in the Almanac, Gardener's
Companion, and Hearth and Home
Companion. Other clients: Timberland,
Lowell Shoe, Houghton-Mifflin, ad
agencies.

Zwinger, Jane
2405 NW Thurman St,
Portland, OR 97210
503 225.9687
fax 503 228.6030
page 139

Zwingler, Randall
1106 Greenway Rd, Wilmington, DE 19803
302 478.6063

Zwolak, Paul
211 E 89th St, NYC, NY 10128
212 289.5514
fax 212 987.2855
pages 292-293

REPRESENTED BY JIM LILIE   TEL 415.441.4384   FAX 415.395.9809

Ron Chan

ROBERT ZIMMERMAN

[704] 252-9689

designed by my friend Barbara deWilde

strictly a nine to five operation

eps at 9600 bps

PH:(212)475-0440 FX:(
194
VICKI
MORGAN
PATTI...
Lafrance
schwarz
Soderlind
Blessin
Bliss
PARISI
Giacobbe
TAYLR

PH: (212) 475-0440 FX: (212) 353-8538
VICKI MORGAN ASSOCIATES
194 THIRD AVE NYC 10003

Matt Foster **design studio** Fax: 215.1257 510.215.1251

SF · Freda Scott 415.398.9121

NY · Daniele Collignon 212.243.4209

Midwest · Lulu 612.825.7564

Matt Foster **design studio** Fax: 215.1257 510.215.1251

SF · Freda Scott 415.398.9121
NY · Daniele Collignon 212.243.4209
Midwest · Lulu 612.825.7564

131 Charlie Parker Place   New York City 1oo09 212~228~2606

CLINT HANSEN

SCOTT HULL ASSOCIATES   USA 513-433-8383   FAX 513-433-0434   NYC 212-966 3604

SCOTT HULL ASSOCIATES   USA 513-433-8383   FAX 513-433-0434   NYC 212-966 3604

Mark
Stearney
FON 312 360 9033
FAX 312 360 9034

Mark
Stearney

FON 312 360 9033
FAX 312 360 9034

BYRON GIN

BYRON GIN

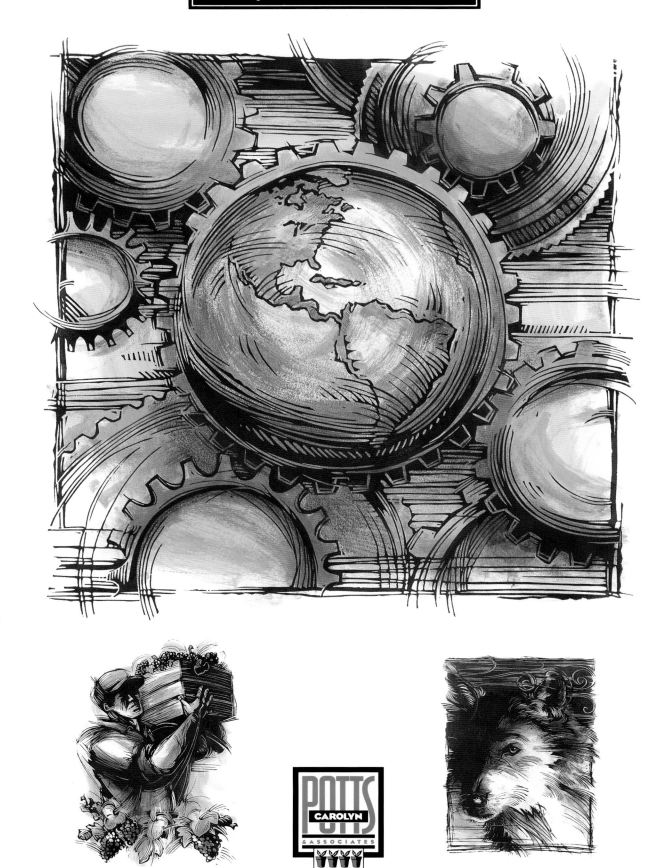

CAROLYN POTTS & ASSOCIATES

312 935-1707

15

RHONDA VOO

POTTS
CAROLYN
& ASSOCIATES

312 935-1707

LESLIE WOLF

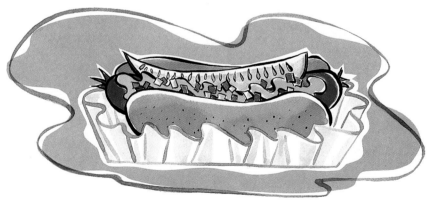

416.530.1500

Nina Berkson

Ken Dewar

416.530.1500

416.530.1500

Clancy Gibson

416.530.1500

Normand Cousineau & Geneviève Côté

REPRESENTED BY LINK

Grant Innes

416.530.1500

Pierre Pratt

23

james f. kraus
art guy studios
[617] 437-1945
boston, ma usa

james f. kraus
art guy studios

[617] 437-1945
boston, ma usa

COCO MASUDA

REPRESENTED BY
JAN COLLIER : 415. 383. 9026

IN THE NORTHEAST & EDITORIAL
CALL
STUDIO: 212. 753. 9331

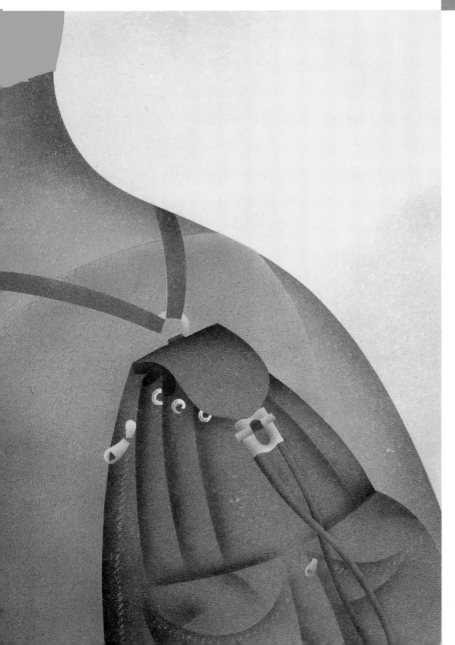

Jan Collier

COCO MASUDA

REPRESENTED BY : 415. 383. 9026
JAN COLLIER IN THE NORTHEAST & EDITORIAL CALL STUDIO: 212. 753. 9331

MICHÈLE MANNING

BUSTAMANTE

ALEX CRO

JAN COLLIER
415.383.9026

Jan Collier

timothy
c o o k

p h o n e

7 0 3 . 8 2 0 . 2 0 4 9

f a x

7 0 3 . 8 2 0 . 3 5 2 1

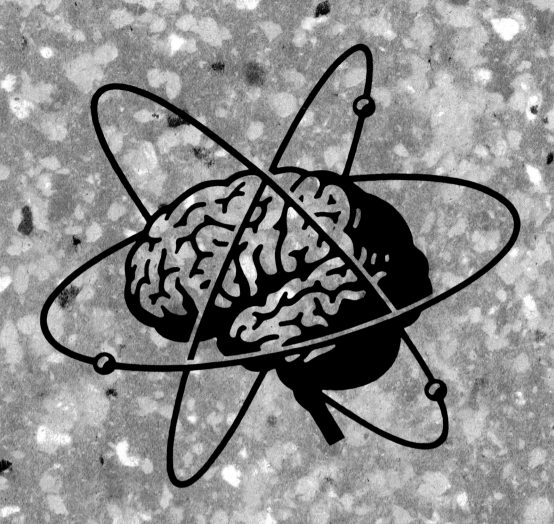

RENARD
REPRESENTS
212.490.2450
FAX 697.6828
NEW YORK

MICHAEL SCHWAB

SCHWAB

THE PRESIDIO
FROM POST TO PARK
OCTOBER 1, 1994

RENARD REPRESENTS
212/490-2450

33

VALERIE SINCLAIR

Renard Represents
Tel: (212) 490-2450
Fax: (212) 697-6828

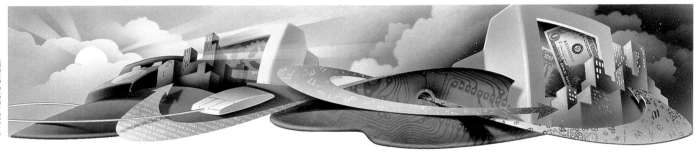

MATSU

Renard Represents
Tel: (212) 490-2450
Fax: (212) 697-6828

THEO
RUDNAK

Renard Represents
Tel: (212) 490-2450
Fax: (212) 697-6828

ROBERT RODRIGUEZ

Renard Represents
Tel: (212) 490-2450
Fax: (212) 697-6828

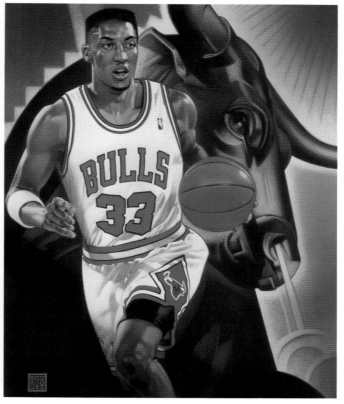

ROB
BROOKS

Renard Represents
Tel: (212) 490-2450
Fax: (212) 697-6828

JONATHAN HERBERT

Renard Represents
Tel: (212) 490-2450
Fax: (212) 697-6828

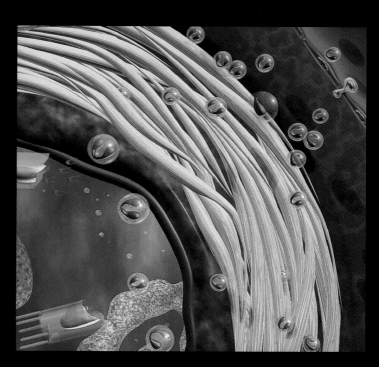

State-of-the-Art 3D
Modeling for Print
and Animation
■

Call for book or reel

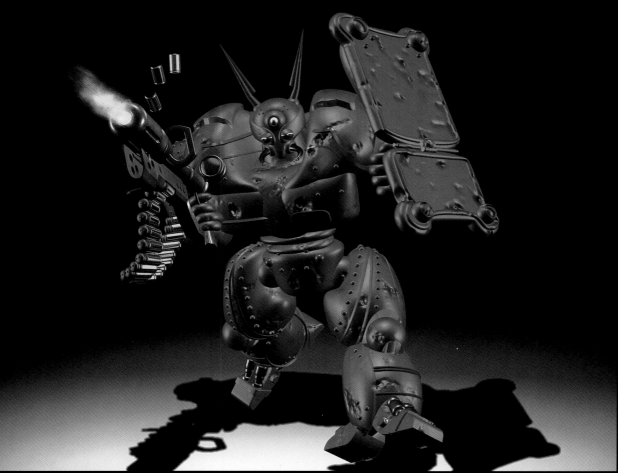

JAMES
BOZZINI

Renard Represents
Tel: (212) 490-2450
Fax: (212) 697-6828

MICHAEL McGURL

Renard Represents
Tel: (212) 490-2450
Fax: (212) 697-6828

JUD
GUITTEAU

Renard Represents
Tel: (212) 490-2450
Fax: (212) 697-6828

KIM
WHITESIDES

Renard Represents
Tel: (212) 490-2450
Fax: (212) 697-6828

43

ROGER
HILL

Renard Represents
Tel: (212) 490-2450
Fax: (212) 697-6828

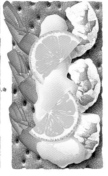

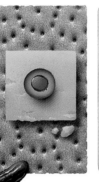

JOHN MARTIN

Renard Represents
Tel: (212) 490-2450
Fax: (212) 697-6828

BILL CIGLIANO

Renard Represents
Tel: (212) 490-2450
Fax: (212) 697-6828

46

WILLIAM HARRISON

Renard Represents
Tel: (212) 490-2450
Fax: (212) 697-6828

HEROES OF THE 20th CENTURY

RENÉ MILOT

Renard Represents
Tel: (212) 490-2450
Fax: (212) 697-6828

© 1995 Rene Milot

48

KAZUHIKO SANO

Renard Represents
Tel: (212) 490-2450
Fax: (212) 697-6828

JOE SAFFOLD

Renard Represents
Tel: (212) 490-2450
Fax: (212) 697-6828

WAYNE McLOUGHLIN

Renard Represents
Tel: (212) 490-2450
Fax: (212) 697-6828

JEFFREY PELO

Renard Represents
Tel: (212) 490-2450
Fax: (212) 697-6828

GARY ELDRIDGE

Renard Represents
Tel: (212) 490-2450
Fax: (212) 697-6828

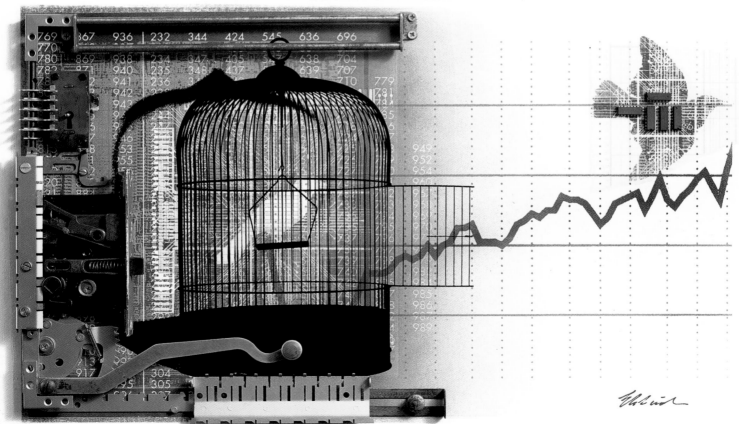

STEVE BJÖRKMAN

Renard Represents
Tel: (212) 490-2450
Fax: (212) 697-6828

DAN GARROW

Renard Represents
Tel: (212) 490-2450
Fax: (212) 697-6828

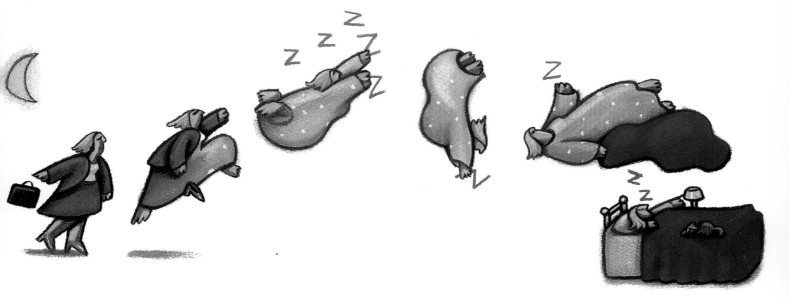

STU
SUCHIT

Renard Represents
Tel: (212) 490-2450
Fax: (212) 697-6828

STÉPHAN DAIGLE

Renard Represents
Tel: (212) 490-2450
Fax: (212) 697-6828

BORIS ЛЮБНЕР
БОРИС LYUBNER

TEL: 80I 649 2129

FAX: 80I 649 8803

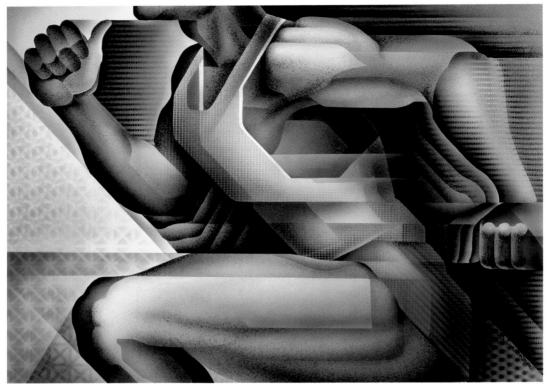

Nike

Oracle

Wadsworth

BORIS ЛЮБНЕР
БОРИС LYUBNER

TEL: 801 649 2129

FAX: 801 649 8803

Perkin Elmer

Epson America

IAN HASTINGS

211 SOUTH RIVERVIEW DR., AMHERSTBURG, ONTARIO, CANADA N9V 3R3

PLEASE CALL FOR ADDITIONAL SAMPLES
TELEPHONE/FAX: 519-734-6276

JIM COHEN ILLUSTRATION　　　　　**708·726·8979**

63

RANDY LYHUS 301·986·0036

We Deliver

James Swanson (708) 352-3081 Fax (708) 352-3082

65

DAN JONES

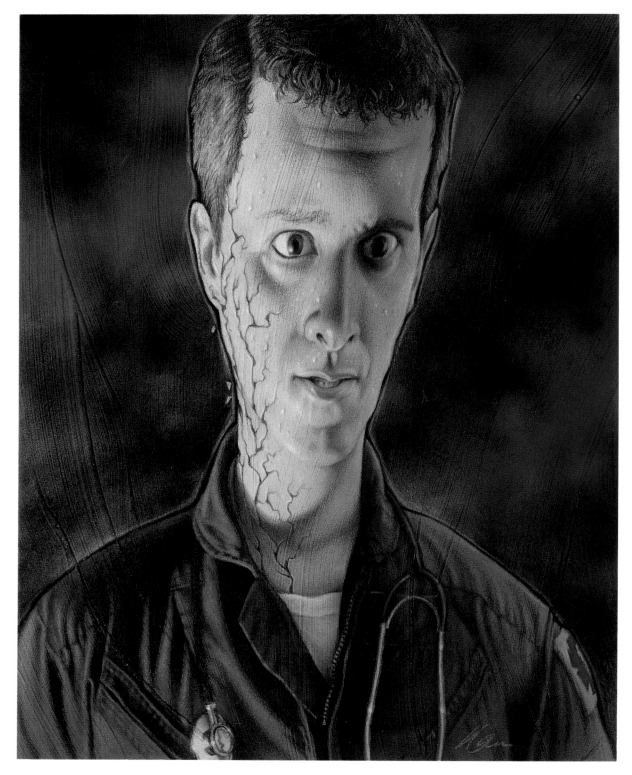

SALZMAN

international

San Francisco 415.285.8267   Fax 415.285.8268   Internet Salzman@designlink.com
Los Angeles 310.276.4298   Chicago 312.252.2244   New York 212.997.0115   London (44) 0171.636.7141

San Francisco 415.285.8267   Fax 415.285.8268   Internet Salzman@designlink.com
Los Angeles 310.276.4298   Chicago 312.252.2244   New York 212.997.0115   London (44) 0171.636.7141

67

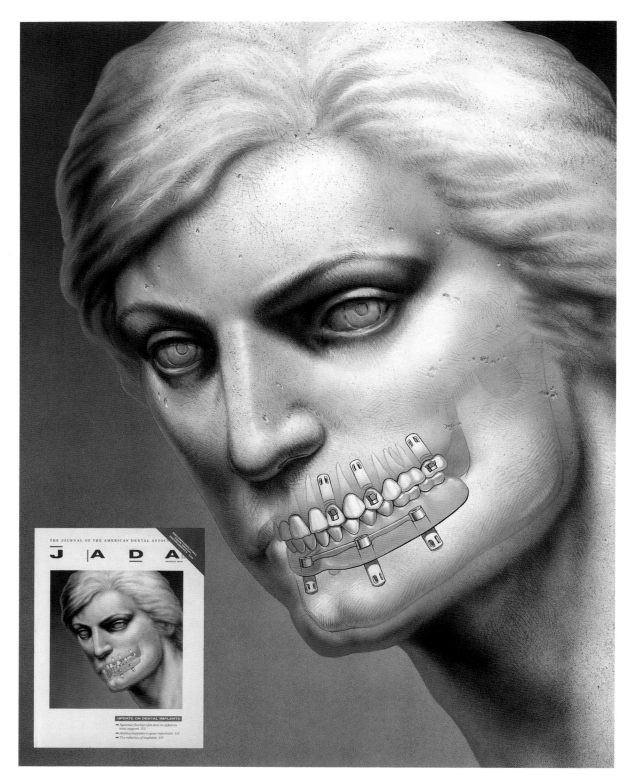

SALZMAN
international

San Francisco 415.285.8267   Fax 415.285.8268   Internet Salzman@designlink.com
Los Angeles 310.276.4298   Chicago 312.252.2244   New York 212.997.0115   London (44) 0171.636.7141

SALZMAN
international

San Francisco 415.285.8267   Fax 415.285.8268   Internet Salzman@designlink.com
Los Angeles 310.276.4298   Chicago 312.252.2244   New York 212.997.0115   London (44) 0171.636.7141

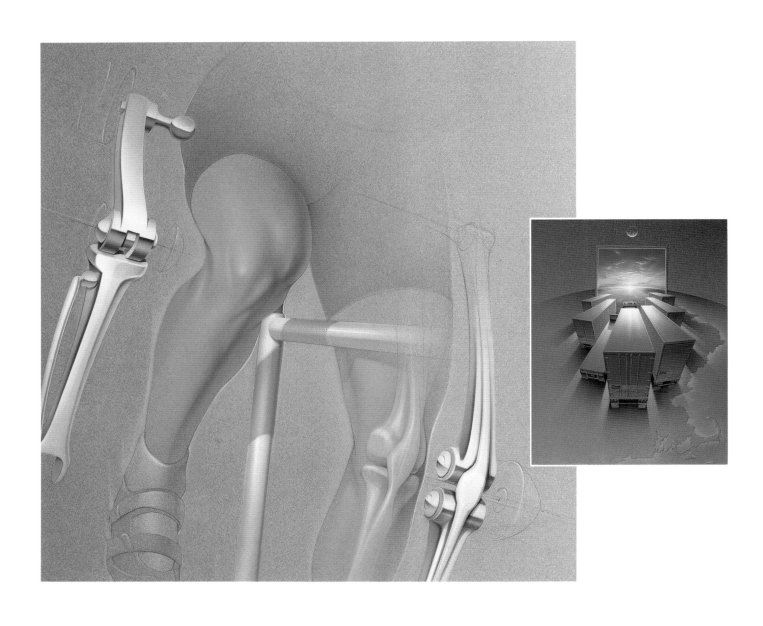

DAVID UHL
ILLUSTRATION STUDIOS

1501 BOULDER STREET, DENVER, COLORADO 80211 • 303-455-3535 • FAX 455-1603

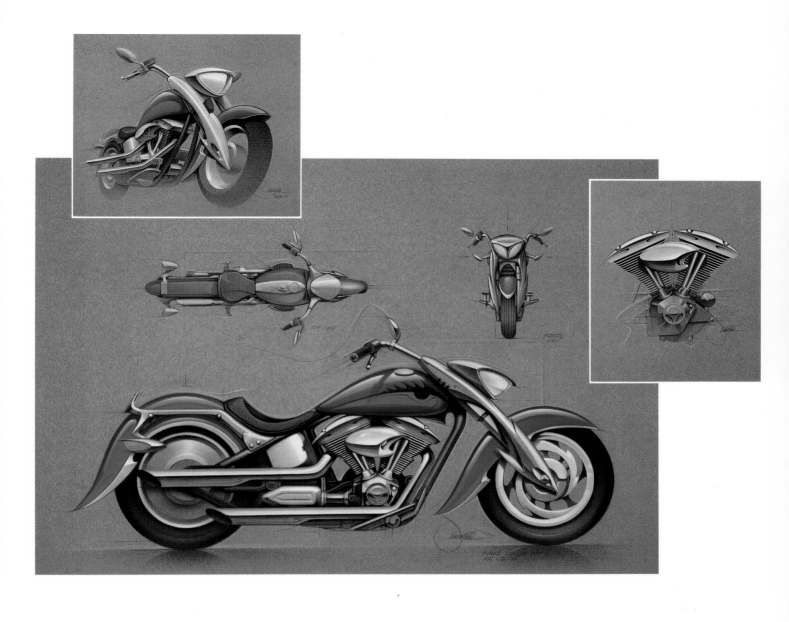

DAVID UHL
ILLUSTRATION STUDIOS

1501 BOULDER STREET, DENVER, COLORADO 80211 • 303-455-3535 • FAX 455-1603

FRED INGRAM

SUSAN AND CO

ARTIST REPRESENTATIVE / PHONE 206 728 1300 / FAX 206 728 7522

SUSAN AND CO

CLIENT: AMERICAN EXPRESS
AGENCY: OGILVY AND MATHER

P.O. BOX 2193
GRAPEVINE, TEXAS 76099

817·481·2212
FAX 817·481·2908

THE·ART·SOURCE

G E N E V I E V E   M E E K

M I C H A E L   H O G U E

D A V I D   M E R R E L L

T E L   &   F A X   9 1 8 . 7 4 9 . 9 4 2 4   **SUZANNE CRAIG** R E P R E S E N T S   4 0 1 5   E .   5 3 R D   S T .   T U L S A   O K   7 4 1 3 5

PAUL CORRIGAN

COCA-COLA®
CONTOUR BOTTLE
CAMPAIGN

ALETHA REPPEL

HUMOROUS ILLUSTRATION
& CHARACTER DEVELOPMENT

© 1995 MGM ANIMATION

CAM McCLELLAND

TEL & FAX 918.749.9424　　SUZANNE CRAIG REPRESENTS　　4015 E. 53RD ST.　TULSA OK 74135

L y d i a H e s s

pacific northwest - Christine Prapas - 503.658.7070

studio - 503.234.4757 *fax - 503.233.1330* *e-mail - lydia hess@aol.com*

VIRGINIA HALSTEAD • 4336 GAYLE DRIVE, TARZANA, CALIFORNIA 91356 • PHONE/FAX 818.705.4353

Clients include American Airlines, Bantam Doubleday Dell, Esquire, New York Magazine, Ogilvy & Mather/Chicago, Pantheon Books, Simon & Schuster, Teen, Weight Watchers

KEViN Pope
PRint and
aNImaTiOn.

812 • 824 * 694 9
812 • 8 2 4 • 6 11.

Mary Ross

Polar Bear

Las Vegas

DIFFA

Rita **G**atlin **R**epresents

Film & Print

USA 800.924.7881 · **SF** 415.924.7881 · **FAX** 415.924.7891

MARJORIE E. PESEK

ROBERT BYRNE

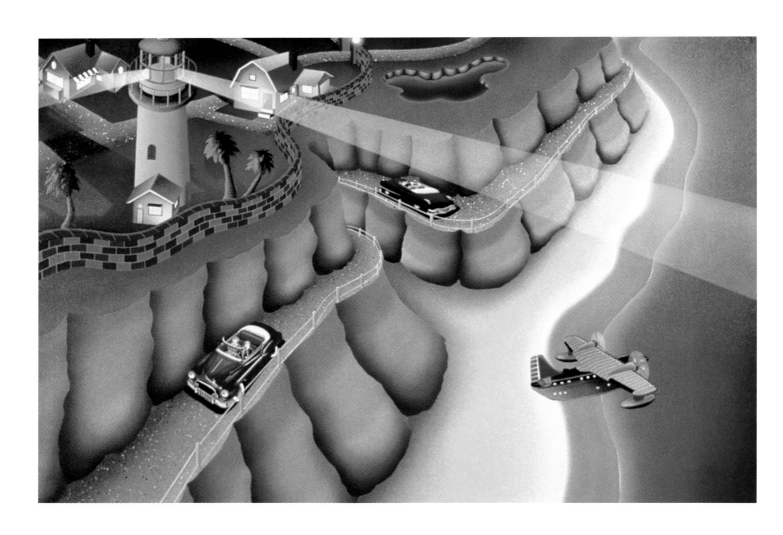

MASAAKI OGAI

Here's where the real work gets accomplished.

TOM VOSS

LAUREN
SCHEUER

617·924·6799

wEndy
grossmAn

212-262-4497

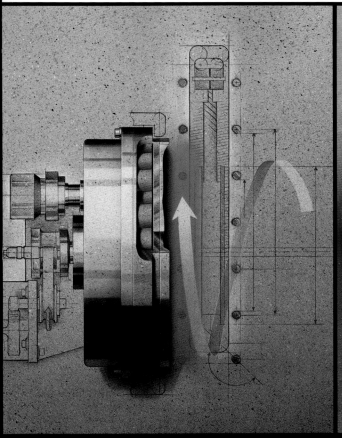

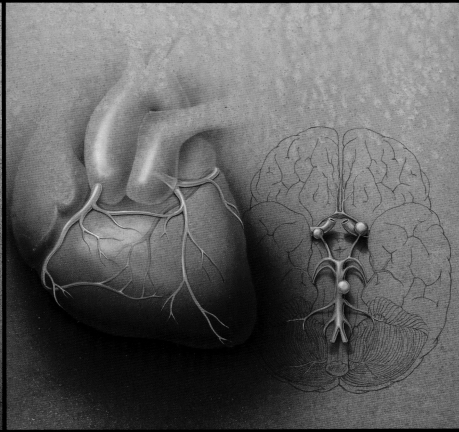

William Graham

Ron Wojkovich

94

ILLUSTRATION

HEDY KLEIN

7 1 8 - 7 9 3 - 0 2 4 6

CARSELLO CREATIVE, INC.
MARGARET CARSELLO
954 W. WASHINGTON BLVD.
CHICAGO, IL 60607

PH: 312.733.5709
FX: 312.733.5736

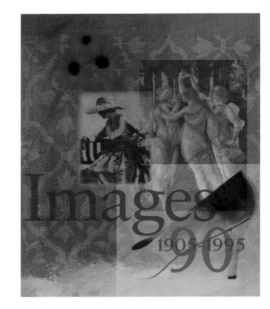

201 / 836 / 4283

LORRAINE RABL

629 Glenwood Avenue, Teaneck, NJ 07666

blaise **JETTE**

artist studio *blaise jette*
phone 503.281.5709

represented by

christine prapas

northwest territory
P 503.658.7070
f 503.658.3960

brian **BATTLES**

See's Candies

Bank of America

OLIVIĀ

represented by

christine prapas

northwest territory
P 503 . 658 . 7070
f 503 . 658 . 3960

artist studio *olivia*
phone 714 . 252 . 1147
fax 714 . 252 . 1260

christine prapas

leslie **WINTER-GORSLINE**

COMPUTER ILLUSTRATIONS MAC OR PC COMPATIBLE.
YOUR CONCEPT OR MINE. I CAN COMBINE COMPUTER
ILLUSTRATION WITH YOUR PRODUCT PHOTOGRAPHY.

northwest territory
p 503.246.9511
f 503.658.3960

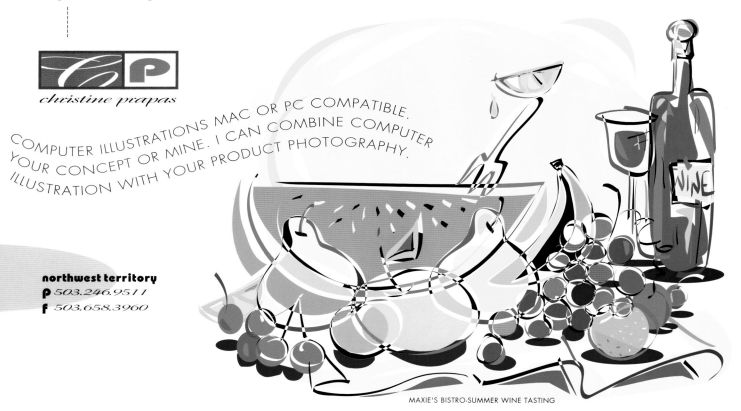

MAXIE'S BISTRO-SUMMER WINE TASTING

SEASON'S GREETINGS FROM U.S. BANK

artist studio *leslie winter-gorsline*
phone 503.245.8464
fax 503.245.2474

steve **ELLIS**

CLIENT LIST INCLUDES

Mid West Airlines

DIRECTV

Hughes Communications

Roland U.S.

Bozell Worldwide - Chicago

Modern Maturity

Please see Showcase 1996

*There is no tenderness in a kiss,
as sweet as a touch from the heart.*

represented by

alan JUST

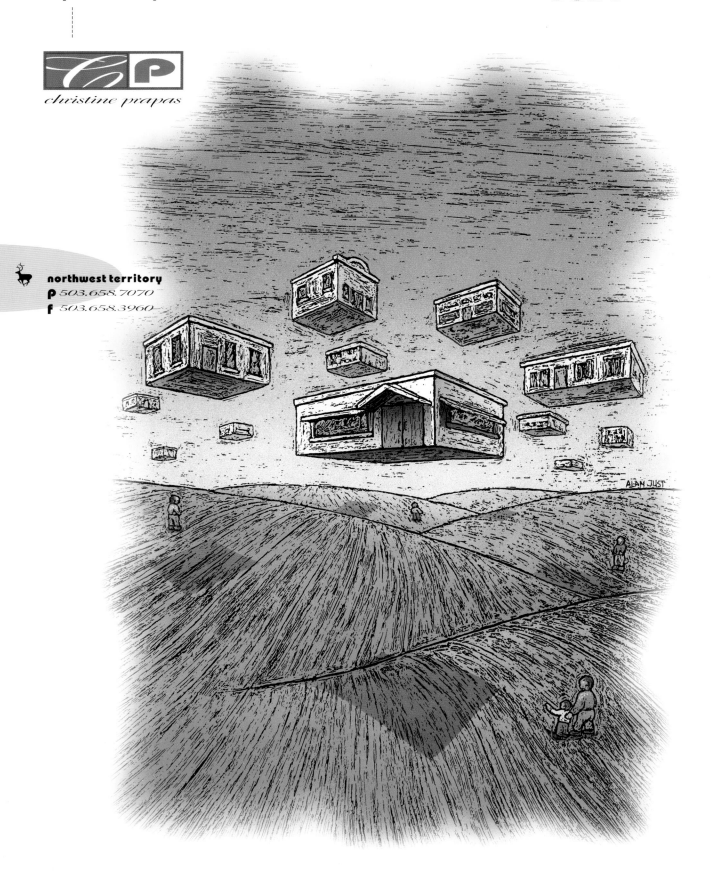

christine prapas

northwest territory
p 503.658.7070
f 503.658.3960

artist studio alan just
phone 503.228.5853
fax 503.221.4296

ðan **BROWN**

represented by

christine prapas

northwest territory
P *503.658.7070*
f *503.658.3960*

artist studio *ðan brown*

phone 360.737.9920

RICHARD A GOLDBERG 15 Cliff Street Arlington MA 02174
☎ 617·646·1041 FAX 617·646·0956

A Paul Verhoeven Film
Showgirls

Mad Love

Mystery of Life

Wild

The Exodus Has Begun

Eric Stoltz   Meg Tilly   Craig Sheffer
Sleep With Me
A comedy brave enough to say those three magic words.

Luther Vandross

Serving

KQED
40 Years

Julio

Milano Collection

107

JOHN WHITE

ILLUSTRATION

THE NEIS GROUP

ILLUSTRATION • DESIGN • PHOTOGRAPHY

11440 OAK DRIVE • P.O. BOX 174 • SHELBYVILLE, MICHIGAN 49344-9625

TELEPHONE 616 - 672-5756 • FAX 616 - 672-5757

JOYCE STIGLICH
ILLUSTRATION

THE NEIS GROUP
ILLUSTRATION • DESIGN • PHOTOGRAPHY

11440 OAK DRIVE • P.O. BOX 174 • SHELBYVILLE, MICHIGAN 49344-9625
TELEPHONE 616 - 672-5756 • FAX 616 - 672-5757

MAPS, CHARTS, DIAGRAMS

 **NIGEL HOLMES**

 203-226-2313

 203-222-9545

 nigelholme @ aol.com

544 RIVERSIDE AVENUE WESTPORT CT 06880

Icons above for *SELF*

Originally commissioned as a black and white map for the inside of Gail Sheehy's *New Passages* (Random House, 1995), this visual description of the stages of life was also used as full-color endpapers to the book.

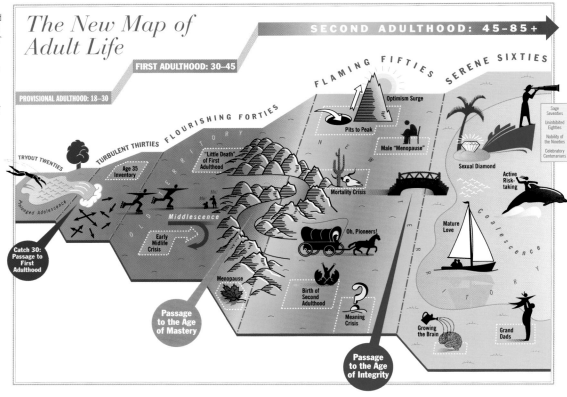

The New Map of Adult Life

SECOND ADULTHOOD: 45–85+

FIRST ADULTHOOD: 30–45

PROVISIONAL ADULTHOOD: 18–30

FLAMING FIFTIES   SERENE SIXTIES

Optimism Surge

Pits to Peak

Male "Menopause"

Sage Seventies
Uninhibited Eighties
Nobility of the Nineties
Celebratory Centenarians

Sexual Diamond

Active Risk-taking

TRYOUT TWENTIES   TURBULENT THIRTIES   FLOURISHING FORTIES

NEW TERRITORY

Age 35 Inventory

"Little Death" of First Adulthood

Mortality Crisis

Prolonged Adolescence

Middlescence

Catch 30: Passage to First Adulthood

Early Midlife Crisis

Oh, Pioneers!

Mature Love

Coalescence TERRITORY

Menopause

Birth of Second Adulthood

Meaning Crisis

Growing the Brain

Grand Dads

Passage to the Age of Mastery

Passage to the Age of Integrity

How to tie your sneaker laces to get a better fit. *American Health.* Art director: Kay Gibson.

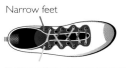

Narrow feet

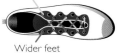

Wider feet

High arch

Toe troubles

Heel problems

Narrow heel
(use two laces)

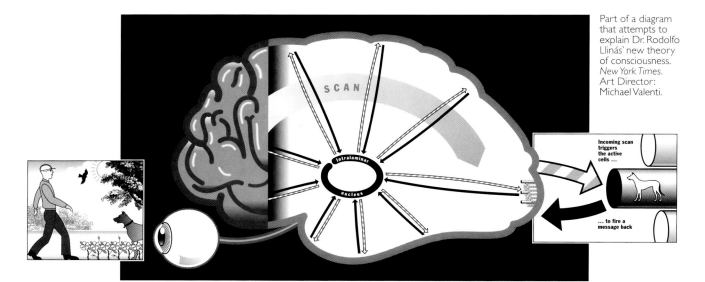

SCAN

Intralaminar nucleus

Incoming scan triggers the active cells …

… to fire a message back

Part of a diagram that attempts to explain Dr. Rodolfo Llinás' new theory of consciousness. *New York Times.* Art Director: Michael Valenti.

ROBIN JAREAUX

BOSTON 617·524·3099

David Milgrim Illustration

Clients include AT&T, Jose Cuervo, Symantec, Random House, American Express,
Adweek, Rodale Press, Gibson Greetings, Baby Talk Magazine, Polaroid.
Call to see more. Call to say hello. **(212) 673-1432**

BEN PERINI

WILFRED SPOON

JUDY UNGER

ANOTHER GIRL REP   (415) 647-5660   BARB HAUSER

COMPUTER ILLUSTRATION ON MAC
COMPUTER ILLUSTRATION IN WINDOWS

MARY CARTER

Stouffer's

J. Walter Thompson

MICHAEL CARROLL

is represented by Steven Edsey & Sons

MIKE DAMMER

represented by Steven Edsey & Sons

121

HAMBLIN

Call 312 • 527 • 0351   STEVEN EDSEY & SONS   *Fax* 312 • 527 • 5468

MICHAEL P. HAGEL

is represented by Steven Edsey & Sons

(212) 677-9100 / FAX: 353-0954

Carol Chislovsky Design Inc.
853 Broadway New York, New York, 10003

CHISLOVSKY

CHRIS GALL

MONTE VARAH

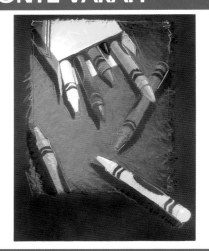

MARK HERMAN

(212) 677-9100 / FAX: 353-0954

Carol Chislovsky Design Inc.
853 Broadway New York, New York, 10003

CHISLOVSKY

GREG TUCKER

TO VIEW MORE WORK, PLEASE SEE "CREATIVE ILLUSTRATION 1995"

Gregg Valley Illustration ☠ Phone: 412•941•4662 Fax: 412•941•3490

CAMERON CLEMENT 501.646.7734

IN AR . OK . KS . MO . TX OR LOS ANGELES CALL SUZANNE CRAIG @ 918.749.9424

NANCY GIBSON-NASH

PHONE (617) 461-4574 FAX (617) 461-5940

Mary Anne Lloyd
207·773·4987

STEVEN NAU

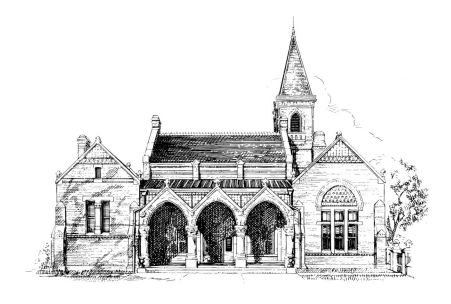

DEBORAH
WOLFE
LIMITED

PATRICK GNAN

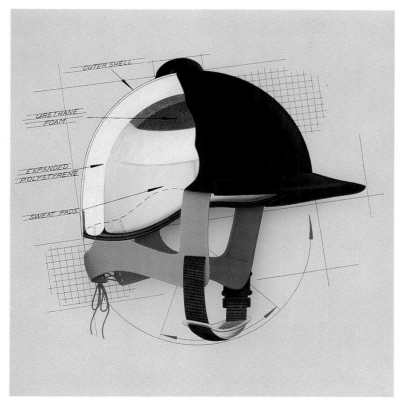

DEBORAH
WOLFE
LIMITED

731 N. 24TH STREET   PHILADELPHIA, PA 19130   215 232 6666   FAX 215 232 6585   131

ANDY LENDWAY

DEBORAH WOLFE LIMITED

731 N. 24TH STREET   PHILADELPHIA, PA 19130   215 232 6666   FAX 215 232 6585

LISA POMERANTZ

DEBORAH
WOLFE
LIMITED

731 N. 24TH STREET   PHILADELPHIA, PA 19130   215 232 6666   FAX 215 232 6585

BILL MORSE
MACINTOSH ILLUSTRATION

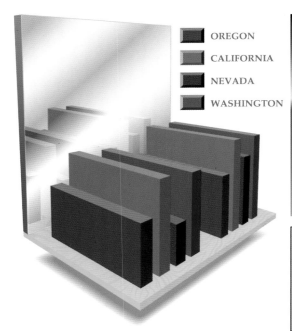

OREGON
CALIFORNIA
NEVADA
WASHINGTON

Production (in millions of tons)

Copper 7.7
Aluminum 18
Zinc 6.2
Iron 600
Lead 3.8

...forever...

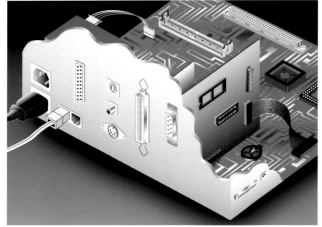

This is it!

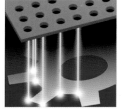

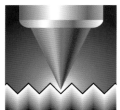

DEBORAH WOLFE LIMITED

134 N. 24TH STREET   PHILADELPHIA, PA 19130   215 232 6666   FAX 215 232 6585

LARRY WINBORG

DEBORAH WOLFE LIMITED

731 N. 24TH STREET   PHILADELPHIA, PA 19130   215 232 6666   FAX 215 232 6585

135

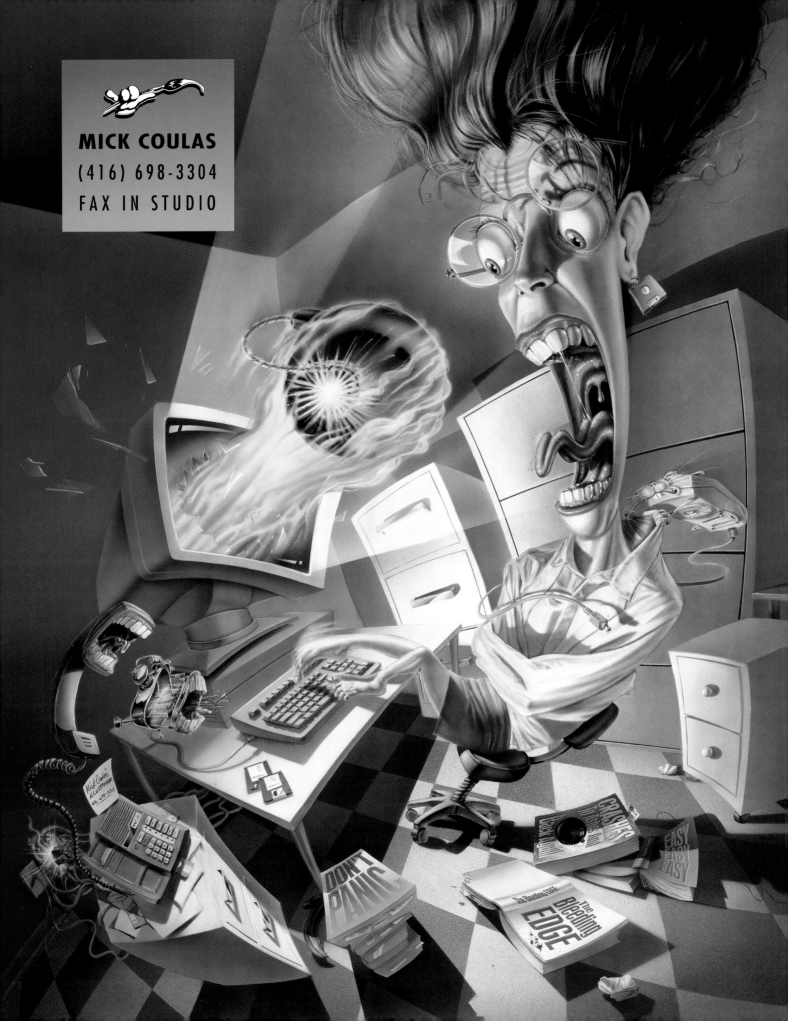

Candace Lourdes · Computer Illustration
(416) 698-3304 · Fax in Studio

STEPHEN F. HAYES

JANE ZWINGER

BEN KILLEN ROSENBERG

DENNIS CUNNINGHAM

Represented by The Art Agency
Cindy Lommasson • *503-225-9687* • *fax 503-228-6030*

©R. Saunders. 95 après T-Lautrec

Rob Saunders

(617) 566-4464 Facques: 739-0040 Drnibs@aol.com

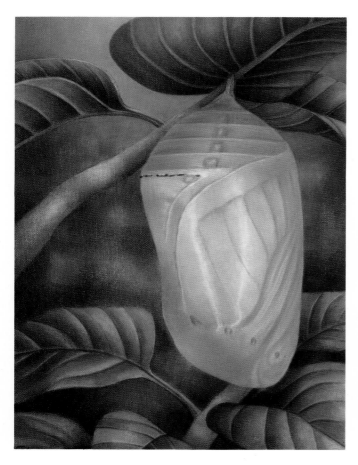

RICHARD

Elmer

RICHARD ELMER, 504 EAST 11 STREET, N.Y.C. 10009, (212) 598-4024

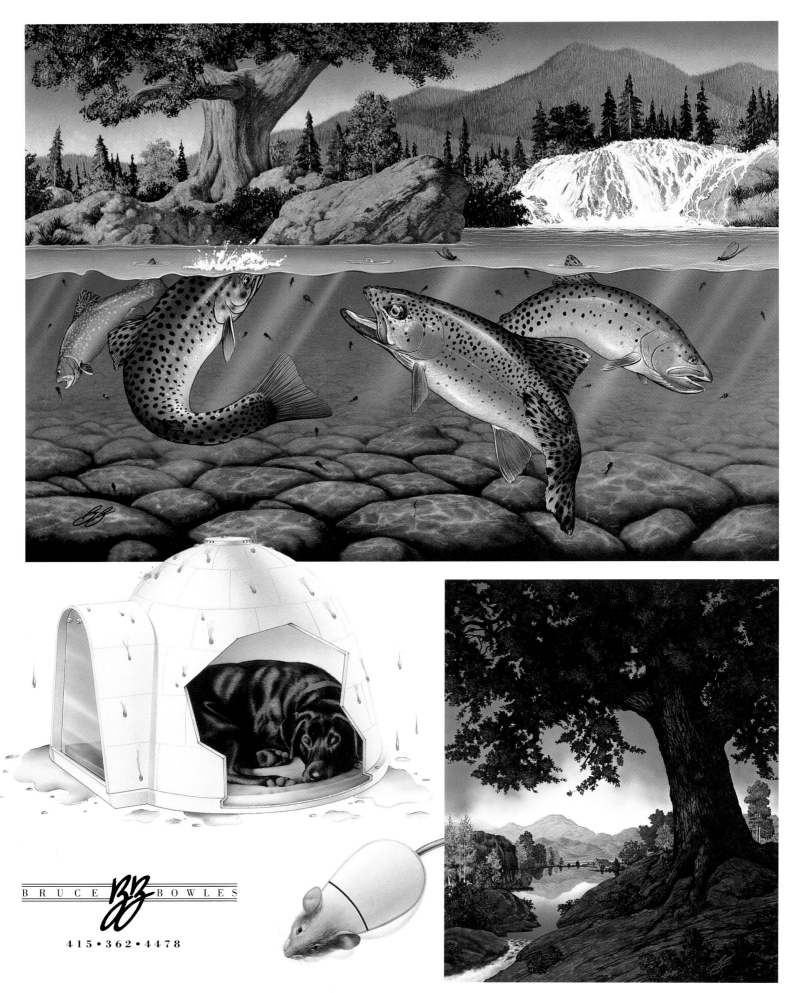

BRUCE BOWLES

415 • 362 • 4478

SLOAN

MICHAEL SLOAN STUDIO
Brooklyn, N.Y.C.
tel. 718·788·5437   fax 718·499·8958

JULIA TALCOTT

PHONE/FAX 617·964·6556

STUDIOS

‹ spain ›
illustration
83 franklin st
watertown Ma
0 2 1 7 2

phone & FAX:
6 1 7 9 2 3 1 9 8 9

portfolio

Financial

CAPITAL

PARTIAL CLIENT LIST

Boston Globe Magazine
Deaconess Hospital
Inc Magazine
Ligature
Nynex
US Magazine
Wang

New Advantage Wonderful flexibility Powerful Application Functionality Upgrade Easy

dizziness

fatigue

STUDIOS

PRENTICE HALL

REDBOOK

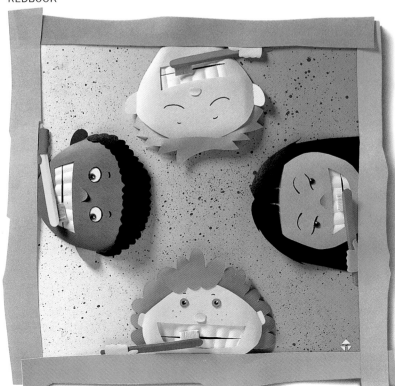

TOBY WILLIAMS

CUT-PAPER ILLUSTRATION

82 FIFERS LANE
BOXBOROUGH, MA 01719
FON 508 263-8106
FAX 508 263-4056

STUDIOS

CLIENT: NEW YORK TIMES

STATE

BANK

Daniel
VASoncellos.

TEL: 617 829.8815

fAX: 617 829.8867

NO JOB
TOO
BIG! ~

AGENCY: ALCONE SIMS O'BRIEN
CLIENT: CALIFORNIA LOTTERY

FOR MORE SAMPLES SEE: SHOWCASE CD#1, SHOWCASE 18 & 19, CREATIVE ILLUST. BK '92.93&94, the DIRECTORY of Illust. 7,10 & 11.
THANK YOU

ZIFF-DAVIS, INC.

PROGRESS
SOFTWARE

NEWSWEEK

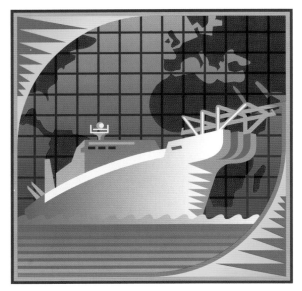

AT&T SUBMARINE SYSTEMS, INC.

FOR EDITORIAL ASSIGNMENTS
PLEASE CALL JEAN DIRECTLY AT 914-693-7681

Osmosis

WORK
NON-STOP

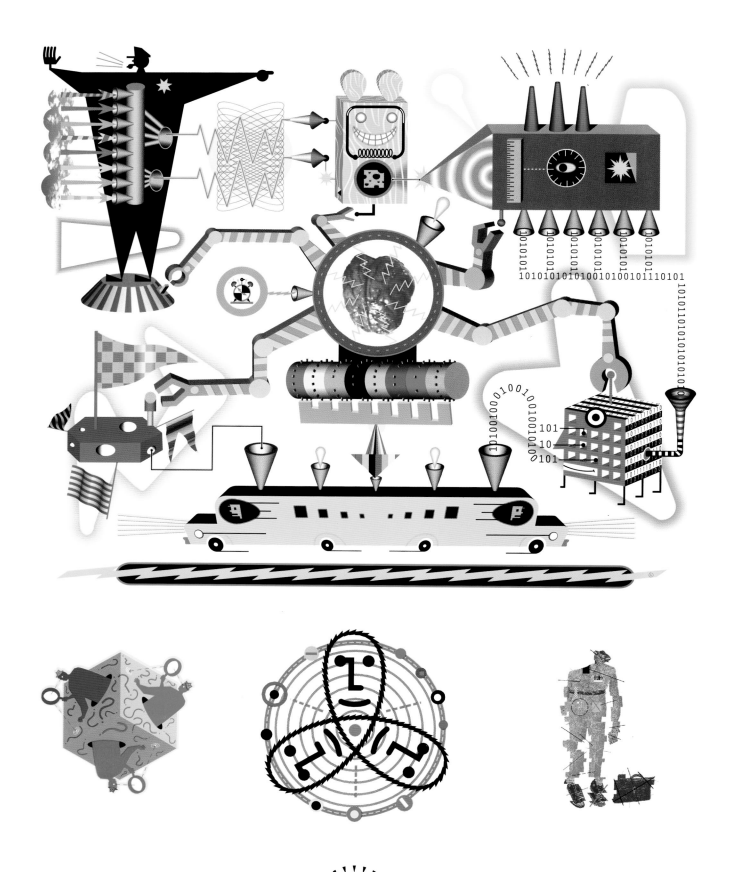

Mike Tyson / Oil

SCOTT MEDLOCK

11522 North Poema Place, suite 201, Chatsworth, CA 91311 Phone/Fax: (818) 341-6207

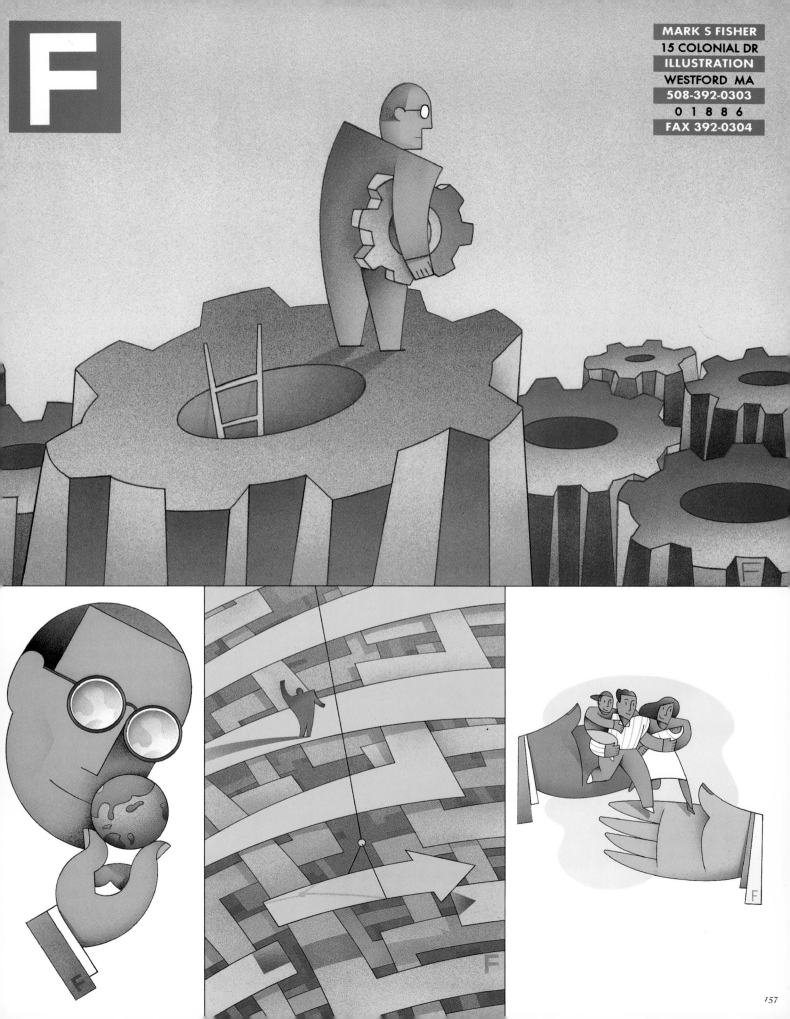

MARK S FISHER
15 COLONIAL DR
ILLUSTRATION
WESTFORD MA
508-392-0303
0 1 8 8 6
FAX 392-0304

FREDERICK H. CARLSON TEL (412) 856 • 0982
FAX (412) 856 • 0983

Linda Helton
7000 Meadow Lake
Dallas, Texas 75214
Phone 214.319.7877
Fax 214.319.6063

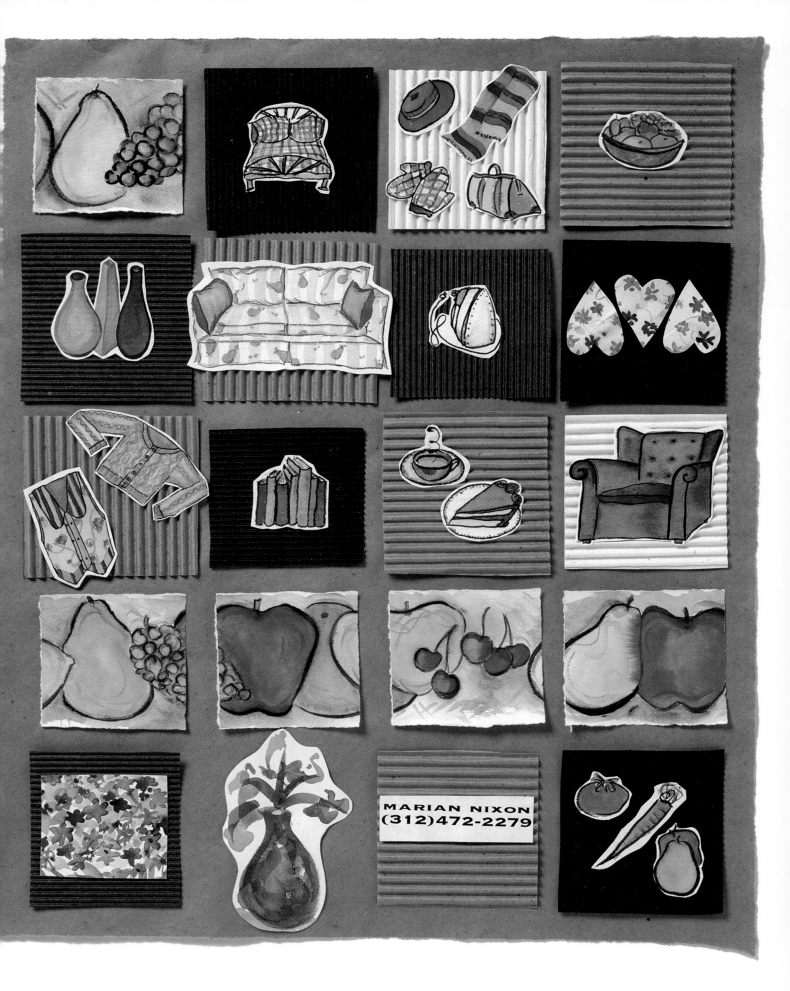

MARIAN NIXON
(312)472-2279

GREGORY
DYE

Studio
303.933.0340

Tom Maloney/Chicago
312.704.0500

MITCH O'CONNELL

CALL TOM MALONEY 312·704·0500

163

DENNAS DAVIS

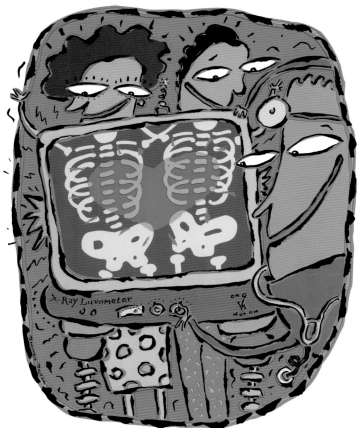

STUDIO
PHONE:
615-386-0444
FAX:
615-386-0430

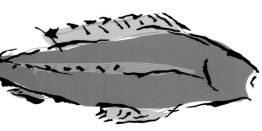

MIDWEST REPRESENTATIVE:
TOM MALONEY
PHONE: 312-704-0500
FAX: 312-704-0501

164

© DENNAS DAVIS

JOHN MARGESON

NEW YORK
CAROL CHISLOVSKY
212 • 677 • 9100

STUDIO
808 • 262 • 7980
(e: JMARGESON@aol.com)

MIDWEST
TOM MALONEY
312 • 704 • 0500

ROD
THOMAS
617·449·0480

16 GRASMERE RD
NEEDHAM MA
02194

NeoWoodcut

VECTOR AIRBRUSH

Wet Brush

SCULPTED LINE

ICON
graphics
INC.

Icon Graphics Inc.
34 Elton Street
Rochester, NY 14607
Phone 716 271-7020
Fax 716 271-7029
All illustrations are produced electronically.

Zoe Worley

212 · 288 · 2011

DAVID DIAZ

ILLUSTRATION

619.438.0070

FAX 619.438.0315

This limited edition "BOOK" is available
upon request. To receive a copy, call or fax
on your company letterhead.

DIAZ ICON

A COLLECTION of EPS ILLUSTRATIONS:

⊙ BUSINESS / TRAVEL   ⊙ NATURE / ENVIRONMENT

⊙ PEOPLE / ANIMALS   ⊙ DINGBATS

EACH DISC CONTAINS 50 ILLUSTRATIONS: $49 PER DISC.

TO ORDER CALL TOLL FREE:

800.474.ICON

Ellen Mueller

phone
707·778
6221

RUTH SOFAIR KETLER
101   BLUFF   TERRACE
SILVER SPRING MD 20902
TEL 301-593-6059
FAX 301-593-1236

THREE CAT STUDIO

SALES TOOL KIT

P.J. MEACHAM

404·299·5842
PHONE · FAX

* illustration with an attitude *

KATHY PETRAUSKAS
312 642 • 4950 • FAX 312 642 • 6391

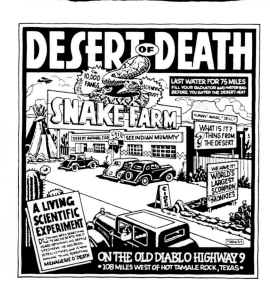

William S. Burroughs, Jr.

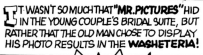

HE DESIGNS 'EM & DRAWS 'EM • THEY AIN'T CHEAP, FOLKS!

GEORGE TOOMER
3923 COLE AVE • DALLAS, TX 75204
214 522-1171 • FAX: 214 528-3588

FRIEND OF THE FRIENDLESS — PROMOTER OF THE SHY — CHAMPION OF LOST CAUSES — GYNOPHILE — PRACTICING DESIGNER, ILLUSTRATOR AND GARDENER.

lisa grothman

phone/fax
(212) 794-2627

pokey-nose people

FREE SPELL-BINDER!

Holm

Call American Artists for your free Sample binder!
212-582-0023

BILL GARLAND

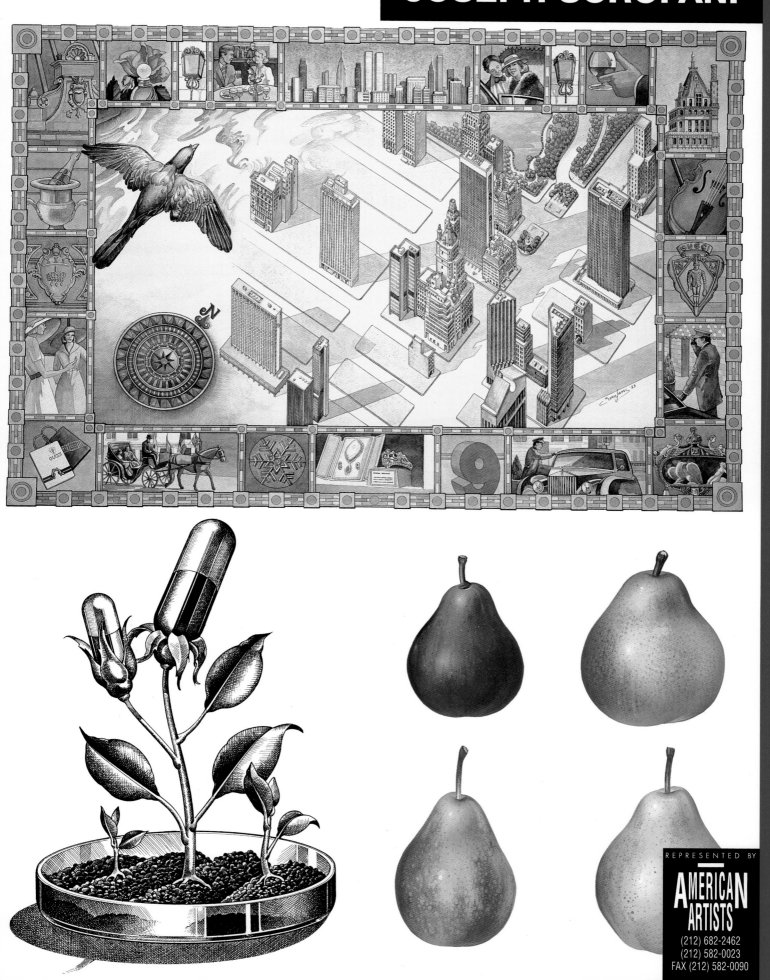

MIKE JAROSZKO

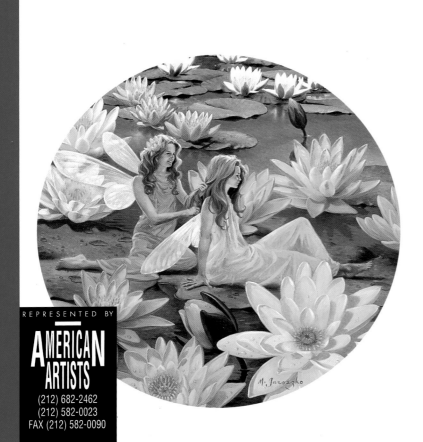

ROGER MARK

ANDREW EDWARDS

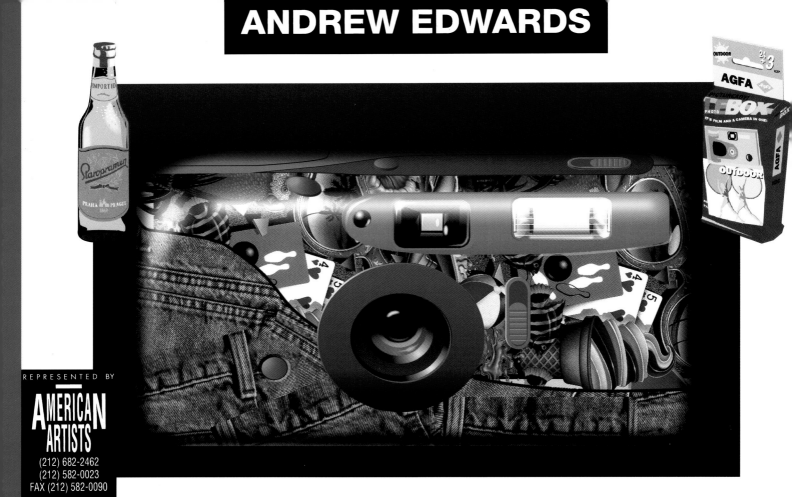

RON MAHONEY

NICKY DUPAYS

ART PROULX

COLIN POOLE

SOUTHWEST:
MELISSA
HOPSON
(214) 747-3122

NORTHEAST:
AMERICAN
ARTISTS REP.
(212) 682-2462

WEST:
LINDA
DEMARETA
(510) 769-1421

SOUTHEAST:
SUSAN
WELLS
(404) 255-1430

STUDIO:
1-800-808-5005

186

Illustration in Fabric

Kate Edwards, 11126 Manhatten Mine Lane, Nevada City, CA 95959 / Fax: 916.265.8118 / Studio: 916.265.4502

phone 916-265-5666 fax 916-265-8118   11126 manhatten mine lane, nevada city, california 95959

Karl Edwards

phone 916-265-5666 fax 916-265-8118   11126 manhatten mine lane, nevada city, california 95959

Karl Edwards

Lee Breuer
I L L U S T R A T O R

Studio Phone (803) 779 - 9669
Studio Fax   (803) 765 - 9308

910 Laurens Street Columbia, S.C. 29201 - 3932
see p. 982 AMERICAN SHOWCASE 18

190

JOHN S. DYKES

17 Morningside Dr. S. ☐ Westport, CT 06880 ☐ (203) 222-8150 Fax 222-8155

IN OUR MARKET, TIMING IS EVERYTHING

MEDICAL ATTRACTION

THE CHARGE FOR BENEFITS

HELEN KUNZE

4 1 7 · 3 5 9 · 5 2 3 3

MARK WICKART

6293 SURREY RIDGE RD. LISLE, IL 60532 ● PHONE (708) 369-0164 ● FAX (708) 369-4004

67 Corvette
STING RAY

427

Don Wieland

A s the creative needs of our clients evolve, so too does the portfolio and services of Mendola Artists. In the past year Mendola has added special effects photography and 3-D animation, both requiring the most sophisticated software and equipment. We have also added interesting conceptual and decorative styles executed with a simple paint-brush. And Mendola continues to represent the finest realistic painters in the industry. Mendola Artists has a staff of expert sales consultants to recommend the right talent for your project. On the west coast, we have a new office to service your needs. You can see the full range of our talent by reviewing the Mendola sections in the major source-books or by requesting our latest promotion book.

MENDOLA LTD.
ARTISTS REPRESENTATIVES
212 **986-5680** FAX 212 818-1246

420 LEXINGTON AVE. NEW YORK N.Y. 10170

WEST COAST 503 236-2645

Steve Cieslawski

Alfons Kiefer

Alfons Kiefer

195

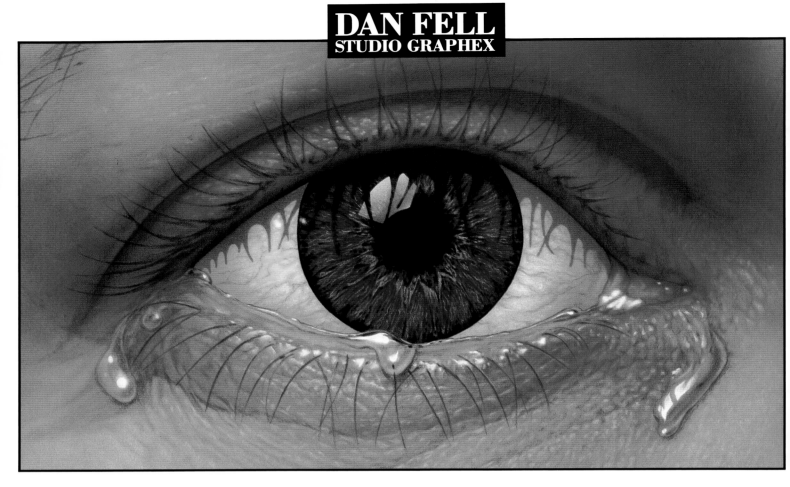

RON BERG

Represented by

MENDOLA LTD.
ARTISTS REPRESENTATIVES
212 **986-5680** FAX 212 818-1246
420 LEXINGTON AVE. NEW YORK N.Y. 10170

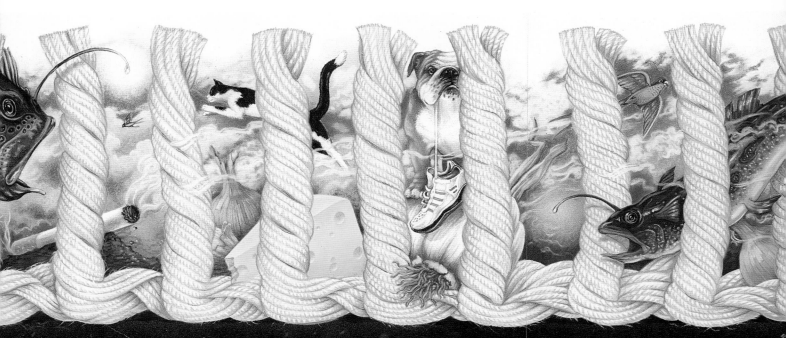

AMY L. WASSERMAN
COLLAGE ILLUSTRATION
413-586-0307
Fax 586-0083

Venus On Line

Your Choice TV

Associates Master Card

In New York City
Mendola Ltd.
212-986-5680 Fax 818-1246

Outside New York City
Amy Frith
617-423-2212 Fax 423-2213

Seth Jaben

New York   *212.673.5631*

Susan Williams

Digital Illustration
Phone: 612-824-6103
Fax: 612-824-2896

KIM LaFAVE

REPRESENTED BY

MAUREEN
MOFFET

TELEPHONE
(416) 691-3242

RogEr RotH

7227 Brent Road
Upper Darby, Pennsylvania 19082
215 352-3235

WALL STREET JOURNAL

NEW YORK TIMES

CALIFORNIA LAWYER

PC MAGAZINE

"THE CAT HALL OF FAME"

MICHAEL W. MARTIS

ILLUSTRATOR

phone
(515) 285-8122

fax
(515) 287-6483

nordstrom **Essentials**

SUSAN GROSS

fon 415.751.5879 fax 5876

Tranquility

i drifted into that other WORLD

Anti-Stress

take my word for it...

Sensuality

and then i opened the door

Revitalizing

i wonder why i love it so much

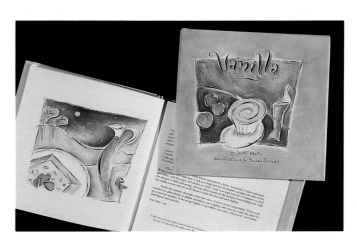

Vanilla

Clients include: Chronicle Books, Nordstrom, L A Times, Running Press, Clarkson N. Potter, Oracle, Harper Collins, Prevention and MacUser Magazine. For additional work see CIB '94 and '95.

MICHAIL
IOFIN

TELEPHONE / FAX
415/386-1984

Joe Boddy

I L L U S T R A T I O N

5375 SKYWAY DR • MISSOULA, MT 59801 • PHONE & FAX 406•251•3587

**katherine
mahoney**

**6 0 hurd
road
belmont, ma
02178**

617·868·7877

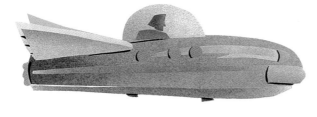

LINDA BRONSON

SCOTT NASH

LAURA DeSANTIS

REPRESENTED BY LEIGHTON & COMPANY CALL 508 921 0887 FAX 508 921 0223

DANUTA JARECKA

214

JOHN BREAKEY

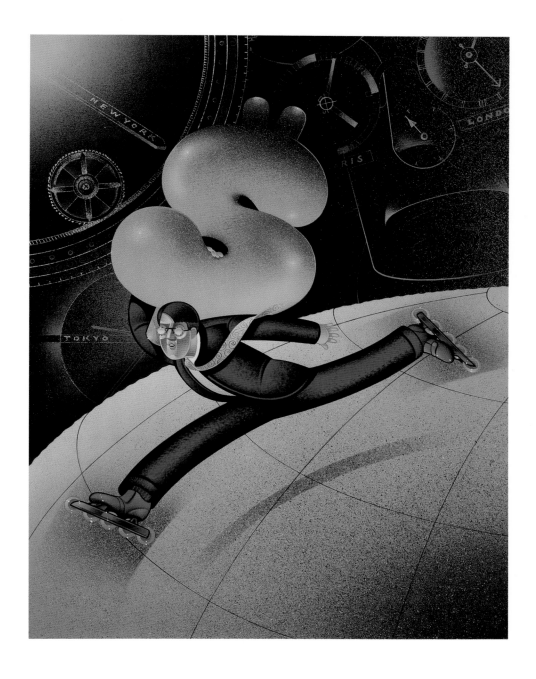

STEVE MEEK

STUDIO
312 477 8055

AUGUST STEIN

217

FRANK FRISARI

TONY DeLUZ

BRUCE SANDERS

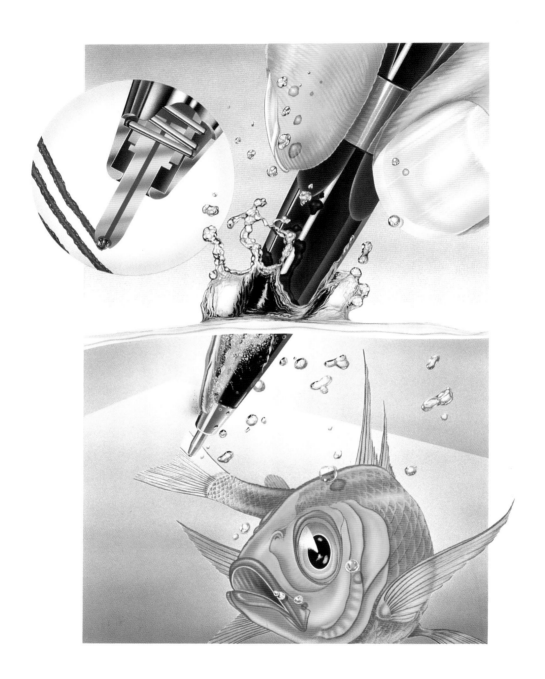

TRADITIONAL & COMPUTER TECHNICAL ILLUSTRATIONS

JOE FARNHAM

REPRESENTED BY LEIGHTON & COMPANY CALL 508 921 0887 FAX 508 921 0223

JAMES KACZMAN

ILLUSTRATION

16 ACRON ROAD

BROOKLINE, MA

02146-7738

T: 617-738-9924

F: 617-738-1585

LISA MANNING
508 927 9990

M.E. COHEN
ph 212•627•8033
fx 212•627•1167

Advertising
&
EDITORIAL

Terry Widener

Represented by Michèle Manasse

200 Aquetong Road
New Hope, PA 18938
Phone: (215) 862-2091
Fax: (215) 862-2641

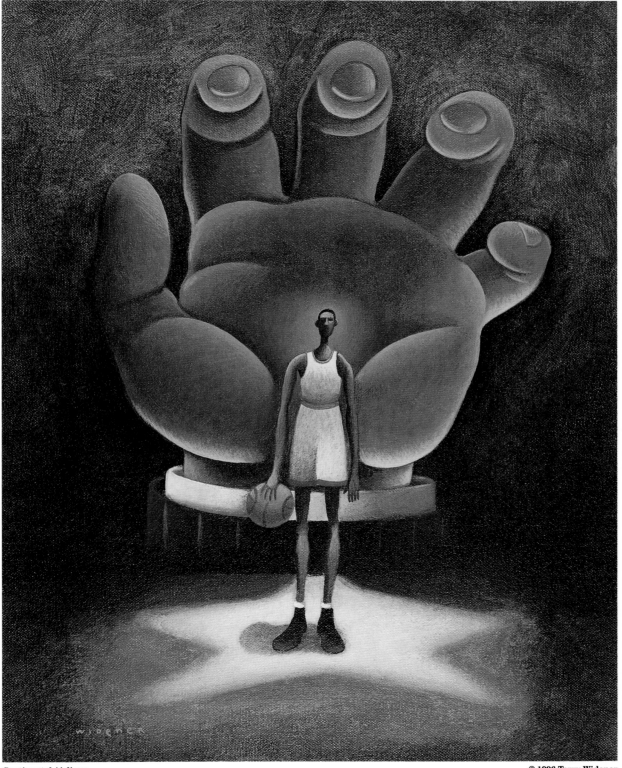

Continental Airlines

Mike Reagan

Represented by Michèle Manasse

200 Aquetong Roa
New Hope, PA 1893
Phone: (215) 862-209
Fax: (215) 862-264

Islands Magazine

Forbes FYI

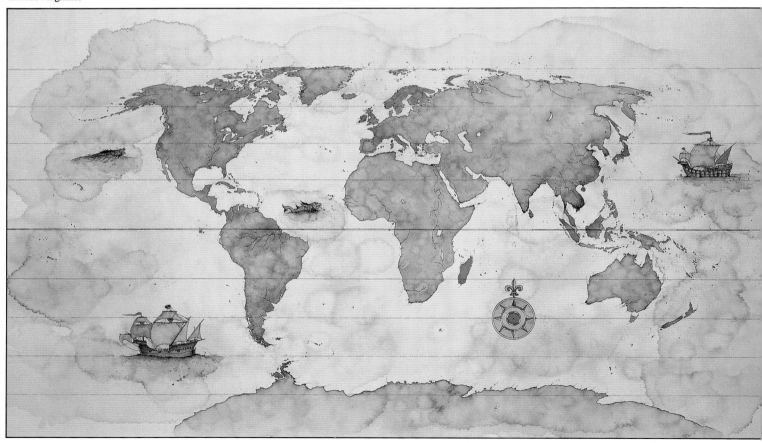

The Greenwich Workshop

1996 ©Mike Reagan

Work

Jacques Cournoyer

Represented by Michèle Manasse

200 Aquetong Road
New Hope, PA 18938
Phone: (215) 862-2091
Fax: (215) 862-2641

Chatelaine Magazine

Actualité Magazine

Business Week

Work

Maxine Boll

Represented by Michèle Manasse

200 Aquetong Road
New Hope, PA 18938
Phone: (215) 862-2091
Fax: (215) 862-2641

Bon Appétit Magazine

Lands' End, Inc.

Kaufman & Broad, Inc.

© 1996 Maxine Boll

228

New Work

Sheldon Greenberg

Represented by Michèle Manasse

200 Aquetong Road
New Hope, PA 18938
Phone: (215) 862-2091
Fax: (215) 862-2641

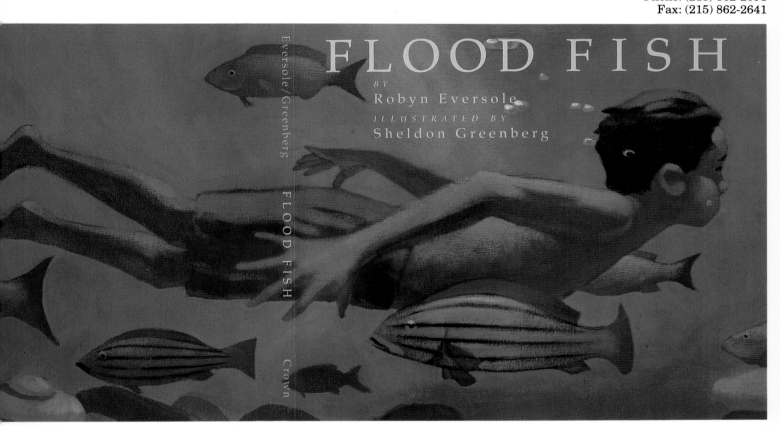

Eversole/Greenberg

FLOOD FISH

FLOOD FISH
BY
Robyn Eversole
ILLUSTRATED BY
Sheldon Greenberg

Crown

Crown Publishers

Family Circle Magazine

Garland/Greenberg

I Never Knew Your Name
by Sherry Garland   illustrated by Sheldon Greenberg

I Never Knew Your Name

Ticknor & Fields

Ticknor & Fields Books

Greg King

Represented by Michèle Manasse

200 Aquetong Road
New Hope, PA 18938
Phone: (215) 862-2091
Fax: (215) 862-2641

Frito-Lay, Inc.

Oregon Ale & Beer Company

Pizza Inn   1995 © Greg King

NEW Work

Eric Dever

Represented by Michèle Manasse

200 Aquetong Road
New Hope, PA 18938
Phone: (215) 862-2091
Fax: (215) 862-2641

The New Yorker

Harvard Business Review

"Justice Via Satellite"

"An American Prometheus"   © 1996 Eric Dever

231

Work

Geneviève Claire

Represented by Michèle Manasse

200 Aquetong Road
New Hope, PA 18938
Phone: (215) 862-2091
Fax: (215) 862-2641

SILVER BURDETT & GINN

SIMON & SCHUSTER

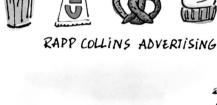

RAPP COLLINS ADVERTISING

PROCTER & GAMBLE

VALENTINE GREETINGS

HANES

PIPER DESIGN inc.

232

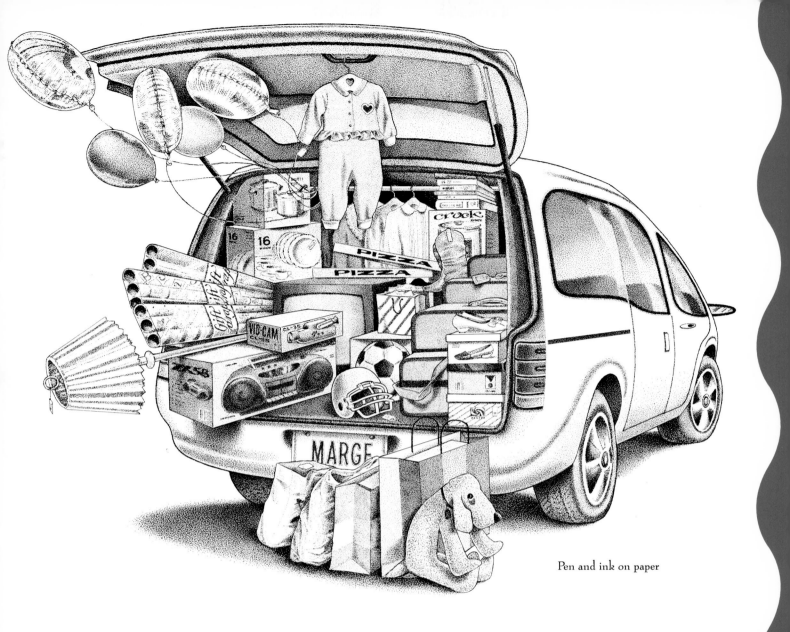

Pen and ink on paper

RICHARD S. HARRINGTON

3612 Kemp Drive • Endwell, NY • 13760-2410
Phone: 607-748-7806
Fax: 607-748-2970

Pen and ink on paper

Jill McElmurry
916·235·0532

Northwest / Max Karst   Tel 206 828 4218   Fax 206 828 9457

DEBRA *Spina* dixon

STUDIO 510.652.6909 REPRESENTED BY FREDA SCOTT 415.398.9121

AMY BRYANT

STUDIO 214. 696.4950 FAX 214. 696.6163

Represented by ANDREA LYNCH 5521 Greenville Ave. #104.338, Dallas, TX 75206
Telephone: 214.369.6990 FAX: 214.369.6938

ZITA ASBAGHI

(718) 275-1995

J F M A R T I N

800 - 360 - 0019

JOEL HARLIB ASSOCIATES

312-573-1370   FAX 573-1445

239

SCOTT ROBERTS ILLUSTRATOR

lindgren & smith

annual report, ad steve martin

lindgren & smith

lindgren & smith

chicago 312.819.0880   new york 212.397.7330   san francisco 415.788.8552

lindgren & smith

lindgren & smith

chicago 312.819.0880   new york 212.397.7330   san francisco 415.788.8552

gti annual report

lindgren & smith

lindgren & smith

lindgren & smith

chicago 312.819.0880   new york 212.397.7330   san francisco 415.788.8552

lindgren & smith

lindgren & smith

chicago 312.819.0880   new york 212.397.7330   san francisco 415.788.8552

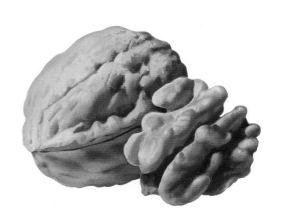

D A V I D   M A Y O   O L M S T E A D

1300 Nicollet Mall • Suite 3046 • Minneapolis, Minnesota 55403 • 612 339-2112 • Fax 612 339-2233

312.384.4676 FAX 384.4643

REPRESENTED BY MUNRO GOODMAN

CHICAGO 312.321.1336 FAX 312.321.1350   NYC 212.691.2667 FAX 212.633.1844

Jody Winger

P. 612.377.4838   F. 612.377.7505

Represented By

Gretchen Harris and Associates

P. 612.822.0650   F. 612.822.0358

G H
& A

© Winger

 Mary Worcester

Represented by Gretchen Harris
612/822-0650 (fax 612/822-0358)

Margaret
Hewitt
Liz Sanders Agency
714·495·3664
FAX-714·495·0129

CAFFEINE ☕ COOL

FRASIER

REMOTE ROYALTY

JOE
FOURNIER
708·848·2756

CALL JOE... CALL JOE...
TRADITIONAL ART?
COMPUTER-READY ART?
ADVERTISING, CORPORATE,
EDITORIAL?
CALL
JOE,

CALL
JOE,

CALL...

Jim Meyer
612-938-0058
Represented by
Robin Ogden
612-925-4174

BILL MAYER, 240 FORKNER DRIVE, DECATUR, GA 30030 (404) 378-0686 FAX (404) 373-1759

265

Joe Baker

35 WOOSTER STREET, STUDIO 2F, NEW YORK, N.Y. 10013

(212) 925-6555

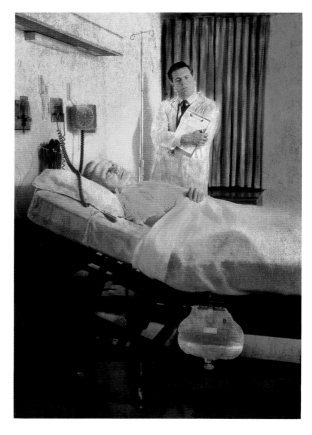

Joe Baker

35 WOOSTER STREET, STUDIO 2F, NEW YORK, N.Y. 10013

(212) 925-6555

MICHAEL WEAVER

913 432 5078

DEREK GRINNELL

IvyGlick
& ASSOCIATES

EAST: 212•869•0214   **WEST:** 510•944•0304
FAX: 510•944•0322

JERRY DADDS

WOODCUTS
WOOD ENGRAVING
LINE ILLUSTRATION

Studio:	**West Coast**	**Chicago/Midwest**	**Philadelphia**
Eucalyptus Tree	**Ivy Glick & Assoc.**	**Dan Sell**	**Deborah Wolfe**
410-243-0211	510-944-0304	312-578-8844	215-232-6666
Fax 243-0215	Fax 510-944-0322	Fax 578-8847	Fax 232-6585

TONY MORSE

Ivy Glick
& ASSOCIATES

EAST: 212•869•0214   WEST: 510•944•0304
FAX: 510•944•0322

MATTHEW HOLMES

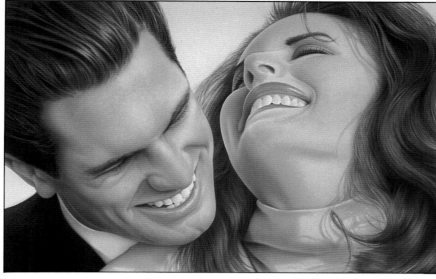

PAUL VISMARA

Chicago, IL TEL FAX **312·248·7084**

BF
·
BILL
FRAM
PTON
·

DANIELE COLLIGNON 200 W.15ᵗʰ NYC 10011
212·243·4209

Nap (Larry) Lajoie   Bob Cox '95

1/422

274

BENIOFF

3311 Jennings Street • San Francisco, CA 94124
Phone: 415 467-5014 • FAX: 415 467-3637

CHRIS SHARP

(212) 505 0649

McDonald s, D.C. Comics, Warner Bros.

Copyright 1995 U.S.P.S.

Pepsico Brazil

McDonald s, D.C. Comics, Warner Bros.

Eloqui

Mark Stutzman

Math Horizons

USF&G

Consultant Pharmacist

Eloqui

Laura Stutzman

301·334·4086   100 G STREET, MOUNTAIN LAKE PARK, MD 21550   FAX·334·4186

Susan Johnston Carlson

Science Illustration & Cartography
(full or computer maps available)

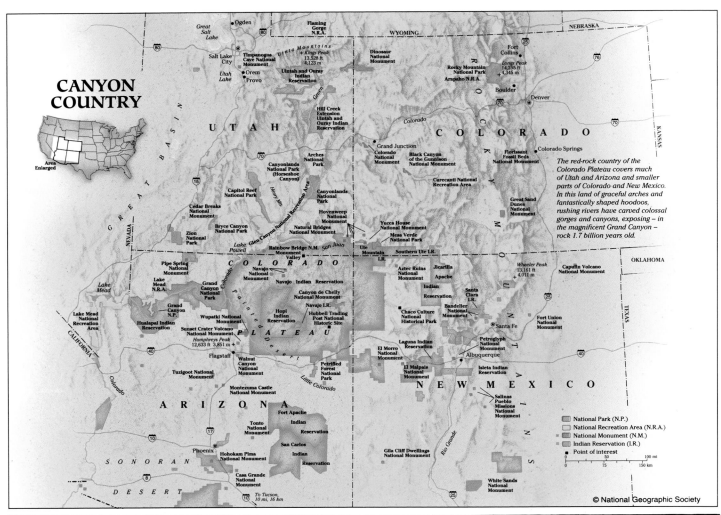

CANYON COUNTRY

Area Enlarged

The red-rock country of the Colorado Plateau covers much of Utah and Arizona and smaller parts of Colorado and New Mexico. In this land of graceful arches and fantastically shaped hoodoos, rushing rivers have carved colossal gorges and canyons, exposing – in the magnificent Grand Canyon – rock 1.7 billion years old.

National Park (N.P.)
National Recreation Area (N.R.A.)
National Monument (N.M.)
Indian Reservation (I.R.)
Point of interest

0   50   100 mi
0   75   150 km

© National Geographic Society

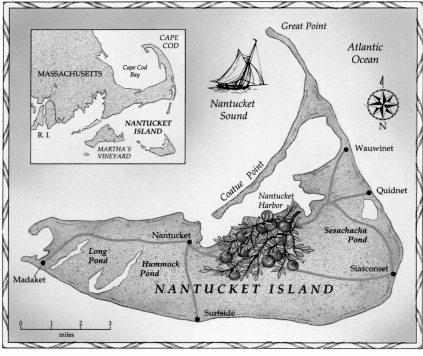

Great Point

Atlantic Ocean

CAPE COD

MASSACHUSETTS

Cape Cod Bay

R.I.

NANTUCKET ISLAND

MARTHA'S VINEYARD

Nantucket Sound

N

Wauwinet

Coatue Point

Quidnet

Nantucket Harbor

Sesachacha Pond

Long Pond

Nantucket

Hummock Pond

Siasconset

Madaket

NANTUCKET ISLAND

Surfside

0   1   2   3
miles

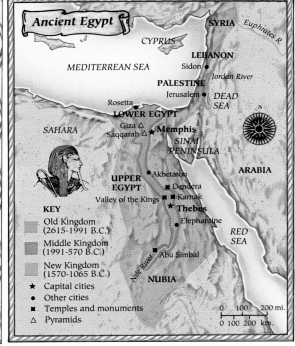

Ancient Egypt

SYRIA

CYPRUS

Euphrates R.

LEBANON

MEDITERREAN SEA

Sidon

PALESTINE

Jordan River

Jerusalem

Rosetta

DEAD SEA

SAHARA

LOWER EGYPT

Giza

Saqqarah

Memphis

SINAI PENINSULA

ARABIA

Akhetaton

UPPER EGYPT

Dendera

KEY

Valley of the Kings

Karnak

Thebes

Elephantine

Old Kingdom (2615-1991 B.C.)
Middle Kingdom (1991-570 B.C.)
New Kingdom (1570-1065 B.C.)

RED SEA

Abu Simbal

Nile River

NUBIA

★ Capital cities
● Other cities
■ Temples and monuments
△ Pyramids

0   100   200 mi.
0   100 200 km.

913 · 539 · 5535

280

Chicago 312•384•3496
illustrations done on mac.
ask about stock illustration availability.

in texas, call star miller at 713•888•0510

281

DALE GLASGOW&ASSOC.
INFORMATION ILLUSTRATION•INTERACTIVE MULTIMEDIA•VIDEO

Dale Glasgow & Assoc.
448 Hartwood Road
Fredericksburg,
Virginia 22406

Voice
(540) 286-2539

FAX
(540) 286-0316

COMPUSERVE
72142,1625

AMERICA ON-LINE
INFOBAN

INTERNET/THE WEB
dglasgow@illuminet.net

To View More Work:
- *Adweek Portfolios*, 1988, '89, '90
- *Creative Illustration Book*, 1991, '92, '93, '94, '95,'96
- *American Showcase*, 1992, '95, '96
- *New Media Showcase* 1993, '94, '95
- *Step By Step Graphics*, Jan. 1990
- *Personal Publishing*, March 1991
- *Washington Sourcebook*, 1992, '94, '95, '96
- *Workbook* 1995,'96
- *Diagraphics*, Volume 2. JCA, 1995
- Published book: *INFORMATION ILLUSTRATION*. Addison Wesley,1994

CALL US FOR A
SAMPLE DISKETTE
OF COMPUTER ART
540-286-2539

CALL US FOR
SAMPLES OF ART
540-286-2539

CALL US FOR A
SAMPLE VIDEO TAPE
OF COMPUTER ANIMATION
540-286-2539

National Geographic Traveler—Flying South

Newspaper Association Of America—Connections of the future

Kiplinger Finance Magazine—The checkbook

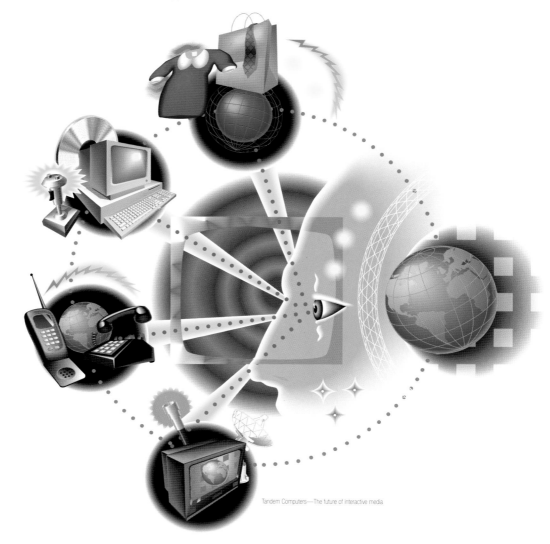

Tandem Computers—The future of interactive media

The May Company—How to grow your money

G&A—The world wide web

KPMG Pete Marwick—Getting the puzzle together

MOST OF THE ART WE CREATE COMES FROM MACINTOSH COMPUTERS AND CAN BE MADE COMPATIBLE IN MOST FILE FORMATS INCLUDING PC, NEXT, SCITEX, SILICON GRAPHICS, SUN AND ALSO INCLUDING VIDEO, BETA, D1

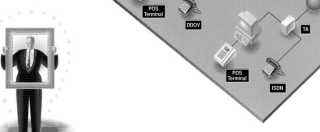

Compuserve—VPL network

CompuServe

LEC Packet Network

DVM

X.75 Gateways

POS Terminal

DDOV

TA

LEC Packet Network

POS Terminal

ISDN

American Diabetes Assn.—Diabetes solutions

US West—Frame yourself

Women-Owned Businesses

Home Office Computing—Women owned business

CUSTOMER SATISFACTION

Xerox—Customer satisfaction icon

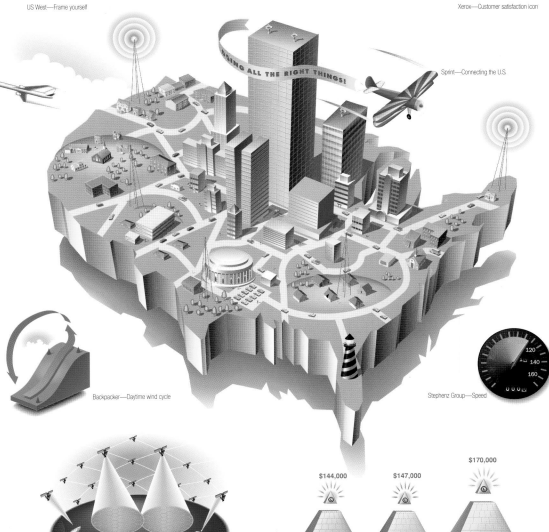

DOING ALL THE RIGHT THINGS!

Sprint—Connecting the U.S.

Backpacker—Daytime wind cycle

120 140 160

Stephenz Group—Speed

$144,000 $147,000 $170,000

1992   1993   1994

Xerox—Profit per employee

Motorola/Iridium—How the network works

Multicom—Animation for broadcast and trade show

MOST OF THE ART WE CREATE COMES FROM MACINTOSH COMPUTERS AND CAN BE MADE COMPATIBLE IN MOST FILE FORMATS INCLUDING PC, NEXT, SCITEX, SILICON GRAPHICS, SUN AND ALSO INCLUDING VIDEO, BETA, D1.

DALE GLASGOW&ASSOC.

INFORMATION ILLUSTRATION•INTERACTIVE MULTIMEDIA•VIDEO

Dale Glasgow
448 Hartwood
Fredericksburg
Virginia 22406

Voice
(540) 286-253

FAX
(540) 286-031

COMPUSERVE
72142,1625

AMERICA ON-L
INFOBAN

INTERNET/THE
dglasgow@ill

To View More Work
• *Adweek Portfolios*
• *Creative Illustratio*
'93, '94, '95, '96
• *American Showca*
• *New Media Showc*
• *Step By Step Grap*
• *Personal Publishin*
• *Washington Sourc*
'95, '96
• *Workbook* 1995, '9
• *Diagraphics*, Volum
• Published book: *I*
ILLUSTRATION. Addis

CALL US FOR A
SAMPLE DISKETTE OF COMPUTER ART

540-286-253

CALL US FOR
SAMPLES OF ART

540-286-253

CALL US FOR
SAMPLE VIDEO TA
OF COMPUTER ANIM

540-286-2

marcie wolf-hubbard

1507 BALLARD STREET   SILVER SPRING, MD 20910   TEL (301)585-5815   FAX (301)585-5060

98

Tom Murray
415.863.8292

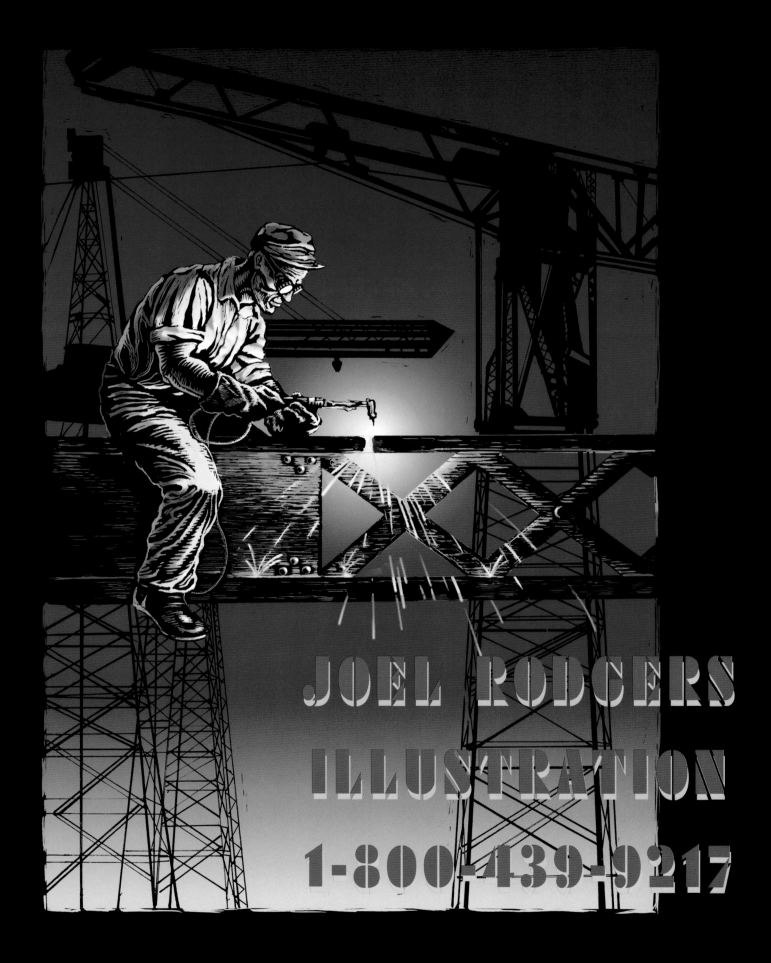

JOEL RODGERS

ILLUSTRATION

1-800-439-9217

JAVIER ROMERO
DESIGN GROUP

24 East, 23rd Street, New York, NY 10010 [212] 420 0656 Fax 420 1168

Zurbarán 10, 4º 2810 Madrid, España 310 5387 Fax 310 5351

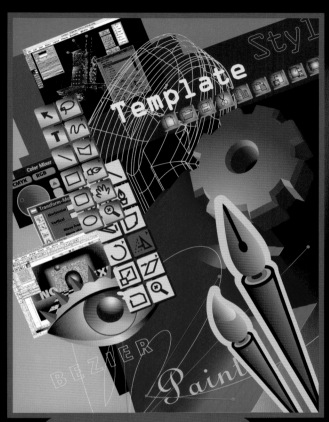

COMPUTER SHOPPER MAGAZINE

COORS BREWING CO.

JWT FOR BELL ATLANTIC

HATMAN ANIMATED TV SERIES

QUEENS FALL FESTIVAL

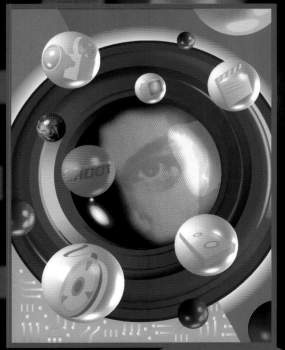

SHOOT MAGAZINE

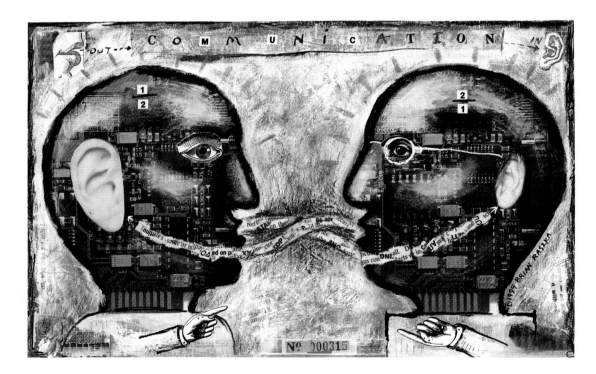

Brian Raszka

(415) 673-4479

Clients Include: Reader's Digest, Los Angeles Times Magazine, Electronic Musician, Advanced
Systems Magazine, Men's Health, Keyboard Magazine, Apple Computer, KFOG Radio and more!

Mark Matcho

ILLUSTRATION

PH 212·529·1318

"In Good Ol' New York City"

FINISHES BY MODEM

SUPAROCKA@AOL.COM

PORTFOLIO ON DISK

ILLUSTRATOR

JaMiE
HOGAN

265 Pleasant Avenue
Peaks Island, ME 04108
(207) 766-9726

marty braun / illustrator

265 PLEASANT AVE
PEAKS ISLAND
MAINE 04108
207·766·9726

PAUL ZWOLAK

MARLENA TORZECKA REPRESENTS **PAUL ZWOLAK** • 211 EAST 89 STREET • SUITE A-1 • NEW YORK • NY 10128
TELEPHONE: 212•289•5514 / FAX: 212•987•2855

Istvan Orosz

Clients:

Brinkley Design, Chiat Day, Chief Executive, Museum of Modern Art/Budapest, New York Magazine, The New York Times, Ogilvy & Mather, Playboy, U.S. Information Agency, W.H. Freeman.

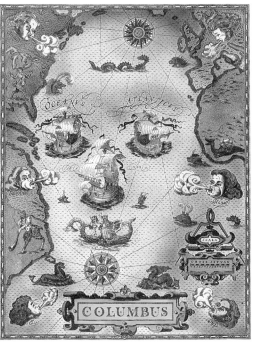

MARLENA TORZECKA REPRESENTS **ISTVAN OROSZ** • 211 EAST 89 STREET • SUITE A-1 • NEW YORK • NY 10128
TELEPHONE: 212•289•5514 / FAX: 212•987•2855

Gerard DuBois

Clients:

Adweek, The British-American Chamber of Commerce, Bloomberg, Family Life, Global Finance, IBM, Karnes Prickett, Microsoft, Oxford American Magazine, P.C. Magazine.

MARLENA TORZECKA REPRESENTS **GERARD DUBOIS** • 211 EAST 89 STREET • SUITE A-1 • NEW YORK • NY 10128
TELEPHONE: 212•289•5514 / FAX: 212•987•2855

ferruccio

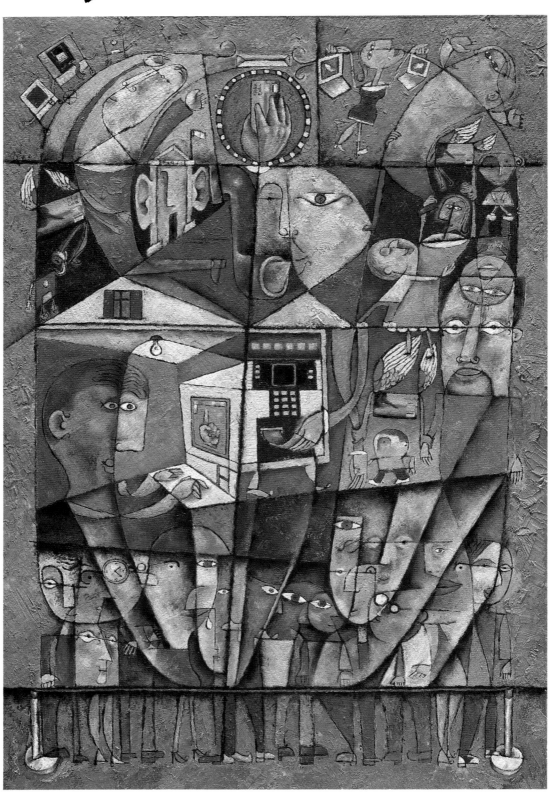

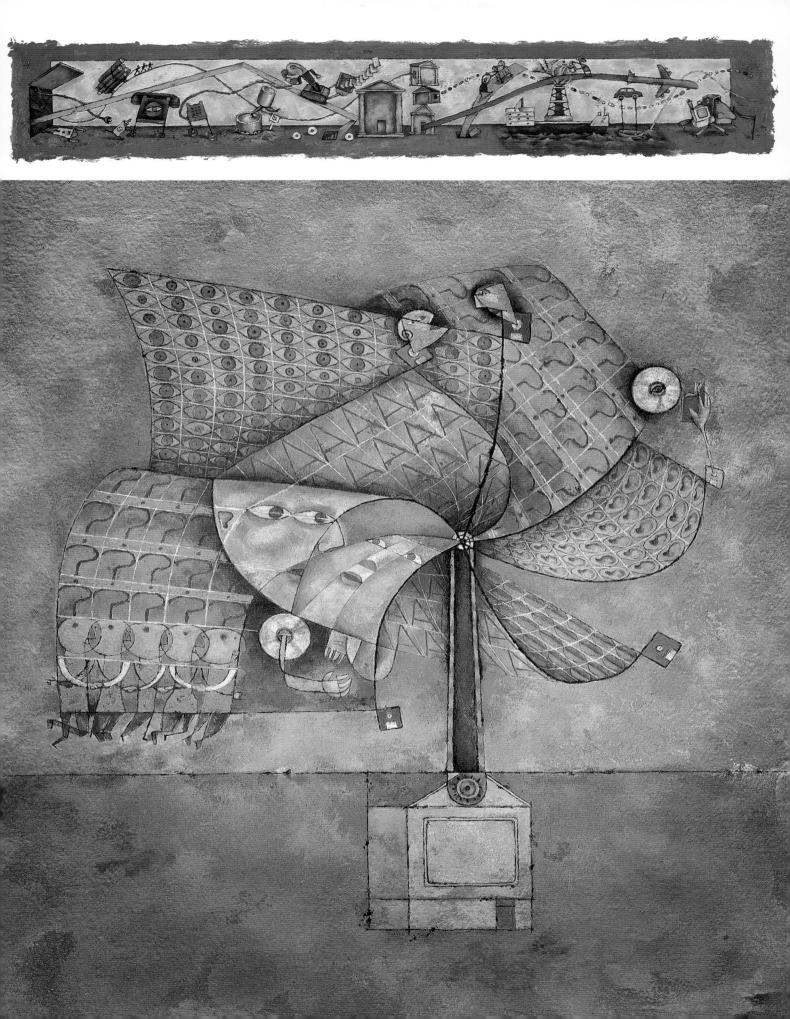

SCOTT MCKOWEN

Clients:

Arena Stage Theatre
Avon Books
Lowe & Partners/SMS
Newsweek
The New York Times
Ogilvy & Mather
Playboy
Red Lobster
Roundabout Theatre
Viking Penguin
Washington Post.

VICTOR SADOWSKI

Clients:

AT&T Collection, Bantam Books, The Center for Global Partnership, Geoffrey Beene Inc., New York City Opera, The New York Times, Playboy, Random House, St. Martin's Press, Time Magazine.

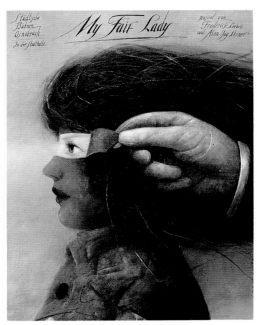

MARLENA TORZECKA REPRESENTS **VICTOR SADOWSKI** • 211 EAST 89 STREET • SUITE A-1 • NEW YORK • NY 10128
TELEPHONE: 212•289•5514 / FAX: 212•987•2855

Clients:

Addison-Wesley, Bell Canada, Bloomberg, Doubleday, Financial Times, Ministry of Health of British Columbia, Newsweek, The New York Times, Teleglobe Canada, US News and World Report.

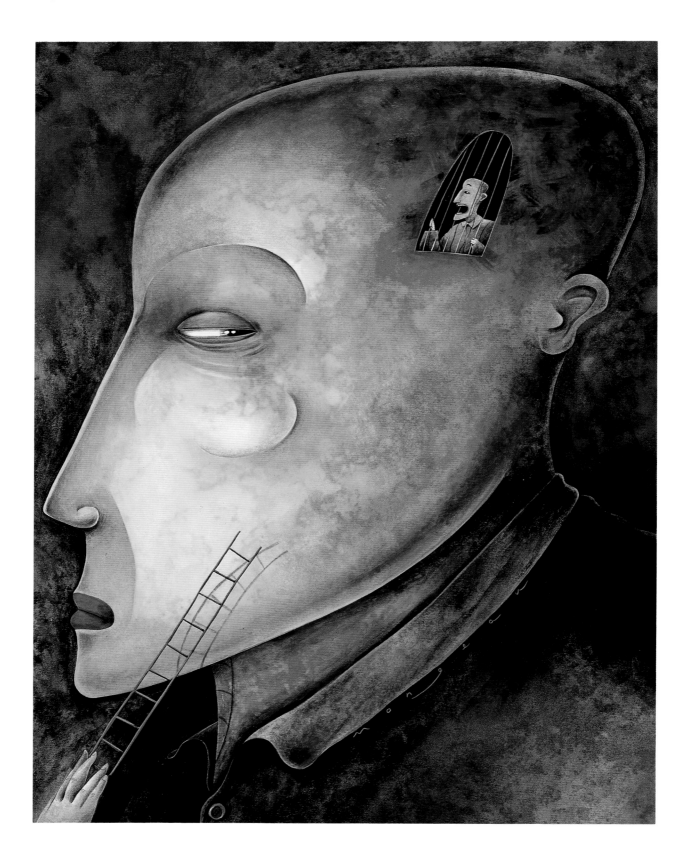

MARLENA TORZECKA REPRESENTS **MARC MONGEAU** • 211 EAST 89 STREET • SUITE A-1 • NEW YORK • NY 10128
TELEPHONE: 212•289•5514 / FAX: 212•987•2855

Susan Melrath

410•785•0797

410•785•1196 FX

3100 Jackson Ridge Court

Phoenix MD 21131

Scratchy Studio · **Fran O'Neill** P.O. Box 990716 Pru Station Boston, MA 02199

MIDWEST Representative LuLu 612.825.7564

617·267·9215

TONAL VALUES INC.

THE FINEST ILLUSTRATION

TAKES YOU TO REALMS

UNCHARTED BY

PHOTOGRAPHY.

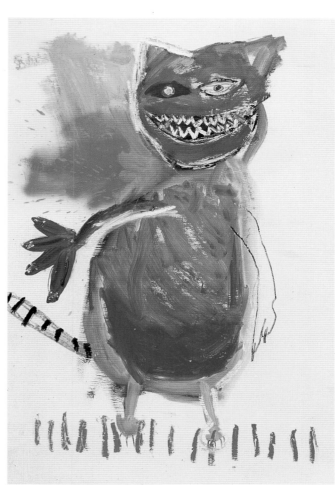

© **Susan Groover**

© **Nikolai Punin**

© **Karen Greenberg**

305

© Christer Eriksson

WEST
(415) 457-3695
(800) 484-8520 Code 1464
Fax (415) 457-6051

EAST
(305) 576-0142
(800) 484-8592 Code 2787
Fax (305) 576-0138

© Anatoly Chernishov

© Pauline Cilmi Speers

© Kevin Peake

© Kevin Peake

© Joan Swan

TONAL VALUES INC.

ILLUSTRATION FOR

A GLOBAL MARKET.

BARRY JACKSON

(818) 769-7321

PATRICIA DOKTOR

(818) 769-7321

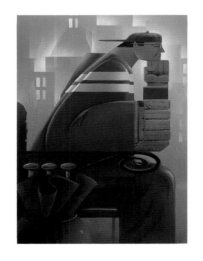

JACKSON•DOKTOR
STUDIO
4118 BECK AVE. STUDIO CITY, CA 91604

HERE KITTY, KITTY, KITTY, KITTY, KITTY, KITTY, KITTY, KITTY, KITTY, KITTY, KITTY, KITTY,

RICHARD COOK

SHERYL BERANBAUM ARTISTS' REPRESENTATIVE TEL 617▪437▪9459 TEL 401▪737▪8591 FAX 617▪437▪6494

SHERYL BERANBAUM ARTISTS' REPRESENTATIVE TEL 617▪437▪9459   TEL 401▪737▪8591   FAX 617▪437▪6494

312

TRAVIS FOSTER, 1209 SHELTON AVE, NASHVILLE TN 37216
STUDIO 615 227 0895 FAX 615 227 2996

LINDA FENNIMORE
ILLUSTRATION

808 WEST END AVE. #801
NEW YORK, NEW YORK 10025
(212) 866-0279

LINDA FENNIMORE • 808 WEST END AVENUE #801 NEW YORK, NEW YORK 10025 • 212-866-0279

B U R T O N   M O R R I S

Studio-412•682•7963   East Coast-Tricia Weber 212•799•6532   Midwest-David Montagano 312•527•3283   Boston-Lori Nowicki 617•497•5336
Washington-Pam Clare 301•365•5422   Texas-Those 3 Reps 214•871•1347   West Coast-Ann Koeffler 213•957•2327

BURTON MORRIS

STUDIO-412•682•7963   EAST COAST-TRICIA WEBER 212•799•6532   MIDWEST-DAVID MONTAGANO 312•527•3283   BOSTON-LORI NOWICKI 617•497•5336
WASHINGTON-PAM CLARE 301•365•5422   TEXAS-THOSE 3 REPS 214•871•1347   WEST COAST-ANN KOEFFLER 213•957•2327

JERRY BLANK

TELEPHONE
408 289 9095
FACSIMILE
4082898532

Matt Brownson

CAROL GUENZI AGENTS GENTS
(303) 733-0128
FAX (303)-733-8154
1-800-417-5120

322

MULTIMEDIA AUTHORING, PROGRAMMING & DIGITAL SPECIAL EFFECTS

PRIMESTAR 30FT BUSSIDE 3D RENDERED ILLUSTRATION. FINAL FILE SIZE 349 MEGABYTES

ZIMA SPECIAL EFFECTS

CAROL GUENZI AGENTS   GENTS   (303) 733-0128
FAX (303)-733-8154
1-800-417-5120

RANDY NELSEN

ANTERIOR VIEW
OF LIVER

LAPAROSCOPE

DIGITAL DELIVERY: SYQUEST, 128 MO, 1.3 GB MO, OR 4X5 TRAN. & DYE-SUB PROOFS

CAROL GUENZI AGENTS

(303) 733-0128
FAX (303)-733-8154
1-800-417-5120

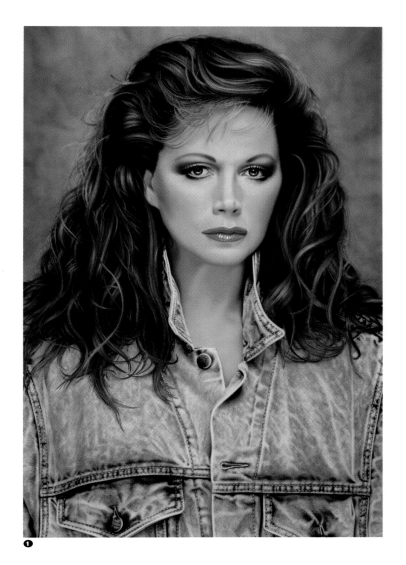

❶ JACKIE COLLINS ❷ KEYSTONE PACKAGING ❸ COORS LIGHT

TODD LOCKWOOD

BF GOODRICH

CAROL
GUENZI
AGENTS
(303) 733-0128

DEAN KENNEDY

ROCKY MOUNTAIN NEWS - COORS FIELD

CAROL GUENZI AGENTS  (303) 733-0128
FAX (303) 733-8154
1-800-417-5120

Doug **HORNE**

Jeff JONES

ZIMA MIRANDA	X-RATED ZIMA	INDUSTRIAL ZIMA
ZIMA FLASHBACK	CUBIST ZIMA	ZIMA WITH A TWIST
A SLICE OF ZIMA	I DREAM OF ZIMA	LEANING TOWER OF ZIMA
CLAUSTROPHOBIC ZIMA	BOWLING FOR ZIMA	ZIMA ON THE RANGE

REPRESENTED BY MARY HOLLAND & COMPANY
FAX (602) 277-0680 · TEL (602) 263-8990

Eric BOWMAN

Shelly **BARTEK**

REPRESENTED BY MARY HOLLAND & COMPANY
FAX (602) 277-0680 · TEL (602) 263-8990

MARY HOLLAND
AGENTS
(602) 263-8990
AND COMPANY INC.

331

946 B STREET PETALUMA CA 94952 707 765 6744 FAX 707 765 0551

HEIDI STEVENS
Illustration

22 TENTH STREET
PETALUMA, CA 94952
707 769-1252

JOHNSTONE'S
COOKiN'

607 666 8120
Anne takes the
ORDeRS

MIKE TOFANELLI
I L L U S T R A T I O N

1100 Howe Avenue #246
Sacramento, CA 95825
Phone/Fax 916.927.4809

For additional work, see The Creative Illustration Book '94 & '95.

Susi Grell

Robert Armstrong

200 East B St • Dixon CA 95620
Studio / Fax 916 678 2955

REPRESENTED BY

ALEXANDER
POLLARD

TOLL FREE:
800-347-0734

ATLANTA:
404-875-1363

FAX:
404-875-9733

REPRESENTED BY

ALEXANDER
POLLARD

TOLL FREE:
800-347-0734

ATLANTA:
404-875-1363

FAX:
404-875-9733

REPRESENTED BY

ALEXANDER
POLLARD

TOLL FREE:
800-347-0734

ATLANTA:
404-875-1363

FAX:
404-875-9733

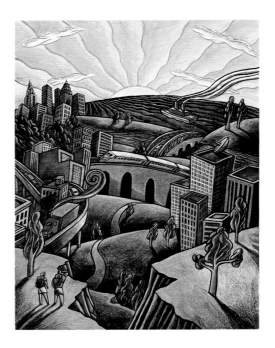

KAREN STRELECKI

REPRESENTED BY

ALEXANDER
POLLARD

TOLL FREE:
800-347-0734

ATLANTA:
404-875-1363

FAX:
404-875-9733

REPRESENTED BY

ALEXANDER
POLLARD

TOLL FREE:
800-347-0734

ATLANTA:
404-875-1363

FAX:
404-875-9733

REPRESENTED BY

ALEXANDER
POLLARD

TOLL FREE:
800-347-0734

ATLANTA:
404-875-1363

FAX:
404-875-9733

REPRESENTED BY

ALEXANDER
POLLARD

TOLL FREE:
800-347-0734

ATLANTA:
404-875-1363

FAX:
404-875-9733

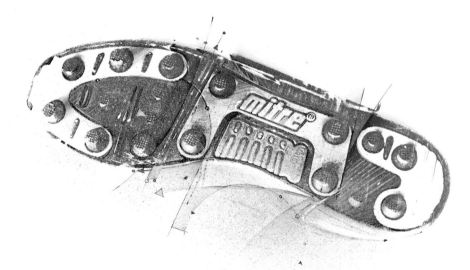

NYC
212.691.2667
Munro Goodman

CALIFORNIA
213.887.8958
Tami Gordon

CAROLINAS
704.372.6007
Kerry Reilly

CHICAGO
312.578.8844
Dan Sell

GEORGIA
404.875.1363
Alexander/
Pollard

W/C STUDIO *florida* 813.579.4499

fax 579.4585

D A P H N E   MᶜC O R M A C K

KAREN WELLS   ARTIST REPRESENTATIVE

713-293-9375 FAX: 713-293-9375*

DEAN WILLIAMS

KAREN WELLS   ARTIST REPRESENTATIVE

713-293-9375 FAX: 713-293-9375*

R A N D Y   R O G E R S

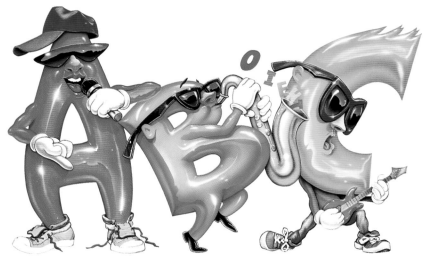

KAREN WELLS   ARTIST REPRESENTATIVE   713-293-9375 FAX: 713-293-9375*

MIDWEST   MARIETTA & JERRY MASON   612-729-1774   FAX: 612-729-0133

348

STEPHEN WELLS

LORRAINE SILVESTRI
508 • 668 • 0111
PHONE/FAX

PATTI GREEN ILLUSTRATION

5222 N. Clark, No. 2   Chicago, IL 60640   **PHONE:** *(312) 275-5895*   **FACSIMILE:** *(312) 878-6857*

Lori Osiecki

Lorio · 123 West Second Street, Mesa Arizona 85201 · Phone & Fax 602-962-5233

GEORGE ABE

KOLEA BAKER
Artists Representative Inc

2814 - NW 72nd Street   Seattle WA   98117   206.784.1136   fax 206.784.1171

DON BAKER

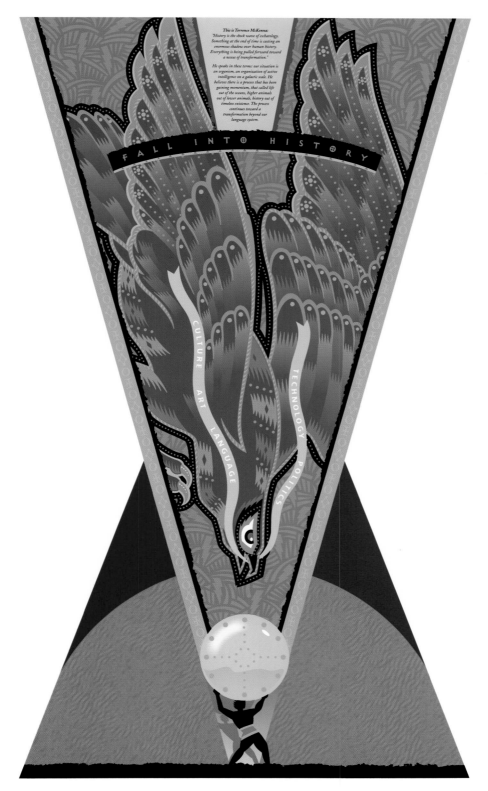

KOLEA BAKER
Artists Representative Inc

2814 - NW 72nd Street   Seattle WA   98117   206.784.1136   fax 206.784.1171

KOLEA BAKER

Artists Representative Inc

2814 - NW 72nd Street   Seattle WA   98117   206.784.1136   fax 206.784.1171

jeff shelly

1202 N. Harper Ave. Los Angeles, CA 90046 • (213)654-7368 • (800)318-3244 • Fax (213)654-8146

Matt Eastwood

MEIKLEJOHN

Brochure and NYC based portfolios featuring Europe's finest available on request

28 Shelton St, Covent Gdn, London WC2H 9HR, UK Tel (01144)171 240 2077 Fax (01144)171 836 0199

Warren Madill
(Fine Art Forger)

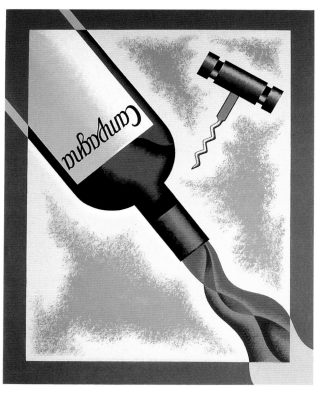

Jake

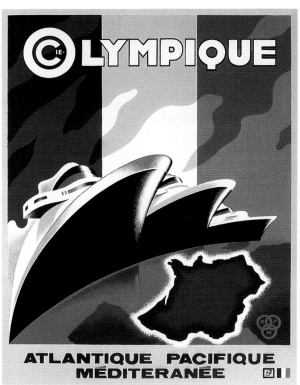

Jake

MEIKLEJOHN

Brochure and NYC based portfolios featuring Europe's finest available on request

28 Shelton St, Covent Gdn, London WC2H 9HP UK Tel (01144)171 240 2077 Fax (01144)171 836 0199

Melvyn Evans

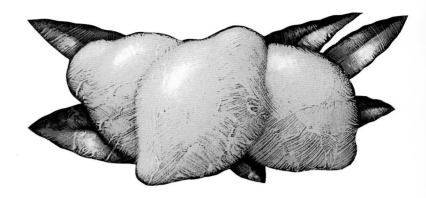

Corinna Reetz

MEIKLEJOHN

Brochure and NYC based portfolios featuring Europe's finest available on request

28 Shelton St, Covent Garden, London WC2H 9HP, UK Tel (01144) 171 240 2077 Fax (01144) 171 836 0199

Gavin Reece

Gavin Reece

MEIKLEJOHN

Brochure and NYC based portfolios featuring Europe's finest available on request

28 Shelton St, Covent Gdn, London WC2H 9HP, UK Tel (01144)171 240 2077 Fax (01144)171 836 0199

Andrew Farley

Andrew Farley

Zig Peterson

MEIKLEJOHN

Brochure and NYC based portfolios featuring Europe's finest available on request

28 Shelton St. Covent Gdn. London WC2H 9HP UK. Tel (01144)171 240 2077 Fax (01144)171 836 0199

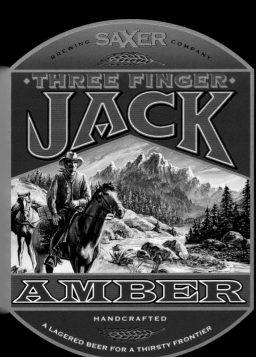

ANTON KIMBALL DESIGN
820 SE SANDY BOULEVARD
PORTLAND, OREGON 97214
503-234-4777 FAX 234-4687

"WHAT DAY OF THE MONTH IS IT?" HE SAID TURNING TO ALICE: HE HAD TAKEN HIS WATCH OUT OF HIS POCKET, AND WAS LOOKING AT IT UNEASILY SHAKING IT EVERY NOW AND THEN AND HOLDING IT TO HIS EAR. ALICE CONSIDERED A LITTLE, AND THEN SAID "THE FOURTH."
"TWO DAYS WRONG!" SIGHED THE HATTER. "I TOLD YOU BUTTER WOULD NOT SUIT THE WORKS!" HE ADDED LOOKING ANGRILY AT THE MARCH HARE. "IT WAS THE *BEST* BUTTER," THE MARCH HARE MEEKLY REPLIED. "YES, BUT SOME CRUMBS MUST HAVE GOT IN AS WELL." THE HATTER GRUMBLED. "YOU SHOULD NOT HAVE PUT IT IN WITH THE BREAD-KNIFE."
THE MARCH HARE TOOK THE WATCH AND LOOKED AT IT GLOOMILY: HE THEN DIPPED IT INTO HIS CUP OF TEA, AND LOOKED AT IT AGAIN: BUT HE COULD THINK OF NOTHING BETTER TO SAY THAN HIS FIRST REMARK, "IT WAS THE *BEST* BUTTER, YOU KNOW."

MARIA KNIER PHONE/FAX 414.284.3449 • IN THE PACIFIC NORTHWEST PHONE TIFFANY REPRESENTS AT 206.441.7701 FX 206.441.3002

NIKKI MIDDENDORF 212 • 683 • 2848

Clients include:
AT&T
Shearson Lehman Brothers
American Express
Nynex
Time Warner
New York Times
Wall St. Journal
Detroit Free Press
Business Week
Ad Week
Vegetarian Times
Golf Illustrated

JEFF SWARTS

308 S. CEDAR STREET   DANVILLE, OHIO 43014-0289
PHONE & FAX 614-599-6516

367

PAUL COZZOLINO

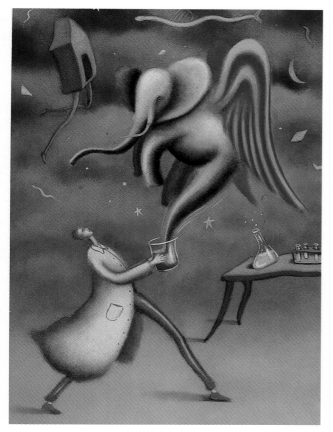

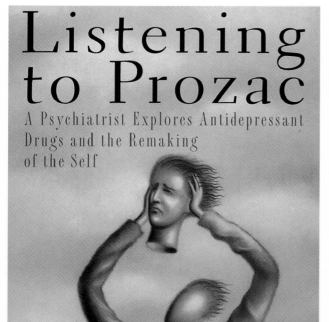

Listening to Prozac

A Psychiatrist Explores Antidepressant Drugs and the Remaking of the Self

Peter D. Kramer

(212) 969-8680

KATHY O'CONNELL

Computer Illustrator
Photoshop & MacroMedia Director
RayDream & Illustrator

Rockets modeled in 3D

Computer Illustration
Kathy O'Connell

Clients Include:
Tyco Toys, Fleer,
M&M/Mars,
Sunshine Cookies,
Johnson & Johnson

COREY WILKINSON

855 Joyce Avenue • Melrose Park, Illinois • 60164
708-562-2512

JOHN
FRANCIS
ILLUSTRATION

1665 Logan Street

Suite 1046

Denver, CO 80203

303-894-8350

FAX 894-8343

Kit Hevron Mahoney • 2682 South Newport Street • Denver, Colorado 80224
Phone and FAX: (303) 757-0689

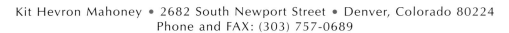

374

MICHAEL CACY

503·233·7715   FAX 503·233·0978

COMPUTER ILLUSTRATION

MAC
NEILL
and
MAC
INTOSH

SCOTT A MACNEILL
74 YORK STREET
LAMBERTVILLE NJ 08530
609·397·4631
FAX 609·397·9982

Call for a floppy portfolio show

378

DAVE WINTER IS REPRESENTED BY DAVE WINTER ☎ 312-527-3900, 275-9529

Kenneth Spengler

2668 17th Street, Sacramento, CA 95818
(916) 441-1932

JEFFREY OH
410-661-6064

San Francisco:
Represented by
Janice Stefanski
415-928-0457

Also see American Showcase, Vol. 14 p.848, Vol. 15 p.863, Vol. 16 p.879, and The Creative Illustration Book 5 p.114.

RICK CLUBB

708 · 690 · 5554
RICK CLUBB ILLUSTRATIONS INC.
310 South Hale Street
Wheaton, Illinois 60187
Fax 708 · 690 · 5553

STEVEN NOBLE

TEL 415.897.6961

FAX 415.892.4449

ADDITIONAL SAMPLES CAN BE SEEN IN THE AMERICAN SHOWCASE VOL.19.

383

Tom Arvis
CARTOONS & ILLUSTRATIONS
11228 TROY RD., ROCKVILLE, MD 20852
PH: (301) 468-0828   FAX: (301) 881-5735

airbrush
acrylics
hand-painted cels
line art
magazine illus.
comic books
storyboards
video art
animatics
marker comps
desktop design

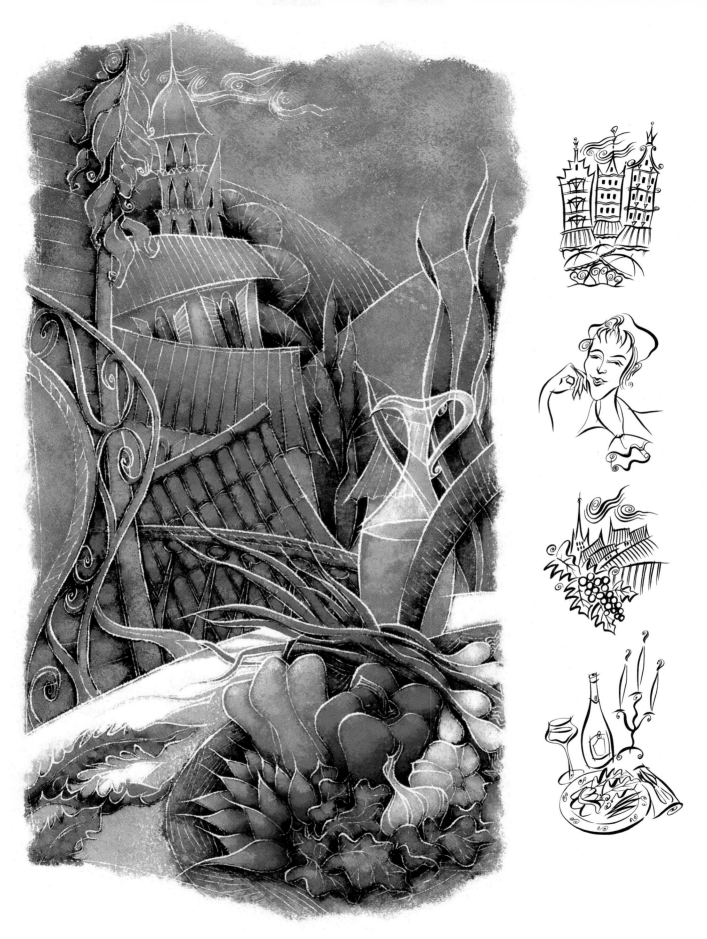

Heather Holbrook   *Tel (416) 467-7098*   *Fax (416) 422-0031*

McDonald's " Be Your Best " program game board

McDonald's " Be Your Best " program bookmark

VitaVision " Lactose Intolerance "

The Flying Tortoise © 1994 Clarion/Oxford/Stoddart

BARBARA SPURLL
ILLUSTRATION
416·594·6594
FAX 416·601·1010

For further samples see CIB'95 P.402

Carl Wiens

416·699·1670

Jackie Snider
(613) 475-4551

STEPHEN SNIDER

613-475-4551

Wayne Mondok

TORONTO

ONTARIO

CANADA

416 • 249 • 2676

WAYNE MONDOK © 1995

S T E P H E N • Q U I N L A N • I L L U S T R A T I O N • L T D
PHONE/FAX (416) 485-8277

Current clients include: The Addiction Research Foundation, American Express, Southwestern Bell, Globe & Mail, IBM, Kodak, Kraft Foods, Molson Breweries, The Red Cross Society, Sunoco, Sunlife Insurance Co., Unicef, Visa.

2453 OLIVE CT. WINDSOR ONTARIO CANADA N8T 3N4 PHONE/FAX (519) 948-2418

ADDITIONAL IMAGES IN AMERICAN SHOWCASE 16, 17 & 18 AND 1995 CREATIVE ILLUSTRATION BOOK

MILES KIMBALL *catalog cover*   POLAR THE TITANIC BEAR (above) *Madison Press / Little, Brown*   LAWRENCE AYLIFFE ADVERTISING

LAURIE M^{c}GAW

(519) 925-5134

NEIL MACLACHLAN ILLUSTRATION
45 Earswick Dr.
Toronto, Ontario
M1E 1C7
Phone 416-269-8141
FAX   416-269-8959

Represented in Canada by Sharpshooter
(416) 703-5300

RICHARD JAMES COOK

PAUL GARBETT 416-431-7034

GSYSTEM**DATA**BASE MARKETING SYSTEM DATA

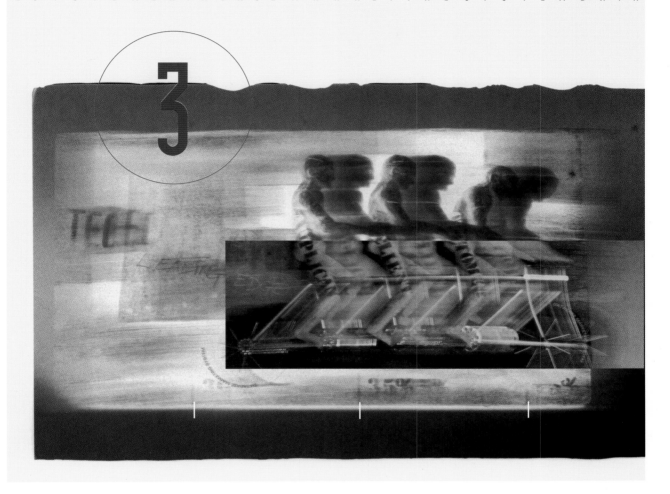

(216) 234-1808

INTL© REVELATIONS
and Holly Hanes Carlson

Holly Hanes Carlson
Studio Telephone & Fax:
(415) 961-4906

Represented by

Jane Klein
Telephone: (510) 535-0495
Fax: (510) 535-0437

ANATOLY

RANDY BERRETT

DICK COLE

JONATHAN COMBS

ROBERT EVANS

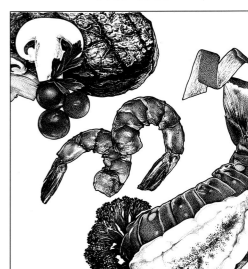

RANDY GLASS

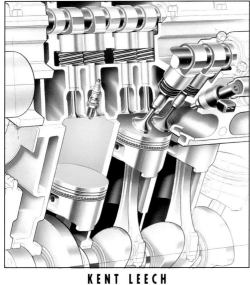

KENT LEECH

WILL NELSON

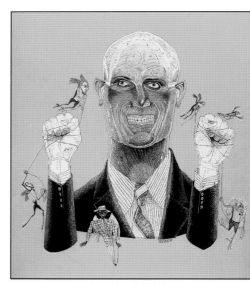

JACK UNRUH

RON SWEET
716 MONTGOMERY STREET
SAN FRANCISCO, CALIFORNIA 94111

Sweet Represents

415/433-1222
FAX: 415/433-9560

Conrad Represents...

DAVID CHEN

T (415) 921-7140 F (415) 921-3939

138 WEST 25TH STREET
BALTIMORE, MD 21218

STUDIO: **410 889 0703**
FAX: 410 889 5498

JIM STARR

NEW YORK	**WASHINGTON, D.C.**	**MIDWEST**	**WEST**
AMERICAN ARTISTS	PAM CLARE REPRESENTS	TOM MALONEY	MARLA MATSON REPRESENTS
212 582 0023	301 365 5422	312 704 0500	602 252 5072
FAX 212 582 0090	FAX 301 365 1653	FAX 312 236 5752	FAX 602 252 5073

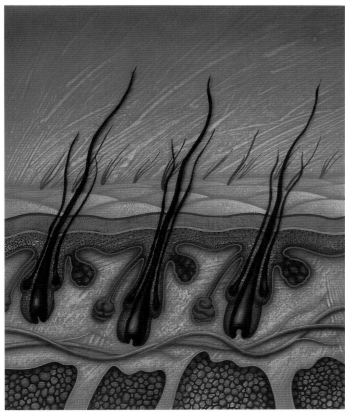

BOB LYNCH 410-366-6535

138 West 25th St. Baltimore, MD 21218

Southwest Clients Call, Marla Matson 602-252-5072

r a y
f r e d e r i c k s

tel: 708.857.8090
fax: 708.857.8111

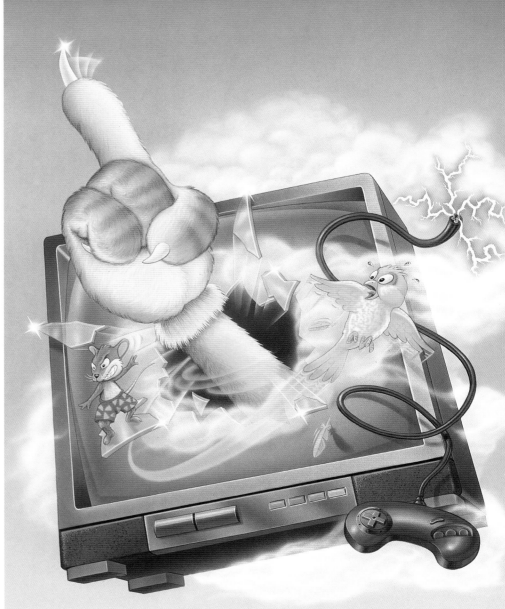

Fredericks Illustration Inc. - 9705 South 52nd Avenue - Oak Lawn, IL 60453

BEN DANN LANDER

Coors Brewing Company

Don Sullivan
ILLUSTRATION
303-671-9257 Fax: 303-752-3037

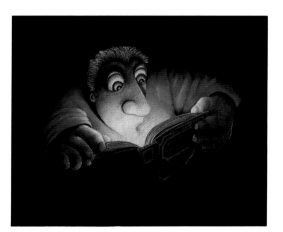
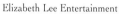
Elizabeth Lee Entertainment

Aunt Ruthie in Oahu

Bloomberg Personal Magazine

Bluestone Records

LA Times Magazine

KEN CONDON

TECH SPECIALISTS

HOME MAGAZINE

PC MAGAZINE

Phone 413-628-4042 Fax 413-628-4043

126 Ashfield Mtn. Rd. Ashfield, MA 01330   In New England call Aurelia Papitto 617-742-3108

For more samples see American Showcase #10, 12, 15 and 16 and the Graphic Artists Guild Directory #5, 6, 10 and 11

CARTOONING / ILLUSTRATION
JIM HUMMEL

3023 Delta Road, San Jose California
Phone (408) 270-2349
Fax (408) 270-2349

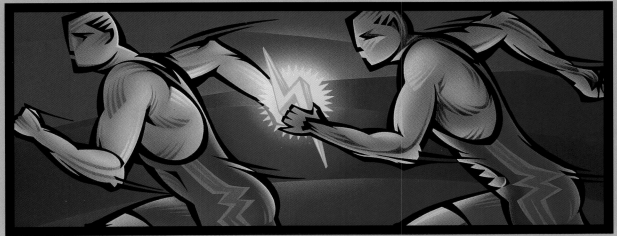

MIKE FISHER

416 NORTH COLUMBIA STREET
COVINGTON, LOUISIANA ◆ 70433
TEL/FAX 504 ◆ 892 ◆ 7557

DOUG RUGH

(508) 548-6684 fax: 457-6394

DARREN THOMPSON

Phone 312-472-7504
Fax   312-472-7508

Call
to see
more

MICHAEL TAKAGI 503·385·3263   REPRESENTED BY REP ART 206·467·9156

chris lensch

209 ford st.

golden, co 80401

303.279.8304

fax 278.6446

digital portfolio

available upon

request

colorado business

self-promo

la times magazine

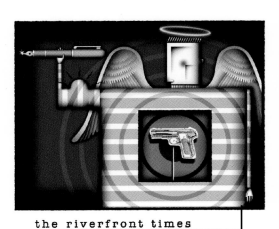

the riverfront times

413

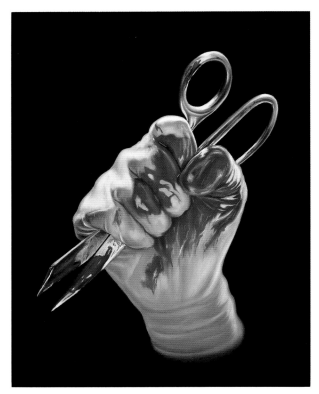

Chris Cocozza

203 • 263 • 2061

DAVID DANZ

REPRESENTED BY SANDY DANZ (916) 622-3218 • FAX (916) 622-4346

TO VIEW ADDITIONAL SAMPLES PLEASE REFER TO AMERICAN SHOWCASE AND THE WORKBOOK.

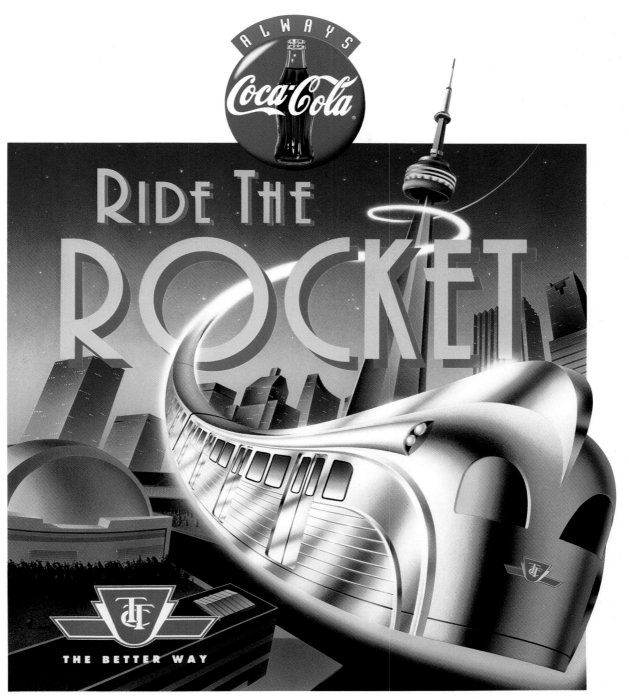

ROCKET: COMMUNIQUÉ GROUP INC. • COKE: COSSETTE COMMUNICATION-MARKETING

mike carter ★ illustration inc.

Phone:[416] 250-5433 • Fax:[416] 250-6919

Jannine Cabossel
ILLUSTRATION

Tuko Fujisaki

ILLUSTRATION

NEW YORK
STUDIO
718 · 789 · 7472

St. Louis
TEENUH FOSTER
314 · 821 · 2278

SAN FRANCISCO
JANE KLEIN
510 · 535 · 0495

· Season's Greetings ·

Winter

Spring

Summer

JANET WOOLLEY

ALAN
LYNCH
ARTISTS
REPRESENTATIVE

11 KINGS RIDGE ROAD/ LONG VALLEY, NJ 07853

TEL (908) 813-8718 / FAX (908) 813-0076

REPRESENTED IN EUROPE BY ARENA:

TEL (0171) 267-9661 / FAX (0171) 284-0486

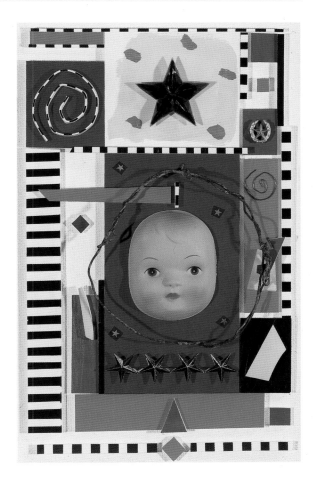

JOHN HARRIS

DAVID HITCH

**ALAN
LYNCH**
ARTISTS
REPRESENTATIVE

11 KINGS RIDGE ROAD/ LONG VALLEY, NJ 07853

TEL (908) 813-8718 / FAX (908) 813-0076

REPRESENTED IN EUROPE BY ARENA:

TEL (0171) 267-9661 / FAX (0171) 284-0486

ALAN
LYNCH
ARTISTS
REPRESENTATIVE

11 KINGS RIDGE ROAD/ LONG VALLEY, NJ 07853
TEL (908) 813-8718 / FAX (908) 813-0076

kirk richard smith

firehouse 101 art + design studio 614 464 0928

492 armstrong street · columbus, ohio 43215

Steve Katz

310 821 5042

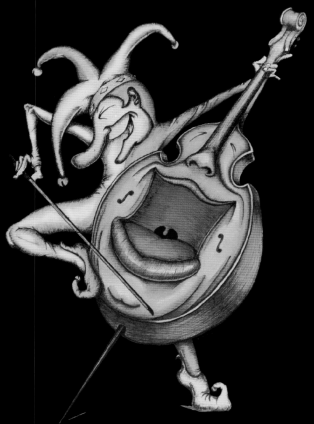

JOSEPH TAYLOR

2117 EWING AVENUE • EVANSTON IL 60201
VOX 708-328-2454   FAX 708-328-2485

J A N E   P .   M i l l e r

4 0 8 - 6 8 4 - 1 5 9 3

San Francisco–based Goodby, Silverstein and Partners contacted the Archive about developing a trademark character named "Captain Weegie" for their client, Norwegian Cruise Line.

Nike 180 Air poster designed using customized CSA Archive illustrations, commissioned through Wieden & Kennedy.

Three of the eight "Adventure Guys," created for Chiat/Day's "Nissan Pathfinder Practical Guide to Outdoor Adventure" campaign. The campaign ran in numerous sporting and outdoor magazines.

A customized illustration for a Subaru print campaign, commissioned through Wieden & Kennedy.

C.S. Anderson Design Co. was asked to create this piece for the Endpapers page in the New York Times Sunday Magazine using images that represent a Midwestern tourist's impression of New York.

These are stills from a TV commercial produced for Levi's by Foote, Cone & Belding.

Archive cuts of literally hundreds of specific objects were used to illustrate a Levi's-MTV sweepsteaks.

All of these images were located and sent out in a single day, and on television the next week.

This ad uses one of 30 customized line art icons created as part of an identity for Turner Classic Movies. Each interchangeable "head" was designed to capture the feel of a different film genré and can be used as an onscreen logo, in advertising, on stationery, or for any other application the network might dream up.

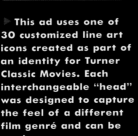

Archive CD Sampler

Magnetic Personalities

Watch Faces Collection

Mouse Pads

Coffee Table

Gary Meyer

21725 YBARRA ROAD, WOODLAND HILLS / CA 91364 — TEL (818) 992-6974, FAX (818) 992-4538

MARGIE SHINNICK · 220 12TH AVE. · SAN FRANCISCO CA. 94118 · 415-221-4208

KIM WILSON BRANDT
ILLUSTRATION

415·824·2055   718·237·8546

See Also Kim Wilson Eversz in Directory of Illustration 9 and American Showcase 13 & 14.

Represented by John Brewster Creative Services 203.226.4724 fax 454.9904

R.M. Schneider

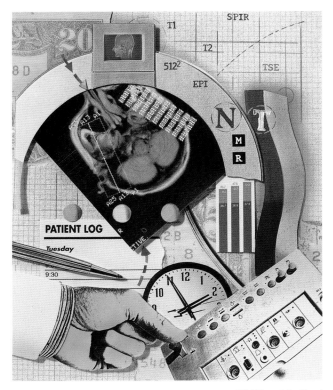

Philips Medical

Merrill Lynch

RCI Software

Sports Forum

Pepsico

JOHN
BREWSTER
CREATIVE
SERVICES

[203] 226-4724 • [203] 454-9904 fax

Lane duPont

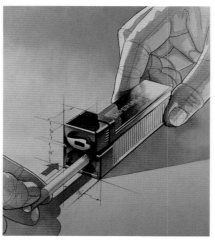
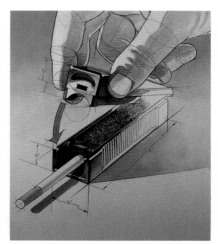

JOHN
BREWSTER
CREATIVE
SERVICES

[203] 226-4724 • [203] 454-9904 fax

Glenn Gustafson

Fisher Controls

Heubien

Nordic Trac-Digital Image

JOHN BREWSTER CREATIVE SERVICES

[203] 226-4724 [203] 454-9904 fax

Ameritech

Miles Parnell

THE WORLD'S YOUR OYSTER

Vacance en France

White Cliffs of Dover

JOHN
BREWSTER
CREATIVE
SERVICES

[203] 226-4724   [203] 454-9904 fax

TOM PATRICK
I L L U S T R A T I O N

Brian Jensen

RKB Studios, Inc.
Call Diane Larson or Rosemary Merrill
Phone (612) 339-7055 • Fax (612) 339-8689

M.

MARLA MATSON

REPRESENTS

602 252-5072

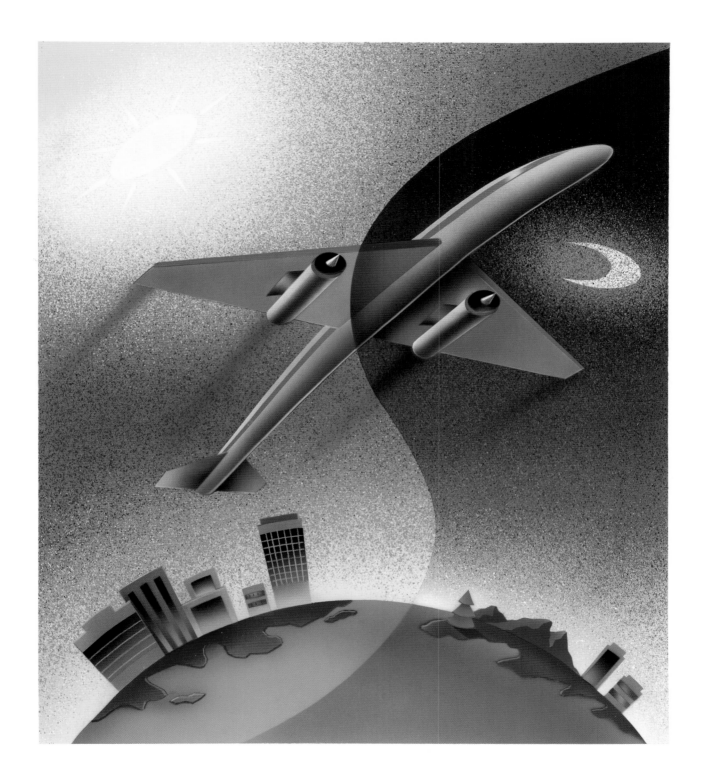

M.
M A R L A   M A T S O N
R E P R E S E N T S
6 0 2   2 5 2 - 5 0 7 2

VIRUSCAN

ASTONISHING ILLUSTRATION
Get the book...don't
wait for the movie!

Deadly
Diseases
are fun →

Healthy Pet Stuff ↗

The green Pet owner.

Animals in Distress

JOGGER

Pasta Amore

Cow flops are dangerous.

Environmental Issues

Romantic Restaurants ↑

ART.
DIR.
CLUB
MAG.
↓

Lonesome chicken →

Photo Safari
↓

A TRUE AND ACCURATE
FARM REPORT by Lee Lee Brazeal

Sometimes · Represented by Dan Sell · Chicago · Tel · 312 - 578 - 8844 · Fax · 312 · 578 · 8847
Other times · Represented by Brooke & Co · Dallas · Tel · 214 · 352 · 9192 · Fax · 214 · 350 · 2101

443

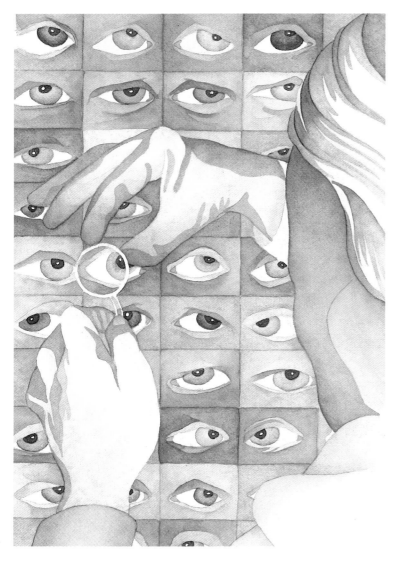

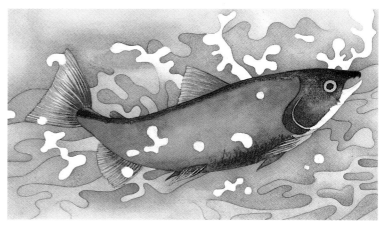

ELSA WARNICK
(5 0 3) 2 2 8 - 2 6 5 9
PHONE AND FAX

STEPHANIE LANGLEY

DONNA JORGENSEN ANNIE BARRETT ARTISTS REPRESENTATIVES
206 634-1880 FAX 206 632-2024

MITS KATAYAMA

DONNA JORGENSEN ANNIE BARRETT ARTISTS REPRESENTATIVES
206 634-1880 FAX 206 632-2024

GOT THE TIME?
©Colin Hayes 1995

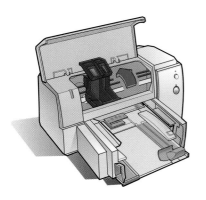

COLIN HAYES

DONNA JORGENSEN ANNIE BARRETT ARTIST REPRESENTATIVES
206 634-1880 FAX 206 632-2024

Oh God! Not another **ART DIRECTOR'S QUIZ**

So you think you're the 'Visual' type, eh? Got a real important job as an Art Director in a big agency, probably never lost a game of Pictionary... right? Well let's see how good you are. The following words are in the illustration above. No fair asking your kids for help.

RESEARCHERS, FAREWELL, PERSUADERS, DINOSAUR, ESCAPE, WRINGER, METAPHOR, AMATEUR, FLOUNDER, MICROWAVE, PHILOSOPHER, CLASSIC, LETTERHEAD, FOREHEAD, CATSUP, QUALITY, FELONY, AMERICAN, GIGANTIC, ILLUSTRATOR, SERIAL KILLER, and MUSHROOM.

For answers, advice, questions, or if you just want to talk about it: Michael Kline Illustration, 316-264-4112. Pictures by modem or otherwise.

SHARON WATTS  718 • 398 • 0451

3301 SOUTH JEFFERSON AVENUE ■ SAINT LOUIS, MISSOURI 63118

314.773.9989 ■ FAX 314.773.6406

OTHER SAMPLES MAY BE SEEN IN CREATIVE ILLUSTRATION 94,95 P. 148

AND AMERICAN SHOWCASE 13 THROUGH 18

david Bamundo   718.370.7726   digital illustration

modem delivery available. . .call for printed samples or disk portfolio

451

816-561-8045 **JIM PAILLOT** FAX 561-6201

SPACEK
PETER
212 962 7383
call for

453

BONNIE HOFKIN

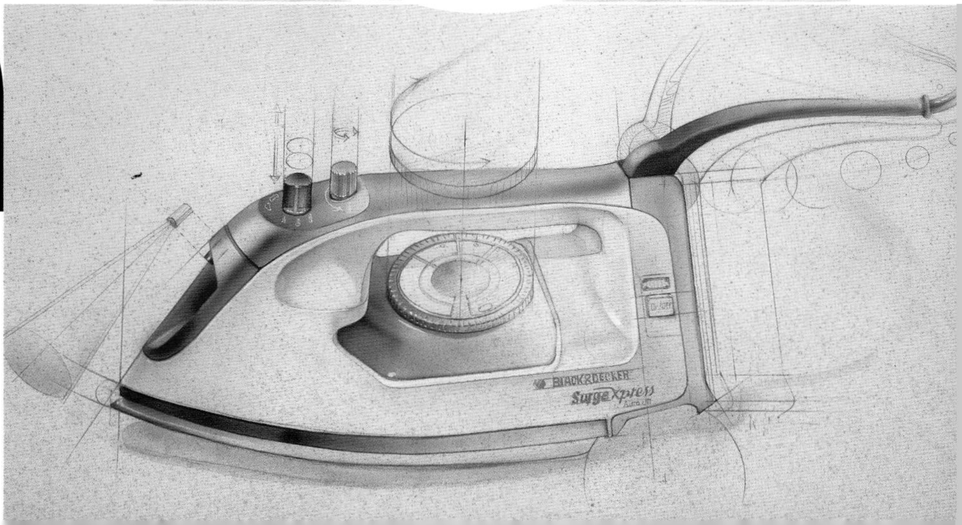

BONNIE HOFKIN

BOOK OF

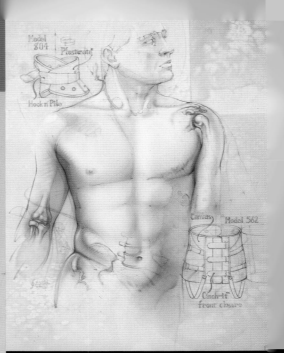

joanne paluliar
representative
212 581 8338
203 866 3734
fax 203 857 0842

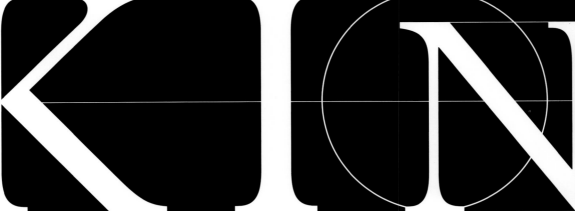

design by elastic 416.488.0270

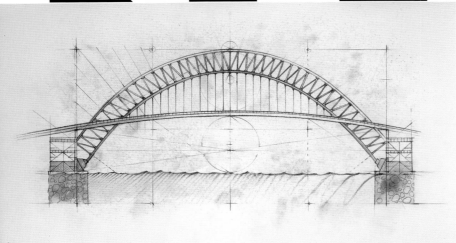

DAVID LESH
David Lesh
D a v i d L e s h

aLL It TaKeS iS a LiTtLe ImAgInAtIoN

yOuRs AnD MiNe

TOP

Represented in the East
by Joanne Palulian
1.203.866.3734
1.212.581.8338

all it takes is imagination
yours and mine

DAVID LESH
5693 NORTH MERIDIAN STREET
INDIANAPOLIS, IN 46208
1.317.253.3141
FAX 1.317.255.8462

Hi
Dad
Joey

gayle**kabaker**

Joanne Palulian
Representative
212 581 8338
203 866 3734
Fax 203 857 0842

459

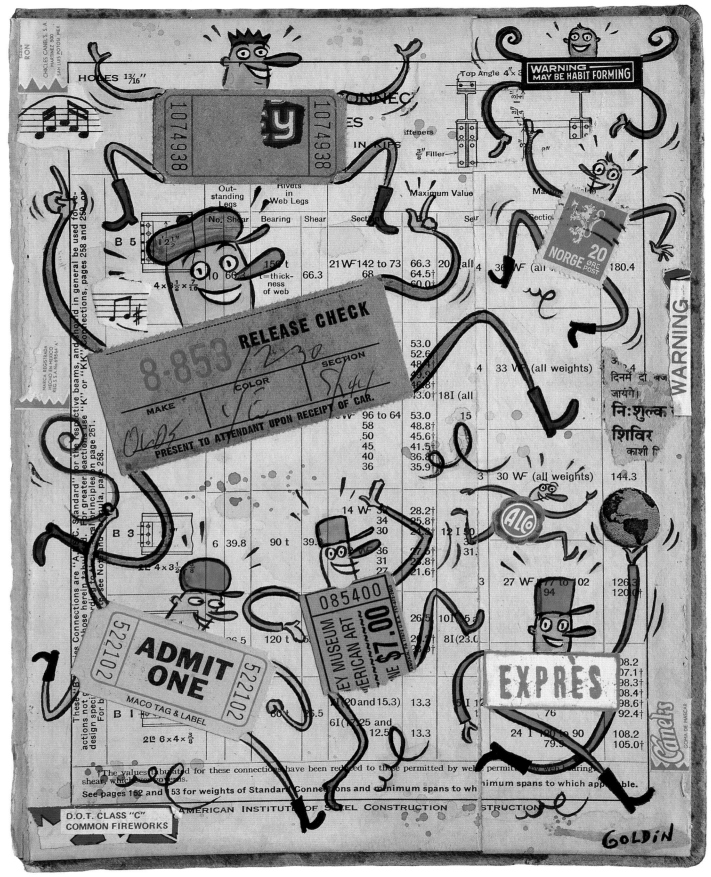

DAVID GOLDIN COLLAGE

STUDIO: 212·529·5195

REPRESENTED by JOANNE PALULIAN: 212·581·8338 OR 203·866·3734 FAX: 203·857·0842

DAVID GOLDIN ILLUSTRATION

STUDIO: 212·529·5195

REPRESENTED by JOANNE PALULIAN: 212·581·8338 OR 203·866·3734 FAX: 203·857·0842

SONY presents... a brief history of shopping

Bonnie Timmons
Represented by Joanne Palulian (203) 866-3734 (212) 581-8338

Dick Palulian

Joanne Palulian
Representative
212 581 8338
203 866 3734
Fax 203 857 0842

Philippe Beha

Joanne Palulian, Representative 212 581 8338 ▪ 203 866 3734 ▪ Fax 203 857 0842